HyperTalk™ Programming

HAYDEN *Macintosh Library* BOOKS

Macintosh® Revealed

**Volume One:
Unlocking the Toolbox
Second Edition**
Stephen Chernicoff

**Volume Two:
Programming with the
Toolbox
Second Edition**
Stephen Chernicoff

**Volume Three:
Mastering the Toolbox
(forthcoming)**
Stephen Chernicoff

**Volume Four:
Programming the
Macintosh® II (forthcoming)**
*Stephen Chernicoff and Geri
Younggren*

**How to Write Macintosh®
Software
Second Edition**
Scott Knaster

**MacAccess: Information in
Motion**
Dean Gengle and Steven Smith

**MPW and Assembly
Language Programming**
Scott Kronick

**The Macintosh® Advisor
(Updated for Multifinder)**
Cynthia Harriman and Bencion Calica

**Object-Oriented
Programming for the
Macintosh®**
Kurt J. Schmucker

Programming the 68000
*Edwin Rosenzweig and Harland
Harrison*

**HyperTalk™ Tips and
Techniques**
Dan Shafer

**The Waite Group's
HyperTalk™ Bible**
The Waite Group

**IBM® PC and Macintosh®
Networking: Featuring TOPS
and AppleShare™**
Steve Michel

**Macintosh® Hard Disk
Management**
Bencion J. Calica and Charles Rubin

Nonlibrary Titles

**Artificial Intelligence
Programming on the
Macintosh®**
Dan Shafer

Understanding HyperTalk™
Dan Shafer

---

*For the retailer nearest you, or to order directly from the publisher,
call 800-428-SAMS. In Indiana, Alaska, and Hawaii call 317-298-5699.*

HyperTalk™ Programming
Revised Edition

Dan Shafer

HAYDEN BOOKS

A Division of Howard W. Sams & Company
4300 West 62nd Street
Indianapolis, Indiana 46268 USA

REVISED EDITION
FIRST PRINTING–1988

International Standard Book Number: 0-672-48439-0
Library of Congress Catalog Card Number: 88-61960

Acquisitions Editor: Greg Michael
Manuscript Editor: Susan Pink, Techright and Katherine Stuart Ewing
Illustrator: Don Clemons
Cover Artist: Celeste Design
Indexer: W. Bjerstedt
Technical Reviewer: James Redfern and David Gewirtz
Compositor: Carolyn Shafer, Apricot Press

Printed in the United States of America

Trademark Acknowledgements

All terms mentioned in this book that are known to be trademarks or service marks are listed below. In addition, terms suspected of being trademarks or service marks have been appropriately capitalized. Howard W. Sams & Co. cannot attest to the accuracy of this information. Use of a term in this book should not be regarded as affecting the validity of any trademark or service mark.

HyperCard, HyperTalk, Macintosh, MacPaint, and SANE are trademarks of Apple Computer, Inc.
HyperNews is a trademark of Training Resources Unlimited.
HyperQuiz is a trademark of Dan Shafer.
Mac is a registered trademark of Apple Computer, Inc.
Menu's for HyperCard! is a trademark of Nine to Five Software, Inc.
Reports for HyperCard is a trademark of Mediagenic
scriptExpert is a trademark of Hyperpress Publishing and Dan Shafer.
scriptView is a trademark of Eldon Benz.
Sound Advice is a trademark of Paul T. Pashibin.
Word is a registered trademark of Microsoft Corporation.

For patience beyond endurance,

support beyond expectation,

love beyond measure,

joy unsurpassed …

For Carolyn

Contents

Preface

Programming the Macintosh just got easier. Thanks to Bill Atkinson and HyperCard and to his colleague Dan Winkler and HyperTalk, programming the Macintosh is no longer the arduous and intricate task it once was.

This book helps you take advantage of this awesome new power to control your Macintosh world the way you want it controlled. If you are an experienced programmer, you will be exposed to the inner workings and object-like concepts in HyperTalk so that the underlying elegance of the language is revealed. If HyperTalk is your first language — or if you are one of the hundreds of thousands of people who learned BASIC but gave up programming since the advent of more difficult-looking Pascal and C — you will gain a ground-level introduction to HyperTalk as a language and be taken all the way through complex script development.

The focus of this book is on the HyperTalk language, not on how to design and build stacks. Shortly after HyperTalk became available, the lack of documentation was evident. Early books had to be printed before some aspects of the language were"frozen" in design. Even the early documents of the Apple Programmers and Developers Association (APDA) had trouble staying current.

This book was completed in a short time in an effort to bring you current and useful information at the beginning of what promises to be a major revolution in the way people view and use the Macintosh. But nothing was sacrificed for the sake of time. Every useful command, function, property, and operator in HyperTalk is covered, along with conceptual material and detailed instructions and examples on the use of external commands and functions written in Pascal and C. You'll find tips, traps, and techniques gathered from the experiences of dozens of "stackheads" who began developing scripts in HyperTalk almost before HyperCard was a known quantity.

What's in Here?

This book has 26 chapters and 3 appendices. Chapters 1 and 2 cover background material about HyperTalk and the HyperCard environment. Chapter 3 is a refresher course in the basics of HyperCard design. Chapters 4 and 5 introduce essential, practical information about HyperTalk programming, such as how to use the script editor and HyperTalk naming conventions.

Then in Chapter 6 we begin our exploration of the operation of the HyperTalk programming language itself. We cover intensively the following topics:

- system messages (Chapter 6)

- keyboard, mouse, and file I/O operations (Chapter 7)

- control structures and logical operators (Chapter 8)

- controlling stack flow, card flow, and interaction (Chapter 9)

- text and data management routines (Chapter 10)

- dialog boxes and their use in HyperTalk (Chapter 11)

- menu management (Chapter 12)

- the use of visual and graphics effects (Chapter 13)

- sound and music (Chapter 14)

- math (Chapter 15)

- action-taking commands (Chapter 16)

- property-related commands (Chapter 17)

- communications commands (Chapter 18)

- script and other related commands (Chapter 19)

Chapters 20-24 cover more advanced topics, including practical advice from experienced HyperTalk programmers, how to extend the power of HyperCard and HyperTalk itself, how to design stacks for maximum effect, and a survey of free and shareware programming tools. Chapters 25 and 26 contain two substantial scripts that you can examine, take apart, modify, and learn from. To order a disk containing these scripts, see the disk offer at the back of this book.

Appendix A is a complete alphabetical vocabulary listing of HyperTalk's commands, operators, functions, messages, and properties. Appendix B is an ASCII chart that comes in handy when you use some of HyperTalk's commands. Appendix C tells you where you can get more information about HyperTalk and HyperCard.

In keeping with one of the key principles of hypertext called chunking, several of the chapters are short. I've done this so that material about one topic is all together without extraneous material to distract you.

Laboratory Exercises

In hands-on exercises throughout Chapters 6-19, you build small demonstration scripts that show how commands work and interact.

These "In the Laboratory" segments are marked by a special icon that looks like this:

When you see one of these icons, plan on being at your Mac and ready to type in a script or message to see how something works. I have emphasized hands-on experiments because HyperTalk is not the kind of language you learn sitting passively and reading this book or any other. HyperTalk, like the HyperCard environment of which it is an integral part, requires interaction on your part. Don't just *read* these lab exercises, *experience* them.

Programs Mentioned

Throughout the book, but especially in Chapters 21, 22, and 24, I mention free and shareware programs. You can usually obtain these programs from several sources, some of which are outlined in Appendix C.

Shareware programs are developed by people who enjoy"hacking" at the Macintosh and like to see some reward for their efforts but who don't want to put their programs into usual marketing channels. Some incredibly good software is shareware. But shareware only lasts if people who use shareware products pay the usually nominal fee to the developer. So if you use and enjoy someone's shareware product, take the time to send him or her a check. You'll contribute to the likelihood that more good shareware will appear over time.

I should add that for the most part, mentioning these programs does not mean that I recommend them, or that they are the best of their kind available. It means only that I've used them, they work for me, and I think you might find them helpful. If you find more useful stacks and programs, let me know.

Contacting Me

I try to be accessible to my readers. After all, you are the most important ingredient in the recipe of whatever success I may ultimately enjoy. This is my twelfth computer book and I've enjoyed each of them. But I've enjoyed more the interaction with readers.

If you find a bug, have a question, want to argue, or have things to share for future editions of this book and related books, please contact me. I can be reached electronically on Compu-Serve (71246,402), GEnie, and MCI Mail (DSHAFER both places). Or you can write me at 277 Hillview Avenue, Redwood City, California 94062. But please don't call me at home; I'm buried under stacks anyway.

Enough of the Commercial Already

I know you're itching to get into scripting, so I won't take any more of your time. Thanks for buying this book and realizing the immense potential of HyperTalk. I think you'll be pleasantly surprised at the elegance of the language and how easy it is to learn and use.

Enjoy!

Acknowledgements

This is my twelfth computer book in about two years. More than any other book I have written, this one has been a group effort. It is only fitting that these persons stand up and take a bow. Unfortunately, unless this book wins me a Pulitzer, they won't get that chance, so they'll have to settle for these heart-felt thanks.

So a sincere vote of appreciation to

- Bill Atkinson and Dan Winkler for creating this fabulous new tool. What a vision!

- Danny Goodman for writing the pioneering book in this field from which we have all learned so much and for being there on CompuServe when I had questions.

- Mike Holm, HyperCard product manager, and Moira Cullen, HyperCard evangelist, both at Apple Computer, for uplifting words, votes of confidence, and lots of information and help.

- David Leffler, manager of the HyperCard test team, for sharing dozens of stacks, lots of insights, and many hours of time he didn't have to help make this book accurate.

- Steve Maller, a fellow laborer at the word processor and a better-than-average hacker, who spent many hours helping me understand XCMDs and XFCNs. Many of the insights in Chapter 22 are his, and the fact that some of his stacks are on my recommended list is a far greater testimonial to his prowess than to my judgment.

- David Gewirtz, president of Hyperpress Publishing Inc., a fellow stackhead and writer, who helped smooth out wrinkles, kicked ideas around, and became a good friend.

- Several people at Apple Computer and elsewhere who reviewed all or parts of my manuscript and provided helpful suggestions. These people, in no particular order, include: Chris Knepper of Apple Developer Technical Support; Mark "The Red" Harlan; James Redfern of Apple's HyperTalk testing team; and Jason Gervich and Alan Spragens of Apple's Customer Publications group. Although each contributed in his own way, I am the only one responsible for any errors.

- Bill Gladstone, my agent, for recognizing the potential in HyperCard as a book topic and hanging in there with me as we designed the book and presented it to Sams.

- My editors, who were, as usual, patient and caring people. I love writing for Howard W. Sams and their Macintosh Library largely because of people like Greg Michael, Jennifer Ackley, Kathy Ewing, Fred Amich, and Susan Pink Bussiere. Despite a crunching schedule, they maintained their sense of humor. They're among the best.

- Celeste Design, who did the incredible cover art (you didn't *notice?* By all means stop right now and take a look). I hope someone offers to give me the original drawing; I'd like to frame it and hang it in my office. It would give this place a touch of class!

- My wife, Carolyn, who always plays a major role in everything I do. I honestly don't know where I'd be without her. But on this book, her contribution was both more tangible and more significant. She handled the page production and brought it in on time despite having to work with me in the next room. Guess it must be love, eh?

- Tomás Hernández, who not only assisted Carolyn in production but saved our necks when we had hardware problems on the weekend when there was no service available. Tomás has also made a number of valuable art contributions and served as a kibitzer and companion during long nights of writing and preparation.

- Finally, people I "met" on CompuServe and a dozen bulletin boards around the country, including especially Michael Long of Nine to Five Software, who have been of immeasurable help.

I hope all these people feel part of this effort. To the extent that they didn't feel that way during the hectic writing and production schedule, I hope this makes up in some small way.

Thanks, all.

Building Your Own Stacks

In this chapter, you will

- examine the step-by-step process of stack creation using HyperCard

- see the role played by scripting in HyperCard's built-in HyperTalk language

Why Build Stacks?

You have some interest in building and programming HyperCard stacks or you wouldn't have bought this book. But you may have some lingering doubts about the wisdom or value of constructing your own stacks as opposed to buying them. Or you may be planning to build stacks for other people and you want some idea of what stacks are likely to be most useful.

1

Build versus buy

The question of whether you should buy a ready-made stack or plunge into this book and the joys of HyperTalk programming is subjective enough that you shouldn't expect a hard-and-fast answer. But we believe that designing and even scripting your own stacks is neither so hard as to be intimidating nor so time-consuming as to be prohibitive if programming isn't your primary occupation.

Still, there are trade-offs. Constructing and scripting a stack for your own use takes time, though it takes substantially less time than programming a Mac application any other way. Particularly when stacks are being sold inexpensively and even given away so freely in the Bill Atkinson-generated spirit of HyperCard, it may be tough to justify to yourself, your spouse, or your boss spending any time developing your own stack. It's the old "build versus buy" decision brought down to real micro-economics. So here are some good reasons for doing your own stackware.

1. If you want something done right, you have to do it yourself. That old saw is another way of saying that some of your needs for a particular stack are probably unique. HyperCard gives you such enormous flexibility about the way the stack looks and how you use it that it seems a shame to let someone else make those decisions for you.

2. You understand better how to use something that you've designed. We all know people who have been using very powerful programs on the Mac but using them in limited ways, not taking advantage of all their capability. Part of the reason is a lack of understanding of what the programs can accomplish. If you design the stack, you will certainly be able to take advantage of all of its functionality.

3. The creative process itself is rewarding and enjoyable.

4. In designing a stack to solve a problem, you will gain some insight into the nature of the problem itself. You may find out that the problem you are trying to solve with the stack is

a completely different one from what you first thought. This added insight makes you a better problem-solver.

Building stacks for others

If you are a programmer or a designer and are asked to develop stacks for other people you don't need to be convinced of the value of stack design. You've been doing custom programming long enough to understand its strengths and weaknesses. Your concern probably lies more with the issue of whether HyperCard is an appropriate vehicle for solving a specific problem.

The brief answer is that you can do anything with HyperCard, particularly with its extensibility (discussed in Chapters 21 and 22) and forthcoming interfaces to other languages, that you can do with any other programming language. Even without extension, HyperTalk is, as you will see in this book, a very powerful programming environment that is rich in functionality. The language also brings an ease to programming Macintosh applications that no other language has approached.

But you have to deal with some realities if you decide to use HyperCard and scripts to solve problems for clients and customers. The biggest single limitation of HyperCard is a function of its pleasant predictability for users. Applications written in HyperCard must permit only one window on the screen at a time and confine the size of that window to the size of the screen. If users have a big screen and run MultiFinder, they can relocate the window. But it will always be one window exactly as big as the standard screen. So if your application demands multiple windows, you are probably not going to choose HyperCard.

But don't be too hasty in deciding that you need multiple windows. We have perhaps become a bit spoiled by the Mac's power in permitting many windows lying around desktops that quickly become as cluttered as their real-world counterparts. But many applications don't require that added window capability. Unless the user needs to see two or more pieces of information in parallel on the screen or look at several different applications or data at the same time, multiple windows can become confusing, especially to the casual user. We've watched Mac newcomers struggle to figure out how to bring a hidden window to the top of the stack and noted the near-panic feeling of perhaps having lost forever not only the window but also its contents!

Another sometimes significant limitation of HyperCard from a programming standpoint is the way it shields you from Macintosh ROM Toolbox routines. This can be a real advantage: the ROM is mysterious and difficult to understand and manage in many ways. And it is true that you can extend Hyper-Talk with external commands and functions that do access the Toolbox (we'll show you some of those extensions in Chapter 22). But if you confine yourself to HyperTalk as it is designed and delivered by Apple Computer, you're apt to feel a loss of control over the application.

A minor but sometimes irritating restriction in HyperCard involves its confining all the text in a given field to a single type font and style. Getting around this problem can be quite a chore in fields that the user needs to be able to access and modify.

All these limitations are minor when you compare them to the staggering power and ease of programming in HyperTalk. But you are probably not going to design the next spreadsheet program in HyperCard. And it's not well-suited to designing a full-powered word-processing program. But tasks that involve the things at which HyperCard excels can be a pure joy to design and program in HyperTalk. Here's a list of some of the particular strong points of HyperCard.

1. You will probably never need to worry about local coordinates, global coordinates, and the location of button's and fields on the screen. HyperCard uses its own set of coordinates anchored to the upper-left corner of the card for almost everything you do. But more importantly, a buttons location has no effect on your scripts. If the user moves the button, your script need not be aware of his action. The script goes with the button, wherever the button goes.

2. Designing the most useful interface objects is as easy as using a painting or drawing program. Even scrolling fields, a difficult and demanding task even for a proficient Mac programmer, snap into place with a few clicks of the mouse.

3. HyperTalk, as we will see, includes powerful control structures, high-quality visual effects, and full program access to and control of menu interaction. It is a complete programming language in its own right.

4. When you write scripts, you can be as verbose (and readable) or terse (and efficient during coding) as you like, within broad limits. Many commands have several forms of syntax depending on how readable you want your scripts to be.

5. The modularity of having each script connected to an object means the notorious "ripple effect" of conventional programming practices all but disappears. If a handler for a particular event connected to a button works in script A, it will work identically in scripts B, C, and D, with little or no modification.

6. HyperTalk is designed so that it tries — very hard, in fact — to make sense out of your code. Only when it has exhausted a fairly thorough search of its understanding of the HyperCard environment are you going to get an error message. And when you do get an error message, you can move with a single mouse click to the script to find the cursor blinking at precisely the point where the error occurred. Debugging is streamlined.

You will discover dozens of other advantages to HyperTalk scripting as you work through this book and begin to build your own stacks. We believe that HyperCard as a paradigm and HyperTalk as its programming environment are a leap in Mac program design. Before you are done with this book, we're confident you will agree.

Step-By-Step Design

Now that you are convinced that designing and scripting your own stacks will be rewarding and pleasant, how do you begin? How do you move from an idea for a new product or a problem to the solution itself?

The steps in building a HyperCard stack are not so different from programming in more conventional languages. They are summarized in Figure 1-1. Those unique to HyperCard or that require further amplification are discussed in the following sections.

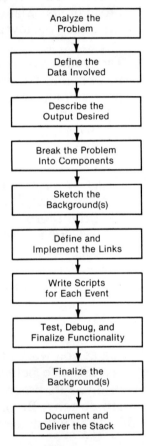

Figure 1-1. Steps in HyperCard stack design and construction

Design process

The first four steps in the process of designing a stack as shown in Figure 1-1 are identical to those in any other application development environment. They are beyond the scope of this discussion.

Any book about basic programming techniques contains information on these steps. There is some information in Chapter 23 about some of the decision-making involved in these steps from a HyperCard standpoint.

Sketch the backgrounds

Every stack has at least one card. Every card has one background. Sometimes the backgrounds in your stacks are graphically elaborate. Other times, they are simple and relatively sparse. Because the background can be detailed in later, it is a good idea simply to rough out the ideas and put in the necessary buttons and fields at this stage.

A word about "borrowing"

One of the principles of Macintosh software design that became established very early in the computer's history was the principle that "nobody does it from scratch." If you've done any serious Mac programming, you know that programmers frequently reuse the main event loops and common procedures of other programmers. There is, by and large, only one way to do many things on the Mac.

HyperCard extends the idea of borrowing to a new level. Unlike almost any phenomenon since the first days of BASIC on microcomputers, HyperCard has fostered a spirit of giving and sharing among its users and developers. We've seen programmers who wouldn't share three lines of their preciously thought-out and painstakingly crafted Pascal code go to great lengths to make sure that anyone who wanted a copy of their latest whiz-bang script got it. As a result of this spirit, you can go to hundreds of places to get ideas for backgrounds and card designs. You may stumble onto one that is exactly what you need for your stack. Or you may find one or more from which you can borrow elements to build what you need. This sort of borrowing — dubbed by one writer as "standing on other people's shoulders, not their toes" — is encouraged and generally positive.

But be careful about what you borrow and for what purpose. The stack, button, and card ideas distributed with HyperCard, for example, are yours to use freely. A great deal of stackware that has developed in the first furious months of HyperCard's popularity is freeware or shareware that you can use at little or no cost. But check your source. "Borrowing" cards, buttons, scripts, backgrounds, and designs from copyrighted stacks may be illegal and is certainly dishonest. If you really need something that a copyrighted stack contains and you are not planning to market the product that incorporates it, drop the copyright holder a note. Quite often, he or she will be happy to give you a release for the limited purpose of your stack; after all, imitation remains the sincerest form of flattery.

Defining and implementing links

If you have worked with HyperCard in its authoring mode, you know that much of the readily apparent power and flexibility of the program stems from its elegant implementation of dynamic links. Connecting one card or idea to another is child's play.

When you design a stack, it's a good idea to think very early about these links. At least two major benefits derive from this approach.

First, deciding on the links often helps you structure the stack in the way that the casual browsing or typing user will find comfortable and natural. Before all the functionality and relative complexity of scripts and dozens or hundreds of cards are in the way, you can think about this issue concisely and somewhat abstractly. Also, this often enables you to gain insight into the design of the stack itself, sometimes leading you to change or enhance the design.

Second, implementing the links is easier when the stack is new and there aren't a lot of visual or conceptual impediments to seeing the path clearly. Efficiency will result.

Writing scripts

This book is entirely about writing HyperTalk scripts. These collections of HyperTalk "code" are not nearly so much like programs in the conventional sense as they are like Pascal subroutines or Smalltalk methods. (We'll have more to say on this subject in the next chapter.)

A script is exactly what its name implies. It consists of a series of handlers, each of which is responsible for dealing with or responding to certain messages from HyperCard objects such as buttons and fields. And a script tells the object to which it is connected how to behave, which is exactly what a TV or theater script does.

You may develop your scripts modularly, dealing with one event at a time. "What do I want to have happen when this button is pressed?" is one question that is answered by a script.

Testing and debugging

Like the first four steps of this process, testing and debugging a script is very similar to programming in other languages and won't be covered in this book. Suffice it to say that you should make sure the script is working under all circumstances you anticipate the end user expecting.

Finalizing the backgrounds

After you're sure the stack and all its scripts are working, you can confidently fill in the graphic, visual, and other details of the backgrounds. We are not talking about the functional or operational aspects of the background such as buttons and fields but rather of cleaning up fixed-text labels, adding graphic interest, detailing existing rough sketches, and the like.

Documenting HyperTalk

As mentioned, HyperTalk permits you to write scripts that are easily read by other people, even those who are not proficient scripters. Throughout this book, we encourage this verbose, readable style for many reasons. If you are interested in some of the most cogent arguments for ensuring the readability of code, get a copy of Dr. Adele Goldberg's article, "Programmer as Reader," which appeared in the September 1987 issue of *IEEE*

Software magazine. Among other things, she says, "Readability is an issue because we read to learn to write, and we read to find information, and we read in order to rewrite." We firmly agree.

But beyond writing your scripts in a verbose way (even though it requires a few extra keystrokes when you're typing the script), you should also be sure to include a Help function in your stack. Users are accustomed to seeing a question mark (see Figure 1-2) on which they can click to get help. The help screen that appears when you click on such a button is just another card or a pop-up field on the current card.

Figure 1-2. Typical HyperCard help button icons

A final level of documentation involves the judicious use of buttons that are intuitive and visual effects that convey information to the user. These topics require an understanding of how HyperTalk works and deals with the user and are left to Chapter 23.

Summary

In this chapter, you examined some of the reasons for doing your own HyperCard stacks and scripts. We discussed the process of designing stacks and examined the steps that are unique to HyperTalk.

Before you begin learning the HyperTalk language however, you will be well-served by taking a more conceptual look at HyperTalk and its HyperCard environment. This process begins in the next chapter, when we relate HyperTalk to the concepts of object-oriented programming.

CHAPTER

2

Object-Oriented Programming

In this chapter, you will learn

- the important new role being played in software development by concepts grouped under the rubric "Object-Oriented Programming" (OOP)

- how HyperCard parallels some of those concepts and goes its way in others

- how an understanding of OOP can help you be a better HyperTalk programmer

HyperCard: Object-Like Programming

Let us be clear at the outset of this discussion. HyperTalk is not object-oriented programming in the "traditional" sense. We know it lacks some essential features of true OOP. But our interest in

11

this chapter is how closely some key ideas in HyperCard resemble those in OOP. The objective is to see what the world of OOP has to offer to would-be HyperTalk gurus.

To describe HyperTalk and its somewhat loose ties to OOP, we have coined the phrase *Object-Like Programming* while not suggesting that we refer to it as OLP. HyperTalk is object-like in that it uses some of the same terminology, adopts some of the same methods and adapts others, and in many ways looks and"feels" like OOP.

Before you can appreciate the validity and utility of all this, though, you need a basic understanding of OOP. The next section presents some of the fundamental ideas in OOP, but it is not an exhaustive treatment of the subject. (For more depth and lots of examples, see Kurt J. Schmucker's *Object-Oriented Programming on the Macintosh,* another member of the Hayden Macintosh Library.) If you are already familiar with OOP, you might want to skim or skip the next section.

OOP Fundamentals

Object-oriented programming is a way of looking at programming tasks that differs from the traditional approach. In procedural programming with Pascal, C, and other similar languages, you describe functions and procedures that operate on certain types of data. The data is separate from the functions that operate on it. In OOP, data and procedures that operate on the data are together, packaged in something called an *object*.

There are five central ideas in OOP: objects, messages, methods, classes, and inheritance. Although we explain each of these ideas briefly, they are so intertwined that an understanding of each depends on an understanding of the others.

What are objects?

Viewed abstractly, an *object* is a single programming entity that combines data and procedures or functions that operate on that data. Viewed from a programming standpoint, objects are the elements of an OOP system that send and receive messages. We discuss messages in greater detail in the next section.

If you write a procedure to invert something in Pascal, you have to know in advance what kind of data the procedure will operate on. For example, inverting text might mean changing it from black letters on a white background to white letters on a black background. Inverting a matrix, however, is a complex mathematical operation unrelated to text color display. Similarly, inverting a graphic object like a pyramid is different from inverting text or numeric matrices. If you want a program to be able to invert any of these types of data, you would write a separately named procedure for each type of data, check in your program for the type of data to be manipulated, and then call the appropriate procedure. This process is depicted in Figure 2-1.

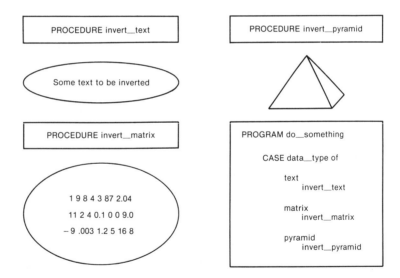

Figure 2-1. Data, procedures, and programs are separate in traditional programming

Object-oriented programming however, permits the designer to say, in essence, "I want to invert whatever object I've been working with, so I'll just use an invert command and let the system take care of the problem." In OOP parlance, this command is referred to as a message. An object called, for example, matrix receives a message called invert and carries out its own processing in response to the message. There are still three separate invert routines, but the part of the program that inverts an object doesn't need to be aware of them. This situation is represented in Figure 2-2.

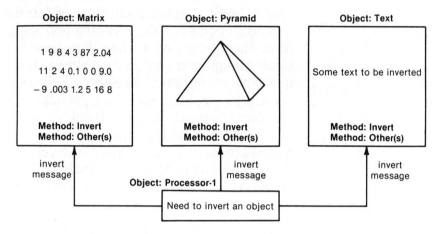

Figure 2-2. Data, messages, and methods in OOP

You can probably see an advantage to the OOP approach. If you want to add a new type of object to a procedural language application — for example, a list of items where invert means "reverse the order of" — you have to define a new procedure and add a new case to the main program. In other words, everything will change. Thanks to the well-known "ripple effect," the consequences of this could take a long time to resolve. In an OOP world, though, you simply create a new object and add to it the ability to invert itself. Any other objects that send this new object an invert message do not need to be modified. The change is isolated and, therefore, manageable.

What are messages?

We have talked glibly about messages as if it were obvious what they are and what they do. Although they may constitute a new *programming* idea, the concept of messages is not novel. When you call a friend across town and she answers the phone, you are sending messages. When you mail a letter to someone and the person on the other end opens it and reads it, you're sending messages. In fact, you probably do most of your work by sending messages of one kind or another to other people and to machinery or electronic equipment.

A *message* in an OOP world corresponds to a procedure or function call in a procedural language. Everything in OOP is accomplished only one way: one object sends a message to another object and the receiving object reacts. There are no alternate ways to get things done. The simple elegance of this model makes programs written for an OOP environment easy to understand.

What are methods?

The idea of a *method* is the easiest of the five basic OOP concepts to explain. A method corresponds almost exactly with a function or a procedure. A method is the code in an object that tells the object how to react when it receives a message with the same name as the method.

In the previous example, each type of object had an *invert* method. When an object receives an *invert* message from another object, it simply carries out the instructions in that method. Sometimes, it sends a message back to the sending object indicating it has completed the instruction. Other times, it might trigger another method in another object, perhaps even a different *invert* method in another object, to accomplish its goals. To do so, it sends a message to that object.

If a message is sent to an object that does not have a method of that name defined, the system generally handles the problem with an error message such as "Object pyramid doesn't understand how to invert." Objects in OOP can have zero to any theoretically large number of methods they understand and that mold their behavior in reaction to messages from other objects.

What are classes?

Groups of objects with sets of common characteristics are called *classes*. The most important thing objects in a class have in common is the way they react to one or more messages. If we had to write the same method for every single object, some of the advantages of OOP discussed in the next section would be lost in a mass of code. But if we define a class, each object we create as a member of that class will already know how to behave in response to the messages the class contains. The class, like everything else in an object-oriented world, is itself an object.

Individual objects are referred to as *instances* of a class. Because a class is also an object, an object can be both a class and an instance of another class. The concept that makes classes significant is the fifth OOP central idea: inheritance.

What is inheritance?

In a true object-oriented world, objects *inherit* behavior from their *ancestors* in an ever-expanding and descending chain of heredity. All objects in OOP have at least one ancestor. The closer an object is to the root object class from which all other objects and classes spring, the fewer ancestors it has. This structure resembles an outline or a classification scheme.

Figure 2-3 depicts a classification structure for a class called Furniture. As you can see, this class has subclasses called Seating, Table, and Lamp. The subclass Seating, in turn, has other subclasses, and so on.

```
Class:  Furniture
    Class:  Seating
        Class:  Chair
                Instance:  armchair
                Instance:  easy chair
                Instance:  secretarial chair
        Class:  Stool
                Instance:  milking stool
                Instance:  bar stool
                Instance:  snack counter stool
        Class:  Sofa
                Instance:  sofa bed
                Instance:  sofa
                Instance:  love seat
    Class:  Table
    Class:  Lamp
```

Figure 2-3.   Typical classification scheme

The key idea in inheritance is that if the class Furniture has a method called, for example, moveIt, every member of every subclass can use that method in the same way. If you send the message moveIt to a love seat, it need not have a method called moveIt. It simply passes the message up the hierarchy to its immediate ancestor (in this case, Sofa), which reacts if it has a method named moveIt or passes the message on if it doesn't have a corresponding method.

Generally, you can override a method that a class has in common so that an individual instance can react differently to that message. If you find yourself doing this too often, the method may be one that isn't really a good one around which to build a class.

Object-oriented programming summary

Let's see if we can capsulize this sketchy look at object-oriented programming. Everything in an OOP environment is an object. Each object (except the one central object from which all others are descended) has at least one ancestor. An object inherits methods from all its ancestors in the chain that tell it how to respond to messages. Everything in an OOP environment is accomplished by objects sending messages to other objects.

Why Object-Oriented Programming?

Why has OOP become such an important idea in the past few years? It really seems to be just a new way of looking at programs and data. So what's all the excitement about?

The characteristics inherent in OOP create numerous advantages in software design and development. Let's take a look at the three main ones often singled out by proponents of the OOP approach to computer programming. These are

- the natural "feel" of the OOP model of the problem

- the high degree of code reusability

- the ease of maintenance and modification

OOP is "natural"

The world in which we live is composed of objects. And as we saw earlier, we accomplish much of what we do by sending messages to other objects in our world and reacting to their messages. Furthermore, we generally do things by telling other objects *what* we want done rather than by explaining in great detail *how* to do them. The *how* describes the procedure and is part of the procedural programming model. The *what* describes the task, the problem, and its solution in descriptive, or declarative, terms, and is part of the *declarative* programming model of which OOP is a prime example. When you give your Macintosh a print message, you don't tell it, "Now I want you to take this document that I've just finished creating and analyze its bit map structure. Got it?" You just tell it to print and expect its behavior to follow.

Similarly, if you give an assignment to a subordinate, you generally say, "I need the quarterly objectives report on my desk by 3:00, Jim." You don't say, "Jim, I want you to sit down at your desk. Take out a piece of paper and a pencil. Now, put at the top of the paper..."

But these descriptions — simplified for illustration — are good summaries of the differences between procedural programming and OOP. The world just doesn't work procedurally. Consequently it is much easier to write programs designed to emulate or simulate reality and intelligence in OOP environments than in more procedure-oriented environments.

NOTE

We should not leave the impression that the dichotomy is between procedural languages and OOP. The distinction is between procedural and declarative languages. OOP just happens to use a declarative style. Prolog, for example, is virtually never used in OOP environments but is a declarative language.

Code reusability

If you can define one object that is usable in several different systems, you can move it from one system to another with great ease in an OOP environment. There is nothing new to declare in the second system, no data structures to worry about, no other objects or procedures to modify. Simply pick up the object from program A and plop it down in program B and run it.

Consequently if a programmer is proficient in and comfortable with OOP design concepts, he or she spends a great deal of time building reusable tools and objects. After that, a large percentage of programming time is spent simply assembling the appropriate objects into new "worlds," or systems. Very little time gets used up by re-inventing wheels.

Ease of maintenance

As we saw earlier, the "ripple effect" that causes so many software maintenance headaches all but disappears in an OOP environment. If the object behaves in a certain way in system A, it is guaranteed to work the same way in system B. Debugging is effectively (though not totally) reduced to finding messages sent to inappropriate objects, messages sent with the wrong number of arguments, and missing or undefined objects and methods.

OOP and HyperCard

So what does all of this have to do with HyperCard and Hyper-Talk? After all, we've already pointed out that HyperTalk is not an object-oriented programming language.

There are some strong parallels between HyperTalk and true OOP systems, though, and these parallels are neither accidental nor incidental. Although the parallels are not exact and don't hold up throughout the architecture of HyperTalk, they are interesting and important enough to merit our attention. Our hope is that by seeing the aspects of design and programming that HyperTalk and more traditional OOP languages have in common, you will see how to take advantage of OOP concepts in designing stacks.

Objects in HyperTalk

There are five types of objects in HyperTalk: stacks, backgrounds, cards, buttons, and fields. Like OOP objects, each of these can send and receive messages. Each type of object can be associated with a *script* that contains *handlers,* which correspond to methods (as we'll see in a moment). So the object and the program code that enables it to respond in a specific and predictable way to a message are packaged together, exactly like objects in an OOP environment.

Messages in HyperTalk

The parallel between OOP systems and HyperTalk continues when we examine the subject of messages. HyperTalk uses the same term to describe the communications that take place between objects.

HyperTalk includes system messages that are sent as a result of events triggered by stack users. Each type of message can be addressed to one or more of the types of objects encompassed by HyperCard.

Conceptually, a stack, like all Macintosh applications, is a single loop (technically referred to as the *Main Event Loop*) that essentially stays on the alert for events to which it must respond. When an event takes place, a system message is generated and sent to the object of which the event is the target. That object reacts as called for in the handlers contained in its script. The parallel with OOP is quite strong.

Methods in HyperTalk

As we have pointed out, each type of object in the HyperCard hierarchy can have a script associated with it. In each script there can be one or more handlers. These handlers correspond closely to OOP methods. A handler is associated with each type of message the object can receive.

There are two types of handlers in HyperTalk scripts: function handlers and on handlers. On handlers are also called *event* handlers in this book because they are typically triggered by an event, as described in the preceding section.

In addition, all HyperCard objects are associated with *properties* (discussed in Chapter 17). Some properties bear a close resemblance to methods as well. For example, a button can have a property of being automatically highlighted when it is pressed. This is a character trait, or behavior, of the object, and so it corresponds at least roughly to a method.

Classes in HyperTalk

There is no strong analog in HyperTalk to OOP's concept of classes. The hierarchical form of inheritance (see the next section) used in HyperTalk is not precisely parallel to that of object-oriented programming, due in part to the lack of classes for objects. For example, there is no class called a button *class* to which all buttons belong and which has individual instances of buttons. Although there is some commonality of behavior among buttons — they all, for example, cause something to happen when they are pressed — there is really no classification scheme resembling OOP classes.

The concept of card *backgrounds,* however, comes close to emulating an OOP class. All cards in a stack with the same background have many common characteristics. They usually look the same, and buttons that appear on backgrounds look and act identically from card to card within the background group. When you design a stack, you generally group cards with similar functions into backgrounds in the stack. Complex stacks almost always have more than one background.

But because you put specific card types into the same background group rather than have them formed by the program as a consequence of their functional similarity or as a direct result of a command, the parallel with OOP classes is not quite complete.

Inheritance in HyperTalk

There is no true inheritance in HyperTalk. Messages pass through a definite hierarchy (see Figure 2-4), and this hierarchy has some of the characteristics of OOP inheritance structures, but the analogy is less complete when it comes to inheritance than on any other point.

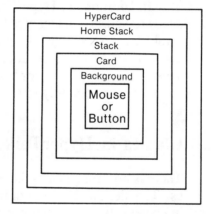

Figure 2-4. HyperTalk hierarchy of inheritance

The hierarchy in Figure 2-4 is up from the button or field, where the action takes place that triggers the event, to the background, card, and stack, then to the Home stack, and finally to HyperCard itself.

A message that originates with the press of the mouse on a button gets passed up the hierarchy until one of two things happens: a handler with the same name is encountered and executed or the top of the hierarchy is reached with no handler having intercepted and acted on the message. This behavior is quite similar to the message processing approach of OOP systems.

But the opposite is not true. In other words, just because a particular button on a card has the ability to respond to a specific type of message does not mean all other buttons have the same capability. The same can be said of backgrounds and cards. If you create a new card using the Edit Menu's New Card option, the new card has the same background as the currently visible card unless you specifically choose not to copy that background (in which case you end up with a blank new card). If the background has a handler for a particular system message, the copy also has that same handler. But this is not inheritance so much as it is copying, because the new card of the same background is not a descendant of the original; both are on the same level of the hierarchy.

How OOP thinking helps in stack design

You can see why we said at the outset of this discussion that HyperTalk is not true OOP but shares enough with that approach to software design to merit consideration of the parallels.

We mentioned that code reusability is a major advantage of OOP systems. Because of the absence of true inheritance, that advantage does not accrue to HyperTalk. Thanks to the Macintosh's marvelous editing power of cut-and-paste, you can easily copy scripts and handlers from one object to another object of the same type (or even a different type). But this manual process, no matter how facile, hardly qualifies as inheritance of behavior from object to descendant object.

On the other hand, the isolated nature of a handler and its ease of modification mean that maintaining scripts is much easier than modifying and managing traditional procedural programs. If the handler works in response to the message it handles in one card or button, it will work correctly in another place. Similarly, if a script has more than one handler, even if they interact, the functionality is isolated to a sufficient degree that software maintenance is quite straightforward.

Finally, and perhaps most significantly to HyperTalk programmers, the language does a remarkably good job of emulating the world of which it is a model: that of the Macintosh application. It makes working with the complex world of objects much simpler, more readable, and more enjoyable than any other Macintosh product since the first desktop appeared on the first 128K Mac screen several years ago.

Partly because of its strong object influence and partly because of the nature of the Macintosh world that lends itself well to such object emulation, HyperTalk removes many of the barriers between programmers and elegant, usable, Mac-like applications.

Summary

In this chapter, we looked at the basic concepts of the new software idea called object-oriented programming (or OOP) and saw how they relate to the HyperTalk programming language. We also saw that the parallels between the two approaches are strong but not complete. We learned some of the advantages of OOP and saw how those advantages translate into the world of HyperTalk design and programming.

Chapter 3 is a refresher course in how HyperCard works from the viewpoint of a browser or author.

HyperCard Refresher

This chapter reviews some of the basic ideas in HyperCard as seen by the users of your stacks. Topics include

- user preferences

- navigation techniques

- links

- using **find**

- authoring tools

- field creation and characteristics

- button creation and characteristics

- copying, moving, and sizing objects

- using HyperCard on read-only media, such as CD-ROM

25

The User's Viewpoint

Before we launch into a discussion of programming in Hyper-Talk, let's pause and take a telescoped look at HyperCard from the perspective of the users who do not generally program their own stacks. Until now, you were probably in this category. So it may seem redundant to spend any time on the *use* of Hyper-Card. After all, you bought this book to learn to *program* Hyper-Card your way, not to learn to use it.

But our objective here is not to teach you to use HyperCard. It is rather to refresh your recollection about aspects of its use that may by now have become so familiar that you don't think about them much. Additionally, we look at some of the authoring techniques you'll need to emulate in your scripts with commands. You are used to performing techniques with explicit mouse-and-tool manipulation. But running these tools by remote control, through a HyperTalk script, has a slightly different feel. By spending these few minutes, you will also understand the user's relationship to HyperCard. That will make the rest of your exploration in this book more fruitful.

What kind of user?

When we talk about the user's perspective, what kind of user do we have in mind? Given that there are several levels of user below that of scripting, what type are we talking about here?

Throughout this book we will focus on designing and providing stacks for users who are browsers and typers. We are convinced that the majority of HyperCard users are in those categories and that most are probably typers. You will probably want to design your stack so that the user who wants to do authoring can't get into your scripts and change anything fundamental. And you will probably not want your users to be able to relocate buttons and fields, particularly if you rely on their position for some of the tasks in your scripts.

So the primary emphasis is on the user who wants to get at a stack of information, put new data into a stack, and use the knowledge stored there without moving things around or changing the way they work.

But we also discuss authoring techniques and tools. By now, you probably have some experience with these aspects of HyperCard. Although we don't expect the user of your stacks to understand these tools, you will often use the techniques described in this chapter to build basic cards and backgrounds. And you'll be doing object manipulation that originates in the authoring environment from within scripts.

User preferences

HyperCard has five levels of user involvement. These are outlined in settings on the User Preferences card in the Home stack, as shown in Figure 3-1. Each higher level of control gives users access to additional tools.

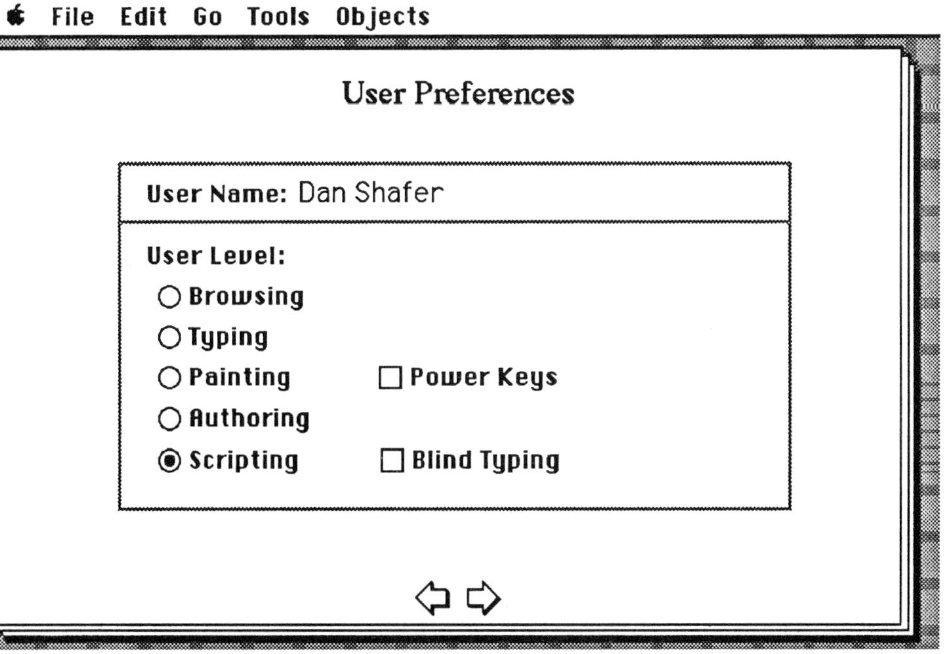

Figure 3-1. User preferences settings

At the *browsing* level, users can only look at information in a stack. This corresponds to traditional read-only access. Moving to the *typing* level, users can enter and edit text in card fields, giving them read-write access to data but still restricting them from changing the stack's structure.

When users have *painting* level control, they can add graphic objects to the stack or any card with the powerful paint tools built into HyperCard. At this point, users can change the stack's appearance but not its functionality.

Users with *authoring* access can modify fields and buttons, create new backgrounds, and generally modify anything about a stack except the scripts attached to objects. This is the highest level of control over HyperCard one can use without learning to program in the HyperTalk language.

Only by setting the level to *scripting* can users gain access to scripts and HyperTalk commands for permanent modification of the stack.

NOTE

To do the work in this book, make sure you have set your user level to scripting on the User Preferences card of the Home stack. It's probably a good idea to do that now if you haven't previously done so.

Modifying the user's level

As you will see in Chapter 17, one of HyperCard's global properties that your script can monitor and modify is the user's access level. You can be in control of this the entire time your stack is running. If you want to disallow access above the browsing or typing level because such access could be dangerous to your stack, you can

• set the user level in your script

• intercept and prevent any effort by the user to modify the level

> ## CAUTION
>
> If you do find it necessary to change the user's access level during the use of your script, be sure to change it back to its original setting when your script is finished and the user is returning to the Home stack or going on to other work. If you fail to do so, you may find yourself with some highly irritated users who find themselves unable to perform tasks they should be able to perform on other stacks after using yours.

Browsing-Level Operation

Even a browsing-level user can perform a number of functions in HyperCard. We will concentrate on two activities that constitute most of those actions and, not coincidentally, the bulk of the browsing-level commands in HyperTalk: navigation (moving between cards and stacks) and finding information in fields.

Navigation functions

As you design and construct stacks, keep in mind the ways in which the casual user is accustomed to moving around in HyperCard.

Most stacks have buttons the user can click to move forward or backward in the stack, to the beginning of the stack, or to the last card in the stack. These buttons often look like those shown in Figure 3-2, though of course they need not look like them at all. The buttons in Figure 3-2 are included with Hyper-Card in the Button Ideas stack.

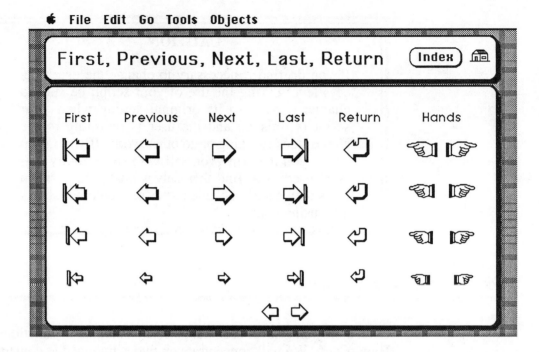

Figure 3-2. Typical navigation buttons

Because browsers are accustomed to buttons of this type for navigation, you should consider including such buttons in your stacks and retaining their usual meanings. Placing a right arrow button in your stack and expecting the user to know that the button increases the value of a number in a field, for example, is not a terrific design idea

On the other hand, feel free to invent new icons or shapes for buttons that are, at least to some degree, self-evident. For example, if you want to let a reader who has clicked on the turned-up corner of a card move forward and backward in the stack, this is relatively easy to do and may be sufficiently evident that the user figures it out easily and becomes comfortable with it.

Clicking on buttons is not the only way users can navigate, of course. They can choose items from the Go menu (see Figure 3-3) or type their keyboard equivalents. All these navigation techniques are available to the browsing user.

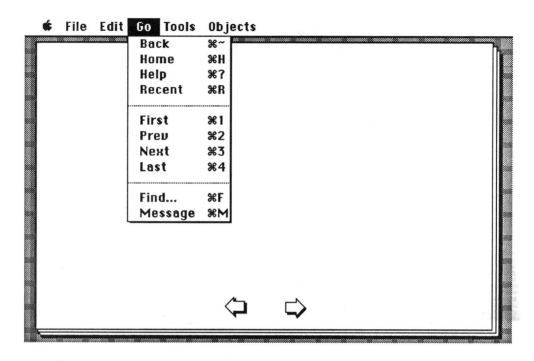

Figure 3-3. Go menu

It is unlikely that you will design a stack in which you don't want the user to be able to navigate. But if you do design such a stack, not only will you want to exclude the usual navigation buttons, you will also want to design handlers to trap key combinations the user can type to navigate as well as menu selections.

Using *find*

Another common task the browsing user performs is locating information stored in fields by using the **find** command. This command can be invoked by a menu selection from the Go menu or by typing Command-F from the keyboard. When the user selects a **find** operation, the Message box appears (if it was previously invisible), with the word *find* already typed and the cursor flashing between two quotation marks (see Figure 3-4). The user then types in the string to be searched for in the stack. When HyperCard finds the string, it stops on the card and draws a rectangle around the located text (see Figure 3-5).

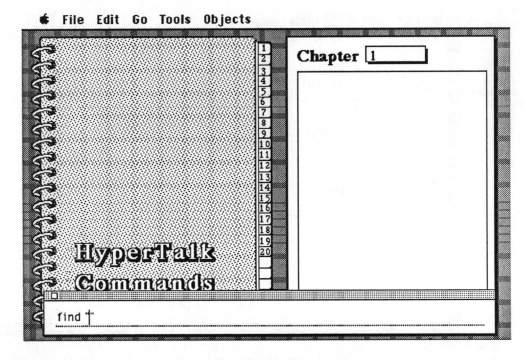

Figure 3-4. The *find* Message box

Quite often the user types in more than one word to find. In that event, HyperCard finds a card on which all of the words appear, regardless of their order, relation to one another, or even if they are all in the same field. For example, if the user searches for New England, a card that describes the new Prime Minister of England is found, with the word new marked.

With HyperCard versions beginning with 1.2, the user can force HyperCard to find multiple-word groups only if they appear in one field and in exactly the order given. This **find whole** function is invoked when the user presses Shift-Command-F from the keyboard or uses the command inside the Message Box or a script.

If you are designing a stack that involves data management (see Chapter 10), you may want to include more sophisticated **find** capabilities in your scripts. You can, for example, let the user confine the search to a single field. But the basic **find** process is the same.

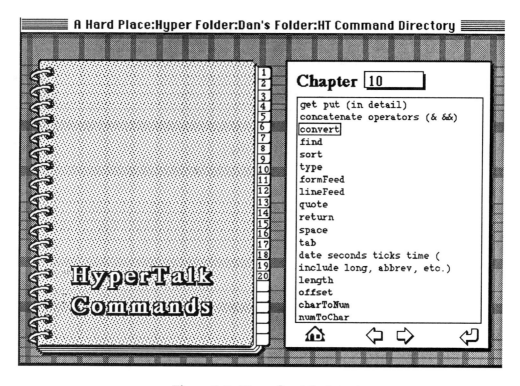

Figure 3-5. HyperCard finds text

Authoring-Level Operations

At the authoring level, the user can perform an almost endless variety of functions. The ones with which we are most concerned, however, involve manipulating HyperCard objects, particularly buttons and fields. Some of these functions in turn involve the use of tools other than the browsing tool. We discuss the following operations in the context of scripting:

- adding and deleting cards

- tool selection and use

- creating fields

- creating buttons

- copying, moving, and resizing buttons and fields

Adding and deleting cards

Because the New Card, Delete Card, and Cut Card options appear on the Edit menu, you might think the browsing-level user has access to them. After all, the Edit menu is displayed when the user is a browser. But there are two different Edit menus in HyperCard, one for browsing users and one for all other levels. The menu on the left of Figure 3-6 shows what facilities the browsing-level user has available. The one on the right is the full Edit menu.

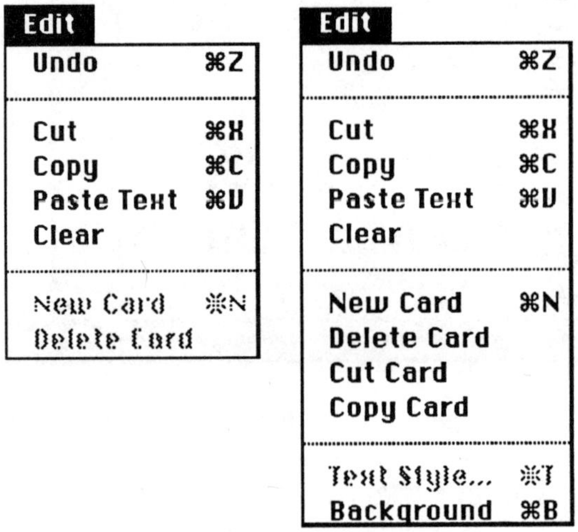

Figure 3-6. HyperCard's Edit menus

As you will see when we begin exploring HyperTalk's commands, you can design handlers to intercept the user's attempts to delete cards, cut cards, or create new ones. Sometimes you want special control over these functions if your stack allows their use. For example, you might not want to let users delete a card that has an outstanding value in a field. Or you might not want to let users delete anything unless they have a special password that the manager of the script-using team only gives to certain members of the group.

Tool selection and use

Authoring-level users of HyperCard can also access the button, field, and painting tools from the Tools menu (see Figure 3-7). Using these tools, users can modify basic information about buttons and fields or alter the appearance of a card or a background.

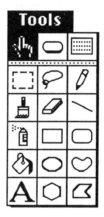

Figure 3-7. Tools menu

The three tools across the top portion of the Tools menu are the browsing tool, button tool, and field tool, respectively. All tools below the dotted line in the menu are painting tools. Depending on the tool selected, the user can perform various tasks using the tools directly or accessing menu options that only appear when a specific tool is chosen.

From within a script, you can choose a tool and then use various commands to manipulate it as if by remote control. You can also intercept an attempt to access a specific tool and either prevent it or post a warning notice that lets users proceed only after acknowledging that what they're about to do could damage the stack or card content.

Creating fields and buttons

Users with authoring-level access to HyperCard can create new
objects besides cards. They can add buttons and fields to a card
or background. (They can also modify them, as we will see in
the next section.) Because these operations can alter the nature
of your stack and the operation of your scripts, you may want to
provide intercepting handlers.

Users can create a new field in two ways. They can choose
the New Field option from the Objects menu, or they can use the
field tool to select and copy an existing field, then move it to a
different place on the card or background. New button creation
is a similar process. Copying can be done either with a menu option or by dragging the selected object with the Option key held
down. If you are faced with users who have authoring-level access to HyperCard, you will want to be sure to either permit such
modifications and plan for them or provide handlers to intercept
the user's attempt to manipulate the stack via menus or tools and
provide appropriate barriers or warnings.

Altering fields and buttons

Besides adding new buttons and fields, users can delete, copy,
move, and resize existing objects if they have authoring-level access to your script. As is the case with creating new objects,
they can modify existing objects either by using the right tool
and selecting the object manually or by using menu choices.

For example, the user can delete a button after it is selected by

- pressing the Backspace key

- choosing Cut Button from the Edit menu

- choosing Delete Button from the Edit menu

- pressing Command-X at the keyboard

Deleting other objects is also easy to do and there are many ways to accomplish the deed. Your script will have to deal with each of these possible situations to avoid serious damage to your stack.

Users can also use the appropriate tool to select an object, then drag it to a new location or resize it or both. Most of the time, this will not affect your scripts, because the object's location on the screen is not vital to your script's execution. Wherever the user drags a button, it will still carry out its task when it is pressed. But if you have script commands that depend on the exact screen locations of objects, you will want to monitor the changing of those locations by the user.

Avoiding User Paranoia

With all this talk about the damage users can do to your stacks and even their scripts if they have proper levels of access and the desire to do so or a lack of understanding of the effects of their actions, you may want to become very defensive in your Hyper-Talk programming. One word of advice is in order: don't.

Macintosh users are accustomed to a great deal of freedom and flexibility when they run applications. The Macintosh's design philosophy is that the user, not the programmer, is the boss. If you design a script so that users can do exactly what you want them to do and nothing else, you may find the script is not well-received, at least by experienced Macintosh users.

We have more to say about this and other design issues in Chapter 23, where we provide a number of design guidelines. But for the moment, simply be aware that you must balance the need for your stack to stay relatively unmolested and predictable against the user's right to and expectation of a great deal of flexibility, freedom, control, and power.

HyperCard and CD-ROM

From the time of its introduction, HyperCard was clearly perceived by many people to be the key for unlocking the potential of such huge mass-storage media as CD-ROM (Compact Disk Read Only Memory) and laser disks. In its first releases, however, HyperCard could not work directly on locked media, which limited its usefulness for such activities.

Beginning with Version 1.2, however, HyperCard can work with locked media.

Summary

This concludes our discussion of how HyperCard works from the user's perspective and how those operations should affect your thinking as you script stacks. You have seen that users can perform many tasks, some of which may be undesirable. And you know there are ways to intercept users' actions and either prevent them or at least warn of the consequences before allowing them to proceed.

Chapter 4 describes the basic building blocks of which all HyperCard applications are composed and begins our study of the HyperTalk programming language.

CHAPTER

HyperTalk Building Blocks

In this chapter, you will learn about the items that make up HyperTalk, including

- action elements

- passive character traits

- objects

This chapter presents an overview of these HyperTalk building blocks; each is discussed in detail in one or more places later in the book.

Naming Things in HyperTalk

Before we begin our examination of the components of the HyperTalk programming language, though, we should pause to discuss the rules regarding the names of things in HyperTalk.

Action elements and variables in the HyperTalk language are generally made up of one word. Action elements include functions, commands, and messages. If you define a new function designed to reverse the characters in a string, for example, you can call it *reverse*, *reverseString*, *reverseIt*, or something similar. But you cannot name it *reverse the string* because that name has more than one word. Similarly, variables, a type of special item called a *container* in HyperTalk, must also have one-word names.

Passive elements other than variables are not generally named; they are more correctly viewed as part of the structure of the language, as we will see in a few moments.

Objects can be named almost anything you wish, using as many words as you like. Thus, you can have a stack named *My Important Stuff* and a card named *Books and Magazine Articles*. Buttons frequently have two-word or three-word names (though you have to watch the length and make sure it can be seen through the button if you have HyperCard show the name on the button). This makes HyperCard friendlier for users. A button named *Do It!* is more communicative than one called *doIt*, which might in fact also be misread.

Several words in one

One naming technique HyperTalk scripters often use is to run two or more words together into one and then capitalize the first letter of each embedded word. You'll see labels like *currentStackName*, *mouseUp*, and *passMeTheSalt* sprinkled through the HyperTalk script examples in this book and other scripts.

This approach to naming things is not unique to HyperTalk. Programmers have been using the technique for many years. But some programming languages have limits on the lengths of names that make the use of such an approach marginally useful at best. In HyperTalk, you won't encounter any limit that will become problematic. A button or field, for example, can have a name up to 253 characters long.

The first character is important

It is a good idea to avoid beginning the name of any HyperTalk item with a number although it is not, strictly speaking, illegal. HyperCard stores everything as strings of characters and tries to interpret the numeric nature of this information from its context. The matter is further complicated because HyperCard automatically assigns numeric identification numbers to objects other than stacks when they are created. Suppose you name a card *1234Alpha* and then try to tell HyperCard to **go** to that card. HyperCard is likely to assume from the first digit that this label is a card ID. As a result, it won't find the card. Begin names with a letter, and you'll avoid a lot of confusion!

Active Elements of HyperTalk

An active element, for the purpose of our discussion, is any component of HyperTalk that results in something happening in the environment. Messages are the basic active element, but there are several others, including

- commands

- handlers

- functions

- scripts

These elements and their use occupy much of our attention in this book. The following brief discussion simply puts those future discussions into perspective rather than provides an exhaustive treatment of each subject.

Messages

We have spent some time in Chapter 2 describing messages and their role in HyperTalk. Now let's examine a message structurally.

All HyperTalk messages consist of only one word. That important idea is sometimes hard to remember. Because Hyper-Talk includes the ability to add *throw-away* words (or, in more traditional programming parlance, *optional parameters*), some messages look like they're longer than one word. For example, in Chapter 13 we'll see the use of visual effects in HyperTalk. These effects can be called with the message **visual**. But they can also use the optional second word **effect** so that the command looks like **visual effect zoom open**.

But only the first word of a message is the message itself. Everything that comes after is either a parameter or additional descriptive information (to tell HyperTalk what object to affect with the message, for example).

The rule that only the first word of a message is its name becomes important when you write handlers to respond to messages. The handler must be associated with a message name. Requiring that all message names be one word makes life much easier for us scripters!

Handlers

There are two types of handlers in HyperTalk: event handlers and function handlers. An event handler always begins with the key word **on** followed by the name of the message it is designed to handle. It also ends with the key word **end** followed again by the name of the message it handles. Most handlers you write will be event handlers.

A function handler begins with the key word **function** followed by the name of the function it defines. The purpose of this handler is to allow you to define new functions that can be used by other event handlers. This type of handler also ends with the key word **end** followed by the name of the function involved.

After you define a function in a function handler, it is available to all other event and function handlers in the same script or lower in the HyperTalk hierarchy. A function handler cannot be defined within another function handler or an event handler.

There are some operational differences between these two types of handlers. This subject occupies much of our attention in Chapter 5.

Functions

Functions are of two types: built-in HyperTalk functions and user-defined functions. HyperTalk has approximately 50 functions that can be used in any handler. These functions involve such tasks as

- mathematical calculations

- locating and managing the mouse and its button

- dealing with date and time

In addition, you can define any function you need. You do this in function handlers, discussed previously and covered in detail in Chapter 19. (It is also legal to define a function with the same name as a predefined one, but then you bear the responsibility for its proper use everywhere in your stack.)

Scripts

A script in HyperTalk is a collection of one or more handlers — some or all of which may be empty — associated with a particular object. Although every object has a script, the script may have nothing in it.

You can think of a script as a program, but as you know from Chapter 2, that is a simplification. There are no programs in a HyperCard stack. Instead, you have one or more scripts, each composed of one or more handlers, which, taken together, constitute the methods describing the stack's behavior in response to messages.

Passive Traits

Not everything in HyperTalk is active. Some elements of the language are for the convenience and use of active elements. These include

- variables

- properties

- control structures

- "chunks"

Variables as containers of information

Throughout this book and other HyperCard and HyperTalk documentation, you will find the term *container* used quite frequently. It is easy, after a brief acquaintance with the term and its use, to conclude that a container is nothing more than a variable in a conventional programming language. That view, however, is too simplistic to be useful or accurate.

A variable is a type of container. But in the broader sense a container is anything that can be a repository of a value. Fields, the **Message box**, and two special HyperTalk variables called **It** and **selection** can also hold information and so are containers.

All programming languages embody the concept of a variable. A variable is any word or symbol whose value can change as the program executes or from one execution of the program to another. This variability of value is where variables get their name.

In many programming languages, you have to define or declare variables explicitly before you can use them. This is not the case in HyperTalk. The rule is simple.

> **HyperTalk Variable Rule**
>
> When HyperTalk encounters a word in a script that
> cannot be interpreted as the name of an object or as
> a chunk of an object's contents, it assumes the word
> is a variable.

It really is that simple. In practical terms, this means that to
use a variable in HyperTalk, you simply use it. No need to
declare it, define its type, or otherwise alert HyperTalk to its
existence or nature. Just use it and HyperTalk takes care of the
details. Attempting to read from or evaluate a container before
putting anything into it, however, generates an error in
HyperTalk just as it would in any other programming language.

There are actually three types of variables in HyperTalk.
Global variables are accessible to any handler in a script and to
other scripts in the HyperCard environment. They must be explicitly declared global using the key word **global** in any script
or handler where they are used. *Local variables* are known only
inside the handler in which they appear and require no special
handling. *Special variables* are furnished by the system and include **It, selection,** and **message box.** We will have more to say
about these variables as they are used in subsequent chapters.

Properties

All objects have certain properties associated with them. For example, they all have system assigned ID numbers (with the exception of scripts) and optional names. They also have properties
such as location, font characteristics, border, shape, and style.

These properties are all accessible to your scripts, and many
can be changed from a script (as well as, more conventionally,
through dialog boxes or other user-oriented means). Properties
are often examined and decisions made based on the outcome of
the examination. For example, you might want to check if a particular object is visible and, if not, to make it visible. Its visibility is a property that your script can both examine and change.

Properties are a very important idea in HyperTalk. We devote all of Chapter 17 to their use.

Control structures

Most programming languages embody elements called *control structures* that permit the programmer to alter the normal sequential flow of processing. HyperTalk is not an exception to that general rule. Both **repeat** loops and **if-then-else** conditional processing constructs are built into HyperTalk. These form the subject of Chapter 8.

Chunks

Chunks: No, we're not talking about the chubby kid in your high school graduating class. The idea of chunking is unique to hypertext; HyperTalk, true to its roots, incorporates the use of chunks in its programming.

Simply stated, a chunk is any arbitrary portion of any container. A *chunk expression* uniquely identifies any given character(s), word(s), item(s), or line(s) in a container. You will come to appreciate chunks as you learn to program in HyperTalk.

Using chunking expressions, you can access individual elements of a container as easily as stringing together a kind of map to their locations. The map is built "inside-out," though, beginning with the smallest unit and moving out to the larger. Here are some examples. (Don't worry if some of the terminology isn't clear; it will be soon.)

```
second character of word 3 of fifth line of field 1 of card "Help"
char 5 to 8 of third word of testVariable
third item of It
```

You can see how powerful an idea chunking is. It permits you to gain precise control over many situations and data elements in a HyperTalk script. Soon after you begin scripting, chunking becomes second nature.

Objects

We have spent a lot of time looking at objects in HyperTalk (see Chapter 2). Most of these concepts are familiar even to a browser of stacks, so they don't bear much further examination. However, we will take a brief look at each object type from a programmer's perspective and spend a fair amount of time on backgrounds, which are largely transparent to users and play potentially important roles in scripting.

Stacks

Every stack has a name. When you choose New Stack... from the File menu, a standard file-creation dialog box appears as shown in Figure 4-1. You must give the stack a name by which it will be known to the Finder.

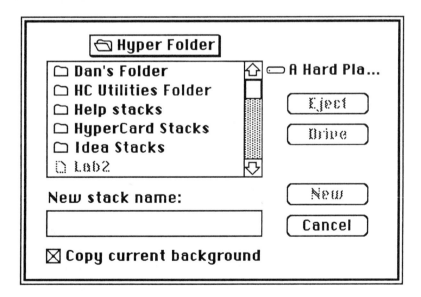

Figure 4-1 Stack creation dialog box

All stacks have a Stack Info... dialog associated with them, which you can view by selecting the menu option with that name

from the Objects menu. Figure 4-2 shows a typical stack information dialog. You'll learn more about individual characteristics of stacks in Chapter 17.

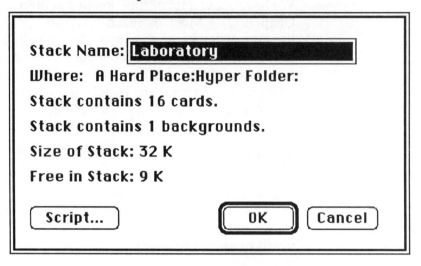

Stack Name: **Laboratory**

Where: A Hard Place:Hyper Folder:

Stack contains 16 cards.

Stack contains 1 backgrounds.

Size of Stack: 32 K

Free in Stack: 9 K

Script...   OK   Cancel

Figure 4-2. Stack Info... dialog box

Backgrounds

If you've built some stacks in authoring mode, you are undoubtedly familiar with the concept of layers in HyperCard. We have
also discussed backgrounds briefly in Chapter 2 as a means of
subclassifying card types within a stack. Now let's take a deeper
look at backgrounds from the viewpoint of the stack designer.

Every stack has at least one background and one card when
it is created. If you create a new stack with the copy current
background check box in the stack-creation dialog box of Figure
4-1 checked, you get a new stack with the same background as
the one that is active when you create it. If you do not check that
box, you get a blank white slate as your background.

The background is the most basic building block of a stack.
It dictates the shape of all cards in the stack (assuming you have
just one background) as well as their default graphic content and
other characteristics. Following the idea of inheritance discussed
in Chapter 2, anything that appears on the background appears

automatically on all cards that share that background. The background is part of the card's appearance unless you specifically remove it.

But layered on top of this background are background object layers. Each button and field you define as a background button or field has its own layer. These layers are transparent overlays on top of the basic background. Like everything else that appears on the background, any background object appears on all cards sharing the background.

Any function or script that you want all cards of a specific background to have should be placed on a *background object layer* or attached to an object there. For example, if you want all cards of a particular background to have a title field at the top where a large, bold type is used to display a brief title, define that field as a background field.

The *contents* of background fields do not carry through to the card level. Typically, background fields do not contain any information. They merely designate the existence of a field on all cards of that background. Data is placed into the field at the card level. If you want text to appear on every card with a common background, place the text on the background directly using paint techniques.

Sometimes you will want all but a few cards of a given background to have a certain graphic or contain a certain field or button. In those cases, define the item as a background item and then use a technique such as designing an opaque button or using a paint tool to obscure it from view on those few cards where you don't want it to appear. This is more efficient than making the item a card-level item and placing it on all the cards you do want it on.

Most of the stacks you have designed in authoring mode probably had one background. In fact, most stacks have one background. But sometimes you will find it advantageous to use two or more backgrounds in a single stack. For example, in the educational stack in Chapter 25 we use different backgrounds for the types of questions and still another for record keeping. You always have to make a trade-off in such situations. You can give a distinct appearance to cards that have different functions or contents by using contrasting backgrounds or by creating new stacks with single backgrounds. We offer some advice on this subject in Chapter 23.

Cards

Every card can have its own fields, buttons, and graphics that don't automatically appear on any other card in the stack. These buttons and fields are accessible only from the card on which they appear, though it is perfectly permissible for them to send messages to objects on other cards, on the background, or higher in the HyperTalk hierarchy.

Like stacks, cards have an information dialog box (see Figure 4-3) that gives you some information about them. This identifying information is often used in scripts.

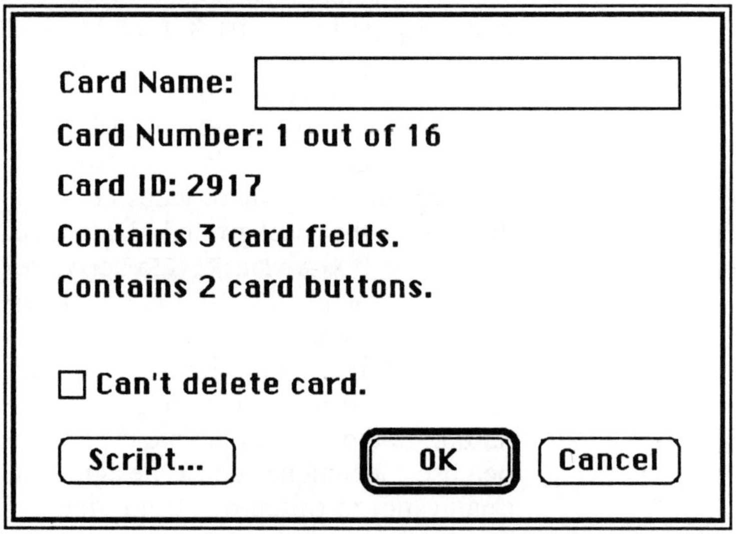

```
┌───────────────────────────────────────────────┐
│ ┌───────────────────────────────────────────┐ │
│ │                                             │ │
│ │  Card Name: [                            ]  │ │
│ │                                             │ │
│ │  Card Number: 1 out of 16                   │ │
│ │                                             │ │
│ │  Card ID: 2917                              │ │
│ │                                             │ │
│ │  Contains 3 card fields.                    │ │
│ │                                             │ │
│ │  Contains 2 card buttons.                   │ │
│ │                                             │ │
│ │  □ Can't delete card.                       │ │
│ │                                             │ │
│ │  ( Script... )   (( OK ))   ( Cancel )      │ │
│ └───────────────────────────────────────────┘ │
└───────────────────────────────────────────────┘
```

Figure 4-3. Card Info... dialog box

Fields

Fields in HyperCard hold information. Everything in a field is stored as a text string. HyperTalk attempts to discern from the context whether it is text information, numeric information, date and time information, or some other form of data.

A field's content is frequently the target of chunking expressions (discussed previously in this chapter). Fields can be any of several types. They also have identifying information associated with them, as you can see in the Field Info... dialog box in Figure 4-4.

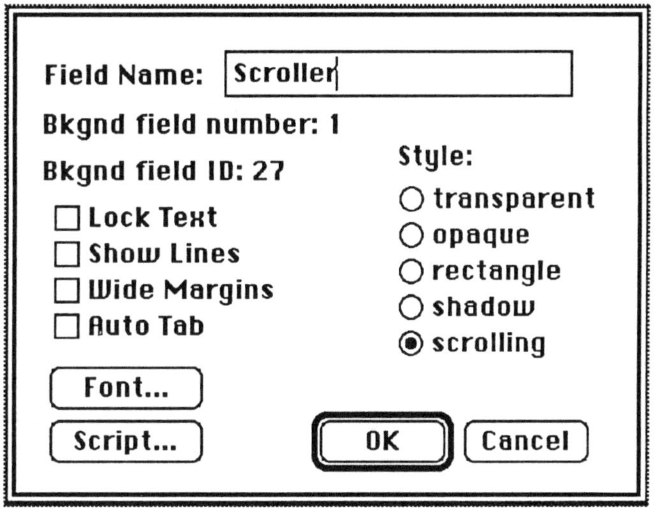

```
╔══════════════════════════════════════════════════╗
║                                                    ║
║   Field Name:  │Scroller│                          ║
║                                                    ║
║   Bkgnd field number: 1                            ║
║                                    Style:          ║
║   Bkgnd field ID: 27               ○ transparent   ║
║     ☐ Lock Text                    ○ opaque        ║
║     ☐ Show Lines                   ○ rectangle     ║
║     ☐ Wide Margins                 ○ shadow        ║
║     ☐ Auto Tab                     ● scrolling     ║
║                                                    ║
║    ┌─────────┐                                     ║
║    │ Font... │                                     ║
║    └─────────┘      ┌──────────┐   ┌──────────┐    ║
║    ┌─────────┐      │    OK    │   │  Cancel  │    ║
║    │ Script..│      └──────────┘   └──────────┘    ║
║    └─────────┘                                     ║
╚══════════════════════════════════════════════════╝
```

Figure 4-4. Field Info... dialog box

Buttons

HyperTalk buttons are the objects most frequently used by browsers and other script users. Most of the scripts you write will be button scripts that activate when the user releases the mouse button. Buttons can be of several types and almost any arbitrary shape. They are the only object that a non-scripter can "program" in the sense of giving them some instructions to perform when they are activated.

Figure 4-5 shows a Button Info... dialog box for a new button. The values shown are the defaults for a button.

A button is the only object whose script starts out with some information in it. Figure 4-6 shows what a button script looks like before you put anything into it. HyperTalk furnishes the skeleton of a **mouseUp** handler because most buttons have at least this handler if they are going to be useful.

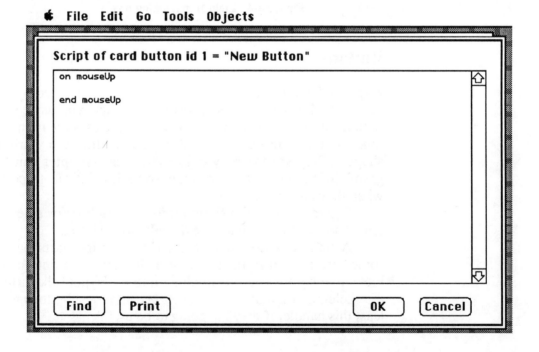

Button Name: New Button

Card button number: 1

Card button ID: 1

☒ Show name

☐ Auto hilite

[Icon...]

[LinkTo...]

[Script...]

Style:

○ transparent
○ opaque
○ rectangle
○ shadow
◉ round rect
○ check box
○ radio button

[OK]   [Cancel]

Figure 4-5. Button Info... dialog box

⬢ File Edit Go Tools Objects

Script of card button id 1 = "New Button"

```
on mouseUp

end mouseUp
```

[Find] [Print]   [OK] [Cancel]

Figure 4-6. Starting button script template

> **NOTE**
>
> Actually, there is no script stored with the button unless you put some commands between the lines HyperTalk provides when you open the script editing window. If you open the script editing window and close it without creating any commands, the script will be empty. HyperTalk simply gives you a helping hand when you open a button's script and no handlers have yet been defined. This becomes important when we consider that messages are "trapped" by handlers and not passed up the hierarchy. The **mouseUp** message is not trapped by an empty button script.

Pictures

Any artwork drawn using HyperCard's built-in painting tools on a card or a background becomes a card or background **picture**. Only one such picture can be associated with each card and each background.

Card and background pictures can be shown or hidden using scripting commands (see Chapter 13) or by setting a property that determines their visibility (see Chapter 17).

Summary

You now have a good idea of all the pieces that make up a HyperTalk script. You know there are active elements that process information, determine the outcome of requests, and manage the environment. You also know that these active elements sometimes use passive elements. Finally, you know more about the functionality associated with each object type in HyperCard.

Chapter 5 introduces the concept of scripting and the basic techniques of HyperTalk stack design and construction.

CHAPTER

HyperTalk Basics

In this chapter, you'll learn about

- the mechanics of entering, editing, printing, and managing scripts

- handlers and their crucial role in HyperTalk scripting

- messages and how they are passed inside HyperCard

- variables and how they are referred to and manipulated

- the special concept of a container and how it is used

- addressing the components of a field in an English-like way

This is a lot of ground to cover, but as you will soon see, learning HyperTalk is enjoyable and far less difficult than learning any other language you've tried. So get comfortable in front of your favorite Macintosh, and prepare to master the basics of HyperTalk.

Script Mechanics

As you already know from our discussions in Chapters 3 and 4, HyperTalk scripts are attached to HyperCard objects. Any stack, card, field, or button can have a script associated with it. Any time you edit one of these objects — and assuming you have scripting access — one of the buttons that appears in its information dialog window is a Script button. Figure 5-1 shows such a button for a HyperCard field. You can gain access to the script for any HyperCard object by clicking the Script button in its Info... dialog.

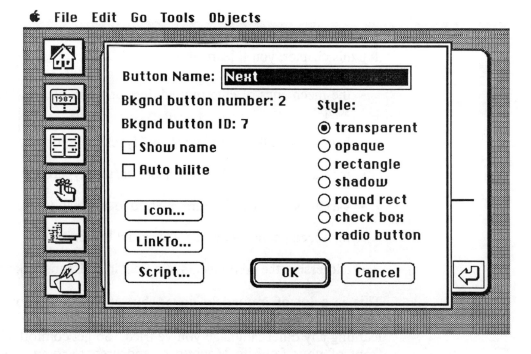

Figure 5-1. Script button gives access to object's script

You can look at the script of an object two other ways. First, you can select the appropriate tool, then double-click on the object while holding down the Shift key. Second, you can use the "peeking" method available in HyperCard Version 1.2 and later. This method uses the Option and Command keys, sometimes in combination with other keys, to open the script editing windows of various HyperCard objects.

The Option-Command key combination with a mouse click opens any button script. Hold down the Shift key with the same combination and open a button or a field script: Option-Command-c opens the card's script; Option-Command-b, the background's script; and Option-Command-s, the stack's script.

Having opened a script-editing window by any method, you can close it one of two ways: by clicking on the Cancel or OK button or by holding down the Option and Command keys and clicking the mouse or pressing any key. If you have changed the script, HyperCard asks whether it should save the changes before it closes the editing window.

After you have opened the script editing window for an object, you will see a screen similar to Figure 5-2. In most cases, the window will be empty. There are two exceptions to this rule. If you open a button script, HyperTalk supplies a framework for the most likely script you'll want to write by presenting a screen like that shown in Figure 5-3. The other exception to the empty-script rule is, when you open the script window for an object that already has a script.

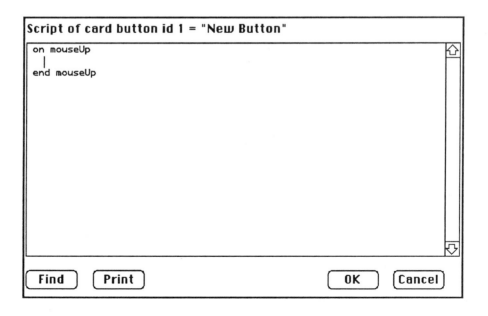

Figure 5-2. Typical empty script window

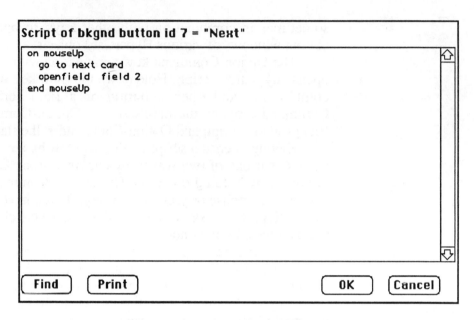

```
Script of bkgnd button id 7 = "Next"
on mouseUp
  go to next card
    openfield  field 2
end mouseUp
```

Find   Print   OK   Cancel

Figure 5-3. Button script window on opening

After you are in a script window, you have the full range of editing capability you'd expect in a Macintosh editor except that the Edit menu's functions are available only with their keystroke equivalents. The menu bar is not active during script editing. But you can still cut, copy, and paste using the usual command-key equivalents of Command-X, Command-C, and Command-V respectively. This slight inconvenience is more than offset by a particularly intelligent feature of the HyperTalk script editor. It"knows" enough about the programming constructs in the language to handle indentation automatically. It places the cursor at the correct position for entering the next line each time you press the Return key. In addition, you can press the Tab key any time and the editor correctly reformats everything in the window.

A side benefit of this capability is that when you press the Tab key, the last line in the portion of the script you are working on — the handler, a term that will become more familiar shortly — is moved flush with the left border of the editing window. If you press the Tab key and the last line of the handler is anywhere but flush with the left border, you know there's something syntactically wrong with your script.

Long lines

Because a single command line in HyperTalk can be any arbitrary length, lines can and often do extend past the right edge of the editing window. Although this does no harm (the scripts still execute), debugging and reading these lines can become difficult. Fortunately, HyperTalk has a way to deal with this problem.

If you are entering a line of HyperTalk code into a script editing window and want to break the line in the middle for readability, simply press Option-Return or Option-L-Return. This places a special symbol (¬) at that point in the text. This symbol is simply a way of notifying HyperTalk that you haven't finished the line. You can use this technique as many times in a single HyperTalk command line as you like. Don't use it in the middle of a text string enclosed in quotation marks, however, or errors will result.

Find and print capabilities

As you can see in Figures 5-2 and 5-3, there are two buttons in the lower-left corner of the dialog that holds the script editing window. One is marked Find and the other Print.

The Find button produces a special dialog with a text-edit window, as shown in Figure 5-4. In this window, you can type any string of characters you want HyperTalk to find in the script. The text-edit window works much like the find command in HyperCard except that it highlights the text when it finds it. So you can't just press Return to find the next occurrence of the word or phrase; doing so inserts a carriage return in place of the located text. Instead, press Command-G to instruct HyperCard to find the next occurrence of the search text. By the way, you can invoke the find feature in the script editing window with Command-F, just as in HyperCard.

An alternate method of using the **find** capability of a HyperTalk script window is to select one occurrence of the text you want to find and then press Command-H. This copies the current text to the **find** dialog window's text-edit field and searches for the next occurrence of the text automatically.

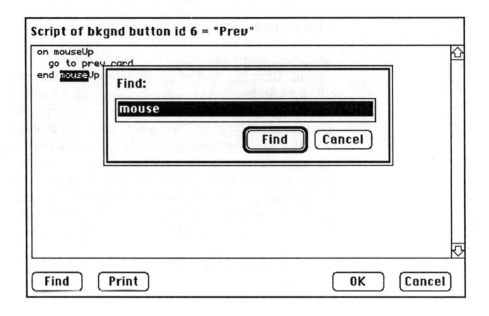

Figure 5-4. Find dialog in script editing window

The Print button works as you'd expect from other Macintosh applications. It sends the contents of the script window to the currently chosen printer. Unlike the **print card** function in HyperCard itself, it does not print the background and surrounding information. It just prints the script and a header that describes the script along with the time and date it was printed. HyperTalk does not display the usual print dialog box requesting format information. Instead, it treats the printout as straight text and just dumps it to the printer, with pagination and a heading.

Syntax checking

The HyperTalk editor does not check syntax when you click the OK button. Syntax and logic errors only show up when you run the script. Other than using the Tab key to confirm that you have matched up beginnings and endings of portions of the handlers correctly, the only way to confirm that a script is correct is to execute it.

Comments

Even though HyperTalk is one of the most inherently readable programming languages yet devised for computers, comments are still in order. You can put a comment anywhere in a script. Comments start with two hyphens (--) and HyperTalk ignores everything that appears to the right of the hyphens. Comments can appear alone on one or more lines or at the end of the line they describe:

```
--This comment is the only thing on this line
put It -- This comment is on the same line as the command.
-- If a comment requires more than one line, each line of
-- the comment must begin with two hyphens.
```

Handlers

Each HyperTalk script consists of one or more *handlers*. A handler is a programming construct that begins with the key word **on** or **function** and ends with the key word **end**. Both key words are followed by the name of the message to which these handlers are designed to respond. The button script template supplied by HyperTalk when you open a button's script window for the first time shows this pattern. It begins with the line **on mouseUp** and ends with **end mouseUp**. The **mouseUp** message is a system message (discussed in Chapter 6) sent whenever the user releases the mouse button.

Commands between the **on** and **end** key words are carried out whenever the object receives the message whose name follows them. This portion of the script handles the particular message for which the script is designed, which is why they are called handlers.

Any HyperTalk script can contain one or more handlers depending on the messages, or events, to which each object responds. These messages can be HyperCard system messages or messages you create just for your scripts.

The key idea to grasp is simply that HyperTalk scripts do one fundamental thing: they respond to messages. Messages are the actions to which a script must respond. Handlers are the intelligent vehicles for responding to the messages. Without handlers, you don't have a HyperCard application.

Where messages originate

We have been talking about messages as if they were all user-generated. Most of the messages for which you will write handlers are a result of the user taking some action. As a result, they handle system messages (see Chapter 6) and have names that identify them as system message handlers. But you can also define your own messages, which then function much as subroutines in BASIC or Pascal. In this case, one handler generates a message that is dealt with by another handler.

This design feature means you can put frequently needed activities in a single handler and then *call* that handler from other handlers. For example, you might have a number of handlers that need to ask users if they really want to quit doing some operation. If you define a handler to do this and call it quitOK, you can then call it from inside another handler like this:

```
on mouseUp
  -- some processing
  quitOK
end mouseUp
```

A second type of handler

Sometimes, you need to define a type of message that can return an answer your script can use. This need is met by the ability to define a **function** handler. A **function** handler is identical to a message handler in form except that it always includes a special **return** statement that sends a result back to your handler. For example, you might need to find out the cube of a number in several different handlers. But you need the answer to be returned to you, not just left in the handler that carries out the calculation. The handler to calculate the cube might look like this:

```
function cube num
  put num * num * num into solution
  return solution
end cube num
```

To use this handler from inside another handler, you would simply write a line like this:

```
put cube 5 into answer
```

You can then take the answer in the container *solution* and operate on it any way you want.

Messages

Without messages, most handlers are irrelevant. Messages are like notices passed from one part of the Macintosh system to another. When the user presses the mouse, a message called **mouse-Down** is generated by HyperCard. When the user releases the mouse button, a **mouseUp** message is generated. These messages are sent along a pipeline, to be intercepted and handled by the first object that has a handler with the same name as the message.

Message hierarchy

At first blush, it might appear that a message such as **mouseUp** would be sent to the object in which the pointer was located when the event took place. Most of the time, that's how HyperTalk scripts work. But it is not necessary that they work that way. For example, if a **mouseUp** message occurs in a field, the field may not be designed to respond to such a message at all. But the card itself might want to do something in response to the user's release of the mouse button anywhere on the card. In that case, the field would not have a **mouseUp** handler but the card would.

So that HyperTalk will know where to route messages as they arise, the language includes a predefined hierarchy through which messages are passed. That hierarchy is depicted in Figure 5-5, an expanded version of the hierarchy described in Chapter 2.

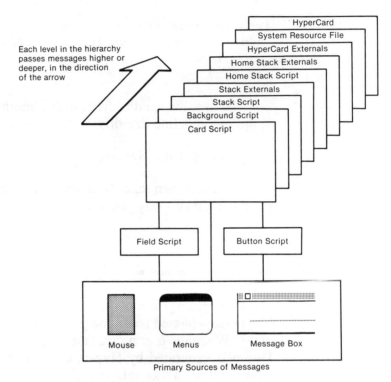

Each level in the hierarchy passes messages higher or deeper, in the direction of the arrow

HyperCard
System Resource File
HyperCard Externals
Home Stack Externals
Home Stack Script
Stack Externals
Stack Script
Background Script
Card Script

Field Script   Button Script

Mouse   Menus   Message Box

Primary Sources of Messages

Figure 5-5. The message hierarchy

The three M's — mouse, menu, and message box — are the primary sources of user-supplied messages. (The keyboard can also be a source of such messages but it generally acts only as a special case of one of the other sources.) Messages originating from the user's interaction with the menu bar or the Message box go directly to the script associated with the active card. This is because almost all such messages have an effect broader than a single field or button.

Mouse messages are the most complex of the three basic types of message. A mouse message — **mouseUp**, **mouseDown**, or **mouseStillDown** — can be sent to a button (the usual case), a field (provided the field contains locked text), or directly to the card. If the mouse message is generated by mouse activity within the confines of a field containing only locked text, the message is sent to that field first. If it occurs within the borders of a button, that button's script gets first crack at the message. If it occurs anywhere outside a field or a button, the card's mouse-message handler (if it has one) is given control.

NOTE

There is a way to override explicitly the normal hierarchy for sending messages between HyperCard objects. The **pass** command serves this purpose. For the moment, though, ignore this possibility and assume that only the natural order of message passing is possible in HyperTalk.

If the first object to receive a message has a handler with that message's name, it handles the message by following the instructions you put into that part of the script. Once this processing is complete, the message that started it all is "swallowed up" by HyperCard and goes no farther unless you force it to do so. But if the object does *not* have a handler for it, HyperCard simply passes the message up the hierarchy to the next level. This process continues until HyperCard either runs out of levels or finds a handler.

EXAMPLE

If a **mouseUp** message is generated in a locked-text field and that field's script does not have a handler beginning with the key phrase **on mouseUp**, Hyper-Card passes the **mouseUp** message to the currently active card. If the card doesn't have an **on mouse-Up** handler, it passes the message to the background of the current card. This process continues until some object along the way *does* have a handler for this message or HyperCard itself is reached. (Hy-perCard is also an object in this sense; it is the default destination for all messages.)

The reason a field can only receive a mouse message if it has locked text may be apparent but is worth stating. If the text in a field is not locked, then a mouse click anywhere in the field is the way users show HyperCard where to put the next text they type or paste. This mouse-click is not designed to be intercepted, so no handler can be devised to do so.

In Figure 5-5, you'll notice references to stack externals, Home Stack externals, and HyperCard externals. These refer to HyperTalk's ability to have its language *extended* by the addition of commands and functions. Externals are new commands and functions written in Pascal, C, and other programming languages and added to HyperTalk. External command creation and use are the subjects of Chapter 22. Do not be concerned about them at the moment except to note where they are in the hierarchy of Figure 5-5.

Variables

As with any programming language, HyperTalk has two types of variables: local and global. Unless you specifically declare a variable to be global, HyperTalk assumes it is local. In this case, local means local to the handler in which the variable is used, not local to the script in which the handler appears. We'll see in a moment how to declare and use global variables.

Naming variables

There are really only three rules about naming HyperTalk variables.

- Variable names must not exactly duplicate HyperTalk reserved words (see Appendix A for a list of the vocabulary of the language).

- Variable names must not begin with a number or special symbol.

- Variable names may not include spaces.

Here are some valid HyperTalk variable names:

```
variable1
temp1
thisIsALongerVariableName
yetAnotherVariable
x
Y
VARIABLE3
```

The HyperCard convention of using uppercase letters in the middle of long strings to show where English words would begin is often a good approach to naming variables. Also, case does not matter in variable names. Three variables named This, this, and ThIs are all the same variable as far as HyperTalk is concerned.

Because variable names cannot include spaces, quotation marks are never needed around the names of variables. You refer to a variable simply by using its name.

Using variables

In keeping with its flexible, forgiving approach to programming language definition, HyperTalk is "relaxed" about the way you declare and use variables. A variable becomes known to the system the first time you use it. No prior preparation is required. If in the middle of a handler you suddenly need to put some value into a variable, just do it:

```
put "Beethoven" into composerName
```

The variable called *composerName* is now known to HyperTalk and can be used later in the same handler by just typing its name.

The special variable, *It*

HyperTalk, in an effort to make scripting more English-like, includes a highly versatile variable called **It** that is shared by your scripts and HyperCard. This variable lets you write natural-sounding script commands such as the following two-line combination that retrieves the user level and puts the resulting value into the field called *Authorization Code*.

```
get userLevel
put It into field "Authorization Code"
```

Several HyperTalk commands put their results into the **It** variable, so you have to remember to be careful when using **It** in your scripts. Typically, you will use this special variable when few, if any, commands appear between the time you put a value into the variable and the time you need that variable. The following HyperTalk commands place their results into **It** by default. (You can almost always supply an alternate destination to avoid overwriting the contents of **It** if you need to do so.)

```
answer
ask
ask password
convert
get
read from file
```

Don't put a value into **It** and then use one of these commands before you have used the original value of **It**.

Displaying variables

To display the contents of a variable so the user can see them, use the **put** command. This is one of the most frequently used commands in HyperTalk. In its simplest useful form, the command's syntax is:

```
put expression
```

where the argument is either a simple source or an expression of arbitrary complexity. In either case, the source or the result of evaluating the expression must produce a string or a number. In this simple form, HyperCard places the expression into the Message box. If the Message box is not visible, HyperCard automatically makes it visible. The HyperTalk command line

```
put "This is a test"
```

will result in the Message box appearing (if it is invisible) and displaying the words *This is a test.*

You may have noticed that we said this was the simplest useful form of the **put** command. You can write the **put** command by itself. In that case, it means "Put whatever is now in the variable It into the Message box." This is seldom a very useful operation.

Assigning values to variables

Another use for the **put** command is the assignment of a value to a variable. In conventional programming languages such as BASIC and Pascal, we use special operators (the equal sign in most versions of BASIC and the := symbol in Pascal) to give a variable a value. In HyperTalk, we use the **put** command in a more complex form than the one we use simply to display a variable's contents. The form of the **put** command for variable assignment looks like this:

```
put expression into variable
```

The **into** preposition causes HyperCard to replace the current contents of the target variable, if it has any, with the value of the expression. The following assignment statements are valid in HyperTalk:

```
put 23 into age
put "This is a test" into testMessage
put 27 * 2 into x
```

The expression assigned to a variable may itself be a variable. After assigning 23 to the variable *age* in the previous example, we could carry out a command like this:

```
put age + 10 into olderAge
```

The **put** statement can use the target variable as part of its expression and as the assignment destination:

```
put age + 10 into age
```

The **put** statement can be used with two other prepositions: **before** and **after**. These are generally, though not always, used with fields of information on HyperCard cards. This use of **put** is described later when we discuss HyperCard containers.

Placing a variable's value into *It*

Because the special local variable **It** is so useful, there are times when you'd like to place the current value of some variable into *It* rather than into the Message box, where a simple **put** statement routes it. To accomplish this, HyperTalk includes a **get** command.

NOTE

The **get** command, like many other HyperTalk instructions, has multiple uses. One primary use is with the properties of HyperCard objects. That subject, along with the role of **get** in that environment, is discussed in Chapter 17.

To use the **get** command, just supply an expression as an argument. HyperTalk will evaluate the expression and put the result into **It.** Here's an example:

```
get age
```

If you carried out this command just after the last use of the *age* variable above, **It** would contain the value 33.

Global variables

Most of the time, variables are by nature useful locally. But when you need to carry information from one handler to another, HyperTalk includes the ability to define variables as global in scope. The **global** declaration must take place before the variable is used the first time, and it must be made in each handler that uses the global variable.

For example, if you want to store the user's age in a variable and then check the age in another button's **mouseUp** handler to determine if a certain action should be taken, the declarations in the two handlers would look something like this:

```
on mouseUp -- Button No. 1's handler
  global age
  get userAge
  put userAge into age
end mouseUp

on mouseUp -- Button No. 2's handler
  global age
  if age > 18 then
  ...
end mouseUp
```

Both handlers declare the *age* variable to be global in scope. Both handlers therefore "know about" this variable and share its value. Note that if you declared *age* to be global in Button No. 1's handler but failed to do so in Button No. 2, the second handler would be working with a different *age* variable than the first handler.

Containers

A HyperTalk variable is a special case of a larger class of objects called *containers*. The inventors of HyperCard had to create a new word for this kind of object because nobody had previously come up with a design that encompassed so many places to put things. Here's a working definition of a container in HyperTalk.

> ## DEFINITION
>
> A container is any place a value can be stored.

Other containers in HyperCard, in addition to defined variables, include several special containers defined by the system. These include **It** (previously discussed), **me, target,** and special containers related to selected text, the current selection, the Message box, and fields.

Using me and target as containers

Prior to the release of HyperCard Version 1.2, two special names that found frequent use in scripts were **me** and **the target.** Both always referred to the objects themselves and not to the contents of those objects, even when the object was a field. With Version 1.2, Apple modified the use of these two special values so that now they can be used as containers.

Generally, **me** refers to the object whose script is now executing, and **the target** refers to the object that received the message now being processed. Most often, these are the same object, but sometimes that is not the case. For example, when a message is passed by one object to another, **the target** continues to refer to the original object that received the message, whereas **me** becomes the designator of the object that is now processing the message.

If **me** or **the target** refers to a field, now you can use **put** to alter the contents of the field in conjunction with one of these containers:

```
put "testing 1-2-3" into me
put "where are you?" into target
```

> ## NOTE
>
> In dealing with this issue in Version 1.2, Apple created a certain amount of confusion. The phrase **the target** continues to refer only to the object itself, not its contents. Without the word **the,** the word **target** refers to the contents of **the target** when it is a field. That means, among other things, that you may not **put** values into **the target** but only into **target.**

Selection as container

Text appearing in a field can be the source or destination for **put** and **get** commands. If the user has highlighted some text in the field, the highlighted text can be referenced as **the selection.** If no text is selected, **the selection** is still recognized by HyperTalk but is empty.

In either case, you can **put** text before or after the selection or replace the selection with other text. All you have to do is change the preposition. Figure 5-6 depicts the effects of the **put** command with its three associated prepositions on the same selected text. In all three cases the text being **put** is *chosen and.* You can see the results of each use of **put** with a different preposition.

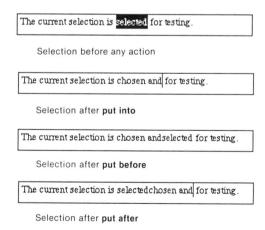

Figure 5-6. **The put command and the selection**

You can also **get** the selection, in which case its contents are placed into the special local variable **It.**

NOTE

Do not confuse the selection explicitly made by the user or your script with text located using a **find** command. Text found with a **find** command can be accessed (in HyperCard versions beginning with 1.2) via several functions that *act* like containers. These are discussed in Chapter 10.

Message box as container

The Message box is also a container. You already know that it is the default destination for the **put** command. But the Message box can serve as a place to display information to the user or to send messages directly to objects or to HyperCard itself.

Like many other HyperCard objects, the Message box has a number of aliases. It can be referred to by any of the following names:

- the Message box

- Message box

- msg box

- the msg box

- the Message window

- Message window

- the msg window

- message

- the message

- msg

- the msg

If you use a **put** command with any of these aliases for the Message box as the destination, HyperCard opens the Message box if it isn't already on the screen and visible. Your program only needs to manage the Message box's visibility in very unusual circumstances.

Field as container

We have already seen how the currently selected text in a field can become the target for a **put** command. Fields can hold two different types of text data: editable text and locked text. If the field holds editable text, the cursor changes to an I-beam when it enters the field, even if the field's boundaries are hidden because it is transparent. Text in an editable field can be the target of a **put** command.

Fields can have names assigned to them when they are created or any time after they are first generated. (We'll have more to say about addressing fields in a few moments.) Suppose we have a field called Author. Our script has just pulled from another stack the information that Asimov is the author of this particular book. Because we've discovered the information somewhat automatically, we don't want to require the user to type it into the Author field. We need a slick way of handling this situation. The following command will do nicely:

```
put "Asimov" into field "Author"
```

The **into** preposition results in the previous contents of the field, if any, being completely replaced with the new data.

Later we find that Asimov's first name is Isaac, and we want to add that information to our growing bits of wisdom. Simple:

```
put "Isaac" before field "Author"
```

As you would expect, the **before** preposition places the expression or source data at the beginning of the field named in the command. Similarly, **after** places its expression or source data at the end of the field named in the command.

Addressing a Field's Contents

Any container, but particularly a field, can hold many words or lines of information. We often want to access specific portions of the contents of such containers. In this area, HyperTalk really shines. It permits us to view a container as consisting of data broken down into items, characters, words, and lines. Furthermore, it permits us to *nest* addresses so that we can refine the focus of our action as much as we want.

The concept of "chunking," mentioned in Chapter 3, is at work here. Each subfield we deal with in this discussion is a chunk.

Although this discussion could also pertain to variables, we will use the term *field* to identify the container type in these examples. This is because fields are the most common places to use these addressing techniques and because doing so simplifies the presentation.

Items in a field

An *item* in a field is defined as any string of text found between commas. If only one comma appears in a field, everything to its left is called *item 1* and everything to its right is *item 2*. In a field without commas, only one item exists. Table 5-1 depicts how items are defined and located in a HyperCard field.

Lines in a field

In many HyperCard fields, text occupies more than one line. Sometimes text "runs over" from one line to the next in a field that's really intended to hold just one piece of information (albeit a large one). For example, a field designed to hold your notes about a book in a bibliographic file might occupy several hundred lines of text, but from your perspective, it's one long field.

Table 5-1. Fields and their item components

Field 1	Item address	Returned value
This is a test	item 1 of field 1	This is a test
A, list, with, commas	item 2 of field 1	list
A, list, with, commas	item 4 of field 1	commas
Everyone is, a comedian	item 1 of field 1	Everyone is
Everyone is, a comedian	item 2 of field 1	a comedian
Everyone is, a comedian	item 3 of field 1	[empty string]

On the other hand, we often break fields into subfields. For example, a field called Address might hold the street address, city, state, and zip code of people in your address book. If you set the cards up so that the person's street address is on the first line of the single field Address, city on the second, state on the third, and zip code on the fourth line, you have created something similar to an array in other programming languages.

But how would you access the city in such a field? Because no commas are used to separate things, using the **item** method discussed in the previous section won't have the desired effect. In this case, you need to focus on a **line** of information; Hyper-Card permits you to do just that.

To get at the city in the Address field, you would simply write a line like this:

```
get line 2 of field "Address"
```

Similarly, you can place information into a field with the **put** command using the same kind of addressing scheme:

```
put "Kalamazoo" into line 2 of field "Address"
```

Characters and words in addresses

If HyperTalk didn't let you do any more than access data in a single field by its item and line, it would have more powerful data retrieval capabilities than many full-blown data processing programs. But it goes two steps farther.

You can access a word or individual characters within a line or field. And you can use the key word **to** to retrieve ranges of words or characters. To access words, you use the key word **word** (oddly enough). To access characters, you can spell out the word **character** or use the shorthand **char**. Let's look at an example, and you will see what we mean about the power in this flexibility of data access.

Suppose you have a field called Grades. Stored in each line of that field are the last name, first name, and test scores for students in a class on (what else?) Macintosh programming using HyperTalk. Figure 5-7 shows a portion of the field, starting with the first line.

```
Bill Adams 93 100 89 77
Cindy North 99 100 99 97
Cal Morrison 72 0 81 62
Heather Hunton 100 90 90 88
```

Figure 5-7. Field containing student information

A **word** can contain letters, numbers, or some combination of characters. If you are used to other programming languages, you must keep this fact in mind. There is no need to define a particular chunk of a field or variable as consisting of a particular type of data.

Extracting a student's last name is as easy as:

```
get word 2 of line 2 of field "Grades"
```

Similarly, getting the grade made by Heather Hunton on the third test requires only that you code a line like this one:

```
get word 5 of line 4 of field "Grades"
```

What if you want to look at the score made by Bill Adams on the third exam to see if it falls in the A grade range? You can extract just the first digit of the grade with a command like this:

```
get char 1 of word 5 of line 1 of field "Grades"
```

Then you could run a check to see if this first digit is a 9 or a 1, in which case an A is probably indicated (assuming nobody scored under 20 on the exam).

Let's change examples. Now we're working with an inventory stack. (A consultant has to be flexible, after all!) You've designed the stack so that the part number is stored as a single string of characters in a field called Part No. on each card. The company's part number design defines the supplier in the first three characters, the part number in the next seven characters, and the next major subassembly of which this part is a member in the last four characters. You can break this part number into its component parts with some lines of HyperTalk code that look something like this:

```
put char 1 to 3 of word 1 of field "Part No." into supplier
put char 4 to 10 of word 1 of field "Part No." into part
put char 11 to 14 of word 1 of field "Part No." into subAssembly
```

(As we'll see in a moment, there are some shorthand ways of doing even this powerful addressing. But for now, focus on the use of the **to** key word to select a range of characters.)

You may combine and nest these addressing schemes to as great an extent as makes sense for the data you are managing with your HyperCard stacks. In general, it makes the best sense to move from the smallest unit (*char*) up to the largest (*field*). Very complex data retrieval is eased greatly with this ability to combine such commands. Take a look at this one:

```
put It into char 3 to 5 of word 2 of item 3 of line 4 ¬
  of field "LargeField"
```

We discuss the use of **put** and **get** with these complex data retrieval schemes in greater depth in Chapter 10.

Ordinal numbers in addressing schemes

The last topic we want to cover in this chapter is the availability of *ordinal numbers* as further shorthand addressing techniques. HyperCard makes available built-in labels so that we can access items, lines, words, and characters more naturally than using constructs like "word 1 of line 3." Instead, we can write:

```
first word of third line
```

HyperCard defines ordinals for the numbers one through ten (first through tenth), as well as the following special ordinals:
  • last

  • mid or middle

  • any (one picked at random)

We find **last** particularly useful. In an address field, for example, we might not know how many names precede the person's last name (depending on things such as whether a title is used and how many middle names or initials the person has). That would drive some database programs insane. But with HyperTalk, we simply code something like this:

```
get last word of line 1 of field "Address"
```

We *know* that the last name is the last word on the line, regardless of how many words precede it.

Remember, too, that all we have said about addressing fields of data applies equally to variables, **It,** the Message box, and **the selection.**

Summary

This chapter has provided a practical framework and beginning point for your study of HyperTalk, the built-in HyperCard programming language. You have learned that scripts are associated with HyperCard objects and that editing them is relatively straightforward. You have become acquainted with the concept of handlers as the building blocks of HyperTalk scripts.

You saw the hierarchy of message passing built into Hyper-Talk. You spent considerable time looking at variables and at a larger class, containers. Finally, you learned to address individual components of a field or container with ease.

Chapter 6 describes all the system messages for which your scripts may want to provide handlers.

System Messages

In this chapter, you'll learn

- what a system message is

- how to choose the destinations for system messages

- how to use all the system messages generated by HyperTalk

- how to transfer messages from their default destinations to other target objects in the HyperCard environment

Messages Galore!

There is always something going on in HyperCard. Even when it doesn't *look* like there's anything happening, HyperCard is sending a constant stream of messages to objects in its environment. If a script isn't active and sending messages of its own and if the user isn't doing something to generate a specific message, HyperCard sends out a continuous stream of messages to let the objects in its hierarchy know that nothing special is happening.

As we saw in Chapter 3, the Macintosh, quite apart from HyperCard, is an event-driven environment. The HyperTalk equivalent of an event is a message. There are only two sources of messages in HyperCard: a script running as part of a stack and HyperCard itself. Messages originating with HyperCard are called *system messages*. In this chapter, we look at all the system messages HyperCard generates. A large percentage of your HyperTalk programming is devoted to responding to or monitoring these messages. Before you read this chapter, make sure you thoroughly understand the concepts of messages and handlers, as discussed in Chapter 5.

Who Gets the Message?

One of the most important ideas to grasp early in our discussion of system messages is that every system message has a *default destination* to which it is automatically sent. As we cover each system message in this chapter, you will see the logic of choosing the default destination for each such message. HyperCard routes some messages to the object in which the event with which they are associated takes place. Others are sent to different HyperCard objects depending on the state of the system. Still others have default destinations that are not dependent on any outside factor.

Every default destination can be overridden in your scripts. If HyperCard sends a message by default to the stack, for example, and you want to override the stack's handling of that message in some circumstances, simply design a handler with the same name in your script and intercept the system message.

> **NOTE**
>
> You should be cautious about writing handlers to intercept and manage system messages. If you do so, you assume all the responsibility for making sure the system reacts appropriately to the message. In some cases, this involves understanding HyperCard at a very deep level. Potential problems will be pointed out in the text.

An Overview of System Messages

System messages usually contain information about the status of some portion of the Macintosh system at the time they are generated. System messages can be divided into the following broad categories:

- mouse messages

- keyboard messages

- action-taking messages

- a menu message

- housekeeping messages

- the "non-event" message called **idle**

Mouse messages

HyperCard generates six mouse messages. Three are actually button messages because they report the status of the mouse button. The other three are location messages that tell your script where the mouse is with regard to specific objects. (There are several built-in functions in HyperTalk to help you pinpoint the exact coordinates of the mouse without regard to objects. These are discussed in Chapter 7.)

Mouse-button messages are among the most frequently used in HyperTalk scripts, because it is often important to know when and where the user has activated the button. The mouse button is the user's primary means of interacting with a Hyper-Card script.

Keyboard messages

Another group of messages reports the pressing of special keys. Three messages let your script know when the Return key, Enter key, or Tab key has been pressed. A fourth informs your script if an arrow key has been pressed (on those Macintosh keyboards that include arrow keys) and, if so, which of the four arrow keys has been used. If your script is run on a Macintosh with the Apple Extended Keyboard, another system message tells you which function key has been pressed.

Action-taking messages

There are two subcategories of action-taking messages: those dealing with objects within a stack and those dealing with the state of HyperCard itself. If the user creates or deletes an object, or opens or closes an object, HyperCard sends a system message to inform your script (and the rest of the system) of the event.

A system message is also generated when HyperCard first starts, when the user or a script chooses to leave the environment, and when the user or a script suspends HyperCard temporarily while another application is run.

Menu message

One system message relates to menu activity. It is a very powerful message — if your script intercepts it, your script becomes responsible for all menu activity from that time until it relinquishes control. By intercepting and handling this message, however, your script gains total control over what happens when the user selects items from the pull-down menus in HyperCard or your stack.

Housekeeping messages

Two messages defy categorization but can be discussed under the rubric of housekeeping. One results from the generation of a message for which there is no handler in the current HyperCard environment. The other permits you to intercept the user's menu-driven request for help.

The *idle* message

When there is apparently nothing going on in a stack, HyperCard sends the **idle** message. Actually, it interleaves this message with a mouse message, as you will see when we explain the **idle** message in greater detail later in this chapter.

Handling Mouse Messages

We will first look at mouse-button messages, which form such a major part of any HyperTalk script. Then we'll examine mouse-location messages, which are used less frequently but with which you should be familiar.

Mouse-button messages

When you click the mouse on a button in any Macintosh application, whether it is written in HyperTalk or a more conventional programming language, you probably think of the task as consisting of one or two steps. Most users think of it as one action called *clicking* the mouse button. An astute observer might point out that there are actually two events taking place: pressing the mouse button and its release.

HyperTalk views this mouse action as consisting of three separate events, and it generates a system message for each. These events and their associated system messages are

- the pressing of the mouse button, which generates a **mouseDown** message

- the continued holding down of the mouse button, however briefly, which generates a **mouseStillDown** message

- the release of the mouse button, which generates a **mouseUp** message

Usually, the user's mouse-button activities are of interest only when they take place inside buttons. That is why most **mouseUp** handlers occur in button scripts and why all button scripts open with an empty handler for this message. But you can supply handlers for any of these messages in a field or even a card as well. It generally does not make sense to include a handler for any of these events in a background or stack script, but there is nothing in HyperTalk to prevent you from doing so.

There are some important rules to remember about how HyperCard processes mouse clicks. First, the **mouseDown** message is sent to the object in which the pointer is located when the button is pressed. Second, all subsequent **mouseStillDown** messages are sent to the *same object that received the mouseDown message* even if the mouse moves outside that object while the button is depressed. Finally, a **mouseUp** message is sent by HyperCard only if the mouse button is released within the confines of the last object to receive a **mouseDown** message. If the user presses the mouse button in, for example, a button labeled OK, then drags the mouse outside that area and releases the mouse button, no **mouseUp** message is generated. This design is in keeping with traditional Macintosh button use, which permits users to change their mind any time before releasing the mouse button.

You will seldom, if ever, write handlers for **mouseDown** or **mouseStillDown**. But **mouseUp** handlers are among the most common in HyperTalk scripts. Virtually every button has such a handler.

To demonstrate how these three commands relate to one another, let's put a handler for each type of message into a single button script in the Laboratory stack we constructed previously. If the stack already has a button (as it should), you can use it for this experiment, or you can add a new button just for this purpose. If it doesn't have a button, add one before proceeding.

Three mouse-button handlers

Here are step-by-step instructions for this experiment in button scripting:

1. Open the button's script window.

2. Type in the following script, which consists of three handlers. When you've entered and proofread it, click the OK button in the scripting dialog.

```
on mouseDown
  put "Down" into Message
  wait 40
  put 0 into Message
end mouseDown

on mouseStillDown
  add 10 to Message
end mouseStillDown

on mouseUp
  beep 3
  wait 20
  put "Done!" into Message
end mouseUp
```

3. Put the pointer over the button and press the mouse button. The Message box appears (if it was previously invisible) with the message "Down." Hold the button down for a few moments and the word "Down" is replaced by a series of rapidly increasing numbers.

4. Release the button. In a moment, the word "Done!" appears in the Message box.

5. Repeat step 3 but after you press the mouse button inside the HyperCard button, drag the pointer outside the button area. Notice that the numbers keep increasing, indicating that the **mouseStillDown** handler in the button's script is still receiving messages. Now release the button outside the button's area. The counting stops but no "Done!" message appears and no beeps are heard. The system message

mouseUp was not sent because you released the button in an area outside the confines of the object in which the mouse button was pressed.

Mouse-location messages

Three messages define where the mouse is when the mouse button is not being pressed. They relate the position of the mouse to objects such as buttons and fields. The three messages and their meanings are as follows

- **mouseEnter**, indicating that the mouse pointer has entered the boundaries of a button or field

- **mouseLeave**, indicating that the mouse pointer was in the boundaries of a button or field but has now moved outside those boundaries

- **mouseWithin**, indicating that the mouse pointer has entered the area and remains there

HyperCard interleaves the **mouseWithin** message with the **idle** message any time the pointer is located inside a button or field. Mouse-location messages are handled exactly like the mouse-button messages described in the preceding section.

Mouse-location handlers

One interesting use for mouse-location messages is the creation of "pop-up" fields that appear when the user simply moves the mouse pointer to a certain area of the screen. Such a handler might be quite useful, for example, in an educational script. You could provide a picture of a part of the human body with no visible labels. When the user points the mouse at a specific location, a previously hidden field appears, showing the user the label for that location. When the user moves away from that area, the field goes away. The user can scan the entire set of labels with the mouse easily, without ever pushing the mouse button.

Although developing such an application is beyond the scope of simply learning about these handlers, we can give you something of the "flavor" of such a script with the following laboratory experiment. Open the Laboratory stack again if it isn't already open.

1. If the card does not have a field you want to use for this experiment, create one. Its location is not important. Give it the name Test Field and define it as Transparent. Then put some arbitrary text into it in Browse mode.

2. Create a new button or use an existing one. Enter the following script into its script editing window:

```
on mouseEnter
  show card field "Test Field"
end mouseEnter

on mouseLeave
  hide card field "Test Field"
end mouseLeave
```

3. Be sure the field Test Field is not showing — open the Message box and type the following command if the field is visible before this experiment begins:

```
hide card field "Test Field"
```

4. Before the experiment starts, the laboratory card should look similar to Figure 6-1. Move the mouse pointer over the button to which you've added the script. (We've called our button, unimaginatively enough, Test Button.) The field should suddenly appear, as shown in Figure 6-2. As you move the pointer outside the button, the field disappears again.

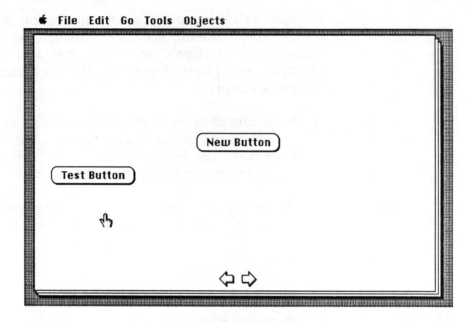

Figure 6-1. Mouse-location test before pointer moves

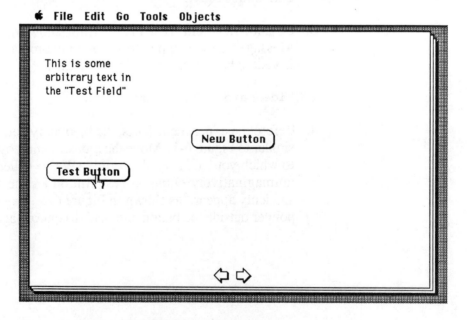

Figure 6-2. Mouse-location test with pointer over test button

Keyboard Messages

The Tab, Return, and Enter keys on the Macintosh Plus keyboard and the fifteen function keys on the Apple Extended Keyboard generate their own messages when they are pressed anywhere except in a text field. The function keys produce their messages even inside a text field, but you recall that the first four keys have specific reserved meanings in editable fields. To avoid conflict, HyperTalk simply does not generate the first four messages when they take place inside an editable text field. The arrow keys on the Macintosh Plus and subsequent Apple-manufactured keyboards also generate messages.

The possible uses for handlers for these messages are not as clear as the uses for mouse messages discussed in the previous section. But some potential uses are hinted at in this discussion.

The keyboard-related messages are as follows:

- **tabKey**

- **returnKey**

- **enterKey**

- **functionKey** number

- **arrowKey** direction label

- **controlKey** number

These are the first messages we've encountered that have parameters. The number that follows the **functionKey** message is a digit between 1 and 15 that indicates which function key was pressed. By convention, function keys 1 through 4 are reserved for editing operations (1=Undo, 2=Cut, 3=Copy, 4=Paste). The direction label associated with the **arrowKey** message is one of the four direction words *up, down, right,* or *left.* The **controlKey** message always carries with it the ASCII code (see Appendix B) of the key held down with the Control Key. If the Control Key is held down with no accompanying key, no message is generated.

All these messages are sent by default to the current card. Among other things, this handler can pass the keyboard-generated message to another object lower in the hierarchy.

Key-button equivalents

One interesting use for message handlers for the Return and Enter keys is to provide a keyboard equivalent for some button selections. Let us assume we have a card with two buttons, one marked OK and one marked Stop. Let's further assume that in documentation or in an onscreen help window (or, better yet, in both places) we have told users that they can press the Return key instead of clicking the OK button and that the Enter key is the same as clicking the Stop button. All we need is a card script that passes these messages to the appropriate button targets when they are received.

> ### NOTE
>
> We will use the **send** command in these examples, even though this command is not discussed until later in the chapter. Its use in this experiment is relatively self-evident, but if you simply can't wait to find out what it does, feel free to read ahead and then come back to this experiment.

Here are the step-by-step instructions for this laboratory experiment in using the **returnKey** and **enterKey** system messages to create keyboard equivalents to button-clicks.

1. It is more efficient to create a new card in the laboratory, though you can go through the process of cleaning all the leftover buttons and fields from the present card if you like. We will not be returning to the previous examples, so choose the alternative you prefer. In any event, it is a good idea to begin this experiment with a clean slate with no handlers or objects.

2. Create two buttons. Size, type, and location are immaterial. Select the Show Name option in the Button Information dialog. Name one button OK and the other Stop.

3. Enter the following script into the script editing window for the OK button:

```
on mouseUp
  put "OK box selected"
end mouseUp
```

4. Enter the following script into the script editing window for the Stop button:

```
on mouseUp
  put "Stop box selected"
end mouseUp
```

5. From the Objects menu, select Card Info... while holding down the Shift key. (Alternatively, select Card Info... and then click the Script button. The result is the same.) Enter the following two handlers into the card's script:

```
on returnKey
  send mouseUp to button "OK"
end returnKey

on enterKey
  send mouseUp to button "Stop"
end enterKey
```

6. Return to Browse mode. Click on the OK button and confirm that the appropriate message appears in the Message box. Then try the Stop button.

7. Press the Return key. The message "OK button selected" appears in the Message box. Now press the Enter key. The message "Stop button selected" appears in the Message box.

Notice that we did not send the **returnKey** and **enterKey** messages to the buttons. Rather, we sent messages that the buttons already had in their scripts. This is not only permissible, it is the most efficient way of handling the task as long as the actions are the same when the user pushes the button with the mouse pointer or uses the keyboard equivalent. You can, however, send the keyboard message on to another object directly. If, for example, you want to highlight the OK button when users press the Return key but not if they use the mouse, you need a handler in the OK button script for the **returnKey** message. You could then simply pass the **returnKey** message to the button from the card script. The other keys operate in an analogous manner.

Uses for keyboard messages

We have already discussed how keyboard messages can be made to work as keyboard equivalents of button presses. The same technique can be used for other actions that have keyboard equivalents.

The arrow keys lend themselves particularly well to a different usage. Because they are usually seen by the Macintosh user as navigation keys, you can intercept these keys to control navigation in ways that make the user's interaction with the stack more understandable. For example, the right arrow key (message **arrowKey right**) can be intercepted at the background or stack level and interpreted to mean "go to the next card with the same background as this card." In multiple-background stacks, this can be quite helpful.

You should never assume that your script will be used on a Macintosh with the extended keyboard. But you can provide handlers for function key messages so that those who do have such keyboards can use the function keys. Users without function key setups will not notice any difference. As with other keyboard messages, **functionKey** messages should be handled at the card level or higher, then transmitted with the **send** command as needed elsewhere in the HyperCard environment.

Action-Taking Messages

As mentioned, action-taking messages fall into two categories. The first group, deals with the management of specific objects in the HyperCard environment. The second is related specifically to HyperCard's own operation.

Object-related action messages

There are typically four things users can do to objects in Hyper-Card. They can open, close, create, or delete objects. Each of these actions can also be performed by a script. Whether the actions occur as a result of the user's instructions or a script's execution, your script may want to intercept the actions by providing handlers for the appropriate messages.

Fields, stacks, cards, and backgrounds can be the recipients of all these messages. Buttons can be created and deleted but not opened or closed. By combining the first part of the message name — the action to be taken — and the second part — the type of object to be affected—we come up with a matrix like Table 6-1, which lists all these system messages by function.

Table 6-1. Action-taking system messages

Action to Take	Button	Field	Card	Background	Stack
Create object	newButton	newField	newCard	newBackground	newStack
Delete object	deleteButton	deleteField	deleteCard	deleteBackground	deleteStack
Open object	N/A	openField	openCard	openBackground	openStack
Close object	N/A	closeField	closeCard	closeBackground	closeStack

As a general rule, your scripts will not contain message handlers to create or delete buttons or fields because this is part of the design process and not usually something you want to do dynamically. (There is, however, nothing in HyperTalk to prevent you from doing so. You may have a specialized application where you need to do just that. In that case, by all means do so.)

NOTE

It is important to note that HyperCard only sends these messages *after* it has taken the action they indicate. In other words, the **newCard** message is only sent after HyperCard has created a new card. So you can't use these messages to prevent the creation of new cards, though you can achieve a similar effect by sending a **deleteCard** message to the newly created card after it has been generated. This also means that you generally have to place the handler for such messages one level higher in the hierarchy than might seem evident. A **newCard** message handler, for example, will not function as expected if it is in a card script. When the new card is created, it doesn't have any scripts. So you have to put handlers for the **newCard** message in the stack's script, not in a card's script.

It is easy to become confused about the role of messages versus the role of commands in the case of these action-taking messages. A **closeField** message is generated when the user presses the Tab key in an editable text field after making some changes and moves to the next such field (if any) on the card. This message is also generated if the user modifies the text in a non-scrolling field whose Auto Tab feature is true, then presses the Return key from the last line of that field. Your script can intercept and handle this message as discussed in the next section. But if you want to order a field closed, you would use the **send** command discussed earlier something like this:

```
on someMessage -- defined by your script
  send closeField to card field 1
end someMessage
```

Typically, your scripts will intercept messages that result from the user taking actions that generate object-oriented action messages and will change the usual manner in which HyperCard processes them. Also typically, your scripts will work with the opening and closing of objects.

Handling a *newCard*

In this experiment, we set up a script that automatically inserts information into any new card created by the user. It's a good idea to start with a new card in the laboratory.

1. Create a background field in the upper-left corner of the card. Define it to be a rectangle and give it the name Today. Give it any other nonconflicting characteristics you wish.

2. Open the stack's script by holding down the Shift key and selecting Stack Info... from the Objects menu or by opening the Stack Info... option from the Objects menu and then clicking on the Script button.

3. Enter the following script for the stack:

```
on newCard
  put the date into field "Today"
  beep 3
end newCard
```

The function called **the date** simply returns today's date in short format. You'll learn about HyperTalk's built-in functions in Chapter 14.

4. Return to Browse mode. Select New Card from the Edit menu or hold down the Command-N keys. Add a few more cards if you like (keeping track of how many there are so you can undo the work later) and confirm that each displays today's date when it is created.

5. Delete the cards you created and the new background you generated to avoid confusion with future laboratory

experiments. If you want to keep them make a copy of the stack using the Save a Copy... option from the File menu and then delete the new background and cards.

Another idea

When HyperCard opens an existing card, it generally does not place the pointer anywhere. The same is true when it creates a new card. Quite often, though, stacks are used in applications when the user wants to simply begin entering data when the card appears. To avoid requiring the user to click the mouse explicitly in a field to begin entering data, you can provide a handler for the **openCard** message that would open a specific field. The simplest way to do this (with what we already know about messages and handlers) is to have the **openCard** handler send a **tab-Key** message to the card. This opens the first field on the card and automatically selects all of its text. If you want to tab to the second field, send two **tabKey** messages.

A handler to accomplish this task is associated with the stack and looks something like this:

```
on openCard
  send tabKey
end openCard
```

As you gain more experience with HyperTalk scripting, you'll find many occasions for the use of these object-related messages.

HyperCard messages

Four system messages HyperCard generates are related to the status of the HyperCard application itself. These four messages and their meaning are

- **startUp**, which is sent when HyperCard is first started

- **quit**, which is sent when the user or a script quits HyperCard

- **suspend**, which is sent when the user or a script runs an external program from within HyperCard and plans to return to HyperCard when the other application has finished executing

- **resume**, which is sent when the external program for which HyperCard has been suspended finishes executing and control is returned to HyperCard

An example of a **startUp** message handler is in the Home stack supplied with HyperCard. That handler simply looks to see if there is an external command called **startUp** to which it is to respond. (We have more to say about external commands near the end of this book.) The **startUp** message goes to the Home stack if you start HyperCard by double-clicking the application's icon on the desktop. But if you double-click a stack's icon, the **startUp** message goes to the first card of that stack.

These messages are seldom used in HyperTalk scripts, so we won't spend much time on them. One note is worth making, however. If you want your script to perform a set of actions when the user first opens it, you may want these same (or a substantially similar set of) instructions followed when the user returns to your script after running an external application. If so, be sure to put a command in the resume handler that carries out those actions because the **startUp** handler is not called when operation of HyperCard resumes after a **suspend** message.

The *doMenu* Message

When the user chooses a menu item or invokes it with its keyboard equivalent, HyperCard sends a message called **doMenu** followed by the name of the menu item, exactly as it appears in the menu bar (complete with the three dots, or ellipsis, that follow many menu choices). Your script can check for the occurrence of any menu item(s) and react accordingly.

This technique can be used to disable menu items to protect your stack scripts or the stack information base itself. You simply intercept the message, check to see if it's an item you want to disable, and do something like **beep** if it is or pass the message to the next level if it isn't a menu option you care about.

WARNING

The **doMenu** message handler must be carefully designed so that it uses the **pass** command (described
in the next paragraph) to pass menu control up the
hierarchy if the user's choice isn't one your handler
is concerned with. If you omit the **pass** command,
you will be unable to open the script editor for that
stack. This Catch-22 "endless loop" is broken only if
you delete the script by typing into the Message box
"set script of this stack to empty." If the script is not
associated with the stack, change the reference
appropriately. Unfortunately this deletes all the
handlers in the script, which can be problematic. So
be careful when you use the **doMenu** message.

An example of the use of the **doMenu** command involves
displaying a special card with a message such as "See you later"
when the user decides to leave your stack by going Home or
quitting HyperCard completely. (There are other ways to leave
your stack; the technique would be the same regardless of the
method.) To handle such a situation, you attach the following
kind of message handler to your stack's script:

```
on doMenu choice
  if choice is "Home"
  then
    go last card
    wait 20
  end if
  if choice is "Quit Hypercard"
  then
    go last card
    wait 20
  end if
  pass doMenu
end doMenu
```

We discuss the **if-then** construction in Chapter 8. For the moment, just accept our word that this handler performs as advertised.

The *help* Message

The **help** message is created and sent to the currently open card when the user chooses Help from the Go menu or types Command-? to invoke help.

The **help** message can be intercepted by your script to route the user's request for assistance to a special stack (or part of a stack) where the user can get customized help or specific references to other sources of assistance. For example, if you have a card called Special Help that contains hints for using your stack, you can send the user there when he or she asks for help. The handler would look something like this:

```
on help
  go to card "Special Help"
end help
```

(In reality, the handler would be a bit more complex because it would involve making sure HyperCard returns to this point when it finishes furnishing the specialized help. The techniques for doing that are covered in Chapter 9.)

The *idle* Message

We have perhaps said enough about the **idle** message. It is interleaved with a **mouseWithin** message if the pointer is located over an object. The two alternate during times that HyperCard is simply waiting for the user to do something to generate an event and a related message.

A handler for the **idle** message lends itself well to such activities as putting the current time into a field. The Home Card furnished by Apple Computer has such a handler. It looks like this:

```
on idle
    put the time into card field "Time"
    pass idle
end idle
```

Be careful of putting too many commands in an **idle** handler. Each executes often and you can greatly slow down your stacks by injudicious use of **idle** handlers.

Summary

In this chapter, you saw how to deal with messages. You then became acquainted with all the messages the HyperCard system itself generates. You saw how to handle mouse-related messages, keyboard messages, and action-taking messages. You saw the power and the pitfalls in trapping menu choices to make applications written in HyperTalk more individualized.

You learned there are always messages being passed around the HyperCard environment. And you learned that although there is a definite hierarchy to message passing based on the individual message, you can use the **send** and **pass** commands to bypass or accommodate the hierarchy.

Chapter 7 discusses input and output in HyperTalk using the mouse, keyboard, disk drive, and printer.

Mouse, Keyboard, and File I/O

In this chapter, you'll learn how to

- handle several messages that involve knowing where the mouse is and what it is doing

- simulate electronically the user clicking the mouse

- determine the status of the Command, Option, and Shift keys

- perform routine file operations on external (non-HyperCard) files containing only text

Monitoring the Mouse

In the last chapter, we learned about several system messages that report on the status of the mouse and its location in relation to objects. Because of the overriding importance of the mouse in any Macintosh application, HyperCard includes a number of other mouse-monitoring routines. Three of these functions — **the mouseLoc, the mouseH,** and **the mouseV** — report on the screen coordinate location of the mouse at the time the function is called. Two — **the mouse** and **the mouseClick** — determine the status of the mouse button at the time they are used in your script. (The word *the* in each of these names is essential. Without it, HyperTalk does not recognize the function.)

The uses for four of these functions — all but **the mouse-Click** — are pretty esoteric. We have seldom seen a need in a HyperTalk script to detect where the mouse is when it is not being clicked except in relation to some object. (Recall our laboratory experiment in Chapter 6 with the field that appears when the user positions the mouse over a button but does not click on it.) This is not to say you will never use them; you may find many uses for these functions. But they are not among the most often-used functions in HyperTalk.

One reason this is true is the object-oriented way HyperTalk works. We are usually interested in monitoring the location of the mouse and its actions with respect to objects in the Hyper-Card environment rather than with respect to the abstract screen position it occupies. Another reason for the infrequent use of these functions in most HyperTalk scripts is that the location they report can change before it is reported. These functions report the location of the mouse *at the time they are called*. But a fast mouser — and there are many such users out there in the world of Macintosh aficionados — may well have moved the mouse out of the relevant screen location before your script can react to its presence.

The lone exception to this rule in this batch of HyperTalk functions is **the mouseClick**. This function tests to see if the mouse button has been clicked since the last time it was checked. If so, it returns a value of true; otherwise, it returns a value of false. The returned value can then be used in a logical operation, usually within a loop, to control the actions of your handler. The implementation of logical operations and loops is discussed in Chapter 8.

Screen coordinates

Before you can use the three mouse-location functions we are discussing, you must understand how HyperCard views and addresses locations on the screen. We could present this information with a few paragraphs and diagrams. But because HyperTalk lends itself so well to exploration, we're going to set up a script in our laboratory to explore the screen, then summarize what we learn.

You can use an existing Laboratory stack card for this experiment or create a new one with nothing on it. Once you have opened the card you want to use, follow these steps.

1. Open the card's script in one of the usual ways.

2. Type the following script into the script editing window and click on the OK button when you're done:

```
on openCard
  repeat until the mouseClick
    put the mouseLoc
  end repeat
end openCard
```

Don't worry if you have no idea what the strange group of lines that begin and end with the word **repeat** are all about. We'll explain this programming technique in Chapter 8.

3. Return to browse mode.

4. Go to a previous card in the stack and then return to this one so that the card is opened and the handler can take effect. As soon as you do, the Message box appears with two numbers separated by a comma (see Figure 7-1). Move the mouse around without clicking the button and watch the numbers in the Message box change. As you roll the mouse to the right, the first number gets larger until the pointer reaches the right edge of the screen and the number reaches 512. Similarly, as you roll the mouse down the screen, the second number increases until it reaches 342.

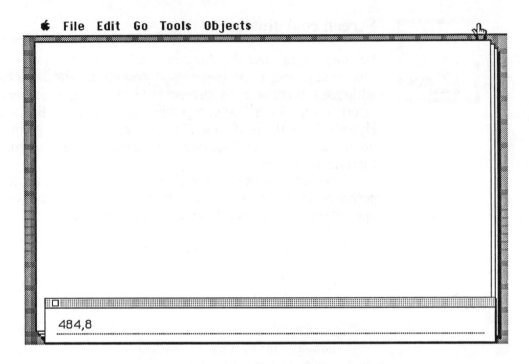

Figure 7-1. Tracking mouse in Message box

5. Put the pointer in the upper-left corner of the screen. You should be able to get the two numbers to reach 0,0. The bottom of the menu bar is at the point where the second number is 20.

6. Click the mouse. Notice that as you roll the mouse around now, the numbers don't change. That's because you've exited **the openCard** handler with **the mouseClick,** so the mouse position is no longer being tracked and reported.

From this experiment, you can probably conclude that the screen is laid out as a gridwork of addresses, with horizontal positions reported in the first part of **the mouseLoc** value and vertical positions in the second part of that value. You can probably also conclude that the screen addresses go from 0,0 in the upper-left corner of the screen to 512,342 in the lower-right corner of the screen. Figure 7-2 depicts this addressing scheme.

Figure 7-2. The Macintosh screen addressing scheme

Each screen location, called a *pixel* (shorthand for picture element), has a unique address. You can see how finely a HyperTalk script can examine and manage screen locations when there are more than 175,000 discrete locations.

One coordinate at a time

Using the same technique we just explored in the Laboratory stack, you can find out that the function **the mouseH** returns only the horizontal location of the mouse and **the mouseV** returns only its vertical position. Just change **the mouseLoc** in the script to one of these functions and observe the results.

Ending repeated commands

You probably noticed in the **openCard** handler in the last laboratory experiment that we used a **repeat until the mouseClick** statement. We'll be discussing such groups of statements in Chapter 8. For the moment, you should note that **the mouseClick** is one of the most useful HyperCard functions for terminating repeating activities because it monitors users and reacts when they click the mouse anywhere within HyperCard's boundaries.

What's with the mouse?

The last of this group of functions is simply called **the mouse**. It returns the value *down* if the mouse button is being pressed when the function is called, *up* if it is not. In some ways, its functions duplicate those of the **stillDown** system message we discussed in Chapter 6.

A key difference is that **stillDown** is a message that can form the argument to the **on** portion of a handler, but **the mouse** is a function that returns a value and is used inside a handler. In other words, **the mouse** gives us a way to perform some steps inside a handler while the mouse is down.

Is user holding down button?

Let's do a little experimenting, without being concerned about what all the commands mean or do. You can use any existing card with a button whose script you don't need or you can create a new card for this experiment. Then follow these steps.

1. Open the button's script in one of the usual ways.

2. Type in the following script and press the OK button when you're done.

```
on mouseDown
  repeat while the mouse is Down
    put empty
    wait 20
    put "Working..."
    wait 20
  end repeat
  beep 3
end mouseDown
```

3. Return to browse mode.

4. Click on the button and hold the mouse button down. Notice that the Message box slowly flashes the message "Working..." as long as you hold down the mouse button.

5. Release the mouse button and note that the system beeps three times.

6. You can also use a **mouseUp** handler in this script to put a message into the Message box when you release the button. For example:

```
on mouseUp
  put "Whew!  I'm glad that's over!"
end mouseUp
```

Obviously, you wouldn't write such a handler this way just to beep the speaker three times. But if you had more complex processing to take care of that you didn't want to carry out while the user was pressing the mouse button, this approach would work fine.

Clicking the Mouse for the User

Sometimes in HyperTalk scripts, you want to put the user in a particular location for some field entry work. Or you may need to simulate mouse clicking that you would normally expect from the user in a demonstration script where you want the user simply to watch what's going on. For these and similar situations, HyperTalk includes the **click** command. Its syntax looks like this:

```
click at location [with modifier key]
```

The location must be an explicit screen address, given as a pair of coordinates like those we have just finished learning about or an expression or variable that evaluates to such an address. If you want to simulate a mouse click as if the Shift,

Command, or Option key were being held down, you can add the key name and the **with** connector. Here is an example of an Option-click command:

```
click at 100,235 with optionKey
```

Modifier key additions are particularly useful when you are using the **click** command while working with one of HyperCard's paint tools.

As with other HyperTalk commands we've looked at, **click** is most useful when viewed with a HyperCard object. Every object has a screen location associated with it. You can find this address with the **location** function, which may be abbreviated **loc**. We have more to say about the **loc** function in Chapter 17 when we discuss the properties associated with HyperCard objects. But for the moment, you need only know that this function returns the screen coordinates of the center point of the object referred to.

If you have a screen button called Button One, you can activate it exactly as if the user had clicked on it by writing a line of HyperTalk code like this:

```
click at loc of card button "Button One"
```

Of course, you can also produce this effect with the **send** command:

```
send mouseUp to card button "Button One"
```

There are a number of ways to accomplish many HyperTalk tasks. This is not the last time we will see such alternatives.

HyperCard includes three functions to help you determine where the mouse was clicked by the user (or, for that matter, by your script). The **clickLoc** returns the location of the click as a point (two numbers separated by a comma). If you want just the vertical position of the mouse click, you can use **the mouseV** and, if you want only the horizontal position of the click, use **the mouseH.**

Is That Key Down?

Having seen that we can use the Command, Option, and Shift keys with the **click** command, it will come as no surprise that we can also check the status of these keys to find out if they are up or down at the time the script checks them. Like **mouse**, the functions that monitor the keys return *up* if the key is not being pressed, *down* if it is. You can use these values in testing and branching operations in HyperTalk.

In fact, you can actually check not only on these keys but also on the **enterKey**, the **returnKey**, the **controlKey**, and the **functionKeys**. These last two are not implemented on all Macintosh systems, but they are part of the extended keyboard design that most Macintosh II owners use. The same *up* and *down* logic that applies to the other keys we've been discussing also applies to these keys with the exception of the **functionKey** message. When a function key is pressed, the message sent in HyperCard includes the number of the key. The resulting handler portion looks like this:

```
on functionKey keyNo
  if keyNo = 5 then
  -- do some processing
  -- etc.
end functionKey
```

Don't use function keys 1-4 for HyperCard activities because most Mac word processors and text editors use these keys for editing operations pre-defined by Apple Computer.

Keypresses modify results

For this experiment, you can use an existing button whose script you no longer need, or you can create a new button on either a new or existing Laboratory stack card. After you have prepared the button, follow these steps:

1. Open the button's script editing window using one of the usual methods.

2. Type the following script into the window.

```
on mouseDown
    put "Mouse is down "
    repeat while the mouse is down
        if the optionKey is down then
            put "with the Option Key" after Message
            exit repeat
        end if
        if the commandKey is down then
            put "with the Command Key" after Message
            exit repeat
        end if
        if the shiftKey is down then
            put "with the Shift Key" after Message
            exit repeat
        end if
    end repeat
end mouseDown
```

3. Press the mouse button in the button you are using. The message "Mouse is down " immediately appears in the Message box. Now press the Shift, Command or Option key. Notice that the Message box adds information after its previous contents about which key you pressed. Confirm that the handler has been executed by continuing to hold down the mouse button and trying the other keys.

4. Release the mouse button. Now repeat the instructions in step 3 for all the special keys. Try holding down two of the special keys simultaneously. Notice that only one of them is acknowledged.

Even though this handler is longer than ones we've dealt with before, it is not very mysterious. The main body of instructions execute as long as the mouse is held down or until one of the special keys is pressed. When one of the keys we are monitoring is pressed, the handler adds some words to the end of the current contents of the Message box indicating which key was pressed. Then it leaves the loop and the handler ends.

Checking for two-key combinations

You can link two key conditions together with the **and** logical operator and check for key combinations. We discuss the **and** operator in detail in Chapter 8. To look for the Shift-Command key combination, for example, you could perform a check like this:

```
if the shiftKey is down and the commandKey is down
```

Saving the key's condition

Given the rapidity with which HyperCard applications execute and the speed with which many people use the Macintosh, it is sometimes useful to store the state of a key and then check later to see if it was pressed when the user made the last selection or took the last action. This is particularly helpful when you write handlers that permit a single button to have more than one effect depending on whether a special key was held down while the button was activated.

Because these operations are functions that return a result, we can put that result into a container. Here is the skeleton for a **mouseUp** message handler that reacts differently to the message depending on whether the Shift, Option, or Command key is held down while the button is activated:

```
on mouseUp
    put the optionKey into optionStatus
    put the commandKey into commandStatus
    put the shiftKey into shiftStatus
    -- some other actions that don't depend on
    -- the keys' status take place here; these
    -- might be commands that are common to all
```

```
      -- variations of the button's theme
      if optionStatus is down then
        -- carry out the optionKey version
      end if
      if commandStatus is down then
        -- carry out the commandKey version
      end if
      if shiftStatus is down then
        -- carry out the shiftKey version
      end if
end mouseUp
```

Text File Operations

HyperTalk's vocabulary includes four commands that permit HyperCard to work with text-only files outside its environment. Data can be read from text-only files and used in stacks. Information from stacks can be exported to text-only files for use by word processors, report generators, spelling checkers, and other similar programs.

Whether you are importing or exporting data, the process is fundamentally quite similar. You use the **open file** command to open the file so you can put information into it or take information out of it. Then you use the **read** or **write** command to perform the actual data transfer. Finally, when you're done, you use **close file** to end the processing. Let's look at these commands in the order in which we just listed them.

Open file

There is nothing mysterious or difficult about the **open file** command. Supply the name of the file — either explicitly as a string or implicitly in a container — and HyperTalk establishes a communications channel between your script and the disk file, creating it if it doesn't already exist.

For example, to open a file called Test File, you could simply write this command:

```
open file "Test File"
```

HyperCard looks in the root level directory of the currently active disk drive. If it finds a file called Test File, it opens it. If not, it creates a new file called Test File at the topmost level of the current disk volume.

A word about path names

If you have set any of the Preferences card options in HyperCard's Home stack, you have already gained at least a nodding acquaintance with path names. The path name of a file is a map that helps the Macintosh File Manager (part of the operating system) locate a file on the disk. To make HyperCard look anywhere but the root level of the currently active disk for files you want to open or create, you must supply a path name.

DEFINITION

A *path name* starts with the name of the disk (also called the volume) on which the file is located and then lists each folder in turn to which a file belongs. If you omit the volume name, you can begin the path name with a colon, and HyperCard assumes you mean the currently active volume. This technique works fine if you are using a hard disk most of the time.

Look at Figure 7-3. It depicts a document called Vendors stored inside a folder called Lists. That folder in turn is found inside another folder called Documents, which is at the top level of the hard disk volume called A Hard Place. HyperTalk can access the Vendors document in an **open file** command by either of the following two lines:

```
open file "A Hard Place:Documents:Lists:Vendors"
open file ":Documents:Lists:Vendors"
```

Hard Disk Name: A Hard Place

Folder Name: Documents

Folder Name: Lists

Document Name: Vendors

Figure 7-3. A document in a hierarchy of storage

Reading from a text file

The full name of the command that reads data from text files is
read from file. It has two alternative forms. The first, which
follows, reads all the data from a file until it reaches a defined
delimiter character. Generally, two delimiter characters are used
in text-only files. Tabs separate individual fields, and carriage
returns mark the ends of records.

```
read from file file name until delimiter character
```

The file name must be placed in quotation marks. The delimiter character must be one of HyperTalk's standard constant
characters (tab, return, lineFeed, or formFeed) or another character you define using ASCII values or a single-character string.
(In case the term ASCII is unfamiliar, it is a standard way of representing characters in computers. Appendix B contains a chart
of all Macintosh characters and their ASCII equivalents.) If you
supply more than one character as the delimiter, HyperTalk uses
only the first character of this string and will stop reading when
it encounters the first instance of that character.
Using the above form of the **read** command, a script would
have to perform two checks. It would read individual files with
a command like this:

```
read from file "Test" until Tab
```

Then it would check as each field was read in to see if it was a
return:

```
if it is Return then
  -- follow with appropriate processing
```

Depending on the file's structure, you might also need a check for an empty field to recognize that the end of the file had been reached:

```
if it is empty then
  -- follow with appropriate processing
```

The second method of reading a text-only file in HyperCard is to know in advance how many bytes of information you want to read. This approach usually works only for small files because larger ones are hard to manipulate into field formats after you bring them into HyperCard through your script. The format of this version of the **read** command is

```
read from file name for number of bytes
```

HyperCard has a 32K-byte buffer limit when performing either type of **read** operation. When the **read** process stops, you may want to check to ensure that you have read to the point you wanted to reach. If the last character of the text stream is the one on which you wanted to stop, you can be confident that the **read** did not overflow the buffer. If it is not the desired character, then you have probably read 32,767 bytes of data without encountering the character you specified.

Writing to a text file

If you need to export text from a stack to a text-only field so that a word processor, a database manager, or some other program can use it, you will find the **write** command quite powerful and flexible. Its form is

```
write content to file filename
```

The content that is written to the file can be either the name of a variable, a text string inside quotation marks, or, more commonly, some file name identifier.

If a field is being written out to the file, you can supply either its assigned name or its field or unique ID number.

The field name can be either the field's assigned name or its field or unique ID number. Locally assigned field numbers are often more useful than names or IDs in **write** scripts because using numbers permits you to loop through all the fields on a card in a small amount of code. The file name must, as usual, be in quotation marks. The comments about locating the file and its path name made in discussing the **read** command apply equally to the **write** command.

You must insert delimiter characters into your outgoing text. If the program on the receiving end of your output expects a tab-delimited file, add a tab after each field is written to the file. One form of the portion of your script that handles this assignment is

```
repeat for the number of cards
  repeat with x=1 to the number of fields
    write field i to file "Test"
    write tab to file "Test"
  end repeat
  go next card
end repeat
```

Summary

In this chapter, you saw how to use several messages about the mouse's location. You also examined the **click** command, which permits you to simulate the user's mouse-clicking actions.

You looked at several messages that let you determine whether the Command, Option, or Shift keys were held down the last time the user clicked the mouse. You learned how they worked, and saw a possible application of this approach in a script. Finally, you learned how to open and close text-only files and how to get information out of such files into HyperCard and vice versa.

In Chapter 8, we take our long-promised look at control structures and their related logical operations.

8

Control Structures and Logical Operators

In this chapter, you will learn

- how control structures are used in HyperTalk scripts to execute groups of instructions repeatedly or conditionally

- what logical operators and related functions are available in HyperTalk

- how to use special HyperTalk commands to gain better control over loops

- how HyperTalk compares with Pascal and other traditional procedural languages in the way it handles control structures

Loops and Conditions: Background

If you have programming experience in Pascal, C, BASIC, or another traditional programming language, feel free to skip this discussion and move to the next section, "If-Then Processing." But if HyperTalk is your first programming language or you're a bit rusty in the fundamentals, reading this section will make the rest of this chapter more understandable.

Most computer programs — and HyperTalk handlers are no exception — execute linearly, starting with the first instruction, then executing the second, then the third, and so on until they come to some kind of logical end. Along the way, procedural programming languages often include branching instructions that send the program to some other part of the code semipermanently (as with the BASIC GOTO statement) or temporarily (e.g., GOSUB in BASIC). These languages also generally include instructions to execute one or more commands conditionally (i.e., only if a certain condition is met) or repeatedly (i.e., until some condition arises, as long as some condition is true, or a specific number of times).

In all cases, these constructs give programmers great flexibility in the way their programs manage data and interact with the user. It can be argued — and often is — that no interesting or useful programs can be written without such conditional processing and looping constructs. Avoiding that philosophical issue, it is clear that meaningful programs are often more difficult and time-consuming to design and write without such constructs.

HyperTalk includes no commands equivalent to BASIC's GOTO and GOSUB commands. It does, however, offer conditional execution and looping constructs, which are the focus of this chapter.

(We should perhaps be a little clearer at the outset. In HyperTalk, it is possible to call procedures from within procedures. In some ways, this resembles calling the BASIC GOTO and GOSUB statements just described. But there is no inherent, built-in command for such branching.)

If-Then Processing

The first control structure we will discuss is the **if-then-else** construct, which in one form or another is part of most major programming languages.

Many of the decisions we make in our lives can be expressed as if-then decisions. *If* it is Sunday, *then* I won't get up early and go to work. *If* it is 95 degrees outside *and* the sky is azure blue, *then* I won't take a raincoat with me when I leave this morning. In each case, notice that we have the conditional"flag" in the word *If*, a word a wag once declared to be the biggest little word in the English language. This word is followed by a description of a state of affairs or sequence of events that is either true or false. If it is true (e.g., if it really *is* Sunday), the second part of the statement is carried out (e.g., I don't get up early to go to work).

If-then-else decisions in HyperTalk are similar to such decisions in our daily lives.

General format and use

To undertake some conditional processing in HyperTalk, you have a choice of two related approaches. The first has one set of conditionally executed commands that are carried out only if some condition is true. Its general form looks like this:

```
if <condition> then
  <series of commands>
end if
```

This format can be abbreviated if there is only one command to be executed. In that event, the **end if** statement is not required. The conditionally executed command can be on the same line as the **if-then**:

```
if <condition> then <command>
```

or on the next line:

```
if <condition>
then <command>
```

The second approach to conditional program processing provides two sets of alternative commands, one is carried out if the condition is true and the other is carried out if it is false. This approach is known as the **if-then-else** approach, which is familiar if you have any experience programming in conventional languages such as Pascal or BASIC. The formatting of this approach is identical to the first one mentioned. The general format looks like this:

```
if <condition> then
  <series of commands>
else
  <alternate series of commands>
end if
```

The simplest form of the **if-then-else** construct is:

```
if <condition> then ≤command_1> else command_2>
```

Formatting, which is generally not an issue in HyperTalk programming, becomes important in dealing with the **if** command and its variations. The issue centers around when you must supply the **end if** statement. Many HyperTalk programmers have had difficulty sorting out this question. If you run into situations where HyperTalk's script editor refuses to indent your **if-then-else** loops correctly and you can't figure out why, ask yourself these questions:

1. How many **else** clauses are there? (Note that if you put the key word **else** on a separate line from the command to be executed with it, HyperTalk sees this as two clauses, not one.) If you have only one line in the **else** clause, you should not include the **end if** statement. In fact, it is wrong to do so. If you have two or more lines in the **else** clause, the **end if** is *required*. If you have no **else** clause, then go to the next question.
2. How many **then** clauses are there? (Again, HyperTalk sees the word **then** on a line by itself as a **then** clause line.) If

you have only one line in the **then** clause, you should not include the **end if** statement. Otherwise, it is required.

You must, of course, separate clauses into lines; you cannot combine commands in one HyperTalk line inside an **if** statement any more than you can anywhere else in HyperTalk.

It is , of course, possible to set up multiple conditions in the **if** clause of an **if-then** or **if-then-else** construct. In the event you need such multiple conditions, you will find it necessary to connect them with the key words **and** or **or.** We'll see some examples of this usage later in the chapter.

NOTE

There are some anomalies in the way HyperTalk formats and treats **if** clauses. If you use such clauses in a script that seem not to execute properly, try reformatting the **if-then-else** clauses. This will quite often erase apparent errors.

Nesting *if* statements

You can nest **if-then** and **if-then-else** statements. In other words, commands executed conditionally can themselves be a set of conditionally processed commands. This ability lends itself to powerful — but potentially complex — programming structures.

Here is an example of a nested set of **if-then-else** statements:

```
on mouseUp
   if the optionKey is down then
      if the shiftKey is down then beep 5
      else beep 3
   else beep 1
end mouseUp
```

The button this script is attached to beeps once when it is clicked, unless the Option key is held down at the same time, in which case it beeps three times. If the Shift and Option keys are held down together when the button is pressed, HyperCard beeps five times. Notice that each **if-then-else** includes only one command in the **else** portion, so no **end if** statements are required.

Nested *if* statements

Let's go back to the Laboratory stack. Pick any card with a button whose script is no longer needed, or create your own. Then follow these instructions:

1. Open the script editing window for the button.

2. Type the following script into the window and click OK when you are done and the handler is syntactically correct:

```
on mouseUp
   if the optionKey is down then
    if the shiftKey is down then
      beep 5
      put "Shift-Option Combination" into Message
    else
      beep 3
      put "Option Key Alone" into Message
    end if
  end if
end mouseUp
```

3. Return to browse mode.

4. Click on the button, first with the Option key held down, then with the Shift-Option keys held down, and finally with no keyboard keys held down. Notice not only the different beep combinations, but also the changing notices in the Message box.

This is the same basic handler script as the one we just looked at in much simpler form. It works the same, but this time we've added multiple statements after each **else**, requiring that each **if** clause be ended with an **end if**. Although this script is simplistic and doesn't do anything to write home about, it does demonstrate the flexibility of multiple nested **if-then-else** statements. A single handler responds to an event that can be sent in three ways: alone, with the Option key, or with the Shift-Option keys.

Conditional Operators and Calculations

Now that we've seen how **if-then** and **if-then-else** combinations work, let's see how we create their conditions.

True or false tests

All conditions in conditional processing must ultimately lead to a true or false situation. Any question that can be answered "yes" or "no" can be used to formulate a condition for an **if** clause in HyperTalk.

You can set up tests for equality (**if** x = 3 then...) or inequality (**if** not x = 3 then...) but generally not for mathematical formulas (**if** x*4 then...) or other expressions that don't produce a true or false, yes or no, 1 or 0 result. Functions and expressions that do return such results are referred to as logical operations or Boolean functions.

Sometimes, you will test the value of a container or variable without using explicit equality or inequality comparisons. A statement such as **if** x **then**... is an acceptable and logical Hyper-Talk statement if x contains the value true or false or the number 1 (which means true) or 0 (which means false).

In HyperTalk, you will frequently test many things in the condition portions of **if** statements. Broadly speaking, all are tests for values stored in containers. But we can divide them more conveniently into tests of

- equality

- inclusion

- status

Let's look at each kind of test.

Equality conditions

The test condition you will undoubtedly use most often in HyperTalk scripts is the **is** command. Actually, **is** is a synonym for *equals*. But most HyperTalk scripters use **is** to keep their scripts readable.

The following examples of equality conditions using **is** are similar to those you will frequently encounter in programming HyperTalk scripts:

```
if field "Name" is empty
if the optionKey is down
if x is 5
if it is "excited"
```

These are identical in effect to

```
if field "Name" = empty
if the optionKey = down
if x = 5
if it = "excited"
```

You can use **is** and = interchangeably, but your scripts are easier to read if you confine your use of = to numeric comparisons and use **is** for all other comparisons.

As you might expect from a language as English-like and flexible as HyperTalk, **is** has an opposite just as = does. The opposite of the equal sign is written as either < > or ≠ and the opposite of **is**, logically enough, is **is not**. In many cases, HyperTalk has values that make the use of **is not** and other inequality operators unnecessary. For example, you hardly need to write

```
if the optionKey is not down
```

when the shorter and clearer

```
if the optionKey is up
```

is available. But in other cases, the inequality operator is exactly what's needed:

```
if field "Name" is not empty
if x ≠ 5
if it is not "excited"
```

Comparison operators

Sometimes, it is not enough to know that an item is not equal to another. You need to know if it is greater than or less than the other object. For these situations, HyperTalk includes the usual programming language complement of comparison operators. These operators are summarized in Table 8-1.

Table 8-1. Comparison operators

Operator	Interpretation	Example
<	Less than	15 < 53 returns true
<= or ≤	Less than or equal to	15 <= 53 returns true
		33 ≤ 33 returns true
>	Greater than	15 > 53 returns false
>= or ≥	Greater than or equal to	15>= 53 returns false
		33 ≥ 33 returns true

Inclusion

Besides equality and inequality, your HyperTalk scripts can test for the presence of a sequence of characters in a field or text container. You can use either **is in** or **contains.** Both operators perform text matches that are not case sensitive. They look at one text string — the container — and see if another text string is located anywhere within it.

The syntax for these two commands is as follows:

```
if <source string> is in <container>
if <container> contains <source string>
```

As you can see, the only syntactical difference between the two commands is that **is in** places the string to be searched for first, but **contains** puts it last.

Testing for inclusion

Use either an existing Laboratory Stack card with a reusable field or create a new field on either an existing card or a new card. Size doesn't matter; leave the field set at the default size HyperCard creates when it brings up the new field. But define it as a rectangle or shadow so its outlines are visible (this makes things easier when you're testing and come back to the field later).

1. Click into the field. Type in the following text with capitals exactly as shown.

    ```
    This is a dumb TEsT
    ```

2. Now open the Message box if it isn't already open, or click in the Message box if it is open. Make sure the box is empty.

3. Type:

    ```
    card field 1 contains "test"
    ```

    and press Return. The Message box displays "True." Clearly, HyperTalk has found the string and ignored the case differences. Try the same thing with other combinations of uppercase and lowercase if you like.

4. Type

    ```
    "dumb " is in card field 1
    ```

    Be sure to include the space after the word *dumb*. Again, the Message box displays "True." You can use this approach to find any combination of characters or spaces in the text of a field.

Status

We have already seen in Chapter 7 how to test the state of the Shift, Option, or Command keys and react accordingly. As we will see in Chapter 17, all HyperCard objects have *properties* associated with them. These properties enable us to find out basic information about the objects other than their contents. For example, using property management commands we can find out if a field is presently visible, the user level for the person accessing the stack, an object's name, how many cards, buttons, fields, or backgrounds are in a stack, and dozens of other useful pieces of information.

Although we defer the discussion of specific properties until Chapter 17, you should be aware that testing the condition of these properties is one of the most frequent kinds of conditional processing you'll do in HyperTalk. The general form for using these properties as conditions is straightforward:

```
if <property name> is <value>
```

To give you an idea of what kinds of things you might test for, here are some sample lines:

```
if card field 1 is visible
if field "Test Field" is empty
if the number of cards > 53
if lockScreen is true
```

Not all properties that can be attributed to HyperCard objects are subject to **if-then** testing or could logically be used in conditional processing statements. In Chapter 17, we make clearer which of the many properties do lend themselves to this treatment.

Using the constants *true* and *false*

When you do conditional processing programming in Hyper-Talk, you can use the built-in constants **true** and **false**. These constants are not often used with most of the conditional processing situations we've discussed in this chapter because the true or false nature of the condition is apparent. A button is either up or down. Writing a line such as

```
if the optionKey is down is true
```

is superfluous.

But sometimes the built-in logical constants are handy. Perhaps the most obvious case is the process of setting flags. In complex programs, we often want to keep track of a condition in the system. For example, we may want to know if the user has clicked on Button 1 because if so, certain processing won't be necessary. So we set up a "flag" variable — call it *pressed* in this example — to keep track of that value. Then we can test it at the appropriate time. The framework for the example we just described is

```
on someEvent
  set pressed to false
  . . .
  if pressed is false then
  . . .
end someEvent
```

Logical connectors

One final topic should be covered to complete our discussion of conditional processing. Oftentimes, a combination of conditions must be tested before a script can proceed with processing. Staying with our by-now-familiar special key checking, for example, we might want to know only if any of the special keys has been pressed. We could get that information by programming a construct such as

```
on mouseUp
  if the optionKey is down then put "Special key down"
  if the shiftKey is down then put "Special key down"
  if the commandKey is down then put "Special key down"
end mouseUp
```

Pressing any combination of these special keys when the mouse button is clicked puts the message "Special key down" into the Message box. (We should note that if more than one special key is used, the message is actually placed in the Message box as many times as there are special keys pressed. But the effect is all but unnoticeable to the user, so it is not significant in this context.)

But this is more code than we need. If we want to display the message if any special key is being pressed, we can use the **or** connector. This connector links logical conditions so that if any one of the conditions connected by **or** is true, the condition succeeds. Thus, the previous handler can be reduced to this:

```
on mouseUp
  if the optionKey is down or the shiftKey is down or ¬
    the commandKey is down then put "Special key down"
end mouseUp
```

Similarly, if we want to display a special message only if all the keys are down, we use the **and** logical connector. Conditions hooked together with **and** only succeed if all the conditions are true.

The third logical connector in HyperTalk is **not**. It is used to negate or reverse logic. It can be applied to any equality condition check to make it a check for inequality. It can also be combined with **and** and **or** to create complex criteria in control constructs.

Using *and*

Go to your Laboratory stack again. Use the same button you've been using for these special key combination tests or create a new one. Then follow these steps:

1. Open the button's scripting window by one of the usual methods.

2. Enter the following script into the window:

```
on mouseUp
  if the shiftKey is down and the commandKey is down then
    beep 3
    put "Two keys down"
  end if
end mouseUp
```

3. Return to browse mode.

4. Try pressing the mouse button with the cursor over the button whose script you just created or modified. Notice that something happens only when you hold down the Shift and Command keys together.

NOTE

We cannot test for all three keys being pressed at once, not because of limitations of the **and** connector but because pressing the Command-Option key combination results in HyperCard suspending operation and highlighting all the buttons on the card. This interrupts script processing.

Looping Commands

Besides conditionally executing instructions in a handler, we might want to execute some particular step or steps more than once. The repeated execution of commands in HyperTalk is accomplished with an instruction that is named, appropriately enough, **repeat**.

This instruction should properly be looked at as four separate instructions. These variations on the **repeat** theme are

- **repeat for**

- **repeat with**

- **repeat while**

- **repeat until**

As we will see, these commands correspond to similar constructs in Pascal, C, and BASIC. HyperTalk, however, includes something most other programming languages lack: two ways to "escape" from an executing loop without finishing some or all of its instructions.

Basic looping concepts

All **repeat** structures in HyperTalk work similarly. They all start with the word **repeat** and end with the phrase **end repeat**. They all execute the commands contained between those key words zero or more times. And they all end when the circumstances under which they are expected to execute are no longer valid, unless they are interrupted sooner by an **exit repeat** command.

Inside a loop, all the rules of program execution apply exactly as they do in a complete handler. Any conditional statement groups involving **if-then** combinations are evaluated and executed as if they were the only statements in the group. Local and global variables known to the handler can be used anywhere inside the **repeat** loop.

Quite often, a handler consists entirely or nearly entirely of a single **repeat** loop. We saw one such loop in Chapter 7 when we performed a Laboratory exercise to track the coordinate position of the mouse pointer in a card. You may recall that the loop executed until you clicked the mouse.

The most crucial idea in writing loops in any programming language, including HyperTalk, is to make sure there is an escape route. There are two ways to create such routes in HyperTalk:

- by including an **exit repeat** condition that explicitly leaves the loop when some event occurs

- by ensuring that the condition under which the **repeat** command is executed eventually changes to a condition under which it will stop

Failure to do one of these results in a dreaded construct called an *infinite loop*, one of the most common mistakes in programming.

Basic repeat conditions

Whether we are talking about HyperTalk or a conventional programming language, there are two general categories of conditions under which loops can be programmed to execute:

- for a specific number of times

- as long as some condition remains true

In the first category of **repeat** loops, it is the reaching of some specific value in a variable or an upper limit on the number of iterations set as a condition. In the second category, the circumstance that causes the loop to stop is the changing of a condition.

Using object-counting in repeat conditions

One of the most useful things you can find out in HyperCard for use in **repeat** loops is the number of some kind of object with which you wish the loop to deal. For example, if you want to zip through a stack and look at each card individually, you want to know when you're done looking at all the cards. If you want to perform some operation or test on all the card buttons on a given card, you want to know how many buttons you have to deal with. Although you can "hard-code" such information, this is practically never a good idea; any future changes to the stack design might not get picked up in the scripts affected by those designs. All manner of confusion can result.

You can have HyperCard supply you with the number of buttons or fields on the current background or card, the number of backgrounds in the stack, the number of cards in the stack, or even, beginning with HyperCard 1.2, the number of cards sharing the current background.

It then becomes easy to write loops such as this one.

```
repeat for the number of cards
  if field "Accepted" contains "Yes" then 1 to total
  go to next card
end repeat
```

You will find frequent need for such repeat-loop counter controls that involve knowing the number of some particular kind of object with which the handler must be concerned.

The *repeat for* command

The **repeat for** command is the most straightforward of the looping constructs in HyperTalk. It simply tells HyperCard how many times to execute a loop. In the absence of an **exit repeat** command inside the loop, the instructions execute exactly the specified number of times, then the handler proceeds with the rest of its processing.

In Pascal, BASIC, or another conventional language, you implement this same kind of loop with a FOR-NEXT construction, starting with the counter value set to 1 and the upper limit set to the number of times you want to execute the loop.

Here is the syntax for the **repeat for** construct:

```
repeat [for] <number> [times]
  <statements>
end repeat
```

Notice that there are two optional words in the command: **for** and **times**. This permits you to make your **repeat** loops as abbreviated as you want or to opt for maximum readability. The following opening lines of **repeat** loops are equivalent:

```
repeat for 11 times
repeat for 11
repeat 11 times
repeat 11
```

The number argument need not be an explicitly supplied numeric value. It can be a container that holds a number. For example, you might ask users how many times they want some action to occur, store the answer in the variable *numberOfTimes*, and then set up a **repeat** loop like this:

```
repeat numberOfTimes times
  ...
end repeat
```

One place you will find this approach to the **repeat** loop most useful is when you are performing some process repeatedly but want to insert a **wait** command to slow things down a bit. (The **wait** command is discussed in detail in Chapter 20. For now, just remember that it delays the number of ticks, or 60ths of a second, supplied as an argument.) You have undoubtedly noticed, for example, that when we use commands such as

```
beep 3
```

in our scripts, the three beeps take place in such close proximity that the effect isn't always what we intended. By putting the **beep** command inside a **repeat** loop, we can separate the sounds by some silence, achieving the desired effect:

```
repeat 3 times
  beep
  wait 4
end repeat
```

Experiment with the value supplied as the time to wait to convey the audio message you want.

Another place where you will frequently use the **repeat for** approach to looping involves scanning through all the fields or cards to look for something or to change the data. For example, you might have a client billing stack that includes on each card a field with the billing rate for that attorney. If the partners decide to increase billing rates by 10%, you could write a small **repeat for** loop like this:

```
repeat number of cards times
  put field "Rate" * 1.1 into field "Rate"
  go next card
end repeat
```

The repeat with command

The **repeat with** command adds another level of complexity to the condition. In the **repeat with** approach, you use a special variable called a counter that you increase or decrease by 1 during each cycle through the loop until it reaches a predetermined value. Then the loop stops executing.

This command is HyperTalk's equivalent of the FOR-NEXT loop in Pascal and BASIC. The only difference is you cannot specify an increment or decrement value in HyperTalk. The variable is always increased or decreased by 1.

The syntax for the **repeat with** command looks like this:

```
repeat with <counter> = <start> [down]to <end>
  <commands>
end repeat
```

If the value for *start* is 1, **repeat with** is the same as **repeat for**. In other words, this **repeat** loop:

```
repeat with x = 1 to 10
  <commands>
end repeat
```

does the same thing as this one:

```
repeat 10 times
  <commands>
end repeat
```

There is an important exception to this equality. If you need to use the number of times through the loop as a value, only the **repeat with** approach will work.

Returning to our time billing example, suppose each attorney's card contained several billing rates and the fields were called (for purposes of simplicity) Field 1, Field 2, and so on. You could update all the fields on a single card with a single **repeat** loop like this:

```
repeat with x = 1 to number of card fields
  put card Field x * 1.1 into card Field x
end repeat
```

But if billing rates start with Field 7 and are the last fields on the card, a simple modification handles that case as well:

```
repeat with x = 7 to number of card fields
  put card Field x * 1.1 into card Field x
end repeat
```

In this last example, it would be difficult, if not impossible, to use the **repeat for** loop to solve the problem.

The *repeat while* command

You use the **repeat while** command to carry out a set of instructions as long as a condition is true. As soon as the condition is false, the loop stops executing.

The syntax for the **repeat while** command looks like this:

```
repeat while <condition>
  <commands>
end repeat
```

The *condition* here is identical in use and form to those we discussed with **if** processing previously in this chapter. It must evaluate to a true or false value, and it can use any of HyperCard's built-in functions to do so. If the *condition* is false the first time HyperCard encounters the loop, the loop never executes.

Using the *repeat while* command

Open the Laboratory stack again. We need a card with a button and a field whose contents you can re-use. Find an old card with this combination of objects or create a new one. The field must be Field 1, or you must make appropriate changes to the following script.

1. Open the button's script editing window in one of the usual ways.

2. Type the following script into the window and click OK when you're done:

```
on mouseUp
   repeat while card Field 1 < 64
      put card Field 1 * 2 into card Field 1
   end repeat
   beep
end mouseUp
```

3. Return to browse mode.

4. Enter the number 2 in the field.

5. Press the button. A series of numbers appear in the window, until the value 64 appears. Then the loop stops, your Mac beeps, and the handler ends. Your screen looks similar to Figure 8-1.

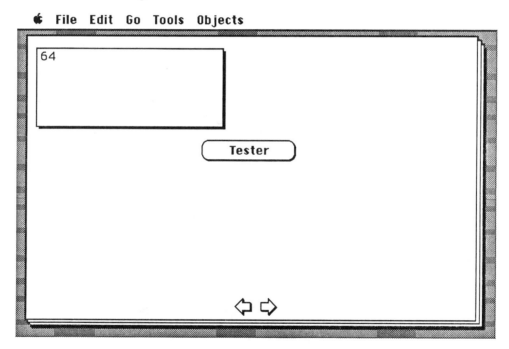

Figure 8-1. The repeat while loop experiment ends

6. Put the number 75 (or any number higher than 64) into the window and notice what happens. The repeat loop is never executed. Instead, you get the expected beep sound and the

handler ends. The first time the repeat loop was entered, the value of the field was greater than 64, so the loop was never carried out.

The *repeat until* command

The last of the four regular **repeat** forms we will examine is the **repeat until** command. It is easy to understand because it is the flip side of the **repeat while** command we have just examined. The commands within its boundaries execute as long as the condition remains false. As soon as the condition turns true, the loop stops. This generally requires a reversal of the logic of the **repeat while** loop's condition.

Here's the syntax for **repeat until**:

```
repeat until <condition>
  <commands>
end repeat
```

To execute the example in our previous Laboratory exercise the same way using a **repeat until** loop, we have to reverse the logic of the condition. Instead of checking for the field's value to be greater than 64, we check for it being less than or equal to 64:

```
on mouseUp
    repeat until card Field 1 >= 64
        put card Field 1 * 2 into card Field 1
    end repeat
    beep
end mouseUp
```

If you want to experiment with this script, simply edit the **repeat** line of the script from our last Laboratory experiment and run the handler.

> **NOTE**
>
> We use the condition "greater than or equal to 64" rather than "equal to 64" in the previous example for an important reason. If you use only an equal condition (i.e., Field 1=64) and if Field 1's value never gets to exactly 64, the loop could become an infinite one. For example, if the user puts a 3 instead of a 2 into Field 1 at the start, doubling the value each time results in answers of 6, 12, 24, 48, 96, 192, and so on. Because 64 never appears, the loop just keeps executing. In the Laboratory example, we were sure that the value 64 would eventually appear. But unless you can guarantee the ceiling value will be reached, use conditions that are met without an infinite loop.

The naked repeat command

You will occasionally encounter one last form of the **repeat** command in scripts: the naked **repeat**. With no *for*, *with*, *while*, or *until*, the **repeat** command means **repeat forever**. (You can even add the word **forever** if you want to make it clearer.)

In 99% of all cases where you use the **repeat** command alone, you will supply a means of exiting the loop using the technique described later in this chapter. And you probably could design the loop as a more conventional **repeat** loop using one of the other ending conditions we've been studying.

But in some limited circumstances, you want to keep all or a major portion of your script's processing in an intentionally infinite loop. Such loops can give the programmer more control over the user's interaction with the program, a decidedly unMac-like thing to do. Because the user can always leave your script by using one of the menu navigation commands to go to a different stack or card, though, you are not really *trapping* the user in an infinite loop. Still, use the concept sparingly. Always ask yourself if there isn't a more straightforward way to deal with the loop requirement.

Control Within Repeat Loops

HyperTalk includes two powerful commands to change the course of action within **repeat** loops. One, **next repeat**, cuts short the execution of part of a collection of repeated statements while continuing the loop at the next iteration. The other, **exit repeat**, causes the loop to stop executing and the script to begin processing at the first statement after the **end repeat** line.

The *next repeat* command

Although most programming languages do not have a command equivalent to the **next repeat** command, it has some handy uses. Within any **repeat** loop, you can use a command such as

```
if <condition> then [<commands>] [end if] else next repeat [<commands>]
```

to make the program go back to the top of the **repeat** loop, without executing any statements between the **next repeat** command and either another **next repeat** command or the **end repeat** command. If any commands appear between **then** and **next repeat**, the **end if** statement is also required, as you will recall from our discussion of **if-then** combinations previously.

Here is a generic example of the use of the **next repeat** command:

```
repeat with x = 10 to 50
  <statement1>
  <statement2>
  if <condition2> then
    beep 3
    next repeat
  end if
  <statement3>
end repeat
```

This loop executes 41 times, once for each value of x from 10 to 50, inclusive, unless the condition specified in *condition2* becomes true before that time. In that event, the system beeps three times and *statement3* is not executed. But *statement1* and *statement2* continue to execute until the loop ends normally. If *condition2* is never changed, *statement3* is not executed again because each time through the loop, the **if** command catches the execution, finds the condition to be true, and returns to the top of the loop.

Again using our time billing example, assume the partners want to not only increase all billing rates by 10%, but also make sure no billing rate is lower than $125. The following loop handles that task:

```
repeat with x = 1 to number of card fields
  put card Field 1 * 1.1 into card Field 1
  if card Field 1 >= 125 then next repeat
  put 125 into card Field 1
end repeat
```

There are more ways to handle this problem, but this solution works, is efficient, and demonstrates the use of the **next repeat** command nicely.

Counting backwards with *downTo*

When you need to count down from a higher number to a lower one rather than in the more common ascending order, you can substitute **down to** for **to** in the **repeat with** loop structure.

```
repeat with x = 10 down to 1
  put x
  beep x
end repeat
```

Defining a different increment

As mentioned, **repeat** loops in HyperTalk that use values with the **with** and **for** approaches do not allow you to increment or decrement the value of the counter by any value other than 1. Sometimes you want to increment a value by another value. In those cases, you can use the **next repeat** function with the **mod** operator to change the increment. (The **mod** operator finds the remainder in a division problem. For example, the result of 6 **mod** 3 is 0 because 6/3=2 with no remainder. But 39 **mod** 2 is 1 because 39/2=19 with a remainder of 1. The **mod** operator is fully discussed in Chapter 14.)

Here, for example, is a loop that effectively increments the counter by 2 each time through the loop:

```
repeat with x = 1 to 100
  if x mod 2 ≠ 0 then next repeat
  put x
end repeat
```

You can confirm that this loop works by attaching it to a button in a Laboratory card. The numbers 2, 4, 6, and so on up to 100 are displayed in the Message box, though you may have to build in a **wait** instruction to see each value displayed. Note that all the usual rules about using **if-then** constructs, described previously in this chapter, apply to **next repeat** commands.

The *exit repeat* command

The **exit repeat** command is straightforward. It is almost always used with an **if-then** construct. The **exit repeat** command causes the loop to terminate immediately.

The syntax for this command is:

```
if <condition> then exit repeat
```

As with other **if-then** constructions, this command can incorporate other commands between **then** and **exit repeat**. If other commands are included, an **end if** is needed.

Continuing with our time billing example, the fickle partners have now decided to increase everyone's fees by 10% in the first three categories (fields) but to bump only the partners' fees by 25% in all remaining categories. The following loop handles the assignment neatly:

```
repeat with x = 1 to number of card fields
  put card Field x * 1.1 into card Field x
  if card Field "Status" is not "Partner" then exit repeat
  if x > 3 then put card Field x * 1.25 into card Field x
end repeat
```

This loop would be part of a larger loop so that when the **exit repeat** command is encountered, the next card is examined and this repeat loop executes again.

Summary

In this chapter, you learned about two of the most important programming techniques in HyperTalk (or any other programming language): conditional commands and loops.

You saw that the **if-then** and **if-then-else** command groups permit you to execute instructions in a handler selectively. You learned there are a wide range of conditions you can check to determine if a command or sequence of commands should be carried out or not.

When instructions need to be carried out multiple times, you learned to use the various forms of the **repeat** command. You saw that each command in a **repeat** loop can be executed a specific number of times or until some condition is true or false.

Finally, you noted that HyperTalk, unlike most programming languages, offers powerful ways to alter the course of a loop's execution, adding another dimension of control.

In the next chapter, we will examine some commands, functions, and operators for controlling the stack and card environments.

CHAPTER

Card Management Methods

In this chapter, you'll learn how to use HyperTalk commands to

- navigate among cards and stacks

- enable the user to return quickly to some pre-determined point in the stack

- show or print one or more cards in a stack

Navigation Commands

In a typical stackware application, the user spends a lot of time moving among cards. The user generally controls this movement with buttons you've designed and connected to arrows and icons. But there are times when you want to control what cards the user accesses and in what order. Sometimes this need is temporary, and other times it is an integral part of the stack's design.

149

When you do want to control the navigation process, you can use one of HyperTalk's built-in commands, possibly with one of the language's constants.

Basically two HyperTalk commands are used for navigation: **go** and **find**. You use **go** to send the user to a specific card that can be named or referred to relative to the user's present position in the stack. The **find** command is used to send the user to a card based on its content.

Using *go* in a Script

You have probably had the experience of typing **go** commands into the Message box. This command can be used to move from your present position in the HyperCard world to any card in the current stack or to any addressable card in any other stack. Using the **go** command in a script is not substantially different from using it in the Message box.

The basic syntax of the command is simplicity itself:

```
go [to] <destination>
```

Notice that you can use the optional word **to** for more English-like syntax. The destination can be a card or a stack. You cannot **go** to a field or any other object.

Addressing a destination

As you may know, any card can be addressed by name, sequence number, or unique ID number. If the seventh card in the current stack is named Directions and HyperCard has assigned it the unique ID 14238, all of the following commands will take you to the card:

```
go to card "Directions"
go to card 7
go to card ID 14238
```

The argument to the go command can be stored in a container so that the addressing is indirect. If the container helpPlace contains the value Directions, this command takes you to the same card as the previous three commands:

```
go to card helpplace
```

If you want to **go** to a different stack from the current one, simply supply the name of the stack in quotation marks as an argument to the go command. In the absence of instructions to the contrary, HyperCard goes to the first card in that stack:

```
go to "My Appointments"
```

The quotation marks are required even if the stack has only one word so that HyperTalk doesn't think you are supplying the name of a container. Also note that to **go** to a stack, you need not use the word **stack** (though you may do so for readability). HyperCard assumes you want it to change stacks when you issue the **go** command and only needs clarification if you want to **go** to a card in the current stack.

You can combine these methods of navigation to take the user to a specific card in a stack:

```
go to card 78 of stack "Employees"
go to card ID 41233 of "Help"
```

Cards with special addresses

Several groups or classes of cards in any stack with special addresses can be used to make navigation easier and more readable. These special addresses include

- positional addresses like first, third, or last

- relative addresses like back, recent, or next

HyperCard includes special constants to address these specific cards.

The *positional* constants include the ordinal numbers 1—10 (**first, second, third**, and so on) as well as the random card address **any** and the address of the last card in any stack, **last**. The middle card in the current stack can also be addressed specially, as **mid** or **middle**, should you come up with a need to do so. All these special addresses are also used to address components of containers. Their use in that context is more fully discussed in Chapter 10. All of the following, then, are valid **go** commands:

```
go to seventh card -- same as "go card 7"
go to last card -- go to the last card in this stack
go to third card in "Ideas"
go to last card in "Ideas"
go to any card -- pick a card at random and go there
go to mid -- go to the middle card in the current stack
```

The *relative* constants include: **next, previous** (also abbreviated **prev**), **forth, back**, and **recent**. For all practical purposes, the last two are identical. The first two — **next** and **previous** — affect the user's position within the current stack relative to the present position. Thus, if the user is at the 14th card in the stack and a script executes the **go previous** command, the user is shown the 13th card in the stack even if the 14th card was reached without going through the 13th card. In other words, **next** and **previous** are not related to the route by which the user arrives at any given point.

On the other hand, **back** and **recent** are both path-related. If the user has been taken or has "driven" through a path like that shown in Figure 9-1, each use of one of these commands backs up the path one step. The **forth** indicator is also path-related. It points at the next card in the Recent stack. If the current card is the last card in the Recent stack, the command

```
go forth
```

takes the user to the Home stack.

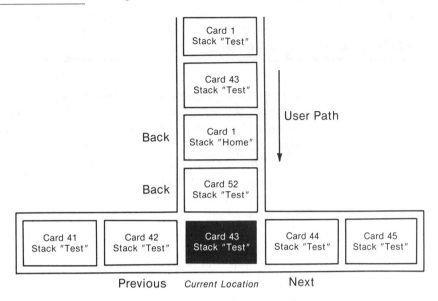

Figure 9-1. The *back, next ,*and *previous* commands

As you can see in Figure 9-1, the user started at Card 1 of the stack called Test and followed the indicated path to reach Card 43 of the same stack. Now, a **go prev** command takes the user to Card 42 of that stack. A **go next** command takes the user to Card 44 of the stack. But a **go back** command (or a **go recent card**) takes the user to Card 52 of the stack, and another execution of that command moves the user to Card 1 of the Home stack.

Non-existent cards

If a **go** command attempts to access a non-existent card, the message "not found" will be returned in a function called **the result**. Good error-trapping strategy dictates that you check for this condition.

```
go to card id 1437
if the result is empty then
  -- some processing
else
  -- error-handling
```

Finding Cards by Content

Sometimes, you don't know the specific card you want to steer the user to, but you do know that it contains some key word or words. In those cases, use the **find** command to locate the desired card.

This command is not mysterious. Almost from the time you began using HyperCard, probably before you were aware that HyperTalk existed, you were using **find** commands to move to cards when you wanted to locate an individual in your Address stack or an appointment in your Datebook stack.

Used within a HyperTalk script, the **find** command is identical, though you may use it with slightly more arguments and sophistication than you were aware was available to you in the Message box. The simplest form of the command is

```
find "<text>"
```

When it is used this way, the **find** command searches through all fields of each card in the stack, beginning with the currently visible one, and locates the first occurrence of the word or words supplied as an argument.

You can add two types of qualifiers to the find command. The first type defines the nature of the search; the second confines the search to a specific field. You use both kinds of qualifiers extensively in scripting. Without these qualifiers, HyperCard locates the text anywhere it occurs, even if it's split over two fields on the same card, as long as the target string is the beginning of a word. Thus, it would find *an* in answer and antidote, but not in *banana* or *Alexander*.

What kind of match to find?

You can add four qualifiers to the find command to tell Hyper-Card what constitutes a "hit":

- whole

- string

- word

- chars

Each of these qualifiers results in a slightly different approach to the **find** command. They may not be used in combination with one another.

We take a look at each of these qualifiers in turn, then we examine an example that clarifies how the qualifiers differ from one another.

The command **find whole** is the most targeted of these commands. Its rules for declaring a combination of characters as a "hit" are as follows:

1. The word or phrase found must match exactly the argument supplied with the command.

2. Spaces are significant.

3. Order is significant.

4. All of the word or phrase must appear in the same field on a card.

This option was added to HyperCard 1.2 to overcome what many users and designers saw as a limitation in earlier releases of the program. Those limitations become clearer when we study an example of the various **find** commands later in this section.

Also added in HyperCard 1.2 was the **find string** command. This command is essentially the same as the **find chars** command (which we discuss next), except that when its argument has one or more spaces in it, HyperCard uses its fastest search algorithm. This addition significantly improves the peformance of complex searches but does not add functionality to HyperCard.

If you want to limit the search to the whole word or words supplied as the search text, use the **find word** form:

```
find word "end"
```

This command only finds the word *end* as a whole word. The words *blender, ending,* and *weekend* are not located.

Finally, if you want HyperCard to find the target string even if it occurs mid-word, use the **find chars** form of the command:

```
find chars "end"
```

This command finds *blender, ending,* and *weekend.*

Specifying the Search

1. Create a new Laboratory stack using the "New Stack" option from the File Menu; leave "Copy Current Background" selected in the resulting dialog.

2. Create two background fields for this new stack.

3. On Card 1, type in field 1 the word *"Irving"* and in field 2 the word *"Glotzbach".*

4. On Card 2, type in field 1 the words *"Irving Glotzbach"* and in field 2 the words *"lives here".*

5. On Card 3, type in field 1 the words *"Ingemar Johansen"* and in field 2 the words *"lived here".*

6. Go to Card 1.

7. In the Message Box, type:

```
find "Irving Glotzbach"
```

8. After it finds the string on Card 1 (notice that it appears split across two fields), press the **return** key. Notice that it finds the string on Card 2 as well. Press **return** again and HyperCard returns to Card 1.

9. Now try typing:

```
find word "Irving Glotzbach"
```

10. Notice that the results match those we encountered in Steps 7 and 8.

11. Change the Message Box so that it reads:

    ```
    find whole "Irving Glotzbach"
    ```

12. Notice that now HyperCard only finds Card 2. This is the only card where the target string, *"Irving Glotzbach"*, exists exactly as provided in the argument to the find command and entirely in one field.

13. Now type the following line into the Message box:

    ```
    find whole "live"
    ```

14. Notice that HyperCard simply beeps at you; it cannot find the word "live" as a complete, stand-alone word. (You can achieve the same result with the **find word** variation in this case.)

15. Return to the Message Box and type:

    ```
    find chars "ing"
    ```

16. Now HyperCard finds all three cards, because all of them have the string *ing* somewhere in one of their fields, though not necessarily at the beginning of a word.

17. Let's change the Message Box to read:

    ```
    find "ing"
    ```

18. Now HyperCard only finds Card 3, because that's the only place that the string "ing" begins a word (in this case, *Ingemar*).

Narrowing the search

When you design stacks, each field will probably have a specific purpose. Each card on which the field appears will store the same kind of information in that field. On an inventory stack's cards, for example, you might store the part number in Field 1, the quantity on hand in Field 2, the price per unit in Field 3 and the date last ordered in Field 4. If you want to find all parts with a 5 in the number, you can write:

```
find "5"
```

But HyperCard would find every card where the quantity on hand was 5 or 15 or 500, any part that cost $49.95, any date that included a 5 — in short, it would find every 5 in every card of the stack. That's not what you wanted. So you might narrow the search to Field 1 like this:

```
find "5" in field 1
```

HyperCard would ignore the contents of all other fields and concentrate its search for 5's only in Field 1. If the 5 were a standalone part of the part number so that it qualifies as a word in HyperCard, then you could even use

```
find word "5" in field 1
```

This is a little more specific, but it will still find any 5 surrounded by spaces anywhere in Field 1.

Limitations on *find*

Unfortunately, the **find** command cannot be forced to confine itself only to a specific component of the field. You may know that the 5 you are interested in is always the third digit, but that's not going to help you with the **find** command. In that case, design a customized search routine that looks at the third character of the field and does something if it's a 5.

When you execute the **find** command within a script, the user cannot continue the search with a simple Return key, though you can design the script to make this possible.

The found card

When the **find** command is successful, it makes the card on which it locates the match the current card. You can then use property-retrieval techniques (see Chapter 17) to find out that card's ID, or examine other fields or parts of the same field to qualify the card before continuing processing. If the **find** command fails, it leaves the current card unchanged.

If the **find** command fails, a message indicating the approximate reason for the failure will be returned in the built-in function **the result**. The specific error is not usually important, so merely checking to see if **the result** has anything in it is sufficient to deal with error conditions.

```
if the result is empty then step1 else step2
```

Using *pop* and *push* in Scripts

In complex scripts with lots of card movement, you often want to mark a card as one to return to after some exploration is complete. Rather than requiring you to keep track of how many **go back** commands it will take to get there, HyperTalk includes the **pop** and **push** commands. In essence, **push** marks a card for later instant retrieval with the **pop** command.

The **push** command does not require any parameters. (You may, for the usual reason of readability, write the command to **push** the current card as **push card**, but that is not necessary.) If you want to mark the current card, simply use the command by itself. If you want to push the most recent card (i.e., the card from which the user got to the current card), you need to add a parameter:

```
push recent card
```

The **pop card** command indicates that you want to return the user to the card to which you most recently applied a **push** command. The **card** parameter is required. The only other use of **pop** is explained later when we describe multiple **push** statements.

The stack created by *push*

You can think of the **push** command as moving the card to which it applies to a special location that in traditional programming terms would be called a *stack*. Only this is not a HyperCard stack. Rather, it is a kind of single-file line in which cards that are pushed stand until they are called again. Figure 9-2 depicts this special location. In such a situation, only the top card — the one nearest the door in the illustration — can be affected by a **pop** command. It must get "out of the way" before you can release any of the cards placed there earlier.

Figure 9-2. Pushed cards go into a special location

The kind of special location shown in Figure 9-2 is called, in computer terms, a LIFO stack. LIFO is an acronym for "last in, first out." The last card pushed into this line is the first one popped out of it. Most of the time, your scripts will not push more than one card at a time. Only very complex applications ever need to handle multiple-card special stacks like that shown in Figure 9-2.

Using *pop* without showing the card

But if you do have an application that uses multiple-card pushes and you want to **pop** a card other than the top one into view, you will need to use the technique of popping the card into a container.

The syntax for this technique is:

```
pop card into <container>
```

When you **pop** a card into a container, the card's ID and stack location are placed in the container and the card is removed from the special stack location without being shown to the user. Later, you can use the information in the container, along with a **go** command, to show the card that was popped into the container.

For example, assume you have executed two **pop** commands. The first one operated on Card 6 of the current stack and the second operated on Card 157. Now you want to take the user to the card that was popped first. The basic handler segment looks like this:

```
pop card into card field 1 of holder
pop card
```

Now the card identifying information for Card 157 is stored in the container called *holder*, in Card Field 1. Now if you want to show that card, use a command like this:

```
go to card field 1 of holder
```

Notice that this does not take the user to the field but rather to the card whose identifier is stored in the field.

Using *push* and *pop*

For this experiment, let's create a new stack that uses the background of the Laboratory stack. After you've done that, follow these directions:

1. Get into Edit Background mode.

2. Add a rectangular field to the background. You don't need to name it because we'll refer to it by its field number. The card should look similar to Figure 9-3.

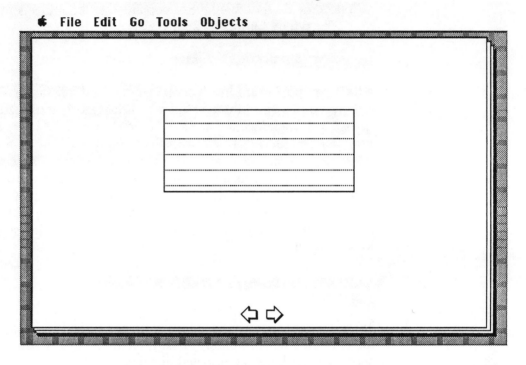

Figure 9-3. New Laboratory stack card

3. Return to browse mode.

4. Create six new cards for the stack so that the stack has seven cards. Name the cards Test 1, Test 2, and so forth, in the Card Info... dialog.

5. Label each card Card 1, Card 2, and so forth, in the field you've created. These are used as visual cues as we go through the experiment.

6. Go to Card 1 and create a new scrolling field. Name it Tracker. Put it anywhere on the card. Card 1 should now look similar to Figure 9-4.

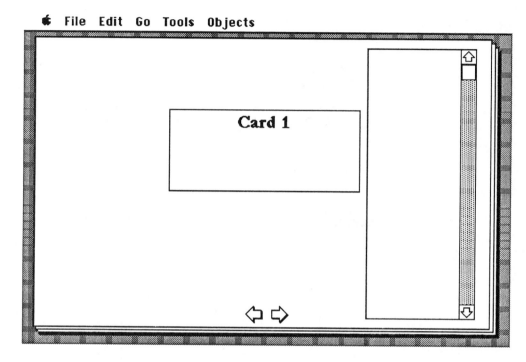

Figure 9-4. Card 1 with Tracker field added

7. Open the Message box. Type the following commands, in the order shown:

```
go to card "Test 1" -- Card 1 should appear
push card
go to card "Test 3"
go to card "Test 4"
pop card -- Card 1 should reappear
```

8. Now we'll try a multiple-push experiment. Type the following commands, in the order shown:

```
go to card "Test 1" -- Card 1 should appear
push card
go to card "Test 3"
push card
go to card "Test 5"
push card
go to card "Test 6"
pop card into card field "Tracker" of Card "Test 1"
```

```
pop card after card field "Tracker" of Card "Test 1"
pop card -- Card 1 should reappear with text in Holder
```

9. Your screen should look similar to Figure 9-5. Notice that identification information, complete with path, is now stored in the Tracker field of Card 1. These are the IDs of the two cards that were pushed onto the stack after Card 1 and then popped into this container. To confirm this, go to those cards and choose Card Info... from the Objects menu. Note the card ID numbers shown there.

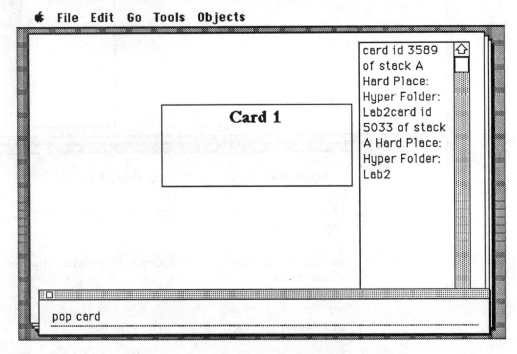

Figure 9-5. Card identification in Tracker field

Using *push* and *pop* between objects

It is not necessary that balanced **push** and **pop** commands work with the same object or one of the same level. It is not only possible but often useful to **push** a card as a result of the user having pressed a button and later to **pop** the card from a card script.

You'll find that judicious use of **push** and **pop** can save you a great deal of unnecessary navigation.

Showing and Printing Cards

You've undoubtedly noticed the icon on many HyperCard stacks that is used to zoom through the stack looking for a specific card. Such an icon is included in the Address stack, for example, and is shown in Figure 9-6 (the second icon from the bottom of the panel of icons along the left side of the Address card). Open this button's script in one of the usual ways. It should look like this (assuming it has not been modified):

```
on mouseUp
  show all cards
end mouseUp
```

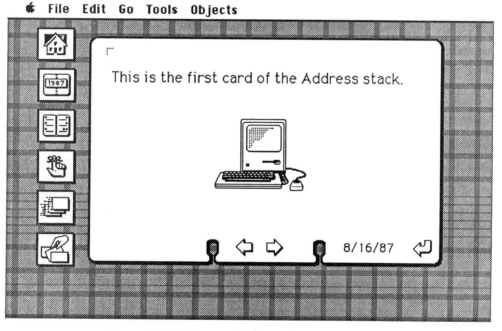

Figure 9-6. Address stack card with "show cards" icon

This **show** command lets the browser skim through a stack. It shows cards until it has shown all the cards it has been asked to display or the user clicks the mouse, whichever happens first. The first card shown is the one after the one showing when the command is issued. You can use it to let the user flip through all the cards in a stack or just through a specific number of cards. In the latter case, the command syntax is

```
show <number> cards
```

If you ask HyperCard to show more cards than are in the stack, it simply recycles through the stack until it has shown the requested number of cards.

The principles that apply to **show** also pertain to the **print card** command. This command has three forms:

```
print card
print card "Test 3"
print 5 cards
```

The first form prints the current card. The second prints any identified card. The last prints a specific number of cards, beginning with the currently visible one, and may use the word **all** in place of a number.

Summary

In this chapter, you saw how to use script commands to move the user through a stack with variations of the **go** command. You also saw how to save one or more cards for quick return and retrieval using combinations of **push** and **pop**. Finally, you learned to use **show** and **print** to display and produce printed copies of cards in various ways. In Chapter 10, you explore a wide range of commands that involve managing information in HyperCard stacks.

Managing Text and Data

In this chapter, you'll learn how to

- read the contents of fields

- get information about data in fields

- find and select field contents

- modify the contents of fields

- use fields to simulate arrays and tables of data

- sort cards by the contents of fields

- deal with date and time data as a special class of information

- trap the use of the Return and Enter keys in a field

167

HyperCard as an Information Base

When HyperCard was first announced, many people, in a sincere attempt to describe what is clearly a new class of product, compared it to conventional database management systems. This turned out to be an oversimplification for at least two reasons:

- HyperCard does much more than manage data, which is what database management systems do.

- Database management systems have other capabilities for data manipulation that exceed those of HyperCard.

Nonetheless, HyperCard does manage data. Its management of information through Hypertext features (the links between cards and stacks that make authoring without HyperTalk more powerful than many kinds of programming) and HyperTalk scripts is its most important feature. In HyperCard, before the release of Version 1.2, the ability to find data and to position the cursor correctly in a data entry field were quite difficult to implement. In Version 1.2, HyperCard added a great deal of functionality to make the **find** command more useful as well as providing a new **select** command. Used together, these two instruction groups significantly improve the data-management capabilities of HyperCard.

In this chapter, we examine HyperTalk commands that manage information. This data is stored in fields on cards because fields are the only places changeable data can be stored and still be visible to the user.

Reading Information in a Field

When information is stored in a card field or background field, it can be obtained by the **get** command. This command is not new to us. We've used it in several Laboratory experiments and in other discussions. But now we will take a close look at how it works and gain more insight into its use.

We can also use the **put** command to retrieve data, even though the action of retrieval sounds contrary to what we usually think of when we use the word *put*. We can use **put** to copy information from a field to another field or a container. The **put** command also serves as the means for permanently modifying information in a field. We'll talk about the **put** command several times from several different perspectives in this chapter.

The *get* command

As you may recall, **get** retrieves data and puts the result into the special *It* variable. From there, your script can access *It* and do whatever it wants, including:

- test the contents of *It* and use the test result in an **if** construct

- use **put** to move data into another temporary container or field

- modify data in *It* and then perform another function

Generally, if your plan for the data after it is retrieved involves moving it from *It* to any other container or field, it is better to use **put** (discussed next) to move it directly. This is true for two reasons:

- This approach requires fewer keystrokes and is a more efficient use of memory.

- The *It* variable is used extensively by HyperCard, so minimizing its use in your scripts is a good idea.

Addressing reminder

As you may recall from our previous discussions, particularly in Chapter 5, data in fields can be addressed in many ways to gain access to very specific information chunks. In the remainder of this discussion, we frequently use the **item**, **line**, **word**, and **char** operators to focus on the information we want to retrieve.

Some *get* practice

For our next exercise, use the same new stack of cards you created in Chapter 9 for the exercise on **push** and **pop**. (If you didn't do that exercise or didn't save the resulting stack, create a new card in the Laboratory stack and add a field called Field 1, using the default size and position HyperCard uses when it creates a new field. If you do this, however, you have now created a *card field* called Field 1 and must modify the directions in this Laboratory exercise accordingly. Remember, HyperCard assumes you mean a background field when you address a field unless you explicitly indicate a card field. Also, name this card Test 2 to match the name we use in the listings. Put the words Card 2 into the field.)

> **NOTE**
>
> You don't need to use the card name when you are referring to the current card. But these are experiments, and in most cases you will use the complete address of the source and destination, including the card identifier. So we use the full address even though we could shorten it. This helps pattern your thinking so you don't make a mistake when writing your own scripts.

After you open the stack from Chapter 9 or create a new one, get to the card called Test 2 that says Card 2 in the field. Then follow these directions.

1. Add two lines of text to the field, as shown in Figure 10-1. The commas in the second text line are important, so be sure to include them. Also, be sure to insert a carriage return at the end of the first text line so that HyperCard won't see the two text lines as one continuous line.

2. Open the Message box if it isn't already visible. We'll be conducting these experiments from the Message box and not from scripts.

3. Type the following commands in the Message box. After each is completed successfully, type the word *It* and press Return. Examine the result and check that it is the same as that shown indented under each command.

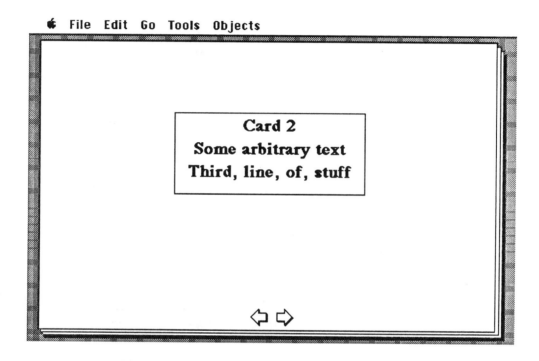

Figure 10-1. Modified field of Test 2 card

```
get line 1 of field 1 of card "Test 2"
     -- it = "Card 2"
get line 2 of field 1 of card "Test 2"
     -- it = "Some arbitrary text"
get first word of line 2 of field 1 of card "Test 2"
     -- it = "Some"
get second item of line 3 of field 1 of card "Test 2"
     -- it = " line" (note the space)
get char 3 to 6 of word 2 of line 2 of field 1 of card "Test 2"
     -- it = "bitr"
```

4. Experiment with other combinations of addresses in Field 1 until you are comfortable with all the component addressing approaches and you know what information they retrieve.

A note on chunking expressions

If the argument that precedes a **to** expression is larger than the value that follows the **to**, you will only extract a single element of the object. For example, a statement like

```
get char 7 to 0 of word 2 of line 2 of field 1
```

will return only the seventh character of the second word on the second line of the field called field 1.

Other uses for *get*

The other major use of the **get** command is obtaining values associated with certain characteristics of HyperCard objects. These characteristics, called *properties*, are discussed in Chapter 17.

The **get** command is also used to retrieve the values of certain functions such as the time and date. This use of the command is explored later in this chapter.

We should point out, too, that the **get** command is something of an anomaly in HyperTalk. Because the **put** command (discussed in the next section) combines the actions of the **get** command with the assignment of the result, you will find that good scripters seldom if ever use **get**.

Using *put* commands to read data

Because the **get** command always puts its results into the special *It* variable, we need an alternate way of retrieving information from a card field. The **put** command is used for this purpose.

You may recall from our discussion of this command in Chapter 5 that it has three basic forms:

- Without any arguments, **put** takes the contents of *It* and places them in the Message box.

- With only a source argument, **put** places the source into the Message box.

- With both a source and a destination argument, **put** places the contents of the source at a specified point in the destination container.

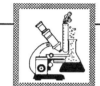

Some *put* exercises

Our next experiment is an exercise with the **put** command. We will use the same Laboratory card and stack for this experiment as we used in the previous Laboratory exercise with **get**. As with that exercise, we will also use the Message box rather than scripts. After you open the new Laboratory stack and arrive at the card called Test 2, follow these instructions:

1. Open the Message box if it is not already visible.

2. Type the following text into the Message box and press Return. The result looks like Figure 10-2.

```
put "silly" into word 2 of line 2 of field 1 of card "Test 2"
```

3. Recalling that the **into** preposition replaces the destination container with the source text or expression and that **before** and **after** place the source text before and after the destination container, try the following exercises in the Message box and compare your results with those shown. This time, you won't need to type *It* into the Message box to see the results; they are immediately displayed in the field.

```
put "interesting" after word 2 of line 2 of field 1 of card "Test 2"
```

(The result of this one should look like Figure 10-3. Notice that the second line of text has wrapped around to accommodate the longer text block and that the third line of text has all but disappeared. We'll fix that problem with the next command.)

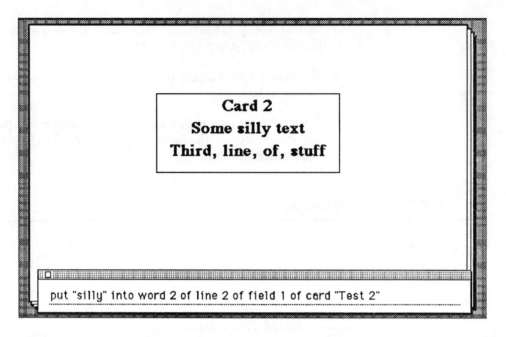

Figure 10-2. Using *put* in Test 2 card

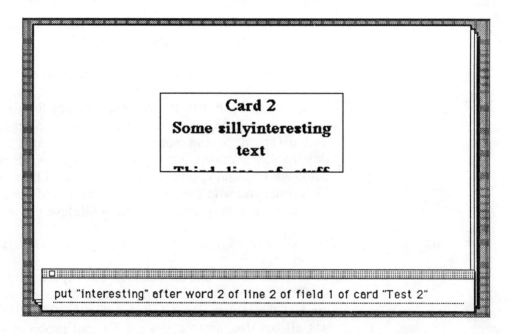

Figure 10-3. Partial result of *put* experiment

```
put "arbitrary" into word 2 of line 2 of field 1 of card "Test 2"
  -- returns card to its contents before these two commands
put item 3 of line 3 of field 1 of card "Test 2" before line 1 of
  field 1 of card "Test 2"
  -- first line now reads "ofCard 2"
put " mess" after line 1 of field 1 of card "Test 2"
  -- first line now reads "ofCard 2 mess" (note the space)
```

4. Use the usual text editing approach to change the contents of
    the field back to the original contents. Or, if you want the
    practice, use **put** statements to accomplish the same thing.

More typical destinations

All the **put** examples and experiments we've seen have used the
contents of a field to change other contents of the same field.
We've done that because the immediate feedback is useful in de-
termining what the **put** statement does. Typically, the destination
for a **put** is not the same as the source. In normal use, **put** is used to
retrieve information from fields and put it into variables or other
fields.

You can experiment with this use of the **put** command by
using the same Laboratory approach we used in the last exercise.
Where we used field addresses, just substitute a variable (for example, *temp*) for the destination. Then after each **put** command,
type the variable name in the Message box to see the results.

How Many Characters in the Field?

The **length** function can tell you how many characters are in any
string, including any addressable component of a field. This is
often useful in reports, in using the **offset** function (described in
the next section), and in ensuring that user-entered data meets
any length limits your script must impose.

The **length** function has two forms. The first spells out the
command in full, readable English:

```
the length of line 1 of field 1 of card "Test 2"
```

The second form uses an abbreviated approach (similar to Pascal or C commands):

```
length(line 1 of field 1 of card "Test 2")
```

The two forms are interchangeable. Your choice of which to use will be governed by your experience and the need for script readability.

In either case, you should know that if you apply the **length** function to a full line in a field, the function does not count the carriage return at the end. This becomes particularly important when you use the **offset** function, because this function does count the carriage return.

Finding and Selecting Text

Starting with HyperCard Version 1.2, the designer's ability to extract and manipulate data based on field contents was significantly increased. Not only was the **find** command enhanced (see the discusion in Chapter 9) with the addition of the new **whole** and **string** parameters, but two new capabilites were included:

- the ability to determine precisely where the text was found by the **find** command;

- the ability to select text based on the results of a **find** operation or on the text's location in a field, or even to position the cursor in a field before or after a particular location.

Where did the *find* take place?

Let's look first at the use of several functions to determine where a particular piece of text for which we have searched has been found. When a **find** operation is successful, HyperCard notes the location of the found text in four special functions:

- **the foundText** (returns the characters enclosed in the box after the **find** command has located the text);

- **the foundField** (returns the identification of the field in which the text was located);

- **the foundLine** (returns the number of the line in the field in which the text was found);

- **the foundChunk** (returns the complete chunking expression to indicate where the text was found).

For example, if we had a field such as that shown in Figure 10-4 and we performed a find operation such as this:

```
find "ran"
```

the foundText would contain the word *range* (because with the unadorned **find** command HyperCard locates the first occurrence of the string at the *beginning* of a word, then makes the entire word the found text). On the other hand, **the foundChunk** would contain the value char 5 to 9 of card field 1, whereas **the foundField** would point to card Field 1 and **the foundLine** to Line 1 of card Field 1.

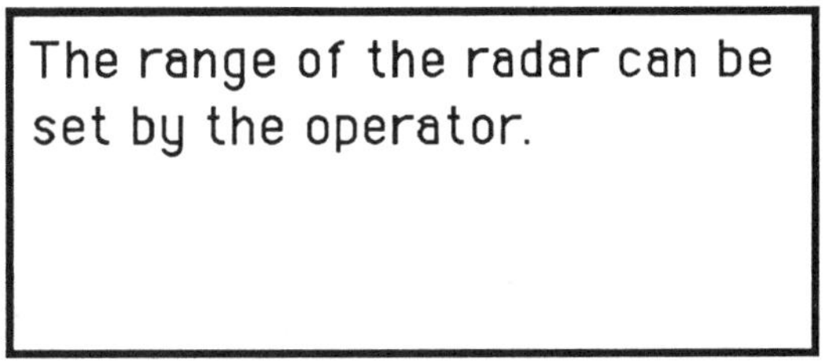

```
The range of the radar can be
set by the operator.
```

Figure 10.4. Sample field to demonstrate *find* options

If we were to change the search from *find "ran"* to *find whole "range of"*, we would see different results. Because of the use of the **whole** qualifier, HyperCard would put *"range of"* into **the foundText** and appropriate values into the other functions. (Strictly speaking, HyperCard actually does not put these values into these functions. Rather, the use of the function returns these values. For this discussion, that is a distinction without a difference.)

Using *select* to pick up found text

Once we've found some text and know where it is located, we quite often want to manipulate it. But we can't manipulate **the foundText** directly. Remember, it's not a container but a function result. So we use HyperCard Version 1.2's newly defined **select** command to accomplish the task.

In essence, the **select** command puts whatever text it is pointed to into **the selection,** a container we discussed briefly in Chapter 5. Once that text is in this special container, we can manipulate it. For example, we can copy it, cut it, or put something new into the container.

Returning to our small field example, once we've found the text *range of,* we can easily turn it into text with which we can work:

```
select the foundChunk
-- puts the located text into the selection
doMenu "Cut Text"
tabKey
doMenu "Paste Text"
```

This little program fragment assumes a **find** has just taken place. It deletes the found text from one field, tabs to the next field in sequence, and pastes the found text into the new field, replacing the contents of the destination field (because the **tabKey** command highlights the entire contents of the destination field and the Paste Text command then replaces that selection).

We used **the foundChunk** rather than **the foundText** here because it makes no sense to tell HyperCard to select words; the **select** command expects an address as its argument.

Using *select* without the *find*

Of course, you don't have to use **select** only with a **find** operation. You can select any arbitrary text that you can address. Both of the following operations, for example, select the words "range of" in Figure 10-4:

```
select word 2 to 3 of line 1 of card field 1
select char 4 to 12 of card field 1
```

Using *select* to position the cursor

Besides selecting text, you can use the **select** command to place the cursor precisely where you want it in a field. This means you can put the user in the right location to enter the next piece of information. You accomplish this with the **select before** and **select after** combinations. They can be followed by any chunking expression. Here are some examples:

```
select after last line of card field 1
-- puts cursor at end of field
select before first line of card field 1
-- puts cursor at start of field
select after word 3 of line 2 of card field 1
select before char 5 of word 3 of line 2 of card field 1
```

Selecting everything and nothing

You can also use the **select** command with the **text of** parameter to put the entire contents of a field into the selection. For example, this line:

```
select text of field "testing"
```

would select all of the contents of the background field called "testing" and put them into **the selection.**

The final form of the **select** command removes any existing selection. To do this, type:

```
select empty
```

Combining *select* and *find* for data management

You should realize by now that the intelligent use of combinations of the enhanced **find** command and the **select** command in HyperCard after Version 1.2 can lead to powerful data management operations in HyperCard.

By using the proper qualifiers on the **find** command, you can narrow the search. With the functions that return the precise location of a successful search, you can locate the targeted text with ease. Then you can select that text and copy it, move it around, replace it, and otherwise manipulate it.

Some more advanced functions can be performed with combinations of these commands and the **do** command described in detail in Chapter 16.

Locating a sub-string's position

As you may recall from our discussion of the **find** command in Chapter 9, locating a card that contains a given string of text in a specific field or anywhere on the card is straightforward. But sometimes we need to know where a particular text string is located in a field by its relation to other known characters or strings. This is quite often useful in decoding formatted product codes and numbers, for example.

To carry out this assignment, HyperTalk includes the **offset** function. This function takes two strings as arguments and returns a number indicating the character position of the beginning of the first string in the second string. The syntax is

```
offset (<string1>,<string2>)
```

Either argument (or both) can be a string enclosed in quotation marks or the address or name of a container that holds a string.

If Field 1 contains the string "Blue Rondo a la Turk" and the variable *lookFor* contains the string "Rondo," then

```
offset("Rondo",field 1)
```

or

```
offset(lookFor,field 1)
```

return the same answer: 6. This identifies the starting position of the source string (string1) in the target string (string2). (Of course, you must *do* something with the returned value of the **off-set** function. Normally you will either **put** it somewhere or test it with an **if** clause group.)

Using the *offset* function

A use for the **offset** function may not be immediately evident. Let's look at an example using our inventory stack analogy. After you work through this example, you will undoubtedly see many places in your stackware that you can use the **offset** command to great advantage.

Assume that the part number field in your inventory stack consists of two or more characters, followed by a hyphen, followed by three to ten additional characters. The first segment of the code, up to the hyphen, is the Vendor Code, which tells you who sells you the part. The second portion of the part number, from the character to the right of the hyphen to the end of the code, is your company's internal part number. There are many places where you want to separate those two segments of the part code and use them independently. Let's do a short Laboratory exercise to see how to do this.

Using *offset* for field decomposition

Open the original Laboratory stack and create a new card for it. Name the card Inventory 1. Now follow these directions.

1. Create a new field for this card. Make it a rectangular or shadow field so you can see its outline. Call it Part Number. We will use only one line of it, so you can narrow its height to one line if you like.

2. Get into browse mode.

3. Type into the Part Number field the following text:

   AB23-00984

4. Create a new button for the card if it doesn't already have one. If it already has a button, you can use it unless you want to save its script.

5. Open the button's script editing window by one of the usual methods.

6. Type in the following handler:

```
on mouseUp
   global vendor, part
   put length(line 1 of card field "Part Number") into len
   put line 1 of card field "Part Number" into temp
   put offset("-",temp) into divider
   put char 1 to divider-1 of temp into vendor
   put char divider+1 to len of temp into part
end mouseUp
```

NOTE

You may be wondering why we put global declarations in this handler when we have never done this before. Because we will want to examine the contents of these variables in the Message box and because the Message box is outside the scope of the handler, the variables must be declared global. Otherwise, HyperCard will complain that it "never heard of" the variable when you type its name into the Message box.

---

7. Get back into browse mode. Press the button to which the new script is attached.

8. Open the Message box if it isn't already visible.

9. Type *vendor* and press Return. The Message box contains AB23. (See Figure 10-5.)

10. Type *part* and press Return. The Message box now contains 00984.

11. Change the contents of the Part Number field so that a different number of characters appear before and after the hyphen. Then retry the button until you are comfortable with how this process works.

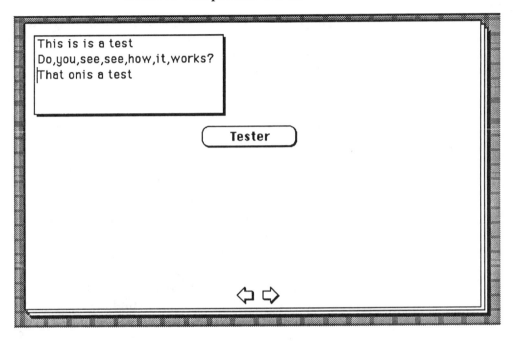

Figure 10-5. Vendor code portion of part number

Modifying the Contents of Fields

It will come as no surprise that the primary command for changing the contents of a field is **put**. This versatile command — arguably the most often used in HyperTalk — can replace the contents of all or part of a field or place new information at any addressable place in a field.

But **put** is not the only command that modifies the contents of fields. Two others, less often used but occasionally helpful, are **type** and **delete**. We've already described the **put** command so this discussion will focus on the other two field-modifying commands.

The *type* command

The **type** command works very much like the **put** command, with two key exceptions:

- The **type** command does not include the ability to address a container as part of its structure. There is no equivalent of the **put into** command (or **before** or **after**, for that matter) for the **type** command.

- The **put** command places data into the field as a single block of text, but **type** places data into the field as if it were being entered by a fast typist.

These limitations make the **type** command less than a critically important tool in your HyperTalk vocabulary. But there are two occasions when it can prove useful.

First, if you are creating a self-running demonstration of a stack and want to simulate for the user the manual entry of text into a field, the **type** command works exactly as desired. To put text into a field, you must be sure the cursor is *in* the field before you **type** anything into it. This can be accomplished with the **click** command (see Chapter 16) or with the **select before, select, after,** or **select empty** commands discussed elsewhere in this chapter. This makes it impossible to experiment with **type** from inside the Message box. If you type, for example:

```
type "Hello, there, world!"
```

into the Message box, the contents of the Message box are immediately replaced by the typed message.

Second, the **type** command is a convenient way of sending certain characters to a field from within a script. For example, you can write a background or stack script that types a Tab character each time a card opens. As a result, each time the user opens a card, the cursor is placed in the first field on the card and the current contents of that field are selected. The next character typed from the keyboard or the script then replaces everything in the field.

The *delete* command

One of the most powerful commands in HyperTalk is the version of the **delete** command that removes text from a field. The command can be used in a similar way to remove text from any other container. You can erase any addressable component — characters, words, items, or lines — of text in a field on any card with this command. The deleted text is *not* placed into the Clipboard. To save the text for later, use a **doMenu** command and select the Cut option, as explained in Chapter 12.

If you use **delete** to cut an entire line of text from a field, HyperCard removes the line and its accompanying carriage return, moving any lines below the deleted line up in the field. If you delete individual words, even the last one on a line, however, HyperTalk does not alter the carriage return. If you delete all the words on a line one at a time, the carriage return remains in place unless you explicitly delete it as well.

Using *delete*

For our first experiment with the **delete** command, let's use the Message box and a variable. Open the Message box if it is not already visible (it doesn't matter what card you are on) and then follow these directions:

1. Type the following line of text into the Message box:

   ```
   put "one two three four five" into temp
   ```

   Press Return.

2. Now type this text into the Message box:

   ```
   delete second word of temp
   ```

   and press the Return key. To confirm that the deletion worked as expected, type *temp* into the Message box. The display should contain: one three four five.

Now let's set up a more elaborate experiment. This time we'll use scripting rather than the Message box. Pick any Laboratory card with a field and at least one button. If you don't have a card with those objects with scripts you are ready to erase, create a new card. In the example, we'll refer to the card field as TD1 (for Test Delete 1) to reduce the amount of typing.

1. Open the button's script editing window in one of the usual ways.

2. Type in the following script and click the OK button when you're done:

```
on mouseUp
    delete second word of line 1 of card field "TD1"
    put "First deletion complete."
    wait 1 seconds
    delete third item of line 2 of card field "TD1"
    put "Second deletion complete."
    wait 1 seconds
    delete char 3 to 7 of line 3 of card field "TD1"
    put "Final deletion complete."
end mouseUp
```

3. Get into browse mode.

4. Type the following three lines of text into the field:

```
This is is a test
Do,you,see,see,how,it,works?
That onis is a test
```

5. Select all the text in the field, and use the Copy Text option from the Edit menu to save it in the Clipboard. Then de-select the text. The screen now looks like Figure 10-6.

6. Press the button and watch the Message box closely. At each deletion, the script displays a message pointing out that the deletion was made and pauses so you can examine the effect. When all deletions are complete, the screen looks like Figure 10-7.

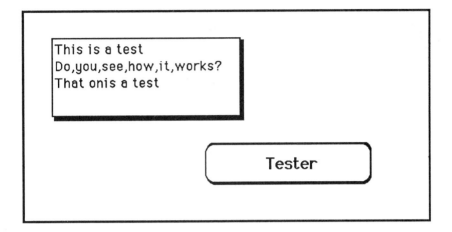

Figure 10-6. Second delete experiment ready to run

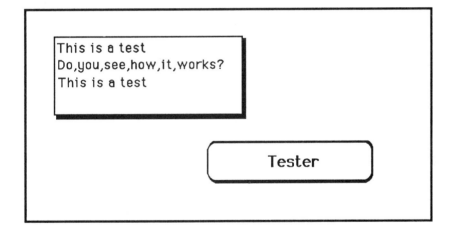

Figure 10-7. Second *delete* experiment completed

7. If you want to repeat the experiment to watch it more
    closely, select all the text in the field, use the Backspace
    key to delete it (don't Cut it or the pre-experiment version
    of the text will disappear from the Clipboard), choose Paste
    Text from the Edit menu, and press the button again. Repeat
    this process as many times as you like. You can also
    modify the script between runs, perhaps increasing the
    amount of time the script pauses or deleting different
    components of the field.

Changing Fields by Concatenation

HyperCard has some of the most powerful text concatenation capabilities of any microcomputer programming language. Using these facilities, you can combine the contents of various containers, components of fields, and string or character constants to modify the contents of fields or other containers.

There are two text concatenation operators: **&** and **&&**. The only difference between them is that the latter adds a space between the concatenated objects and the former concatenates them exactly as it finds them. Thus:

```
put "test" & "ing"
```

displays the word "testing" in the Message box, and

```
put "test" && "ing"
```

displays "test ing", with a space between the two strings, in the Message box.

The items to be joined by concatenation can be any combination of addressable field components, actual strings, or containers of text. The resulting concatenated text can be placed into a field or into a variable using the **put** command. Or it can be displayed, tested, or manipulated in the same ways as any text field. There is no difference between a field created by user entry and one synthesized by concatenation.

Uses for concatenation.

There are dozens of places in scripts where it is useful to join two or more pieces of text. Three such possible uses are discussed here for illustration.

Recall our inventory example with the part number divided into two components separated by a hyphen. If you think about it for a moment, you might have the user enter the vendor code separately from the internal part code. In fact, it may be essential to do it that way given the normal operation of business. The user might know the internal part code but have no idea who the product is purchased from without checking another source of information during data entry.

To accommodate this need, assign two global variables, for example, *Ven* and *IPN* (for Internal Part Number). After the user enters those values for a new part being added to inventory, your script would have a command like this one:

```
put Ven & "-" & IPN into Field "Part Number"
```

The result is the concatenation of the vendor code (e.g., AYS29), a hyphen, and the internal part number (e.g., 90087) so that the Part Number field contains the full part number: AYS29-90087.

Another use for concatenation is personalizing a card in a stack that is used by several people. Suppose three different people use your stack and all have personalized information stored in it. The cards are named in such a way that the person's last name forms the first part of the card name and the card type forms the second part. Thus, Yeats's expense card might be named YeatsExp. At the beginning of a session or when the user changes, your script asks the user for his or her name and saves the last name in a variable called *User*.

Now when a button is clicked to take the user to his or her expense account card, the script does a simple concatenation to get the name of the card:

```
go card User & "Exp"
```

Each user may be unaware that other people using the stack have similar cards to theirs. Yet this is far more efficient than creating separate stacks for everyone.

The last example involves the extraction and display of information from several different fields or even several different cards in such a way that the user only sees the result, not the work that goes into it. For example, a button called Summary on a card might indicate that a manager wants to see the employee's name, hire date, salary, and last review date. The stack's only job is to get those fields and put them into the Message box. Using concatenation, it can do so with one simple **put** command:

```
put field "Name" && field "Hire Date" && field "Salary" && field¬
  "Last Review" of card "Evaluations"
```

Special constants for concatenation.

In addition to text containers, fields, and strings, concatenation can also include built-in HyperTalk constants that represent special characters frequently needed in text streams. These special constants are

- **quote**

- **return**

- **space**

- **tab**

- **formFeed**

- **lineFeed**

You can insert these special constants anywhere in a stream of text being concatenated. You probably won't have a lot of use for the **space** constant in view of the double-ampersand concatenation and the ability to place spaces inside literal strings. But the others will come in handy at one time or another.
The **quote** constant is particularly useful when you want to place a quotation mark into a field but are frustrated in your attempt to do so because HyperTalk sees the quotation mark as marking the end of a string. Simply embed the **quote** constant in the stream of text:

```
put "The" && quote & "boss" & quote && "is here."
 -- Message box shows:  The "boss" is here.
```

Inserting carriage returns to mark the end of one line and the beginning of another in a field is another good use for concatenating with special constants. The **formFeed** and **lineFeed** characters, as well as **tab**, are useful in telecommunications and the design and printing of script-managed reports. These techniques are used in the scripts in Chapters 25 and 26.

Treating Fields as Arrays and Tables

Card and background fields, beyond their usefulness as flexible, addressable containers for text, can be used in your stacks exactly as if they were two-dimensional arrays or tables in other programming languages. HyperTalk does not specifically define a variable type that can contain a two-dimensional array of data. Many experienced programmers, before they examine the language closely, decide this omission is a fatal flaw. But it turns out that using the text field in HyperTalk as such an array is relatively trivial.

By setting up the contents of a field carefully, you can create the same effect as a two-dimensional array. Here is part of such an array. We will use it in a Laboratory exercise in a few moments, but for now just examine it as we discuss it.

```
Record,LastName,FirstName,Employee#,HireDate,Salary
1,William,Genevieve,3904,2/10/79,49575
2,St. Germaine,Elmer,4001,7/11/79,36099
3,Butler,Karl,8977,3/14/82,46230
4,Yeats,Stephanie,9998,5/1/82,28900
```

There are two noteworthy aspects of this collection of data.

First, the first line is different from the others. It contains some labels that describe the contents of each field in the table. This line is not required in HyperTalk, but we have found it quite useful in helping to keep track of exactly what is where in a table several months after we've written a script.

Second, notice that all items in each line are separated by commas. This permits us to address them as individual objects (*items* in HyperTalk parlance), which means we can retrieve any single piece of information in the field discretely from the others.

Having set up the field this way, we can make flexible use of its contents. In fact, proper use of fields as arrays can lead to some database-like applications of HyperCard.

Setting up an array

Open your Laboratory stack and add a new card with only the direction-arrow buttons and no other objects. Because we will stay with this card during our experiments, you need not give it a name, though in practice you would probably append a card name or identifier to many of our sample commands.

Now follow these instructions:

1. Create a new scrolling field nearly as wide as the card and occupying about 3/4 of the card's height, as shown in Figure 10-8. Choose a suitably small font to allow lots of information to be placed in the field. Name the field Table 1.

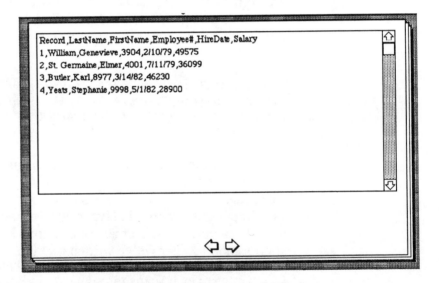

Figure 10-8. New field for array exercise

2. Get into browse mode.

NOTE

The **number of** function we are using is quite significant when dealing with fields as arrays. We'll have more to say about it soon.

---

3. Enter the text in the small employee table, as shown in the previous listing. Proofread after you're done.

4. Open the Message box and type the following line into it:

```
put number of items in line 1 of card ¬
field "Table 1"
```

5. Make sure the answer is 6. If it isn't, you've made a typing error. Find and correct it.

6. Repeat step 4 for the other lines in the field, ensuring in each case that the answer is 6.

7. Type the following command lines into the Message box and observe the results. After each line, the contents of the Message box should be as indicated beneath each line:

```
put item 2 of line 3 of card field "Table 1"
  -- Message box should read "St. Germaine"
put item 4 of line 3 of card field "Table 1" ¬
&& item 4 of line 4 of card  field "Table 1"
  -- Message box should read 4001 8977
```

Loops and the *number of* function

When your script deals with arrays of data, it will probably execute one or more loops (see the discussion of control structures in Chapter 8) as it scans through data looking for some information or accumulating answers in a container. Before it can begin such loops, however, it has to know how many lines or items it must examine. Obtaining this information is the job of **the number of**, a HyperTalk function with many uses.

In fact, **the number of** can be used to find out how many characters (**chars**), words, lines, or items are in a field or in an addressable component of a field.

Generally, you'll **put** the results of **the number of** function into a local variable and then use that variable to control the looping process. Let's go back to the Laboratory stack and run an example to demonstrate what we mean.

Looping for data retrieval from arrays

Return to the same card we used in the last exercise. Close the Message box if it is still visible. Now follow these instructions:

1. Create a new button and name it Total Salary. Make it whatever shape you want, but be sure the Show Name check box in the button definition dialog is checked. Position the button outside the field Table 1. Figure 10-9 gives you an idea how it should look.

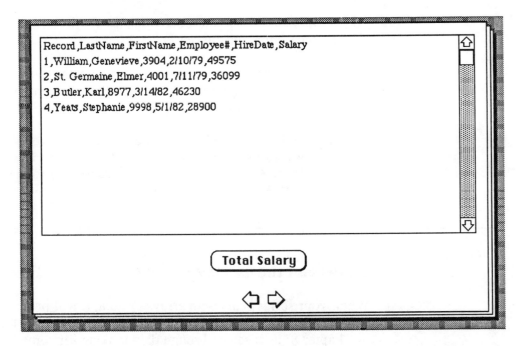

Figure 10-9. Adding a Total Salary button

2. Open the script editing window for the Total Salary button in one of the usual ways.

3. Type in the following script, proofread it, and confirm it is syntactically correct by pressing the Tab key. Then click the OK button to return to the card.

```
on mouseUp
    put number of lines of card field "Table 1" into maxLines
    put empty into totSal
    repeat with count = 2 to maxLines
        put totSal + item 6 of line count of card field "Table 1"¬
into totSal
    end repeat
    put "Total salaries =" && totSal
end mouseUp
```

4. Return to browse mode.

5. Press the Total Salary button. After a moment, the screen looks similar to Figure 10-10. Notice the use of the local variable *maxLines* to control the loop and the use of another local variable, *count*, to determine which line to read. This is a common looping technique when dealing with arrays of data in any programming language.

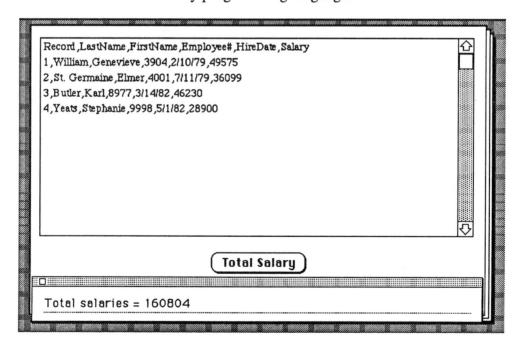

Figure 10-10. Array experiment concluded

Sorting Stacks

Given the flexibility of the HyperText approach to data management, which is the very essence of HyperCard, it may seem a little out of character to include a sort capability in HyperTalk. But in two situations, sorting may be important to your stack's users: flipping through the stack one card at a time and expecting to find the cards in some particular order, and producing reports where the cards appear in some particular order.

To accommodate either need, use the HyperTalk **sort** command. Although this is one of the easiest commands to use in HyperTalk, it offers a large array of possible arguments, or parameters. In its simplest form, the **sort** command looks like this:

```
sort by <expression>
```

The *expression* argument must be a text expression. In other words, it must either *be* text or *evaluate* to text. This expression can be as complex a field component address as is needed. If each record in our employee database example is stored on a separate card, with the information still in one field called Employee Data, you could sort the stack by employee last name with a command like this:

```
sort by item 2 of card field "Employee Data"
```

Beyond this simple use of **sort**, there are two other sets of parameters that can be added to the command. The first set concerns the sort direction, and the second concerns the data type of the sort expression.

Selecting the sort direction

By default, any **sort** ordered in HyperCard is assumed to be in ascending order. But you can override this assumption with the word **descending**. Thus, to sort the employees (assuming, again, that they are on separate cards) according to salary, with the highest-paid employee at the top of the list, you would write a command statement like this:

```
sort descending by item 6 of card field "Employee Data"
```

Defining the data type

From HyperTalk's perspective four different types of data can be sorted:

- text (the default and most often used)

- numeric

- dateTime

- international

If you don't supply a second parameter, HyperTalk treats the sort expression as text. This results in a straight ASCII sort sequence. (See Appendix B for a chart that defines what this sort sequence is.)

Numbers don't fall in numeric order in the ASCII sort sequence. If you want HyperCard to treat the sort expression as numeric, you must tell it so by supplying the **numeric** parameter to the **sort** command.

As you will see in the concluding section of this chapter, HyperTalk treats date and time data differently from other types of information. This leads to some very powerful applications. But if you want HyperTalk to treat a particular sort expression as a date or time data type, you must use the **dateTime** sort parameter.

You will probably never have occasion to use the **international** parameter. It is only necessary if you are sorting data that contains special characters called *ligatures* or *umlauts*. English has neither of these special types of characters, so **text** is adequate for most applications involving alphanumeric data.

Naming the sort field

In most cases, you will either supply the name of a background field explicitly or program a container name with the name of the field in it. It is possible to sort by the contents of a card field but that is not often done since fields that appear on multiple cards are almost always designed as background fields.

You must be careful about one thing in naming the field by which to sort. If you supply a variable that has not been initialized or if you use a string with no *field* identifier preceding it, HyperTalk appears to complete the sort but the order of the cards isn't changed. For example, the line

```
sort by "Date"
```

appears to work but does not. You must explicitly tell Hyper-Talk that the word Date refers to a field.

Some complex sorts

The following examples are self-explanatory and straightforward, but they show how the **sort** command can become quite complex and specific.

```
sort dateTime by card field "Hire Date"
sort descending numeric by item 3 of card field "Table 3"
sort descending dateTime by chars 1 to 5 of line 4 of field 1
```

Date and Time: Special Data Types

We will conclude our discussion of HyperTalk data management techniques and commands by turning our attention to the use of dates and times as special data types. As we just saw, data which is intended to be sorted as if it were a date or time must be pointed out to HyperTalk as part of the **sort** command. Other considerations must be watched also when you deal with such data.

Five functions are involved in managing date and time data, and most of them have several versions. The five basic functions are

- **date**

- **time**

- **seconds**

- **ticks**

- **convert**

We will discuss each of these in the order shown.

The *date* function

In its simplest form, **the date** simply returns the current date in what is called *short format*. This format is the one you are probably most accustomed to writing: mm/dd/yy. Thus, January 15, 1988, appears as 1/15/88.

The next simplest form of the command is **the abbreviated date**. This command can be written out completely or shortened to **the abbrev date** or even **the abbr date**. A date retrieved in this form includes the day of the week and the month (both abbreviated) and the year. Neither abbreviation includes a period. January 15, 1988, written in an abbreviated HyperCard form is: Fri, Jan 15, 1988.

Finally, there is **the long date** function. This command spells out all of the date's components: Friday, January 15, 1988.

Usually, you will put the date, or some portion of it, into a field on a card in an **openCard** or **openStack** script. There are, of course, many other uses for this function.

You can extract the individual items in either **the abbreviated** or **the long date**. For example, to pull out the day of the week and put it into a card, you would write something like this:

```
put item 1 of the long date into card field "Day of Week"
```

If you use **the abbreviated date** rather than **the long date**, the abbreviation for the day of the week is retrieved and **put** where you direct it to be placed. Individual items cannot be extracted from the short form of the date, which exists entirely as one item. When you extract such information from a date field, it must then be treated as text and not as a date on which special mathematical operations can be performed.

The *time* function

There are two forms of time functions. The first function, **the time,** has no qualifiers and returns the current time in hours and minutes. The second is written **the long time** and adds the seconds to the end of the time. In all other respects, they are identical.

How the time is displayed — for example, as 5:15 P.M. or as 1715 — is determined by the settings in your Control Panel and may not be altered in HyperTalk. Individual components of the time functions' return values may not be retrieved.

The *seconds* function

The seconds function can be written as either **the seconds** or **the secs.** In either form, it returns the number of seconds that have elapsed since January 1, 1904. This is the date Apple Computer used as the basis for its internal clock. Because of that, **the seconds** returns incredibly large numbers; billions of seconds have passed since January 1, 1904.

One useful application for this function is in stacks where you want to time the user's response or usage time. Simply store the value of this function when a process begins, then store its value when the function ends. A simple calculation reveals how much time has elapsed between steps.

The *ticks* function

Every time you turn on your Macintosh, it begins keeping track of how long the system is turned on using a special unit of measure called a *tick*. A tick is 1/60 of a second. You can use the special function **the ticks** to obtain the current value of this counter. The function has no arguments and returns a number — generally a very large number — that you can use like any other number.

Like **the seconds** functions, **the ticks** can be used to time the distance between two events. It is 60 times as fine a measurement as **the seconds**, so it can be used when you need very accurate timing. One such situation is programming the Macintosh double-click mechanism. Much of what takes place in Hyper-Card uses only single clicks, but many Macintosh users are accustomed to double-clicking on items. Because HyperCard doesn't penalize the user for double-clicking (it simply ignores the second click), the usefulness of a double-click mechanism is marginal.

Using *convert* to reformat dates

We have seen date and time information in HyperCard in six formats:

- seconds

- long date

- short date

- abbreviated date

- long time

- short time

All of these represent the time elapsed since the Macintosh base date and time of January 1, 1904, at 00:00:00. Sometimes you will want to convert a date stored in one format into a more readable or usable format. To perform such a task, HyperTalk includes the **convert** command. Its syntax looks like this:

```
convert <container> to <format>
```

The container must contain data in a date or time format. The **convert** command converts this information into the form specified by the format argument. The converted result replaces the contents of the container, so you will usually want to do conversions of dates and times in variables rather than in fields on the screen. Imagine the consternation of the uninitiated user who sees a nice, readable date such as Jan 15, 1988, suddenly turn into the staggering number 2652048000!

We haven't looked at one of the most useful conversions in HyperTalk. The **dateItems** format is a special form of the date that can be used easily in arithmetic. When you convert a date to this format, HyperTalk returns a comma-separated list of seven items, beginning with the year, continuing down to seconds, and ending with a number indicating the day of the week. The day of the week assigns Sunday as 1, so Monday is 2, Tuesday is 3, and so forth.

To see the **dateItems** conversion work, go to any card and stack in HyperCard and open the Message window. Type in these three lines:

```
put "1/15/88" into date1
convert date1 to dateItems
date 1
  -- Message box shows 1988,1,15,0,0,0,6
```

Notice that because we didn't store a time in the field, HyperTalk simply substitutes zeros for the three time fields. You may be surprised to see that happen if you've worked with more stringent programming languages that return an error if you try to convert something without enough data in the original value. The number 6 at the end of the **dateItems** list tells us that January 15, 1988, is a Friday.

The real value of the **dateItems** format is that you can perform math on any item in the list. Want to know the date 45 days from now? Type the following lines into the Message box and see the answer. (We used January 15, 1988, for our current date.)

```
put the date into date1
convert date1 to dateItems
put item 3 of date1 + 45 into item 3 of date1
convert date1 to date
date1
  -- Message box contains February 29, 1988
```

If you are curious about how this works, go through the same process, but after you perform the addition (the third line of code) and before you restore it to a readable format, type *date1* into the Message box. Look at the third item. Don't be surprised if it is larger than the number of days in any month! Yet, when you perform the conversion back to a readable date format, HyperTalk takes care of this discrepancy and produces a logical answer.

Trapping the Return and Enter Keys

During data entry into a card with more than one field, the experienced Macintosh user expects to be able to press the Return key or the Enter key to move from one field to another. In versions of HyperCard prior to 1.2, this was not possible; HyperCard reacted to either key being pressed in an editable field by simply placing a carriage return in the field. But beginning with Version 1.2, HyperTalk has two field-specific system messages to enable you to create real-world data entry environments. (System messages are discussed more broadly in Chapter 17.)

The two messages are **returnInField** and **enterInField.** The first message is sent whenever the user presses the Return key while typing in an editable field. The other is sent in response to the user pressing the Enter key in an editable field. You can write handlers to respond to these messages so that you can customize how your stack responds to these commonly used keys. For example, if you want to simulate a word processor's reaction to the Return key so that HyperTalk adds a second carriage return and "tab" five spaces, you could write a handler like this:

```
on returnInField
  send returnInField to HyperCard
  send returnInField to HyperCard
  type "     "
  -- number of spaces desired to simulate tab
end returnInField
```

Notice that we have used the command

```
send returnInField to HyperCard
```

twice in this handler. The effect of this command is to pass the **returnInField** message up the hierarchy directly to HyperCard, where it simply creates a carriage return (because there are no contrary instructions). If we tried something like this instead:

```
on returnInField
  type return
  type return
  type "   "
end returnInField
```

we would encounter an error condition. Each time one of the command lines that send another Return key to the field was executed, the handler itself would be issued. Eventually, you encounter an error message informing you that you have created "too much recursion." To get around this problem, send the message outside the handler.

If you wanted the Return key to be used to move from one field to another, write a handler like this at the card level or higher:

```
on returnInField
  send tabKey
end returnInField
```

This moves the cursor to the next field and selects all of the text of that field. But if you wanted instead to position the cursor at the end of that field, you could improve on this handler substantially. Assuming you want to move the user around the card in field-sequence order (i.e., field 1 to field 2 to field 3, etc.), a handler like this at the card level or higher does the trick:

```
on returnInField
  put the number of the target into holder1
  -- the target is the field receiving the message
  if holder1 = 6
  -- or whatever the highest-numbered field is
  then
```

```
  go to next card
  exit returnInField
end if
select after text of field (holder1 + 1)
end returnInField
```

You could as easily change the last line before the end of the handler to:

```
select before text of field (holder1 + 1)
```

and place the cursor at the beginning of the next field. It should not be too difficult to see how you could use combinations of the returnInField message and the select command to do very sophisticated data-entry management in HyperTalk.

Everything we have said about **returnInField** is equally true of **enterInField.**

Summary

This has been a full chapter. You learned many tasks that make it possible to use HyperCard as a competent database management system. You learned more than a dozen new commands and functions and gained more insight into the use of commands and functions we discussed earlier.

You now know how to use **get** and **put** to read and alter the contents of fields in stacks. You know how to use the **length** and **offset** functions together to track down strings inside fields and set them up for recovery or modification.

You have seen how to combine the powerful **find** and **select** commands to perform data management tasks, such as locating and manipulating textual informantion in fields

You saw that even though HyperTalk does not include an explicit data type that handles two-dimensional arrays (tables), you can easily use fields to mimic such a data type. You not only learned how to set up fields for such use but also saw a complex, real-life example of how to get data from a table in HyperTalk.

You learned to use the **sort** command to rearrange the order in which cards are stored in HyperCard stacks for the times when the user wants to go through a stack in some predetermined order rather than use the HyperText techniques that are the heart and soul of HyperCard.

Finally, you learned to deal with dates and times: how to obtain them, how to convert them to usable forms, and how to use the special **dateItems** format to perform useful arithmetic on date and time fields.

Chapter 11 continues the process of examining techniques that make HyperCard stacks usable as applications. We also look at how to implement the classic Macintosh-style dialog box in HyperTalk.

Dialog Boxes

In this brief chapter, you will learn to use three new HyperTalk commands

- **answer**, for dialog boxes requiring only that the user press a button to give your script some information

- **ask**, for dialog boxes requiring that the user type something to give your script some information

- **ask password**, for a special type of **ask** dialog box

Dialogs and HyperCard

As anyone who has spent more than five minutes with a Macintosh knows, dialog boxes are a crucial component of designing good applications. Dozens, perhaps hundreds, of kinds of dialog boxes have appeared in Macintosh applications over the few years the system has been available. Some are standard, built-in dialogs (as dialog boxes are often called) such as those you see when you want to open a file (Figure 11-1) or print a document (Figure 11-2). Others are specific to the application, such as Microsoft Word's character formatting dialog (Figure 11-3).

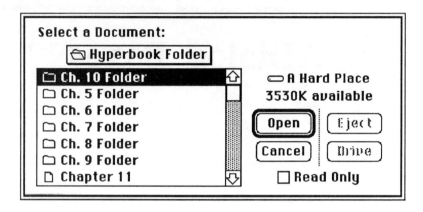

Figure 11-1. Standard open file dialog

Figure 11-2. Standard print dialog

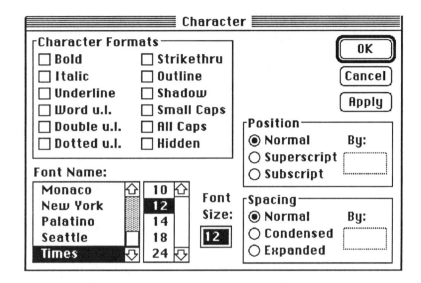

Figure 11-3. Microsoft Word's character formatting dialog

Few Macintosh applications, if any, operate without dialogs. But in our exploration of HyperCard so far, we have not seen any way to obtain information directly from a user in an interactive way. We learned in Chapter 10 how to read information the user had placed in fields. And we know the Message box can be used as a type of mini-dialog where we display a request for information and read the user's response. But the Message box only works for HyperTalk commands, so its use is limited.

Fortunately, HyperTalk includes the ability to produce two basic kinds of dialogs. Both have limitations that don't exist in more conventional approaches to Macintosh dialogs. Nevertheless, they give us a way to ask users for information and all but force them to give us a reply we can use in our scripts.

Three kinds of Mac dialogs

In the world of the Macintosh, there are three types of dialogs. There are *alert* dialog boxes, which are generally used for error messages. These frequent Mac screen visitors (see Figure 11-4) usually have an icon that lets us determine the seriousness of the error or message and a single OK button we can click in to remove them from the screen.

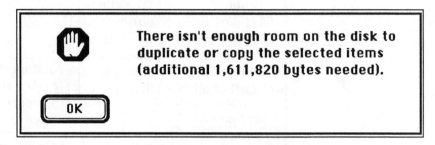

There isn't enough room on the disk to duplicate or copy the selected items (additional 1,611,820 bytes needed).

OK

Figure 11-4. Typical alert box

Second, the Macintosh displays *modal* dialog boxes, so named because they put the Macintosh into a mode in which only the dialog box responds to user input. Modal dialogs do not have a close box, so users can't simply dismiss them. They must respond to their presence. Alerts are a special category of modal dialogs.

Finally, there are *modeless* dialogs designed to assist the user in some types of processing. These boxes are more like document windows on the Macintosh. A modeless dialog generally has a close box, and the user can make it inactive by clicking in another window to make a different window the active one. A common example of a modeless dialog is the Find box in most Macintosh word processors. If you bring up a modeless dialog and then click in another window, the modeless dialog doesn't get put away; it simply goes behind the newly active window. You can prove this by opening a document window in your favorite word processor and collapsing it so it occupies only part of the screen. Then call up the Find dialog and click in the document window. You will see that the Find dialog is still on the screen, but it's not the topmost (active) window.

All HyperCard dialogs are modal. The user must respond to them before continuing any processing. They have no close boxes. Clicking anywhere outside the dialog results only in a Macintosh system beep (or perhaps some other sound if you're using a Macintosh II).

Two modal dialogs in HyperCard

There are two styles of modal dialogs in HyperTalk. One, like that shown in Figure 11-5, poses a question to the user and displays one, two, or three labeled buttons to use as a reply. This is the dialog created using the **answer** command. The other, like that shown in Figure 11-6, is generated with the **ask** command and allows the user to enter text in a small text editing rectangle before accepting the entry.

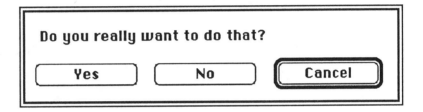

Figure 11-5. An *answer* dialog

Figure 11-6. An *ask* dialog

Using Dialogs in HyperTalk

When your script executes an **ask** or **answer** command, the user's response is placed into the special *It* variable. You can then store the response, test it for conditional processing, or do anything else with it that you like. (Remember our frequent cautions about the use of the *It* variable. Don't keep things in *It* any longer than necessary.)

The **answer** dialog can also act much like a standard Macintosh alert, though without the usual icons that give users a visual clue as to the type of warning they are being given.

The *answer* Dialog

The syntax for the **answer** dialog looks like this:

```
answer "<question>" [with "<reply>" [or "<reply>" [or "<reply>"]]]
```

As you can see, **answer** requires only one parameter: the question to be posed to the user. If you supply only the question and no possible responses in the form of **with** parameters, HyperTalk displays a dialog with only one default response: OK.

You can display dialogs from within the Message box. Let's see what a one-answer dialog looks like. Open the Message box in any card or stack and type the following line:

```
answer "This makes no sense!"
```

When you press Return, the dialog shown in Figure 11-7 appears immediately. You can see why this is very much like a Macintosh alert box. It has only one response the user can make, so its job is obviously to inform the user of something, make sure the user has noticed it, and then slip quietly away into the nether reaches of the program.

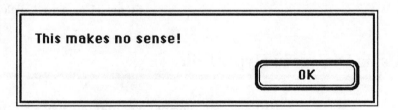

Figure 11-7. One-answer *answer* **dialog**

Just out of curiosity, you might want to click in the OK box and then type *It* in the Message box. The OK response is stored there.

Some rules about *answer* dialogs

Now let's create an **answer** dialog with two responses in it. In the Message box, type:

```
answer "This makes more sense!" with "OK" or "Oh yeah?"
```

The result looks like Figure 11-8. Notice that the OK button is listed first in the **answer** command line but shows up in the middle of the dialog, not at the right where we expect to find OK buttons. Also notice that the Oh yeah? button is highlighted. These two observations come about because of two basic rules in **answer** dialogs:

1. The options fill in the dialog box as if they were being inserted into the dialog box from the right and pushing existing options to the left. If you put in all three options, as we will in a moment, the one listed first in the command line ends up in the first, or leftmost, spot.

2. HyperCard always highlights the rightmost button, which is the last one listed.

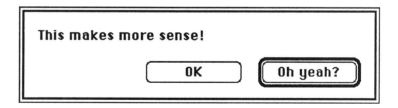

Figure 11-8. Two-answer *answer* dialog

So if you want the dialog in Figure 11-8 to look like other Macintosh dialogs, you have to write:

```
answer "This makes more sense!" with "Oh yeah?" or "OK"
```

Text in *answer* dialogs

In designing *answer* dialogs, it is important to consider the limitations on the size of text fields for the question and the responses. HyperCard uses the standard but space-hungry Chicago 12-point font for all text in its dialogs. As a result, you should keep the question to under 40 characters or even less if the question has a lot of capital letters.

Similarly, the buttons are intended to hold very short replies. Ideally, buttons should contain one word or two short words. Keeping the button text to 10 or 11 characters works best. Also, remember that the Mac centers text in these buttons.

Tailoring text in a single *answer* dialog

The question displayed in an **answer** dialog is a text field like any other in HyperCard. Thus, you can use concatenation to tailor the text in an **answer** dialog without having to create a separate dialog for each possible event. For example, suppose you need an alert to notify the user that a problem exists in a file. You can simply create a standard format for a dialog and have it add the file name when it is displayed:

```
answer "Error in file " & filename
```

Figure 11-9 shows such a dialog when the file name is Words. Again, remember the size limitations for the text string so you don't end up with an unreadable dialog or one missing vital information. You can also tailor the text in a button. The same principles apply, but you must be vigilant against button text overflow!

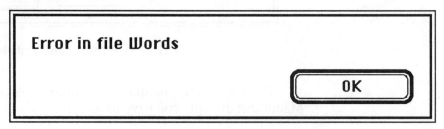

Error in file Words

OK

Figure 11-9. Tailored *answer* dialog

Macintosh design consideration

There is a final point to make about these HyperCard dialogs. Most Mac users are accustomed to being able to cancel all but alert dialogs. So it is very important that your script include a Cancel button as one of the options in an **answer** dialog. (You need not concern yourself with this issue in **ask** dialogs because HyperCard automatically furnishes such a button in those.)

The *ask* Dialog

Aside from the fact that users type an answer in response to an **ask** dialog rather than press a button to select a reply from among those you've offered, this type of dialog is similar to the **answer** dialog. In fact, everything we've said about **answer** dialogs can be applied to **ask** dialogs except for the issue of how buttons fill in the dialog. There are two predetermined buttons in an **ask** dialog, and you have no control over what they say or where they are placed.

Syntactically, the **ask** dialog command differs only in that it permits only one optional **with** argument:

```
ask "<question>" [with "<reply>"]
```

Generally, you will not use the **with** option when you write **ask** dialogs. But if you do supply a **with** argument, the text it contains becomes the *default* text in the dialog's text editing rectangle when the dialog appears. The text you supply is selected, as is the case with standard Macintosh dialogs of this type, so if the user types any key except Return, the typing replaces the text you supply as the default. Users can also edit the text your script places in the rectangle. First they must click somewhere in the

---

text field to remove the selection. Thereafter, they can use any standard Macintosh editing technique to modify the text.

As usual, pressing the Return key or the OK button accepts the text, storing it in the *It* container. From there, you can process the text.

Example of the *ask* command

Open the Message box any place in HyperCard and type the following line. The resulting dialog looks like Figure 11-10.

```
ask "Which computer has the best stuff?" with "Macintosh!"
```

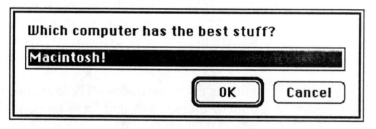

Figure 11-10. Typical *ask* dialog

The *ask password* variation

The only difference between **ask** and **ask password** lies in what happens to the user's answer. Before HyperCard places the response into *It*, the program converts the reply to an integer value and then encrypts it. This encrypted integer can then be compared with a previously stored encrypted integer to see if the person has used the proper password to gain access to the script or some portion of it.

For example, suppose that the first time a new user runs a script, the user is asked for a password of his or her own creation. After the user enters the password, you store the encrypted integer HyperCard places in *It* in a card field called Protect. The next time the same person uses the stack and reaches the password point, he or she enters a password. Your script then simply examines the password value entered this time against the one stored previously. If they are equal, all is fine and the user can proceed. If not, you may want to give the user more chances to enter the correct password or take some other action.

Summary

In this chapter, you learned to post dialog boxes during Hyper-Talk script execution as a way of obtaining information from the user. You saw that the language has two different modal dialogs. The one created with the **answer** command presents users with one or more options in the form of buttons they can press to supply an answer. The one generated using **ask** or its variation **ask password** permits the user to type a response.

Chapter 12 explains how to manage menus and access the other tools available in HyperCard.

CHAPTER

Managing Menus and Using Tools

I n this brief chapter, you'll learn how to use the

- **doMenu** command to carry out from within a script any action that can be taken with a menu selection in HyperCard

- **choose tool** command to switch among the various tools used in authoring HyperTalk scripts

Running Menus from Scripts

Like most well-designed Macintosh applications, HyperCard invests a lot of its power in menus from which the user can choose functions. But unlike most Mac programs, HyperCard gives you the ability to carry out menu-driven operations from scripts. Any function that can be performed from a menu can be performed from within a script.

219

The command that allows you this flexibility and power is the **doMenu** command. It takes only one argument, the exact name of the menu choice as it appears on the pull-down menu. Among other things, the requirement for an exact match means that menu choices that end with an ellipsis (three periods), indicating that a dialog box of choices is displayed when it is chosen, must have those three dots included in the **doMenu** command. The **doMenu** command is not, however, case-sensitive.

Figure 12-1 is a menu map of HyperCard with all its menu choices (unless a particular stack adds menus of its own). Not all of these menus are on the menu bar at one time, of course. Sometimes, you have to be in a particular mode (e.g., painting mode) for a specific menu or menu item to be available.

If the stack with which you are working is write-protected (see Chapter 3) against changes, the following menu choices are not available. An attempt to invoke them with a **doMenu** command produces an error:

- on the File Menu, the "New Stack...", "Compact Stack", and "Delete Stack..." options;

- on the Edit Menu, tne "New Card", "Delete Card", Cut Card", "Copy Card", and "Paste Card" options;

- on the Objects Menu, the "New Background" option.

- on the Options Menu, "Edit Pattern..."

In addition, neither the script nor the user may rename a stack, change any scripts in the stack, or sort the stack if it is write-protected. Additionally, any editing changes the user or a script makes are lost when a card movement takes place.

You can use **doMenu** in a script even if you've turned off menus in your stack. (This might give you a clue about how to access menus when they are hidden in a stack designed by someone else. Because **doMenu** can be executed from the Message box, you can invoke menu access even when direct use of menus is disabled.)

To prove this, open the Message box anywhere in Hyper-Card and type

```
hide menubar
```

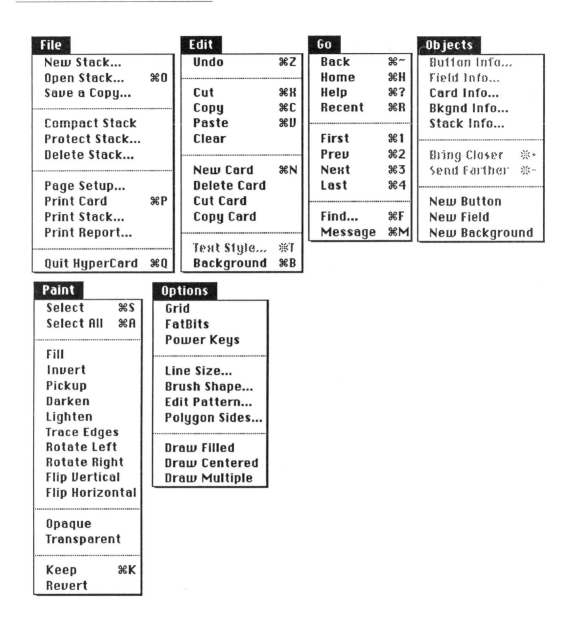

Figure 12-1. Complete menu map of HyperCard

and press Return. The menu bar at the top of the display disappears.
Now type the following in the Message box:

```
doMenu "Open Stack..."
```

The usual file opening dialog appears. Press Cancel, because
you really don't want to open a stack at this point. To redisplay
the menu bar, type

```
show menubar
```

You can also open desk accessories with the **doMenu** command. From the Message box, type

```
doMenu "Control Panel"
```

and watch as the standard Macintosh control panel appears on
the screen.

NOTE

At this point, you are facing one of the most discon-
certing dilemmas in HyperTalk scripting. You can
enable the user to open a desk accessory but you
cannot cause HyperCard to do anything at this point.
You can't click in the Control Panel somewhere to
change a value (e.g., the blinking rate for the cursor). You can't even get rid of the Control Panel.
The user is in charge and HyperCard is essentially
sitting back waiting for control to return to it. You
must be very careful of this problem, particularly
when designing stacks for people who are not
Macintosh-proficient.

Using *doMenu* in scripts

You are not likely to encounter many places where the **doMenu**
command is useful in your HyperTalk scripts. Virtually everything that can be done from the menus is in one of two categories:

- actions that are done only or primarily during script authoring rather than script execution;

- actions that are available as HyperTalk commands and for which **doMenu** is therefore a redundant and less efficient way of accomplishing a task.

But four tasks are occasionally useful, not accessible from HyperTalk commands, and therefore good candidates for the **doMenu** command. These tasks are: compacting the stack, protecting the stack, adding a new card, and deleting a card.

Compacting the stack

As the user works with a stack, adding and deleting cards can cause free space to develop. If this free space becomes excessive, it can slow down the execution of a script and the movement among cards in a stack. The Compact Stack option on the File menu eliminates this free space. As a result, stacks run more efficiently.

You can check the amount of free space in a stack by using the **freeSize** property. (HyperCard properties are discussed fully in Chapter 17.) If the **freeSize** property has a value greater than zero, free space can be recovered from a stack. That doesn't mean you should compact the stack any time this value is more than zero. But you may want to keep an eye on the situation, particularly if the stack is prone to become quite large.

Some successful stack designers report that if they check the amount of free space that has accumulated in a stack and find that it exceeds 20% of the stack's current size (which can be obtained as the stack's **size** property), they either compact the stack or advise the user to do so. A partial script to handle this task — probably best included in a **closeStack** handler — might look like this:

```
put size of stack "Laboratory" into stacksize
put freeSize of stack "Laboratory" into freespace
if freespace > .2 * stacksize then doMenu "Compact Stack"
```

Protecting the stack

Most of the time, you will protect a stack before you make it available to end users, if you protect it at all. By *protect*, HyperCard means not to prevent copying, but just to control access. But sometimes users of your stack may create a new stack (perhaps a copy of the one you've furnished or one generated by the operation of your stack) that they want protected or that your design requires to be protected. In that case, you can use the **doMenu** command to force stack protection. In fact, **doMenu** is the only way to accomplish this objective other than relying on the user to handle it.

When users encounter a script that carries out a **doMenu** command to set up script protection, they will see a dialog box like that shown in Figure 12-2. If the user then clicks on the Set Password button, a new dialog appears (see Figure 12-3).

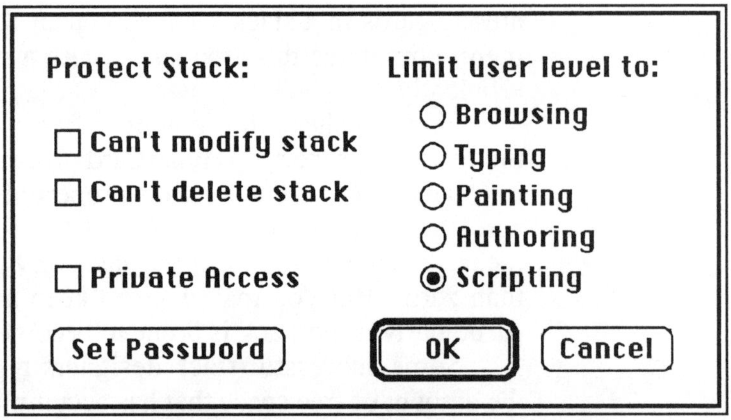

Protect Stack:

  ☐ Can't modify stack

  ☐ Can't delete stack

  ☐ Private Access

  [Set Password]

Limit user level to:

  ○ Browsing
  ○ Typing
  ○ Painting
  ○ Authoring
  ⦿ Scripting

  [OK] [Cancel]

Figure 12-2. The Protect Stack... menu dialog

Besides setting a password, the user can also protect the stack from deletion, modification, or both by selecting the appropriate check boxes in the dialog shown in Figure 12-2. (The "Can't Modify" option is available only in HyperCard 1.2 or later.) If the user or the designer specifies a stack as not subject to deletion, the stack cannot be deleted, even with a proper password. The same is true of modification. Password protection applies only to accessing the stack.

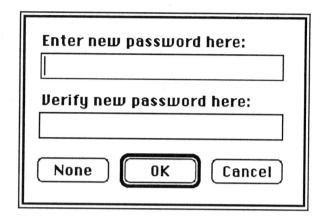

Figure 12-3. Setting a password

If the "Can't Modify Stack" check box is selected as part of stack protection, the "Can't Delete Stack" check box is also selected automatically by HyperCard.

Any attempt to modify a stack that has been protected against modification is met with an alert dialog. Menu items for deleting the stack and compacting it are dimmed on the File menu if the stack is protected. (You can use scripting techniques to allow temporary modification of protected stacks. See Chapter 17.)

NOTE

Any protection the user puts on a stack takes effect the *next* time HyperCard is started. The protection is not in effect during the same session. If, for example, it is critical that a password protection be effective immediately, you could insert a **doMenu** command to quit HyperCard after notifying the user and telling the user how to recover. This is a little drastic, though, so you should consider using it only where security is critical.

Adding and removing cards

In the extensible, flexible world of HyperCard, it is not unusual for a stack user to be increasing and decreasing the size of a stack routinely. Most HyperCard users know how to add a new card or delete one. But what if you want the menu bar hidden or you want to do something out of the ordinary when new cards are created or old ones are deleted?

As you know from our earlier discussions, particularly those in Chapter 6, you can intercept the user's interaction with menus to carry out peculiar processing needs. But sometimes you need to allow the user to use stack buttons that have an effect similar or identical to using menu commands.

For example, you might have a project planning stack that works on the basis of weeks. If the user clicks on a button labeled New Card, Extend Stack, or some similar text, your script might need to create seven new cards, perhaps with different backgrounds. The only way to accomplish this is with a script, part of which looks something like this:

```
repeat with count = 1 to 7
  doMenu "New Card"
end repeat
```

Another possible use for the New Card menu command arises if your stack creates a card to store information temporarily while your stack's script is being executed. This can be a very efficient way to store information that might otherwise be in variables, where confusion among names and uses might arise.

But if you create new cards during execution of the script, particularly if you do so without the user's knowledge, you should get rid of them later so the stack is returned to its original state. To do this, you can use the **doMenu** command with the Delete Card option from the Edit menu. This **doMenu** option is also useful when your script deletes cards on its own or because of a user request. For example, a calendar stack might have a Purge Appts. button that goes through the stack, finds appointments older than some set number of days, and deletes them.

User level and *doMenu*

As mentioned, before a **doMenu** command can be issued for a particular menu option, that menu option must be available to the user. In part, this is a function of whether the user is using the right tool (the subject of the next section of this chapter). But it is also related to the user's level when the menu command is needed. If, for example, the user is limited to the browse level and you want to carry out in your script a menu command that requires a higher level of access than the user's, you must modify the user level. You can do this with a script fragment like this:

```
put the userLevel into currentLevel
-- save current level for later
set the userLevel to 5
-- execute doMenu and other commands here
set the userLevel to currentLevel
-- restore former level
```

Using *choose* to Select HyperCard Tools

Many tools are available to the HyperTalk programmer and the HyperCard user at the authoring level and above. You may be wondering what we could possibly mean by *many*, given that there are only three basic tools: the browse tool, button tool, and field tool. During the creation of stacks, you use these tools frequently.

But from HyperCard's perspective, 15 other tools are available. These are all painting tools. Figure 12-4 shows all of them, as they are arranged in the Tools tear-off menu, along with the name(s) by which each tool is called in a HyperTalk script.

The syntax for the **choose** command is:

```
choose <tool name> tool
```

The word **tool** is mandatory. The tool name must be spelled correctly according to the names shown in Figure 12-4.

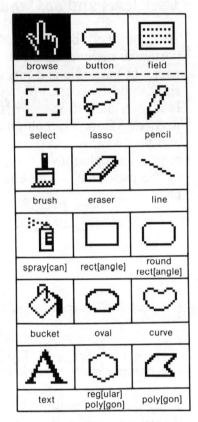

Figure 12-4. HyperCard tools and their HyperTalk names

Duplicating tool use and menu calls

Sometimes you will want to do something that requires one of
the general tools — the button tool or field tool — and you will
assume the program should look something like this:

```
choose button tool
doMenu "New Button"
```

But that is not necessary. The **doMenu** command automatically
selects the appropriate tool for its execution. So in this example
you essentially end up selecting the button tool twice, which is
inefficient.

Using *select* to choose a tool and an object

In HyperCard versions above 1.2, a new command is included. Use the **select** command to pick a button or a field and simultaneously choose the appropriate tool. This command comes in handy if your script is designed to perform operations on specific objects. For example, to select a button named "Choose" for copying, you could either use the "old" approach:

```
Choose button tool
click at the loc of button "Choose"
doMenu "Copy Button"
```

or the new approach:

```
select button "Choose"
doMenu "Copy Button"
```

Either approach works, but the latter is much faster to program and execute.

Returning to the browse tool

It is very important to return users to the browse tool after you have changed the current tool in your script. If you forget to do so, you may end up with frustrated users who suddenly find themselves unable to click buttons, activate fields, or type into the Message box. If your script, or someone else's script that you are using, should leave a tool other than the browse tool selected, press Command-Tab to return to the browse tool so you can correct the mistake.

Using a container to name the tool

You can store the name of the tool you want to use in a HyperTalk container and then use the contents of the container to **choose** the desired tool. For example, suppose your script has a variable called *useTool*. Based on any number of events taking place in the stack, you might put any of several values into this container. Then one command can use the appropriate tool:

```
choose useTool tool
```

Summary

In this chapter, you learned to access menu items and tools from inside HyperTalk scripts. You saw how to use the **doMenu** command to carry out menu operations from within scripts, and you learned about the **choose** command and how it can be used to select a tool from HyperCard's range of tools.

In Chapter 13, you put these techniques and others to work in creating graphic and visual effects from within your scripts.

Graphic Commands and Visual Effects

In this chapter, you will learn

- how to program visual effects in a script

- when to use each visual effect

- how to create artistic paint effects in a script, including setting various painting properties

- how to animate objects on a card

- how to manage card- and background-level pictures

A Graphic Computer

You've heard it a million times. The Macintosh is an all-graphics computer. Everything that appears on its screen, regardless of how much it looks like text, is graphics.

231

With that formality out of the way, let us say that Hyper-Card offers the casual user and application programmer more graphic capability and control than almost any other Macintosh program. If you've run through a few good stacks, you've seen these effects. They resemble television production techniques, which is no accident. If you don't know the names of these effects, get ready to learn about wipes and dissolves, barn doors and irises.

Beyond the visual effects HyperCard uses every time it moves from one card to another, HyperTalk programmers also have complete access to the paint tools and techniques that are such an integral part of HyperCard. As we saw in Chapter 12, you can choose different tools from the menu bar, and you can use the **doMenu** command to carry out any menu function. These techniques become particularly important as we turn our attention to the graphics power of HyperCard.

Programming Visual Effects

Perhaps the most noticeable thing about a stack as compared to many other Macintosh applications and environments is the smooth transition from one card to another using sophisticated visual effects. Those visual effects can only be placed into a stack by writing HyperTalk handlers, so users, even at the authoring level, miss out on these capabilities. The command to cause these effects is **visual**, usually written in its full-name variation, **visual effect**. Its syntax is

```
visual [effect] <effect name> [<speed>] ¬
[to black | white | gray |inverse |card]
```

We will explore each parameter to the **visual effect** command shortly. First, you need to understand some rules about its use and operation.

Basic rules for the *visual effect* command

When HyperTalk encounters a **visual effect** command in a handler, it stores that effect and uses it the next time a card switch takes place. You also can, with HyperCard Version 1.2 and later, encapsulate visual effects within an **unlock screen** command, in which case the visual effect is executed immediately.

Generally, a card switch is dictated by a **go**, **find**, or **pop card** command that results in a different card being displayed. However, you can create a visual effect using a **go** command that goes to the same card in which the command is executed. In other words, if you have two lines like this:

```
visual effect dissolve
go to this card
```

HyperCard displays the visual effect without the card changing. You seldom need to do this, however, particularly with Hyper-Card Version 1.2 and later, where you can create visual effects that seem to apply only to selected objects on a card.

To alter the visual effect HyperCard uses in the transition from card to card, you must include the **visual effect** command in your script before the next **go** or **find** command appears. Many HyperTalk programmers keep the **visual effect** command immediately before the card switching command whenever possible so that it is easier to find the effects later if they need modification.

During idle time — when HyperCard is between handlers and messages — any visual effect is forgotten. As a result, it is a good idea to include an initial **visual effect** for your stacks in a **stack open** handler.

If you are working with HyperCard Version 1.2 or later, you can also attach a visual effect to a specific object or group of objects by locking the screen, hiding or showing objects to which you want the visual effect to apply, then unlocking the screen with the visual effect as an argument. We see an example of this process later in this chapter.

Effects you can program

The first parameter you must supply to the **visual effect** command is the name of the effect to be used. There are nine basic effects, five of which are associated with two or more directional descriptors. The nine basic effects are as follows:

- **wipe**

- **scroll**

- **zoom**

- **iris**

- **barn door**

- **dissolve**

- **checkerboard**

- **venetian blinds**

- **plain**

The first five effects in this list require that you define the direction of their animation. Both **wipe** and **scroll** have four directional descriptions: *up*, *down*, *left*, and *right*. The other three — **zoom**, **iris**, and **barn door** — permit you to instruct them to **open** or **close**. In the **zoom** effect, you can substitute **in** for **open** and **out** for **close**. *In* and *out* are television production terms that are often used in audio-visual circles to describe the **zoom** effect, so HyperCard permits you to use either the internally consistent **open** and **close** or the TV standards **in** and **out**.

The **plain** visual effect cancels any special effects and returns to normal card-to-card transitions. We discuss the visual impact of the other effects shortly.

Varying the speed

Some effects can be made more dramatic or interesting by varying the speed with which they occur. HyperTalk recognizes four speed commands:

- **very slow** (or **very slowly**)

- **slow** (or **slowly**)

- **fast**

- **very fast**

You probably won't notice much difference between **fast** and **very fast** except on a Macintosh II system.

Changing the image

If you include the last parameter associated with the **visual effect** command, it is preceded by the key word **to** and followed by one of these words:

- **white**

- **gray**

- **black**

- **card**

- **inverse**

Most of the special effects you can program in HyperTalk do not benefit much from this parameter, but the use of black and gray as the image to which to make the transition can have a nice impact with the **dissolve** approach.

HyperCard moves through one of these intervening images as it moves to the next card. Thus, if you insert a command such as:

```
visual effect dissolve to black
```

in a handler, the next card transition results in a totally black screen appearing for a moment, followed by the image of the next card.

Chaining effects

For extra-special visual effects, you can chain these commands in a handler. HyperCard simply accumulates them and then executes them one at a time at each card transition. A fairly soft transition can be achieved by this combination:

```
visual effect dissolve to black
visual effect dissolve to white
```

This combination gives the impression of an image fading slowly and then reappearing in a new form.

Flashing a card

One more effect occurs not on the next card transition but immediately when it is executed. The **flash** command inverts the Macintosh screen area occupied by HyperCard and then returns it to its original state. The command takes an optional numeric argument that tells it how many times to go through the flashing process.

The *visual effect* command in card switches

Open the Laboratory stack and create two new cards. Each should have a button approximately in the middle of the card. Then use the HyperCard paint tools to create some different shapes and patterns on each card. Fill a substantial part of the card with these patterns and be sure they are sufficiently different from one another to make it obvious which card you are looking at. (You don't need to get artistic. The idea is simply to have contrasting cards so that when you perform visual effects you can see clear transitions between cards.)

Next, follow these instructions:

1. Open the script editing window of the card that has the lower number in the stack sequence. (If you're not sure which one this is, use the Card Info... option from the Objects menu.)

2. Type the following script into this editing window:

```
on mouseUp
    ask "What visual effect?"
    put it into request
    do "visual effect" && request
    go next
end mouseUp
```

3. Click on the OK button for that script, move to the next card, and open the script editing window for its button.

4. Type the following script into this editing window (it is the same except for the **go** line, so you can use copy-and-paste methods to edit it):

```
on mouseUp
    ask "What visual effect?"
    put it into request
    do "visual effect" && request
    go prev
end mouseUp
```

5. Close the script editing window by clicking OK. Use the left arrow at the bottom of the card (or any other method) to return to the first cards.

6. Press the button. An **ask** dialog like that shown in Figure 13-1 appears.

7. Type in the following line in response to the query:

```
dissolve
```

8. Watch as the card dissolves into the next. Press the button on this card. Another dialog box appears. Enter into that dialog box:

```
zoom in slowly
```

9. You can repeat this sequence as many times as you like. If you enter a visual effect command HyperTalk doesn't understand, it greets you with an error alert box like that shown in Figure 13-2. Just click the Cancel button and go on.

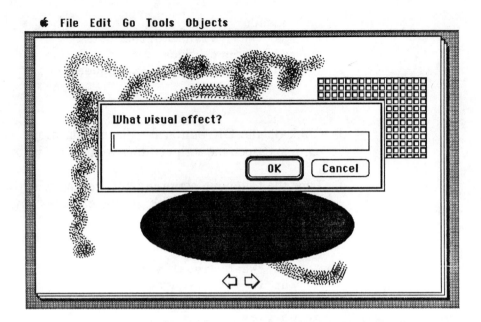

Figure 13-1. Visual effect testing *ask* dialog

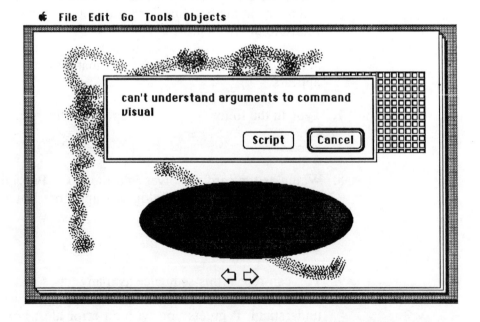

Figure 13-2. Error message during visual effect testing

Using *visual effect* on objects

As I indicated earlier, you can cause HyperCard to use visual effects as it hides and shows various objects (buttons, fields, and pictures). The framework for the portion of a handler that would accomplish this task looks like this:

```
lock screen
-- hide or show one or more objects
unlock screen with visual efect dissolve
-- or other visual effect
```

All of the objects you hide or show while the **lock screen** command is in effect--i.e., until the **unlock screen with visual effect** command is encountered--appear and disappear at the same time, using the single visual effect called for in the **unlock screen** command. You can include only one visual effect in this case. You cannot stack them as you can card-switch visual effects.

The *visual effect* command with objects

Open the Laboratory stack to any card with three or more card buttons on it. If you don't have such a card, create one. Resize two of the buttons so that they are large enough to be visible when the transitions take place.

1. Be sure that the buttons are numbered card button 1, 2, and 3 and that you use card buttons 2 and 3 as the buttons to hide and show. If necessary, use the **send farther** and **bring closer** menu items from the Objects Menu to set up this alignment or create a new card.

2. Open the script window of card button 1.

3. Type the folowing script into this editing window:

```
on mouseUp
  lock screen
  hide card button 2
  wait 15
```

```
unlock screen with visual effect dissolve
lock screen
hide card button 3
show card button 2
wait 15
unlock screen with venetian blinds
lock screen
show card button 3
wait 15
unlock screen with checkerboard
end mouseUp
```

3. Click the OK button of the script editing window.

4. Return to the browse tool if necessary.

5. Click card button 1.

Choosing Visual Effects

With such a variety of visual effects, how do you decide which to use? The answer is complex. Many psychologists and media experts have spent years studying the issue of special effects and how they affect people. At the same time, much of the answer is quite subjective: what works for you may leave others cold, bewildered, or unfocused.

There are, however, some basic guidelines you can follow with some assurance that they will be successful, thanks in large part to research in this area. In the next few sections, we focus on the more traditional visual effects — scrolls, wipes, dissolves, irises, and zooms — and some tips about their usage. The others are more "gimmicky" effects. (We're not using the term *gimmicky effects* to demean them or to suggest they shouldn't be used. It is just a way to categorize them.) You should use them sparingly and primarily for variety.

Scrolls

If you've experimented with scrolls — and if you haven't, you should go to the Laboratory and work through the previous experiment with some scrolls, especially at slow speeds — you probably had the feeling that the new card was shoving the old one out of the way. Scrolls are particularly effective when you want to make the browser feel that a change in content or emphasis has taken place with the transition, that the old is being bumped aside for the new topic. Scrolls are also effective in slide show presentation stacks, because the scroll is similar to a slide projector as it moves from slide to slide.

Wipes

When you carry out a wipe, the browser's impression is of a card sliding into place over another card, rather than bumping another out of the way and replacing it (as with scrolls). As a result, wipes usually work best when you want transitions between cards that are less abrupt than those signalled by a scroll effect.

When the subject matter remains the same and you're providing additional content at about the same level of depth as the previous card, the wipe is a good effect to choose. Browsers feel like they are on the same level as before and that a new card has simply shuffled into view.

Dissolves

The dissolve is one of the most artistic effects in HyperTalk and, as a result, is one of the most often used. It is also, unfortunately, one of the most abused.

You should consider a dissolve as representing a gradual transition in material or content between cards. In that respect, it is midway between wipes and scrolls. It gives the browser the feeling of one thing metamorphosing into another without any"rough edges" or clear borders.

Unlike most other effects, dissolves work best when there is either a great graphic contrast between cards or when only one small part of a design changes from one card to another.

Irises and zooms

We'll discuss irises and zooms together because they are quite similar. The only difference is that a **zoom out** begins its "telescoping" where the mouse is clicked to activate the effect, and **iris open** always focuses on the center of the card.

NOTE

Even though some documentation on the **zoom in** effect says that it returns to a point other than the center, that is not the case. A **zoom out** emanates from the point where the command is activated, but **zoom in**, like **iris close**, always goes to the center of the card.

An **iris open** and a **zoom out** give browsers the sense of going deeper into something. They are quite useful when browsers click on a button that takes them to a card displaying more detailed or focused information. The sensation is of a door opening as you walk through it. An **iris close** and a **zoom in** reverse that effect. If you use a series of **zoom in** or **iris close** effects to take browsers several levels into a stack, use a corresponding number of **zoom out** or **iris open** effects to bring them out.

The **zoom out** and **iris open** effects are also useful if you want to give the illusion of magnifying a small part of a card by moving to a card with a more detailed, close-up look at that portion.

A general observation

None of these principles is hard and fast, of course. Occasionally there are good reasons to disregard them and do something out of the ordinary. Sometimes, it is a good idea to have a graphic artist — particularly one with experience in film or TV — look at your stack and give you some advice.

If you think about the effect you want to create and the feeling you want the browser to have, and if you concentrate on keeping the effects simple and clean, you'll have no trouble designing interesting stacks that furnish your browser with visual cues as to what is going on.

Painting from a Script

HyperCard's designer, Bill Atkinson, built in some very powerful painting capabilities. This is no surprise because Atkinson also wrote Apple's popular and widely emulated MacPaint program, the first software to show off the real power of bit-mapped graphics and the Macintosh interface.

All painting techniques available to the user at and above the painting level can also be accessed through HyperTalk commands in scripts. If your stack could benefit from animation on a single card, use the painting tools.

Why paint in a script?

Most painting and artistic design takes place within the realm of stack development rather than stack use. By the time a user gets to the stack, the painting and drawing are done. In fact, of the dozens of scripts we have built and examined during the preparation of this book, not one undertook any artwork while the stack was executing. But in at least three circumstances, script-generated artwork may be a useful feature of HyperCard.

First, if you are designing a stack and are a better mathematician and programmer than an artist, you might want to write scripts that generate some of the graphics in your stack. This is particularly true if precision in the graphic is important. For example, if you need to draw a series of equidistant rectangles, writing a small script to do so is easier than creating a single rectangle, duplicating it, and moving it into the proper position.

Second, if one of the purposes of the stack is to enable the user to design something that requires graphics, you want to access the paint properties and tools we discuss in the rest of this chapter.

Finally, if the animation of objects on a single card has some value in your stack, you may want to be able to select and move an object within some constraints you establish.

Choosing painting tools

Recall that in Chapter 12 we discussed the **choose tool** command. In that discussion, we pointed out that each painting tool has a distinct name by which it can be invoked and used. To refresh your memory, Figure 13-3 lists the tools as they appear in the tool palette, along with the HyperTalk names for each.

To choose the paint brush, for example, just write a line like this in your script:

```
choose brush tool
```

Until you change the tool explicitly, the script will use the brush tool. You generally perform three basic functions with paint tools:

- **get** and/or **set** properties

- **click at** card locations with the tool

- **drag** the tool to card locations

Paint properties

As you know from our discussion in Chapter 3, an important idea in HyperCard is *properties*. Many objects that make up the HyperCard world have properties associated with them. We take an in-depth look at properties and their management in Chapter 17. But for the moment, we will quickly examine the use of properties to carry out painting tasks in HyperTalk scripts.

Each property in HyperCard can assume a range of values. You can discover the current setting of a property with the **get** command:

```
get brush
```

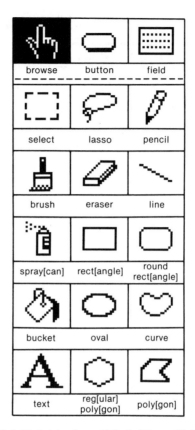

Figure 13.3 Paint tools and their HyperTalk names

You can change the current setting of a property with the **set** command, which generally takes the form:

```
set <property> value
```

For example, if you want to change the brush shape, just insert a HyperTalk command like this:

```
set the brush to 12
```

Table 13-1 summarizes all properties associated with painting tasks in HyperTalk and the range of values each can assume.

Table 13-1. Paint properties and their ranges

Property Name	Values
brush	1 - 32
centered	true or false
filled	true or false
grid	true or false
lineSize	1, 2, 3, 4, 6, or 8
multiple	true or false
multiSpace	1 - 9
pattern	1 - 40
polySides	number larger than 2
textAlign	left, right, center
textFont	font name
textHeight	numeric value
textSize	numeric value
textStyle	any combination of bold, italic, underline, outline, shadow, condense, extend, and plain

Most of these properties are self-explanatory, particularly if you've used the Options menu in HyperCard. Some, however, require further explanation.

The **brush** property can have any of 32 shapes. The shapes are numbered in the order in which the brush shapes are listed in the mini-palette that appears when you select Brush Shapes... from the Options menu or double-click on the brush tool. The brush shapes and their corresponding numbers are shown in Figure 13-4.

Line widths are set with the **lineSize** property, which can have a value of 1, 2, 3, 4, 6, or 8, corresponding to the line weights shown in Figure 13-5.

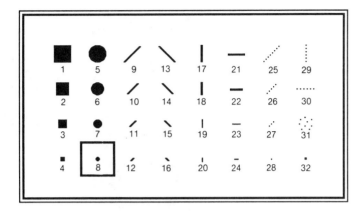

Figure 13-4. Brush shapes and their values

Figure 13-5. Line widths and their values

Similarly, **pattern** properties are numbered in a matrix that matches the pattern palette that appears under the Pattern menu and which may be torn off to be available during paint operations. Pattern numbering begins in the upper left-corner with the number 1 and continues down the first row to 10. It then resumes numbering at 11 with the top pattern in the second column, and so forth. Figure 13-6 depicts the standard paint patterns and their numbering scheme.

The **multiSpace** property determines how many pixels to leave between each copy of a shape generated as the tool used to create it is dragged through a drawing area when **multiple** is set to true.

The **polySides** property determines the shape of the regular polygon to be drawn when that tool is selected. The property may have any numeric value larger than 3. The higher the number, the more nearly the shape approaches that of a circle.

Finally, the **textStyle** property sets combinations of characteristics for text as follows:

```
set textStyle to bold,italic,underline
```

Figure 13-6. Patterns and their values

One more property is not strictly a paint property, but its use is primarily confined to painting activities. It is referred to as a global property and is a member of a group of properties discussed in Chapter 17. Its name is **dragSpeed** and it can take any numeric value you like, though experience shows that values larger than 144 cannot be distinguished by most people. When used with the **multiple** and **multiSpace** properties, **dragSpeed** can determine how regularly spaced your drawings look when you use multiple images.

Properties, then, determine the characteristics of drawings produced with basic paint commands. After you set the properties and select the tool, drawing is a matter of clicking, dragging, or both, depending on what you want to accomplish.

Clicking and coordinates

The Macintosh screen consists of a collection of addresses 512 pixels wide and 342 pixels deep. Each position on the screen is addressed by a two-part number. The first part is the horizontal location, or coordinate, and the second is the vertical. They are separated by a comma. The upper-left corner of the screen is address 0,0, and the lower-right corner is 512,342.

In Chapter 7, we saw how the **click** command could be used with a set of coordinates to simulate button-pressing. You can also use the **click** command to select a location on a card that does not contain a button or a field. You can then execute a painting command, using the clicked-at location as the starting point.

Most of the time, you will only use **click** to draw with tools that do not work by dragging. The text tool and the bucket tool do not work by dragging.

Dumping paint and drawing text

We'll use the Message box for our next experiment, though you can also create a button script for it. In the Laboratory stack, create a new, blank card containing only the background arrows. Open the Message box if it isn't already visible and type the following sequence of instructions, observing what happens after each.

```
choose rectangle tool
drag from 150,150 to 300,200
choose bucket tool
set pattern to 6
click at 151,151
```

The result should look like Figure 13-7. The bucket tool, as you probably know, simply spreads its associated pattern from the point where it is clicked to the borders of the area in which it is clicked.

Stay in the same Laboratory stack, with the same card showing, and type the following commands in the Message box, observing what happens after each:

1. `choose text tool`

2. `set textFont to "Times" -- use a font you have installed`

3. `set textSize to 18`

4. `set textStyle to bold,italic`

5. `click at 50,50`

At this point, the cursor should be flashing near the upper-left corner of the card. Anything you type at this point is displayed on the card using the text characteristics you set with instructions 2-4.

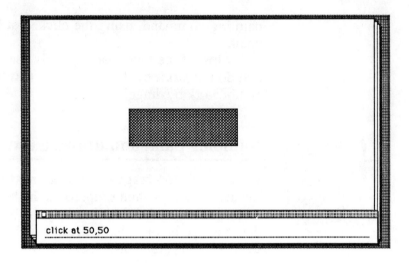

Figure 13-7. Using the bucket tool and the *click* command

Figure 13-8 shows what happens when you type the words *this is a demonstration of painting text.*

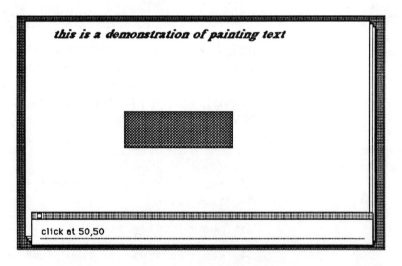

Figure 13-8. Using commands to add painted text to a card

To return control to the Message box, you have to click in it because anything you type at this point is displayed on the card.

Dragging tools for effect

All painting tools, except the text and bucket tools, are used by dragging them from one location to another. Depending on whether the **centered** property is true or not, they draw a shape that starts at the first set of coordinates and ends at the second, or they draw a shape centered on the first set of coordinates and extending in one direction to the second set.

We have already seen the rectangle tool used with the **drag** command to create a place to dump paint from the bucket. But just to be sure we understand what's going on with the **drag** command, here is its syntax:

```
drag from <point> to <point> [with <key>[,<key>]]
```

The point parameters are two-number coordinate addresses, with the numbers separated by a comma. You can specify one or more keys that will be simulated as held down during the drag. Here are some examples of the **drag** command:

```
drag from pt1 to pt2 with shiftKey,optionKey
drag from 0,0 to 512,342
drag from 50,50 to 200,275 with commandKey
```

Although a discussion of all the painting techniques in HyperCard is beyond the scope of this book, it might help to refresh your memory about the use of the special keys with paint operations.

If you **drag** with the **shiftKey** parameter, you constrain the movement of the dragging to the 15-, 45-, or 90-degree axis in which it begins movement. The angle of constraint depends on the shape and the tool, but in general you can think of the Shift key as being a constraint key.

Dragging with the **optionKey** parameter makes a copy of the selected item(s) and drags the copy. If you are using the lasso tool to drag with the **optionKey** parameter, lasso operates differently from its normal use. Generally, using the lasso tool on an object selects only the object and not the surrounding white pixels. But if you use the lasso, press the Option key, and then drag to select an area, the white pixels are also selected.

Using the usual selection marquee tool to **drag** with the **commandKey** parameter, the marquee "hugs" the outline of the

enclosed item rather than selecting everything inside the marquee. This technique is particularly helpful if you know within a
small tolerance the location of a painted item on the card, but
need some margin of error.

If you are dragging with drawing tools such as any of the
shapes — filled or not — use the **optionKey** parameter to cause
the drawing to take place in the currently selected pattern rather
than in black. To refresh your memory about the use of special
keys with paint tools, refer to the *Macintosh HyperCard User's
Guide* from Apple Computer.

Brush painting and drawing with a border

Get a clean Laboratory stack card, open the Message box if it
isn't already visible, and type the following commands into the
Message box, observing what happens after each:

1. `choose brush tool`

2. `set brush to 5`

3. `set pattern to 12`

4. `drag from 60,60 to 350,60`

5. `drag from 80,60 to 280,60 with commandKey`

After step 4, the screen looks like Figure 13-9. After step 5, the
screen looks like Figure 13-10. When the Command key is held
down while the paint brush is in use, it reverses the pattern and
essentially erases what lies under it.

Stay in the Laboratory stack and either create a new blank
card or simply erase the contents of the one you just used.(Remember you can double-click on the eraser tool to erase all the
graphics in the current layer.) Now type the following instructions into the Message box and observe what happens after each.

```
set the filled to false
drag from 50,50 to 150,150
drag from 160,50 to 260,150 with optionKey
```

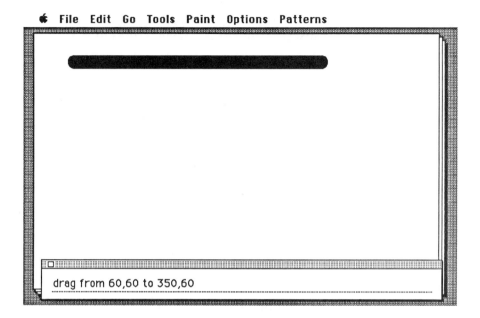

Figure 13-9. Screen after regular paint brush use

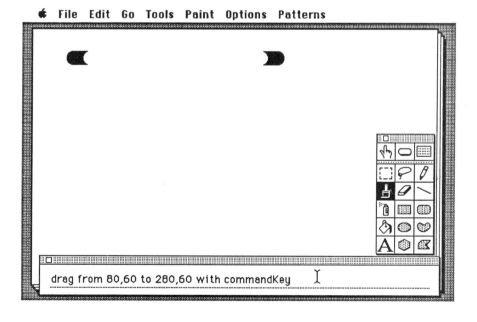

Figure 13-10. Screen after Command-key paint brush use

Notice that using the Option key while dragging a drawing tool causes the line to be drawn in the currently selected pattern.

Animation with Selecting and Dragging

The last topic we will cover in this chapter is the use of selection and dragging to make objects in HyperCard appear animated. Generally, the process of animating HyperCard paint objects involves three steps:

1. Select the item(s) to be moved. This sometimes involves a simple process using **doMenu,** but other times it is more complicated.

2. Set the **dragSpeed** to a rate that is appropriate to the effect you want to achieve. You can only really find this value by trial-and-error. Start with something like 100 and work from there.

3. Use **drag** to move the object.

You may also want to be sure the object reverts to its original position when the animation sequence is finished.

Selecting items to animate

If the object you want to animate is the only paint object on the card or you want to animate all the painted objects, the selection process is greatly simplified. Choose a painting tool, then carry out these two instructions:

```
doMenu "Select All"
doMenu "Select"
```

(The reason for the first menu command selection is that if you haven't de-selected the last object drawn, the **doMenu "Select"** command automates only that object.) A **doMenu "Select All"** command de-selects any object that may be selected. A subsequent **doMenu** call then selects all the painted objects on the screen and prepares them for animated movement.

If there are multiple objects on the screen and you only want to animate one of them, you must use one of the other selection methods. Use a **choose tool** command to switch to the marquee (select tool) or the lasso. Then **click** and **drag**, using the **optionKey** parameter, to select the object.

Setting *dragSpeed*

The **dragSpeed** property can take almost any value. If it is set to 0, it is at the fastest speed. At that speed, the movement of objects is not smooth and gradual. Instead, the object disappears from one point and instantly reappears at the other. If that's the effect you want, use a **dragSpeed** of 0.

For the most part, though, you will want a speed between 72 (which is quite slow) and about 400 (which is smooth and fast). You'll have to experiment with various speed settings to decide what works best for a given effect.

After you select a speed, use the **set** command to assign it to the **dragSpeed** property:

```
set dragSpeed to 200
```

Using *drag* to move objects

We've already covered the **drag** command. When you use the **drag** command in animation, you must make sure your starting point for the dragging motion is within the boundaries of the object you want to move. You will also want to ensure that you don't drag some portion of the image beyond HyperCard's boundaries so that it becomes partially invisible.

Animation experiment

Return to the card you used for the last experiment or create a new one with one or two rectangles near the upper-left corner of the card area. If you create a new object, be sure to choose the

Keep option from the Paint menu. This ensures that when you revert to the image, the objects return to this position. Then follow these instructions:

1. Create a new button called Animate it! and position it wherever you like on the card.

2. Open this newly created button's script editing window by one of the usual methods.

3. Type in the following script:

```
on mouseUp
    choose select tool
    doMenu "Select"
    set dragSpeed to 200
    drag from 100,100 to 300,200
    drag from 300,200 to 350,100
    doMenu "Select All"
    doMenu "Revert"
    choose browse tool
end mouseUp
```

4. Click OK and then activate the button. Watch as the objects move from the upper-left corner to the right-center portion of the card to the upper-right corner, pause for a moment, and then return to their original location.

Managing Pictures on Cards and Backgrounds

Beginning with HyperCard Version 1.2, you have the ability to hide and show all the artwork you have created on a given card or background. All the art you create in Version 1.2 or later, or that is contained on stacks designed using an earlier version, then compacted using Version 1.2 or later, is defined as a single picture for each card or background. In other words, if you create some paint text and graphic shapes on a card, the entirety of that artwork is defined and managed as a card-level picture. The same is true of artwork on a background.

You have no choice in the matter; the artwork is treated as a single unit for the purposes of the commands discussed in this section. You cannot hide and show selective portions of the card or background art with these commands.

If you wish to hide the picture on a card, you can use one of two forms of the **hide** command. To hide the art on the currently visible card, write:

```
hide card picture
```

If the card whose picture you wish to hide is not the currently visible card, you must use the alternate form of the command:

```
hide picture of <card description>
```

For example, to hide the picture on the fourth card in the current stack before going to that card, you could write a command like this:

```
hide picture of card 4
```

The same logic applies to showing a card-level picture. The current card's picture can be shown by the command

```
show card picture
```

but to show the picture on another card you must designate that card with a description:

```
show picture of <card description>
```

Background pictures have their own set of equivalent commands. To hide the art on the current background, write:

```
hide background picture
```

To hide the background picture on a different background, designate that background by a description:

```
hide picture of <background description>
```

Showing background pictures works similarly.

Because a picture is treated in some respects as if it were an object, it can be shown and hidden in concert with visual effects. Earlier in the chapter, we talked about the **lock screen** and **unlock screen with visual effects** commands. You can use those commands with the **hide** and **show** commands discussed in this section to achieve some interesting visual effects without changing cards.

Summary

In this chapter, you were introduced to the use of visual effects and graphic commands from within HyperTalk scripts. You saw how to use **visual effect** commands and variations and learned something about when and where they are best used. You also examined the use of graphic tools and their associated commands. In addition, you learned about properties and how they are changed to create specific graphic images. Finally, you saw how **click** and **drag** working together with selected objects can be used to animate objects on cards.

Chapter 14 explores another area of creativity in HyperTalk, the use of sound and music in scripts.

Sound and Music Basics

In this chapter, you will learn how to use the:

- **beep** command

- **play** command

- **sound** function

You will also gain some insight into the appropriate use of sound in HyperCard stacks.

Using the *beep* Command

We have used the **beep** command throughout this book without providing a formal explanation of its use. One is probably not mandatory at this point. But let's note its syntax for the record:

```
beep [<number>]
```

259

The number you supply can be a numeric value, an expression that evaluates to a numeric value, or a container that holds a numeric value. If you don't supply a number, HyperCard assumes you want a single beep.

The only "tricky" thing about the **beep** command is that if you want to use multiple beeps to alert the user to different conditions, you may find that HyperCard's timing puts them too close to differentiate them. That's particularly true if you use more than five beeps.

If you need a large number of beep sounds in a script, you should probably put them into a **repeat** loop (see Chapter 8). An example of such a loop might look like this:

```
on mouseUp
  repeat with counter=1 to 15
    beep
    wait 30 -- 30 "ticks", about 1/2 second
  end repeat
end mouseUp
```

The half-second delay in this loop might be too long or short for your purposes. You can supply almost any value for the **wait** command.

The **beep** command has limited application. It can't vary in duration or pitch, so it can't be used for music. But it can be quite useful as an audible device to get the browser's attention when he or she has done something untoward.

Using the *play* Command

If you've explored many HyperCard stacks, you've probably come across a range of sound effects people have used to make their applications more interesting or fun. HyperCard has one of the most powerful and versatile sound-reproducing capabilities of any programming language we know.

The **play** command is one of the most complex in HyperTalk. It can have as many as five separate sets of arguments, and one of them can contain a large number of individual notes, so the commands tend to be long.

Here is the basic syntax of the **play** command:

```
play "sound" [tempo <speed>] [<notes>]
```

As you can see, the only mandatory parameter to the **play** command is the first one, called sound. The sound parameters must be enclosed in quotation marks and must match exactly the name of the sound resource to be used (more on sound resources later in this chapter and in Chapter 21). Let's look briefly at each optional parameter.

Tempo

The **tempo** parameter applies only to a series of at least two sounds. It dictates how quickly the notes are played after one another. If you don't supply a value for the speed, preceded by the key word **tempo**, HyperTalk uses a tempo of 200. This is considered an average tempo, a little faster than a waltz is usually played. Above the value of 800 or so on a Macintosh Plus, the notes simply blend into one another. Increasing the number after that has little or no audible effect.

Unfortunately, there is no relationship between Hyper-Card's **tempo** settings and any standard musical measurement. In music, the term *tempo* means "beats per minute," but that is not the case with the **tempo** parameter in the **play** command. You'll just have to experiment with ranges of values to see what works for each composition you use.

Notes

You will almost always want to give HyperTalk one or more musical notes to play when you use the **play** command, though it is not mandatory that you do so. If you do not supply a note (i.e., if you simply use the **play** command with a sound name), Hyper-Card uses middle C as the note.

The string of notes you want played must be enclosed in quotation marks. You can have (theoretically) as many notes as you like. Each note has the following syntax:

```
<name>[# | b] [<octave no.>] [<duration>]
```

For the name of the note, use the name of the note on the scale, just as you'd expect. The seven letters a, b, c, d, e, f, and g are used to name the notes of the scale.

Each note name can be optionally followed by an *acciden-tal*. This is a special symbol for a sharp or a flat. A note that has a sharp accidental is played one-half step higher in the scale than the name of the key indicates. A flat note is played one-half step lower than expected. In HyperTalk music notation, the pound sign (#) signifies a sharp, and a lowercase letter *b* signifies a flat.

Using this notation and starting with middle C on the piano keyboard, the next few notes up the scale could be written as follows:

```
c c# d d# e f f# g ab a bb b
```

We have deliberately mixed the use of the sharp (#) and flat (b) signs so you see how they look. All the intermediate notes have two names, one refers to the note below and uses a sharp symbol, and one refers to the note above and uses the flat symbol. This means A-sharp and B-flat are the same note.

The octave number tells HyperCard where along the piano keyboard to play the note. The piano is divided into collections of octaves spanning from one C note to the next and encompass-ing seven keys. The octave that starts with middle C is referred to as octave 4 because it's the fourth up from the lowest C note on the piano. The octave beginning with the C note that is one octave up from middle C is the first note of octave 5.

If you don't supply an octave number, HyperCard uses oc-tave 4. After you change the octave, however, the change stays in effect until you insert another octave number in the note string.

The duration parameter uses something akin to standard musical notation, allowing you to use the first letter of the spelled-out name of the note duration. Thus, a quarter note is signaled by a *q* and an eighth note by an *e*. You can add a period after any duration to extend its value by 50% (the equivalent of dotted notes).

Table 14-1 shows you several musical notes expressed in HyperTalk notation, their English names, and their musical notation.

Table 14-1. Some musical notes in HyperTalk, English, and music

HyperTalk	English	Music
g#c	G-sharp, octave 4, 8th note	
c5h.	C, octave 5, dotted half note	
aq	A, octave 4, quarter note	
bbt	B-flat, octave 4, 32nd note	

Notes in HyperTalk can also be represented as numeric values, in which case the octave and accidental parameters are not used. Middle C has a numeric value of 60, and each step up or down represents a half-step. Thus, the E above middle C is 64, B-flat is 70, and the C one octave above middle C (the one that starts octave 5) is 72. You still need duration values unless you are happy with HyperTalk's defaults.

One advantage of using numeric values for notes is that you can calculate sounds, enabling you to play scales and other mathematically related musical groups in a loop. You can also set up generic loops that work from a starting numeric value and play major scales, minor scales, and transposed tunes.

Some familiar tunes

For our next exercise, we need a Laboratory stack card with a single field and a single button. The field can be called Field 1 and the button should be named Play It! (just for variety). Either create a new card or modify an existing one. Make Field 1 big enough to accommodate several lines of typing. Now follow these instructions:

1. Open the script editing window for the Play It! button in one of the usual ways.

2. Type in the following short script and click OK when you've proofread it.

```
on mouseUp
    do "play" && "Harpsichord" && card field 1
end mouseUp
```

      (We use the *harpsichord* sound here because it is one of the built-in sounds in HyperTalk and because it comes the closest of any of those sounds to playing notes that sound like music rather than sound effects.)

3. Return to browse mode.

4. The melody lines for several well-known musical tunes written in HyperTalk notation follow. Pick one and type it *carefully* into Field 1 of the experiment card.

5. Press the Play It! button.

      If all goes well, you will hear the melody line you chose played with HyperCard's harpsichord sound. You can change the instrument or voice by a simple edit of the button's script. (Some of these tunes could stand some tempo improvement. You can easily modify the button script to take care of this if the tempo jars your ears.)

      Here are the melody lines:

1. "America, the Beautiful"
   gq gq. ee eq g gq. de dq e f g a b gh. gq gq. ee
   eq g gq. de dq d5 c5# d5 e5 a4 d5h g4q e5q. e5e
   dq c5q cq. b4e bq c5 d b4 a g c5h. c5q cq. a4e
   aq c5q cq. g4e gq g a c5 g4 d5 ch.

2. "When the Saints Go Marching In"
   cq e f gw gq cq e f gw gq cq e f gh e c e dw dh
   eq d ch. cq eh gq g g fw fq eq f gh e c d cw cq
   e f gw gq cq e f gw gq cq e f gh e c e dw dh eq
   d ch. cq eh gq g g fw fq eq f gh e c d cw

3. "Skip to M'Lou"
   bq b g g be b bq d5h a4q a f# f# ae a aq c5h b4q
   b g g be b bq d5h a4q be c5e b4q a gh gq

4. "Frere Jacques" (3 rounds)
   cq d e c c d e c e f gh eq f gh ge a g f eq c ge
   a g f eq c c g3 c4h cq g3 c4h cq d e c c d e c e
   f gh eq f gh ge a g f eq c ge a g f eq c c g3
   c4h cq g3 c4h cq d e c c d e c e f gh eq f gh ge
   a g f eq c ge a g f eq c c g3 c4h cq g3 c4h

The play stop variation

Because the **play** command continues executing while other script commands are carried out, you can sometimes find sound effects being played at inappropriate times. If you want to control some precise time when the sound should simply stop playing, use the *stop* parameter. The command **play stop** immediately stops whatever sound is playing. If no sound is playing, no action is taken but no error results.

Sound Resources and HyperTalk

When you receive HyperCard from your Apple dealer, it has four built-in sounds: **harpsichord, boing, silence,** and **dialing tones.** You can supply any of these as the sound name in a **play** command and get a response (though in the case of the **silence** choice it will be hard to tell unless you intersperse it with other sounds). But there are dozens of other sound effects available for inclusion in stacks. Where do these come from and how are they used?

To answer that question, we need to explain that all sound effects accessed by **play** commands must be stored as *resources*. (If you don't know what resources are, don't panic. In Chapter 21 we take a close look at them. For now, just think of them as stored instructions that have a name associated with them.) Each resource that has a type called SND can be used by HyperTalk as a sound effect. What is actually stored in the sound resource is a waveform pattern that describes the sound to HyperCard.

If you have a sound resource called, for example, *applause*, you can create a command like this:

```
play "applause"
```

HyperTalk finds the resource and plays the sound it finds represented there.

Sound resources can be copied from other stacks, other Macintosh programs, and special files of sound effects you can obtain from electronic bulletin board systems (BBSes), user groups, and similar places. They are often created by digitizing real sounds using one of several pieces of Mac software.

In Chapter 21, we examine resources and how HyperCard accesses and uses them. We also discuss how you can move a resource from another stack or application into your stack or even the HyperCard Home stack, where more than one stack in your HyperCard environment can access it.

Testing *the sound*

When HyperCard encounters a **play** command, it starts the sound and then continues with processing even while the sound continues to play unless you issue the **play stop** command. You can thus have "background music" behind your script as it executes. This is a nice feature of sound effects in HyperCard.

Sometimes you want the sound to be more synchronized with the screen's activity. Controlling the sound's pace to match the screen action can be tricky. To assist in this process, Hyper-Talk includes a function called **the sound**. Like all HyperTalk functions, it requires no parameters and returns a value. The value it returns is the name of the currently playing sound or the string "done" if no sound is playing.

You can use this function to control a loop as follows:

```
repeat until the sound is "done"
  <statements>
end repeat
```

Alternatively, you can use **the sound** in a conditional processing structure so that nothing happens until the sound is finished playing:

```
repeat
  if the sound is "done" then
    <statements>
  else wait 1 -- or any other reasonable number
end repeat
```

(In this example, the statements should include an **exit repeat** and may consist of only that command depending on what you are trying to accomplish.)

Using Sound Effects Wisely

Like any good thing, sound effects can be overdone. On the Macintosh, with its wonderful sound capabilities, it is an easy thing to do. But you should guard against using sound in a way that confuses the browser.

Unless the stack's primary purpose is to perform music or create or reproduce sound effects, you should only use the **play** command where it will add value to the stack from the browser's viewpoint.

For example, in a stack designed to quiz a child about the letters of the alphabet, playing the well-known "Alphabet Song" at the beginning and end will probably be well received by the young browser. But if you play the song every time he or she gets a question right, you're going to bore the tot.

Associating single sounds with buttons can add dimension to your stacks. Browsers become accustomed to hearing a certain sound as they move "down" into a stack for more information and a different sound signalling that they are moving "up" toward the top and the beginning of their browsing experience.

Summary

In this brief chapter, you learned how to use **beep** and **play** commands to create sound effects from the simple to the symphonic. You also saw how to use **the sound** to determine when a sound effect is finished playing so you can proceed with another aspect of your script where the sound is unneeded or unwanted. In Chapter 15, we shift our attention to mathematics.

CHAPTER

Math Functions and Operators

In this chapter, you will learn about a host of HyperTalk functions and operators that enable your scripts to perform mathematic operations. These include tools to perform

- simple arithmetic calculations

- number manipulation

- advanced mathematics, including trigonometry

- financial math

An Aside to Mathephobiacs

Many people put off learning more about computers because computers seem so inherently mathematical. But a majority of computer programs involve no math more complicated than you probably learned in the fourth or fifth grade. Still, *mathephobia* is a sufficiently widespread phenomenon that many high schools and community colleges offer courses in how to overcome it. They report the courses are jammed and the students largely successful.

Let us be clear at the outset about the role of mathematics in programming most HyperTalk applications. First, you don't need to learn any math to program in HyperTalk. If you have an occasional need to perform a simple calculation, you can quickly and easily look up the proper operator or function, use it with a minimal understanding, and go on with your life as if math never existed. If you want to skip this chapter, feel free to do so. We promise you won't hurt our feelings.

Second, HyperTalk takes some of the "scary stuff" out of math by making operations more English-like and by reducing the number of special characters (operators) necessary. You might find that learning a little about math using HyperTalk isn't nearly as difficult as you may now think.

How Numbers Are Represented

In the discussions in this chapter, we will deal with numbers. Functions and operators work on numbers, and they produce numbers. A number in HyperTalk is stored as a string of characters, all of which are numeric. A number can be up to 73 characters long, which means it can have 73 digits if it's positive and 72 (to allow for the minus sign) if it's negative. It's not likely you'll need larger numbers than these! If you attempt to calculate a value that exceeds this maximum, HyperTalk returns a question mark as the answer.

Any number used in this chapter can be thought of as being represented in the Macintosh in any of the following ways:

- a number stored as text (e.g., 17234511.2)

- a container holding a number stored as text (e.g., sumTotal)

- an expression containing numbers and operators that evaluates to a number (e.g., 2 + 8, which evaluates to the number 10)

This last case is a special situation. If a field on a card contains an expression such as 2+8, and you really want to put the result of *evaluating* that expression into your math calculations, you must use the HyperTalk **value** function. The **value** function evaluates a string containing numbers and (usually) operators and returns the numeric value. (In a moment, we'll have more to say about the concept of returning a value.)

If card field 3 contains an arithmetic expression such as 2+8, and you want to put its value into a container called *temp1*, you could do so this way:

```
put value(card field 3) into temp1
```

When HyperTalk encounters this command in your script, it looks in card field 1, finds the arithmetic expression there (it must be the only thing in the field if you've addressed the entire field as in the example), carries out its calculations, and does what it's told with the result.

Another aspect of representing numbers follows Hyper-Talk's pattern of making programs more readable. Instead of using the digits 0, 1, 2, and so forth, you can write out their names: zero, one, two, and so on, up to ten. You can enter expressions like this:

```
put three + nine into answer
```

and expect the value of *answer* to be 12. You can even concatenate these numbers to make larger numbers (i.e., one and three combine to make 13).

We should point out that the way a specific number is represented can be affected by the setting of a global property called **numberFormat**. This value determines the number of decimal points of precision to which the number will be displayed and used in calculations. We discuss this property in more detail in Chapter 17.

Bringing Order to Things Numeric

Mathematicians spend a lot of time dealing with — and designing systems to avoid — ambiguity. An ambiguous situation arises in mathematics when there are two or more ways to evaluate an expression. For example, if we gave the problem 2+4+8*3 to two different students, one might answer 42 and the other might answer 30. The first student added the first three numbers and then multiplied their sum, 14, by 3. The second student decided to multiply 8 and 3 first, then add this result to the other two numbers. Both are reasonable results. But if you put the problem to HyperTalk, it will reply, unequivocally, 30.

That outcome is determined by something mathematicians call *precedence*. The term applies to decisions about what mathematic operations will be carried out in what order. HyperTalk, not unlike many other languages, applies some fairly simple rules.

RULES OF PRECEDENCE

1. Operations contained within parentheses are performed before those outside parentheses.

2. Exponentiation (raising a number to a power, which is discussed under "Advanced Math Operations") is the highest-priority math operator.

3. Multiplication and division are the next most important math operators.

4. Addition and subtraction are the least important math operators.

5. When you have operators of equal precedence, perform calculations from left to right.

There are many non-mathematic operators among HyperTalk's total set of rules about precedence, but these are the ones that concern us here. Now you can see why HyperTalk got 30 when it evaluated the expression 2+4+8*3. It scanned the line and found a multiplication, which it determined was the highest-priority operation in the expression. So it performed it first in accordance with rule 3. Then it found it had two addition operations, so it applied rule 5 and did them left to right (although the order in which numbers are added doesn't matter), resulting in the answer, 30.

When you want HyperTalk to alter its normal order of precedence in mathematic calculations, use parentheses and take advantage of rule 1. To force HyperTalk to come up with the answer 42 in the simple example we've been following, you would write it as (2+4+8)*3. Now, rule 1 means that HyperTalk will perform the two additions first because they occur inside parentheses. That reduces the expression to 14*3, which is 42.

You can nest parentheses inside parentheses practically to your heart's content. HyperTalk begins with the innermost set of parentheses and works its way outward until it is left only with expressions outside parentheses. Then it applies rules 2 through 5 as appropriate.

Functional HyperTalk

One final point needs to be made before we begin our first experiment. There are three kinds of actors in HyperTalk, as we have seen. There are commands (such as **put**) that usually require one or more arguments, or parameters. There are **operators** (such as +) that simply perform operations on objects. And there are *functions*. Functions are like special kinds of commands. The difference is that a function provides information about something, and a command changes the state of an object. A function in itself never alters anything in the HyperCard environment. In programming parlance, we say that a function "returns a value" as part of its operation. It determines something we ask it about and provides us with the information.

We've seen a few functions already. All the date-related tasks we worked through in Chapter 10 used a function that looked at the Macintosh clock and calendar and gave us the information stored there.

Building a math lab

If you want to try out any or all of the functions, commands, and operators in this chapter, you can do so in two ways. Because of the many topics covered in this chapter, we won't interrupt the flow of the presentation to suggest that you try each one. But if you're curious about how a function works, what its return value is or how it affects a number or expression, feel free to experiment.

First, you can type the examples given in the text into the Message box. Sometimes, this requires you to type **put** commands so you can examine the result. Second, you can follow the instructions in the next section and build a math laboratory card in your Laboratory stack. Then just type numeric expressions into the field on the card, press the button, and the answer appears in the Message box.

A math function tester

Create a new, blank card in your Laboratory stack. Add a field and a button to the card and give the field a rectangle outline. Name the field card field 1. Name the button whatever you like. Then follow these instructions:

1. Open the script editing window for the button by one of the usual methods.

2. Type in the following short script and press OK when you're satisfied it has been typed in correctly.

```
on mouseUp
  put value(card field 1)
end mouseUp
```

3. Return to browse mode.

4. Test your script with a simple arithmetic expression. Type something like 3+9 into the field. The Message box appears (if it was invisible) and contains the answer, 12. Figure 15-1 shows how our card looked with this answer returned.

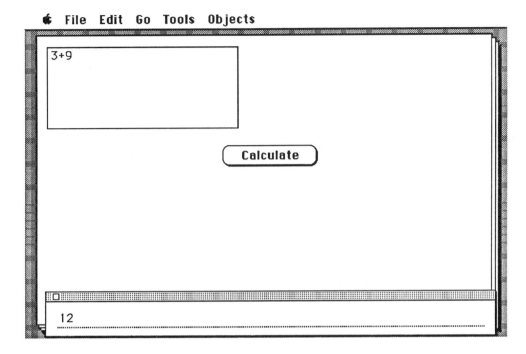

Figure 15-1. Card used to test math functions

Simple Arithmetic Operations

Enough background information. Let's get into some serious calculations! In this section, we'll discuss the simplest arithmetic operators, which carry out addition, subtraction, multiplication, division, modulo, average, minimum, and maximum functions. If some of these terms are mysterious, don't worry. We'll explain the math as we go.

Addition

There are two ways to perform addition in HyperTalk: with the **add** command or with the + operator. They are slightly different in terms of syntax, but both perform basic addition.

The **add** command syntax shows that it involves at least one container:

```
add <number> to <container>
```

When the **add** operation is finished, the container is changed by the value of the number. Notice that the original value stored in the container before the math operation is carried out is lost in this calculation. This is the key difference between **add** and the + operator. With **add**, HyperTalk knows what to do with the answer. With + it must be told explicitly what to do with the result.

The + operator appears between two numbers, as you've become accustomed to seeing. But an expression such as:

```
8 + 45
```

all by itself on a line in a HyperTalk script or in a field makes no sense. It violates a basic rule of HyperCard: everything is done with messages. There is no message here and no receiver. You generally write addition expressions using the **put** command:

```
put 8 + 45 into answer1
```

or, if you wish to use the **add** command instead:

```
add 8 to variable1 -- assuming variable1 has value 45
put variable1 into answer1
```

This will have the same effect as the previous **put** command using the + operator.

The same logic holds for the other math operators that don't include a destination for the answer.

Subtraction

As with addition, so with subtraction. There are two subtraction methods: one uses the **subtract** command and includes a destination, and one uses the minus sign (−) and does not include a destination.

The syntax for **subtract** is logical enough:

```
subtract <number> from <container>
```

Note, again, HyperTalk's readability. This is exactly how we would say a subtraction problem: "subtract 15 from 38."

If we perform a subtraction with the minus sign, we typically use a **put** command to instruct HyperTalk where to place the result:

```
put temp1-value3 into result4
```

NOTE

Another use of the minus sign is to perform negation(i.e., to make a positive number negative). In that case, there is no number to the left of the minus sign, and the minus sign applies to the number to its right. Thus, $13-(-3)$ is the same as $13+3$ because subtracting a negative number is the same as adding it.

Multiplication

The two ways to multiply in HyperTalk are to use the **multiply** command and the * operator. (The asterisk is the most commonly used character for multiplication on computers. In writing out such problems, we usually use a lowercase letter x. But because that is difficult, if not impossible, to distinguish from an intent to use a real letter, it was discarded as a possible multiplication operator by early system designers.)

The syntax for the **multiply** command again stresses readability:

```
multiply <container> by <number>
```

The asterisk multiplication symbol works with the **put** command:

```
put factor1 * factor2 into product
```

Division

It will come as no surprise to those who struggled with long division through high school that division has some peculiar"wrinkles" that don't apply to the other simple arithmetic operations we've discussed so far. HyperTalk has a total of four operators, commands, and functions for division. Let's dispose of the expected two — **divide** and the slash sign (/). The use of the slash sign for division on computers derives from the difficulty of displaying the usual division sign (÷) on conventional computer keyboards. (The Mac has no problem with this special character. But the slash mark was defined a long time before the Mac was a reality.)

The **divide** command has the same two parameters we've seen in other HyperTalk math commands:

```
divide <container> by <number>
```

The result is what you expect: the original value of the container is replaced by the result of the division of the two numbers.

Using the slash operator usually requires the **put** command so that HyperTalk will know what to do with the answer:

```
put number1 / number 2 into quotient
```

You can use two other operators to carry out division and get different kinds of results. The two operators are **div** and **mod**.

As you may remember from your early days of learning division before decimals made any sense (if they do yet), a division problem can be thought of as producing two answers rather than one. The first answer is the whole number of times one value goes into another. The second is the amount left over after the division is complete. This latter value is called the *remainder*.

There are still times when you'd like to be able to get these answers. In Chapter 8, we saw an example where we wanted to execute a portion of a repeat loop every fifth time through. We used the **mod** operator with the promise that we'd explain it later.

The **div** operator produces the whole-number result of the division, with the remainder ignored. The **mod** operator produces the remainder. The statements:

```
put 39 div 7 into temp1
put 39 mod 7 into temp2
```

place the value 5 in the *temp1* container and the value 4 into the *temp2* container, because 39 divided by 7 is 5 with a remainder of 4.

Now you can see how and why we used the **mod** operator in the repeat loop example in Chapter 8. If we want to simulate the STEP operation in BASIC and Pascal so that we execute a loop only when the controlling value changes by 5, we can set up a construct as follows:

```
repeat with counter = 1 to 50
  if counter mod 5 <> 0 then next repeat
  <loop statements>
end repeat
```

The expression *counter mod 5 < >* is 0 only when *counter* is evenly divisible by 5. Any other time, it has a value of 1 through 4 and the *loop statements* are not carried out.

This same technique is often used to determine values when fractions and decimals are not very helpful. For example, if we know how many hours are required to complete some task and want to know how many days are required, we probably don't want the answer to look like 4.125 days. Instead, we want the answer to be 4 days, 3 hours. So we use the **div** and **mod** operators. With *duration* containing the value 99, the following lines produce the answer 4 days, 3 hours:

```
put duration div 24 into numberOfDays
put duration mod 24 into numberOfHours
put "The task took" && numberOfDays && "days,"¬
&& numberOfHours && "hours to complete."
```

Average

If you have your right arm in a bucket of ice and your left arm in a flaming pit, on the average, you're comfortable. That's an old saw about statistics. It describes graphically the meaning of *average*. The average is calculated by adding all members of the list and dividing by the number of members in the list. Thus, the average of 2 and 4 is 3, because 2+4 is 6 and 6 divided by 2 is 3.

HyperTalk, not surprisingly, has an **average** function. It takes an argument — a list of numbers separated by commas — and returns their average value. Its syntax is

```
average(<number1>,<number2>...<numberN>)
```

If we write a HyperTalk script line such as:

```
put average(30,70,20) into avel
```

the container *avel* has a value of 40 when the script has executed. Like all functions, note that we must tell HyperTalk where to store or display the result of its efforts.

Maximum and minimum

We will discuss together the last two simple arithmetic operators — maximum and minimum — because they are nearly identical in operation. In programming it is often important to know the largest value in a list of numbers. Similarly, it is sometimes valuable to be able to find the smallest number in a list.

HyperTalk includes the **max** and **min** functions for these purposes. Each function takes a list of numbers, separated by commas, and returns the appropriate value. Their syntax, then, is identical:

```
max(<number1>,<number2>...<numberN>)
min(<number1>,<number2>...<numberN>)
```

The **min** and **max** operators come in handy when you need to find the range of a set of values. The range is frequently used in statistics. Given a list of test scores stored in a container called *Scores*, the following calculates and displays the range of scores:

```
put max(Scores) into top
put min(Scores) into bottom
put "Range of scores is:" && top && "to" && bottom & "."
```

Number Manipulation

HyperTalk includes three functions that change the value of a
number, **abs**, **round**, and **trunc**, and one that creates new numbers
on demand, **random**.

The *abs* function

When you need to find out the value of a number, regardless of
its sign (positive or negative), use the **abs** function. This function takes a number or numeric expression as an argument and
returns the result with a positive sign.

This function is often useful in finding the difference between two numbers when you don't know in advance which is
larger or if one or both are negative. For example, suppose you
have weather data stored in such a way that yesterday's high
temperature is in a container called *dayHigh* and its low temperature is in *dayLow*. If you live someplace where one or both of
those temperatures could be below zero, and you want to know
the total number of degrees by which they differ, you could
write:

```
put abs(dayLow-dayHigh) into dayRange
```

Rounding and truncating numbers

Two functions reduce a number with a decimal part to an integer.
The **round** function takes a number or numeric expression as an argument and returns its value rounded to the nearest whole number.
If the decimal portion is 0.5 or larger, it rounds the integer up to the
next whole number. If the decimal part is less than 0.5, it leaves the
integer unchanged. Here are three examples. The comment lines
show the value the variable has after the expression is executed.

```
put round(15.7) into t1
  -- t1 = 16
put round(15.5) into t1
  -- t1 = 16
put round(15.3) into t1
  -- t1 = 15
```

Sometimes, we don't want the nearest whole number for a decimal value. Rather, we want the equivalent of its value rounded down regardless of the size of the decimal fraction. For example, if we are trying to determine how many shares of stock to issue to an investment club where the rules require that each member receive whole numbers of shares and the fractions stay in a common pool, we would use HyperTalk's **trunc** function. Its name stands for what it does: it *truncates* a value, or discards the decimal portion. Here are two examples, with the resulting values shown in comment lines:

```
put trunc(15.99999) into t1
  -- t1 = 15
put trunc(15.00001) into t1
  -- t1 = 15
```

Generating random numbers

Occasionally, you may need to create a number at random. This need frequently arises in game programs, but sometimes business and personal applications need a number with which to begin some decision-making. (We know one person who uses a random number approach to seat people at parties. She reports as much success as her friends who spend hours agonizing over seating charts!)

When you need a random number, use HyperTalk's **the random** function. Its syntax looks like this:

```
[the] random of <number>
```

This function returns a number selected at random between 1 and the value of the number parameter, which may not be larger than 32,767.

Advanced Math Operations

Eleven HyperTalk functions and operators deal with what we call "advanced math." They can be divided into four categories: square root, exponentiation, logarithms, and trigonometric functions. (We use the term "advanced math" somewhat arbitrarily, but it serves to divide arithmetic operations most people know how to do and that they perform with some frequency from those that are more obscure.)

The square root function

To find the square root of a number (i.e., the value that, when multiplied by itself, returns the number whose square root is being calculated), use the **sqrt** function. It takes a number or numeric expression as an argument, as do most of the other functions in this chapter.

The numeric argument must be positive. An attempt to find the square root of a negative number leads to an error message that is uncharacteristically cryptic for HyperTalk (see Figure 15-2). This is because in implementing many math functions, HyperTalk relies on the Standard Apple Numerics Envronment (SANE), which has built-in error messages.

The error message abbreviation NAN, also sometimes seen as NaN, is SANE shorthand for "not a number" You'll run into it if you try to apply math functions to text arguments, for example. In this case, the square root of a negative number is what mathematicians term an imaginary number and SANE isn't equipped to deal with it. You can guarantee that you won't encounter this error if you use the **abs** function described earlier.

Here are two examples of the use of the **sqrt** function, with the comment lines again indicating the results:

```
put sqrt(900) into temp1
  -- temp1 = 30
put sqrt(abs((182))) into temp1
  -- temp1 = 13.490738
```

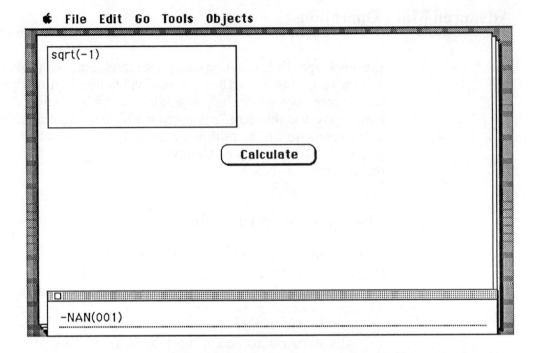

Figure 15-2. Error message for square root of negative number

Exponentiation functions

Three functions and one operator handle exponentiation in HyperTalk. The operator performs the most common type of exponentiation, where one number is raised to the power indicated by another number. This operator is indicated by the ^ symbol placed between the two numbers.

Raising 3 to the fourth power, for example, is written:

```
3 ^ 4
```

In advanced math, several other types of exponentiation are needed for specialized types of calculations. Two involve something called the natural exponential, also referred to as base-e exponentiation. These calculations are based on the natural number 2.718282. A discussion of the reason for the use of this number as a base for logarithms is beyond the scope of this book, but it is related to the fact that many natural phenomena can be measured as a function of this number. But if you need the *natural exponential* of a number, use HyperTalk's **exp** function. If you need the natural exponential minus 1 (another frequently needed calculation in complex math), use the **exp1** function.

Finally, HyperTalk includes the ability to raise 2 to any power with the **exp2** function. It is faster and easier to write this function using the usual exponentiation with the ^ symbol, though, and you'll rarely need the SANE equivalent. (The **exp2** function is negligibly faster, but if you are writing a routine where there is a great deal of this calculation, the cumulative effect could become significant.)

Logarithms

HyperTalk includes three functions that return logarithms of numbers. A logarithm is the mathematic inverse of an exponent. There is no HyperTalk function for the logarithm of a value to base 10, which is the most commonly used logarithm in math below the very complex. This is undoubtedly because the primary use of logarithms is to assist in speeding calculations, and one doesn't need that help with a computer. In fact, using logarithmic calculations to speed math operations in a computer is counterproductive.

But the SANE library, which is part of HyperTalk's world, includes logarithm functions that correspond exactly to the other three exponentiation functions discussed in the preceding section. The **ln** function returns the natural logarithm of the number supplied as an argument, and **ln1** first adds 1 to the argument and then computes the natural logarithm. The **log2** function returns the power to which the number 2 would be raised to calculate the number supplied as its argument.

Trigonometric functions

Included in HyperTalk are four basic trigonometric functions from which all others can be derived: **atan, tan, sin,** and **cos.**

They all operate the same way, taking an argument that is the size of the angle in radians (1 radian = 57.295 degrees) and returning the appropriate trigonometric value for that angle.

The constant pi

The numeric constant *pi* is defined in HyperTalk. It has a value of 3.14159265358979323846. Its precision in a specific calculation can be affected by the setting of the global property **numberFormat**, discussed in Chapter 17.

Financial Math Operations

If the SANE library includes some obscure functions and produces some strange error messages, why was it included in so elegant a programming language as HyperTalk? Aside from the fact that it is a very efficient way of making available some functions that are occasionally needed in higher math, it also includes two handy financial functions that find more everyday use in business stacks. These functions are **annuity** and **compound**.

The *annuity* function

To calculate the present value of one payment unit into an annuity fund, you would use the **annuity** function. Its syntax is

```
annuity(<interest rate>,<periods>)
```

The interest rate must be expressed so that it reflects the rate per period that coincides with the periods. In other words, if you are expressing periods in months, the interest rate must be the monthly rate.

The value calculated by the **annuity** function must be multiplied by the size of a single periodic payment to calculate the net present value of the annuity, which is the most common reason for wanting to carry out this calculation. To figure out today's value of your savings account in 10 years if you save $100 per month at an annual interest rate of 6%, for example, enter this line in a HyperTalk script:

```
put 100*annuity(.06/12,120)
```

The answer is 9007.345333, which, rounded off to the nearest cent, means that the present value of this savings plan is $9,007.35.

The *compound* function

The **compound** function returns the future value of a current periodic payment unit. Future value is a frequently used financial equation. Its syntax is as follows:

```
compound(<interest rate>,<periods>)
```

As with the **annuity** function, you can multiply the answer from **compound** by the amount of each payment to determine the future value of an ordinary investment.

Summary

In this chapter, you have learned how to use about 30 mathematic operators, commands, and functions in HyperTalk. Chapter 16 takes a look at a few action-taking HyperTalk commands that don't fit neatly into any of the niches we've examined to this point.

C H A P T E R

Action-Taking Commands

In this chapter you will learn about several HyperTalk commands that have only two things in common. First, they take some kind of action in a script (as opposed, for example, to providing information or controlling program flow). Second, they don't fit neatly into any of the categories into which we have divided HyperTalk's other operations. These commands include

- **do**

- **wait**

- **open** (with applications and documents)

- **print** (document)

- **open printing**, **print**, and **close printing**

289

The *do* Command

We have used the **do** command already in our discussion. But it is time to examine it more closely and see when and where it can be used.

The syntax of this command is as follows:

```
do <string>
```

The string is usually the name of a field, though it can also be any other addressable component of a field or a variable containing text. If a field name is used, the **do** command applies only to the first line of the field.

You need to keep in mind two basic rules about the **do** command.

RULES FOR *do* COMMAND

The text referred to by the address argument must be on one line. The text must contain or evaluate to a valid HyperTalk command.

There are some restrictions on the kinds of commands you can put into a field and execute with the **do** command. We haven't tried every command combination in a **do** instruction, but there are some things we have learned.

For example, you cannot expect HyperTalk to deal with containers in commands stored in fields unless the containers are global. The action in the field is outside the scope of the handler, so any variable known to the field is not known to the handler and vice versa.

Another limitation of the **do** command is that the **visual effect** command does not "take." The command is accepted by the **do** command but the effect does not appear.

Math operators cannot be used in standalone calculations inside fields to be executed with the **do** command. If you put a command such as:

```
33 * 84
```

into the field and use the **do** command to execute it, you'll get an error message indicating HyperTalk "can't understand 33."

Using the *do* command

Open the Laboratory stack. Create a new card with a single button and a single field or use a card you don't mind dismantling from a previous experiment. In the example script, we call the field Field 1. If you change the field's name, be sure to change the name in the script as well. After you have such a card, follow these instructions:

1. Open the button's script editing window in one of the usual ways.

2. Type the following script into the editing window and click OK after you've proofread it.

```
on mouseUp
  global t1
  do(card field 1)
end mouseUp
```

3. Return to browse mode.

4. Click in Field 1 and type in the following commands to test your card. After each command is entered into Field 1, press the button. The comment lines describe the commands' actions.

```
doMenu "Open Stack..."
  -- brings up the standard file open dialog.  Click Cancel
put 43*3 into t1
  -- nothing visible happens
put t1
  -- Message box appears if it was invisible; 129 is shown.
type "Hello from the Message box."
  -- The text appears in the Message box as if typed.
go previous
  -- Previous card appears.  Use usual methods to Go Next.
```

5. Experiment with other commands.

6. This is a good card to have during script design because you can use it to find out quickly which commands execute from a field with the **do** command and which don't.

Why use *do*?

You might be wondering why you'd ever want to use the **do** command when you can simply execute instructions directly in your handler. The most likely use of the command is when you ask the user a series of questions or gather input from the user or another source without asking questions, and then execute a series of instructions based on the responses. Because you can't anticipate the answers or perhaps even the number of answers, coding this kind of process directly into your script is difficult, if not impossible.

The *wait* Command

The **wait** command is another action-taking command we've used without describing it. As you'll see, we've only used this command in its simplest form. Here is its syntax in that form:

```
wait [for] <number> [ticks | seconds]
```

You can use two units of time with the **wait** command. If you don't specify one or the other, HyperTalk assumes you want to use **ticks**, units that are approximately 1/60 of a second. If you want to use seconds, you must provide that key word in the command.

NOTE

A *tick* is only *approximately* 1/60 of a second. The exact time varies from model to model of the Macintosh. In addition, disk accesses during the handler's execution can alter the timing. Seconds are more accurate and more often used.

In some ways, **wait** is like a loop with nothing going on inside it. The **wait** command has two other forms that resemble the control structures we examined in Chapter 8. The syntax for these two variations is as follows:

```
wait until <true/false>
wait while <true/false>
```

These should be reminiscent of **repeat until** and **repeat while** loops. They cause HyperCard to go into a holding pattern until the true/false expression is true (in the case of **wait until**) or to stay there only as long as it *is* true (in the case of **wait while**). These commands can be used to wait for the user to do something to trigger the script to continue processing. A common use is to have the script wait for the user to click the mouse as a signal to go to the next card or step:

```
wait until the mouseClick
<next command>
```

Opening Applications and Documents

Many people first used HyperCard to replace the portion of the Finder that most of us use all the time: program launching. This was made possible by variations of HyperTalk's **open** command.
The basic syntax of this command is as follows:

```
open ["<document name>" with] "<program>"
```

As you can see, you can open a specific document and furnish the name of the application that document is designed to run with, or you can simply open the application program without an attached document.

The program name must be identical to the name of the application as it is stored on your Desktop. Special symbols, punctuation, and spacing are all significant, although capitalization is not. If you spell the name of the program incorrectly, HyperCard is unable to locate it. One way to ensure that the name is correct is to go to the Desktop, copy the application's name to the Clipboard, then go to HyperCard and paste the name into the **open** command line. Notice, however, that the name of the application must be enclosed in quotation marks.

A classic new launcher

We couldn't go on with our discussion of the **open** command without a brief mention of one of the best-designed Finder replacement stacks we've seen. It's called *Home Desk,* and it is the creation of Russell A. Lyon. When you first open the stack (Figure 16-1), you find yourself in a dark room with a light switch.

Figure 16-1. Home Desk stack opens on a dark room

Press the switch, and your own rolltop desk is revealed (Figure 16-2). Press the lock on the desk, and it opens to reveal a typical desktop (Figure 16-3).

Buttons include the pencil holder (which activates your word processor), a calculator (which opens a desk accessory calculator if one is available), and more than two dozen other application-suggesting buttons. Some are hidden in drawers. There's even a private safe where you can hide documents, applications, and other items that only a person who knows the combination can browse.

Each of these buttons uses the **open** command. Just studying the script can give you a lot of good ideas for places to use this versatile HyperTalk command. More than any other HyperTalk command, **open** makes it possible for you to consider using HyperCard as the focal point of your Macintosh world.

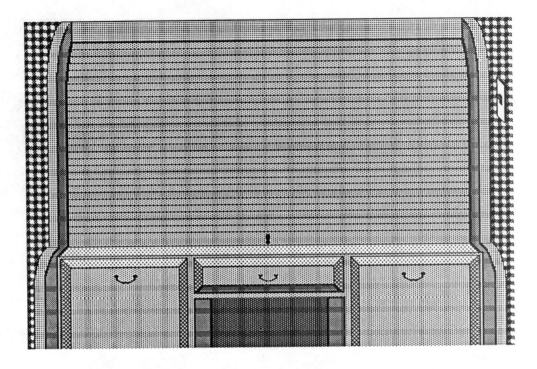

Figure 16-2. Home Desk ready for opening and use

What happens when you use *open*?

When HyperTalk encounters an **open** command in a script, it sends a special message called **suspend system** to the current card. It then notifies your Macintosh System File that when you quit this new external application, control should be returned to HyperCard. Finally, HyperCard clears itself from memory.

After you finish using the application you launch from HyperCard, control returns not just to HyperCard but to the very card that was active when you executed the **open** command.

Figure 16-3. Home Desk desktop

NOTE

If you run HyperCard under MultiFinder or with a
mini-finder present, the system does not return control to HyperCard when the opened application
quits. Instead, control returns to the top level of
your system.

Specifying a document to open

If you want to open a specific document by using the application
that created it, add the middle parameter to the **open** command
along with the key linking word **with**. Here is a typical example
(don't type this command into your stack unless you have the
same document and application pair).

```
open "Chapter 16" with "Microsoft Word"
```

HyperCard's processing in this case is identical to that described earlier, except when it has opened the application, it loads the document file listed in the first parameter.

Helping HyperCard find files

Before you settle into long-term use of a particular **open** command, be sure you place the full path name where the document and the application can be found into Look for Documents In... and Look for Applications In..., two Home Stack cards. If you don't do this, the first time you try to use the **open** button, HyperCard interrupts the processing to ask where the files are located.

Printing Non-HyperCard Documents

In addition to opening other documents and applications, you can order HyperCard to print a document prepared in another application (using that application) and then return to HyperCard when the printing is complete. The **print** command makes this possible. Its syntax is nearly identical to that of the **open** command:

```
print "<document name>" with "<program name>"
```

The **print** command has no optional parameters. HyperCard must know both the document to print and the name of the application whose print routines are to be used.

All of the caveats we discussed when we explained the **open** command apply equally to **print**, including spelling and setting up the paths correctly.

Printing with the **print** command from a HyperTalk script is akin to printing from the Finder with the Print command from the File menu. The application launches, opens the document, prints it (often pausing for a print dialog in between), and then returns to the Finder or, in this case, to the same card you were using when HyperCard encountered the **print** command. Generally, you cannot do other tasks while the external application is running and before control is returned to HyperCard.

Printing Cards from a Script

Anyone who has used HyperCard for more than a few hours of browsing knows that full-blown reports are not a particular strength of the program. HyperCard was not designed to be a database, so this is not surprising.

But printing is not completely unavailable from within HyperCard. Your scripts can include the ability for users to request that certain cards, or even entire stacks, be printed. The process of printing two or more cards from a script requires that you use a structure similar to the following:

```
open printing
  print first card
  print card ID 50128
  go to card "Report File"
  print 23 cards
close printing
```

Notice that there are three separate HyperTalk commands. The first, **open printing**, sets up the printing operation. Its syntax is simple:

```
open printing [with dialog]
```

If you include the **with dialog** argument, the command displays the standard HyperCard printing dialog (see Figure 16-4) before it begins printing, waits for the user's responses, and then initiates printing with the parameters set by the user. If the **with dialog** parameter is *not* included in an **open printing** command, printing proceeds without user intervention and uses the current settings for HyperCard stack printing.

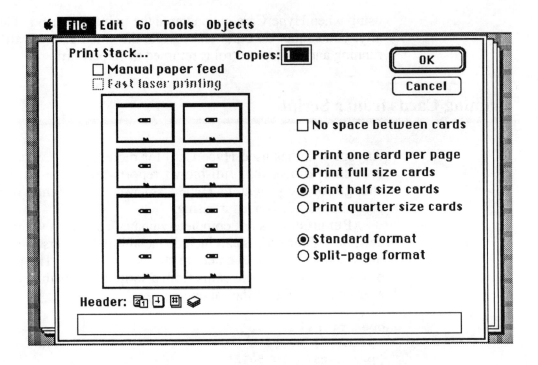

Figure 16-4. Standard HyperCard printing dialog

After printing has been opened, your script executes one or more **print** commands with this syntax:

```
print [all | <number> cards | this card]
```

The **print all cards** command is equivalent to **doMenu "Print Stack..."** except you can bypass the print dialog box with the first approach. You can also supply a number of cards to be printed, starting with the current card. Or you can simply instruct HyperCard to **print this card** or, more concisely, **print**, which it interprets the same way.

When you have ordered your last **print**, you must execute a **close printing** command. This not only ends the printing process and returns control to your stack where it left off, but also ensures that no unprinted cards end up in computer hyperspace. If you order the printing of fifteen cards and selected to print half-size cards so that eight fit on one page, HyperCard stores each group of cards in a buffer in memory until it has eight cards in a group, then it prints them. If you didn't **close printing**, HyperCard would reach the end of the printing operation with seven cards in a buffer waiting to be printed. They would never print.

Summary

In this brief chapter, you learned how to use two of the most powerful and versatile HyperTalk commands: **do** and **open**. They make flexible scripting possible and facilitate using Hyper-Card as the centerpiece of your Macintosh environment. You also saw how to print documents outside HyperCard and cards inside the program.

In Chapter 17, we learn a range of special characteristics of HyperCard objects called properties and how to manage them in scripts.

CHAPTER

17

Properties and Their Management

In this chapter, you will learn about

- HyperCard properties and the important role they play in scripts

- the 45 properties besides the painting properties previously discussed that you can manage in your scripts

- the two commands — **get** and **set** — that manipulate those properties

Role of Properties in HyperCard

HyperCard is, as we have said, highly graphic, interactive, and object-centered. All these facts about the program, combined with a desire on the part of Bill Atkinson and Dan Winkler to give the script-level user a great deal of flexible control over the environment, lead to the important role of *properties* in Hyper-Talk.

A property is a characteristic of an object. If your previous programming experience includes Logo or LISP, you understand properties because they play an important part in those languages. As human beings, we have thousands of properties. Genetic engineers are learning how many of those properties are determined and how they can be either predetermined or altered. Human properties include such diverse things as eye color, height, propensity to gain weight, many diseases, and nose shape. Other properties are not part of the genetic process but are shared by all of us: age, physical condition, abundance or absence of hair, place of residence, whether our parents are still alive, and so on.

Put together a sufficient combination of properties and you can identify any individual. The same is true of HyperCard properties. Every window, stack, background, card, field, and button has properties. Identifying each is a much simpler task than identifying a human individual, of course, because each has an ID number that is guaranteed to be unique (this ID is one of its properties). But other properties more fully describe the object.

HyperCard also has *global* properties that apply to all objects for which they are relevant. These can be viewed as analogous to the traits that make us human: our physical makeup as members of the human race, for example.

How important are properties?

Putting aside for the moment global properties (which we will discuss separately) and painting properties (which we discussed in Chapter 13), HyperCard properties by and large describe what the objects to which they are attached look like, rather than how they behave. Behavior is dictated by scripts. Even the famous link capabilities of buttons create script commands. These scripts actually execute the links we create by mouse clicks.

Properties determine whether an object is visible, its location on the card or background, and its appearance to the user. In a graphic environment like HyperCard, this means properties are vitally important. Understanding properties and how to manipulate them will go a long way toward not only streamlining your stack creation but also making your stacks intuitive and useful.

Virtually any value you can determine in an object's dialog box or in the HyperCard Preferences card can also be set from a HyperTalk script.

General usage

In general, you will find yourself using most of the properties available to you in HyperCard in similar ways.

Often, you will want to retrieve the value of the property with the **get** command and then test that value in a conditional **if-then-else** construct (see Chapter 8). Then, based on the value it *now* has, you may want to change the value with a **set** command. This means much of your property management scripting takes place within a structure like this:

```
...
get some property
  if it is what you want it to be
    then proceed with processing
    else set it and proceed with processing
  end if
...
```

Terseness versus readability

Perhaps nowhere else does HyperTalk offer as much flexibility as in naming properties. You can be almost as terse or as verbose as you like. Many of the property names have short and long forms. For example, **rectangle** can be spelled out or abbreviated **rect**. Because the use of **the** is optional with property names in **get** and **set** commands, both of these instructions have the same effect:

```
get the rectangle of the Message box
get rect of Msg
```

Using *the* in property names

HyperTalk novices are sometimes bewildered by what appears to be a willy-nilly use or omission of the definite article **the** before property names. If you've examined any scripts, you have probably noticed this apparent arbitrariness and wondered about it.

Well, it turns out not to be so mysterious after all. There are some basic rules you must follow when deciding when to use **the** and when to omit it. Those rules follow.

RULES FOR USING *the* IN PROPERTY NAMES

1. The word **the** is never required in a **get** or **set** statement.

2. If the property has parameters, **the** may be included or omitted.

3. If the property has no parameters and appears in any statement other than a **get** or a **set**, **the** is required.

The easy method is to adopt the convention we use throughout this book. Use **the** in the interest of both safety and readability. It is *never* wrong to include it, and it is wrong to omit it often enough that it causes aggravation when scripting.

Order of discussion of properties

In this chapter, we discuss properties in the following order:

- global properties

- properties common to two or more classes of objects

- unique stack properties

- unique field properties

- unique button properties

- unique picture properties

There are no properties that are unique to windows, cards, or backgrounds.

Table 17-1 summarizes all non-painting properties in HyperTalk, defining the class or classes to which each belongs and the possible values it can have. Syntax for those with arguments is discussed in the text rather than the table.

Global Properties

Global properties, as you can deduce from their name, apply throughout the HyperCard environment. They can be changed almost any time from any script or the Message box (or, in some cases, from the Preferences card in the Home stack), but when you change them, they stay in their changed state until they are changed again. Whether you change stacks or even quit Hyper-Card and return later, these values remain the same until they are changed. There are fifteen global properties, four of which are related to Preferences settings.

The *userLevel* property

One global property you may have encountered in your Hyper-Talk scripting is the **userLevel** property. It determines which of the five levels of access the user has. Each level increase is indicated by an increase of 1 in the value of **userLevel** and represents a step upward in complexity and power. Table 17-2 depicts the five values of **userLevel** and how they relate to the Preferences card settings.

Table 17-1. HyperTalk properties and their values

Property Name	Classes	Legal Values
autoHilite	Bt	true or false
blindTyping	G	true or false
bottom	F, Bt, W	numeric
bot[tom]Right	F, Bt, W	two numbers separated by a comma
cantDelete	S, Bk, C	true or false
cantModify	S	true or false
cursor	G	numeric or string (see note 1)
dragSpeed	G	numeric
editBkgnd	G	true or false
freeSize	S	numeric, read-only
hilite	Bt	true or false
icon	Bt	numeric
id	Bk, C, F, Bt	numeric, read-only
language	G	text (name of language)
left	Bt, F, W	numeric
loc[ation]	F, Bt, W	two numbers separated by a comma
lockMessages	G	true or false
lockRecent	G	true or false
lockScreen	G	true or false
lockText	F	true or false
long Version	G, S	when applied to HyperCard, one number; when applied to stack, same as version property
name	S, Bk, C, F, Bt	string
number	Bk, C, F, Bt	numeric, read-only
numberFormat	G	see note 2
powerKeys	G	true or false
rect[angle]	F, Bt, W	four numbers separated by commas; read-only for windows
right	Bt, F, W	numeric
screenRect	G	four numbers separated by commas; read only
script	S, Bk, C, F, Bt	entire script

Table 17-1. (continued)

Property Name	Classes	Legal Values
scroll	F	numeric
showLines	F	true or false
showName	Bt	true or false
showPict	P	true or false
size	S	numeric, read-only
style	F, Bt	see note 3
textArrows	G	true or false
top	Bt, F, W	numeric
topLeft	Bt, F, W	two numbers separated by comma
userLevel	G	numeric, 1-5
user Modify	G	true or false
version	G, S	when applied to a stack, five numeric values separated by commas; when applied to HyperCard, one numeric value.
visible	F, Bt, W	true or false
wideMargins	F	true or false
width	F, Bt, W	numeric

Key: Under Classes, the following abbreviations are used:
Bt=button, G=global, S=stack, C=card, F=field,Bk=background, W=window, P=picture.

Notes:
1. Eight pre-defined cursor names permissible. See Text.
2. The value of **numberFormat** is a pattern described in text.
3. The value of **style** depends on whether the object is a button or a field. See text.

Table 17-2. Meanings of *userLevel* settings

Value	Level
1	browsing
2	typing
3	painting
4	authoring
5	scripting

The *powerKeys* property

When users are using the painting power of HyperCard, implying that they have a **userLevel** setting of 3 or higher, they can also enable the use of power keys to accelerate their painting control. Normally, users check the check box in the Preferences card to indicate when they want this feature enabled. But you can use the **powerKeys** property to do so if you wish. This property can be either true or false. The default is taken from the Preferences card in the Home stack.

The *blindTyping* property

You have probably had the experience of starting to type something into HyperCard with the Message box hidden only to have HyperCard beep. If you check the check box next to Blind Typing on the Preferences card of the Home stack, you can get around this problem. The **blindTyping** property gives you a way of accomplishing the same thing in a script. When it is true, you can type and send messages to HyperCard by typing as if you were entering text into the Message box.

You must be careful in using this feature, however, because syntax errors you produce are not easy to detect if the Message box is hidden. Fortunately, you can always press Command-M and request HyperCard to display the Message box. When you do so, the last message entered into the Message box is available for inspection and editing if necessary.

To **set** the value of **blindTyping**, the **userLevel** must be 5. The property can be either true or false. The default is taken from the Preferences card in the Home stack.

The *textArrows* property

In Version 1.1 of HyperCard, Apple Computer added the capability of using the arrow keys on the keyboard in one of two ways. They also added a check box to the Preferences card of the Home stack opposite the **Typing** user level label. By checking this box, the user can decide that the arrow keys on the keyboard will be used to move the cursor inside fields and script editing windows. By leaving it unchecked, the arrow keys remain as they were permanently set in earlier versions of the program, namely to navigate among cards.

The script version of this process uses the **textArrows** property. It can be either true (equivalent to the check box being checked) or false. If it is set to true, the user can still navigate with the arrow keys by using them with the Option key. The opposite is also true, so that if **textArrows** is false, the user can hold down the Option key with an arrow to use it as a cursor moving key.

Regardless of the setting, holding down the Command key and the left arrow key moves to the beginning of the stack, and pressing the Command key and the right arrow key moves to the end of the stack. The Command-up arrow combination pops a card, and Command-down arrow pushes the current card.

The *cursor* property

We move now to global properties that are not equivalent to settings in the Preferences card of the Home stack. The **cursor** property may only be **set**; the **get** command does not work with this property. This is also one property that cannot be usefully **set** from the Message box; the effects of its modification can only be seen within a script. This is because HyperCard reverts to normal cursor settings when the script ends and the system begins to send **idle** messages (see Chapter 6). This means even though you *could* set the cursor from the Message box, it would be difficult to see the effect because the system would begin sending **idle** messages immediately after the Message box message was handled.

When you **set** the cursor, you must use the number or name of a cursor resource that is available in the current stack or in the HyperCard file. (See Chapter 21 for a discussion of resources and HyperCard.)

HyperCard (after Version 1.2) predefines eight cursor shapes, one of which actually consists of a group of shapes repeated in an animated sequence. These eight shapes are called **none, hand, watch, arrow, iBeam, plus, cross,** and **busy.** You may use the **set** command to change the cursor to any of these shapes simply by referring to them by name:

```
set cursor to watch
set cursor to iBeam
```

Figure 17-1 depicts six of the eight shapes. The cursor shape called **none** results in an invisible cursor. This was a request made by many early users of HyperCard prior to Version 1.2. In earlier versions, it was not possible within HyperTalk to make the cursor disappear. The cursor **busy** is an animated sequence of several shapes that result in the appearance of a rotating "beach ball", a shape with which most HyperCard users are quite familiar.

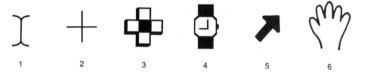

Figure 17-1. Six of HyperCard's predefined cursors

You will probably change the cursor very seldom, if at all. When you do, though, the chances are pretty good that you'll be changing it to the watch (cursor 4 in HyperCard parlance). As you know as a Macintosh user, you don't mind waiting for a process to complete if the watch cursor is showing (for some reasonable period of time), but even relatively brief delays without the watch cursor make you nervous. You wonder if something has gone wrong to hang up the system. So if you're executing something in a script that takes longer than a second or two, you are well-advised to change the **cursor** shape to 4 with a **set** command, then execute the function. Design your scripts so that if you do reset the cursor's shape, the cursor reverts to its normal, idling shape when the handler ends.

The *dragSpeed* property

We dealt with the **dragSpeed** property in Chapter 13. It is included here only for completeness, because it is a global property, although it is used exclusively by painting operations.

The *editBkgnd* property

If your script undertakes a painting, button, or field modification that operates on the background rather than the current card, you must **set** the value of **editBkgnd** to true. Otherwise, your changes alter only the current card.

Your script can only access this property if **userLevel** is 3 or higher. The **editBkgnd** property can be either true or false. The default setting is false.

The *language* property

It is unlikely you will have any occasion to use the **language** property. Language translators for HyperCard became available beginning with Version 1.1, but unless you either write scripts for multiple languages or are translating scripts, you will have no need for this property.

The **language** property can take the name of any valid language translator as a value. If translators are installed in your version of HyperCard, they appear on the Preferences card in the Home stack. If you attempt to **set the language** to a language for which your version does not have a translator, an error message like that shown in Figure 17-2 results.

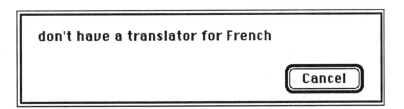

don't have a translator for French

Cancel

Figure 17-2. Language translator error message

The *lockMessages* property

There are occasions in advanced scripting when you want to supress the execution of messages designed to trigger when a card or stack is first opened. By setting the value of **lockMessages** to true, you effectively intercept and bury all messages that deal with opening these objects.

This is sometimes necessary, for example, if you want to let the user navigate through one or more stacks where cards, backgrounds, or stacks have **on open** handlers. If **lockMessages** is false, these scripts will execute even though the user doesn't want them to when he or she is just browsing through the stacks.

The value of **lockMessages** does not affect any other kind of system or other message.

The *lockRecent* property

As you navigate in HyperCard, whether in one stack or among multiple stacks, HyperCard saves the most recent 42 cards you've visited in a special place it knows by the name **recent**. Stored there is a miniature of each of the last 42 cards you've displayed (see Figure 17-3). By clicking on any of these images, you can move directly to that card.

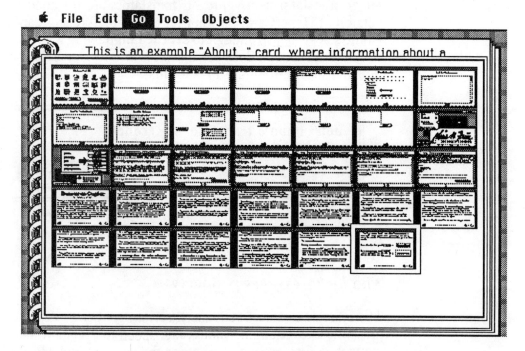

Figure 17-3. The *recent* display

If you want to suppress the user's ability to examine specific cards in your stack or if you just don't want to clutter up the user's **recent** area as you carry out some specialized processing, you can use the **lockRecent** property.

This property can be true or false. The default, of course, is false. If you find it necessary to **set** this property to true, be sure it is returned to its normal false state before returning control to the user.

The *lockScreen* property

You'll find the **lockScreen** property one of the most useful in HyperTalk's repertoire of properties. It can take a value of true or false, with its default being false. When you **set** it to true, any activity you undertake in your script that normally updates the screen becomes invisible to the user.

You can open other cards, read data from them, modify them, even open new stacks, and none of this activity is evident to the user. This approach is often useful to avoid confusing the casual browser. It is also a form of protection from too-easy delving into your scripts and their actions. (Although it is not a very strong form of such protection, it prevents the nontechnical user from being aware anything is happening.)

It may be a good idea to use the **lockScreen** property in conjunction with the **lockMessages** and **lockRecent** properties. It is also a good idea to consider setting the **cursor** to the watch with a **set the cursor to 4** command before you begin processing complex operations with the screen locked. Otherwise, there is almost no way for users to know something is happening, and they may decide the system is "hung" and reset the Macintosh at an inopportune time.

To keep things in balance, you should make sure that your script sets **lockScreen** false for each time it sets it true. In effect, **lockScreen** sets up a value which is decreased by one each time the property is set to false. Only when the value reaches 0 is **lockScreen** set to false. This enables handlers that call other handlers to rely on the status and value of the **lockScreen** parameter not changing unless it is specifically modified by the individual handler.

You can also lock the screen with the **lock screen** command in HyperCard Version 1.2 and later. The effects of **lock screen** and **set the lockScreen to true** are identical. Whether you have used the property or the command, you can use the **unlock screen,** optionally with a visual effect, to unlock the screen (see Chapter 13 for a discussion of the use of the **lock screen** and **unlock screen** commands.)

The *numberFormat* property

The **numberFormat** property controls the degree of precision with which numbers are stored and consequently displayed in HyperCard. It also determines the way they are formatted when they are displayed. Its format is as follows:

```
set the numberFormat to "<format string>"
```

In its default mode, HyperCard formats all numbers with up to six digits to the right of the decimal point and no *required* digits to the left of the decimal point. You can change this by using three pattern characters:

- the number 0, which means HyperCard must put a 0 in that position if it would otherwise be empty

- the decimal point

- the crosshatch, or number sign (#), which is only used to the right of the decimal point to determine maximum precision without regard to trailing zeros

You can use the **set the numberFormat** command to establish any format that makes sense for the numbers you are calculating and displaying in a stack. When the script is finished executing and HyperCard returns to its **idle** state, the system resumes the default pattern. This means you must set the **numberFormat** in a script and not from the Message box.

Table 17-3 presents some typical number formatting patterns and shows how the values 11.9752 and 0.85629371 are displayed in each.

Table 17-3. Typical numeric formatting patterns

Format Pattern	11.9752	0.85629371
"0.00"	11.98	0.86
"0.#########"	11.9752	0.85629371
"0.000000000"	11.975200000	0.856293710
".###"	11.975	0.856

The *userModify* property

In a locked stack, the user is prevented from making any changes to field contents or to artwork. But there are times when you want to offer the user the *illusion* of being allowed to make changes or you want to capture information from him for some other purpose without modifying the stack. When a stack is used as a "front end" to some other product, for example, it might be useful to allow the user to enter data into a HyperCard stack, capture the information, and place it in another program's storage area. But you might not want the user to be able to make any modifications to the appearance of or content in your front-end stack.

To deal with this problem, HyperCard Version 1.2 and later includes the **userModify** property. In a locked stack, this property is set to *false* unless your script specifically sets it to true. If it is set to *true,* the user can make modifications to cards and fields in the stack, but those changes are discarded on leaving the card.

Combining the use of the **userModify** property and a **close-Field** or **closeCard** message (see Chapter 6), you can capture information from the user without permitting modification of your stack. The basic approach would look something like this:

1. The user opens your locked stack. An **openStack** handler sets the **userModify** property to *true*.

2. The user enters some information in one or more fields.

3. In a **closeCard** handler or in individual **closeField** handlers for each field involved, your script uses a **put** command to take the information entered by the user and place it in another stack or write it into an external file.

Here is an example of the salient part of such a script. We assume that the user can enter information into two fields and that we are capturing his entries when he indicates that he is done by pressing a button that appears to take him to the next card in the stack.

```
on openStack -- this handler goes at the stack level
  set userModify to true
  -- perhaps do other processing as well
end openStack
on closeCard -- this handler goes at the card,¬
background or stack level
  set lockScreen to true
  put field "Customer Name" into nameEntered
  put field "Amount Due" into dueEntered
  push this card
  go to stack "Updates"
  put nameEntered & return after field "New Names"
  put dueEntered & return after field "New Amounts"
  set lockScreen to false
  -- not required but good form
end closeCard
```

It is not necessary to clear the fields "Customer Name" and "Amount Due" on the entry stack (which could be a one-card stack) because HyperCard automatically discards the user's changes when he or she leaves the card. Thus, a single stack could be essentially re-used for hundreds or thousands of data entries, which would then be placed elsewhere for processing later.

The *screenReact* property

Beginning with Version 1.2 of HyperCard, you can determine the dimensions of the screen the user has by means of the **screenRect** property. This read-only property returns a rectangle as a value, so it consists of four numbers, separated by commas. The first two numbers are both zero.

For the Macintosh Plus and SE with the standard Macintosh nine-inch monochrome monitor, **screenRect** returns 0,0,512,342. For a Macintosh II with a standard Apple color monitor, the value is 0,0,640,480. Other screens will return different values, of course.

The *version* property

Since the introduction of HyperCard Version 1.2, the differences between versions of the product have become significant to the developer. Some functionality peculiar to Version 1.2 and later will cause difficulties if used in stacks running under HyperCard 1.1 and earlier. Similarly, stacks created under versions earlier than 1.2 and then run under later versions need compacting under the new version before they work as expected.

You can determine the version of HyperCard now in use with the **version** and **long Version** properties. Each can take an optional parameter, **of HyperCard.** The **version** property returns a single decimal value with the actual version number (e.g., 1.2). The **long Version** property, on the other hand, returns an eight-character number. For example,

```
put the version
```

places the value "1.2" into the Message box, assuming you are running HyperCard Version 1.2. With the same version, the command

```
put the long Version
```

places the value "01208000" into the Message box. As later versions are released, this number will increase accordingly.

There is also a stack property called **version,** which is discussed later in the chapter. Using its return values and the stack's version information, you can determine when a forced compacting should take place.

Shared Properties

Eight properties are shared by two or more classes of HyperCard objects. Rather than duplicating the discussion of each of these properties by dividing the chapter by object type, we present these common ones before we discuss those that are unique to each type of object.

The *id* property

All backgrounds, cards, fields, and buttons have associated with them a number that is guaranteed to be unique for a particular object type in a particular domain of a stack. This means no two backgrounds in a stack are assigned the same ID number. Two background fields also do not share the same ID number, though there could be a background field and a card field with the same ID. This guarantee makes IDs a very safe way to address these objects.

You can only **get** an **id** property of an object. It can never be **set**. It is assigned automatically when the object is created and is never changed. Even if the card or other object is deleted, the unique ID number is never used again in that stack for another object of the same type in the same domain.

Don't confuse the ID number of an object with its *sequence number,* which determines its relative position within a card or stack. Sequence numbers can be changed by the Bring Closer and Send Farther selections in the Objects menu.

The *location* property

All fields, buttons, and windows have a specific **location** (also abbreviated **loc**) that describes their relative position on the screen. Recall that HyperCard views the Macintosh's 9-inch display (built in on all but the Macintosh II) as beginning at the location 0,0 in the upper-left corner and extending to the location 512,342 in the lower-right corner. The **location** property uses this addressing scheme.

If you **get the location** of any of these objects, HyperCard returns two numbers separated by a comma, e.g., 100,250. These numbers give the horizontal and vertical offset, respectively, of the *center* of the object. This location can be useful for clicking and dragging operations. Or you can relocate an object with the **set the location** command. For example, Figure 17-4 shows one of our familiar Laboratory stack cards after the **set the loc** command shown in the Message box has been executed. The button, formerly near the center of the card, has shifted 100 pixels to the right.

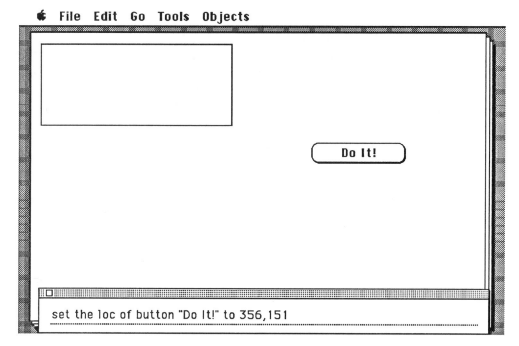

Figure 17-4. Moving a button by altering its location property

This method of relocating buttons, fields, and windows is faster and more efficient than changing the tool and dragging the object. It does not, however, work with painted objects. They must be moved as described in Chapter 13.

The *name* property

You can find out or change the name of the current stack, background, or card or of an identified field or button by examining and altering its **name** property.

You define the name of a stack, background, card, field, or button any time after you create it, and you can always alter it. HyperCard leaves the names of these items blank unless you supply a name. It does not insist that these objects even have names.

There are two forms of the **name** property. One is called **the long name** and the other, **the short name**. If you don't specify which you want to use, HyperTalk generally (but not always) assumes you want to see **the long name**.

Looking at names

Go to any card in the Laboratory stack with a button and a field. Find out the sequence numbers of each object you want to experiment with so you can address them correctly. In the example, we assume you have a button and a field and that each is the only object of its kind on the card. We also assume the field is named Test Field and the button is named Do It! Now type the following lines into the Message box and examine the results.

1. ```
   put the name of card field 1
   -- Message box displays card field "Test Field"
   ```

2. ```
   put the short name of card field 1
   -- Message box displays Test Field (no quotation
   marks)
   ```

3. ```
   put the long name of card field 1
   -- Message box displays card field "Test Field"
   of card id 6001 of stack "A Hard Place:Hyper
   Folder:Laboratory"
   ```

4. Repeat the previous steps with the button field.

As you can see, if you ask for **the name** of an object, HyperCard returns the entire name, including the type and domain (card field, background button, etc.). But if you specify **the short name**, HyperCard returns only the name as it appears in the Info dialog box.
   ```

The *number* property

To find out the sequence number of a background, card, field, or button, you can use the **get** command to return the **number** of that item. The sequence number is the one the system assigns in the order in which objects are created and should not be confused with the ID number discussed earlier (see "The **id** property").

As with the **id** property, the **number** property cannot be changed in a script. Only the Bring Closer and Send Farther options in the Objects menu alter this value.

The *rectangle* property

The **rectangle** property is closely related to the **location** property described earlier. The difference is the **rectangle** property describes the upper-left and lower-right corners of the rectangle enclosing a field, button, or window; the **location** property only defines the center point of those objects.

You can move an object using the **rectangle** property just as you can with the **location** property. With **rectangle**, however, you can also resize the object. If you use the **set** command to change the **rectangle** property of an object and if you modify the proportional distances between the corners, you will resize and perhaps reshape the object. You can, of course, do this without relocating the object. Another use of the **rectangle** property is with the **drag** command using the appropriate tool to resize the object.

The **rectangle** property has four numeric values, separated by commas. The first two define the horizontal and vertical position, respectively, of the upper-left corner. The last two define the horizontal and vertical position, respectively, of the lower-right corner. Both sets of coordinates are essentially offsets because the upper-left corner of a HyperCard screen is at 0,0.

A very important use of this property involves clicking in a field. If you use the **location** property, you will find yourself clicking in the center of the field, which results in the cursor appearing either in the center of a line in the center of the field or at the left margin but centered vertically. If you want to click in the upper-left corner of the field, use the **rectangle** property, then use **delete** to remove items 3 and 4 (or, alternatively, use **put** to extract items 1 and 2) of the address group. Then you can use **click at** with those two values to place the cursor in the upper-left corner of the field.

Other location and size properties

Beginning with Version 1.2, HyperTalk added eight new properties related to the location and size of HyperCard objects. These properties allow you to access specific portions of the information returned by the **rectangle** property for a given object. These properties are as follows:

- **left**

- **top**

- **right**

- **bottom**

- **topLeft**

- **bottomRight** (may be abbreviated to **botRight**)

- **width**

- **height**

Each of these properties, as with all other properties related to objects, is followed with the key word **of** and then with the identifier that names the object whose property you wish to **set** or **get**. The next Laboratory exercise makes this clear.

Using *size* and *location* properties

For the next experiment, you'll need a Laboratory stack card with at least one button and one field. Create a new one or find one whose script you don't mind overwriting. Then follow these instructions.

1. Open the script editing window of a button in one of the usual ways.

2. Type the following handler into the script editing window. Click OK when you have proofread the script.

```
on mouseUp
    put the rectangle of card field 1 into r1
    put third item of r1 -1 into corner
    put "," & fourth item of r1 -1 after corner
    choose field tool
    put "Click the mouse where you want the corner."
    wait until the mouseClick
    drag from corner to the mouseLoc
    choose browse tool
end mouseUp
```

3. Return to browse mode.

4. Click on the button. The Message box appears (if it was invisible) and requests that you click the mouse where you want the lower-right corner of the field to be located.

5. Click the mouse where the field won't cover up the button. The corner moves immediately there. Experiment with different screen positions. If you move the mouse inside the field and click, the field gets smaller.

6. When you've experimented enough with the **rectangle** property, create a card field and name it "Where". Make it a scrolling field so that if the information we're going to put into it gets lengthy, you'll be able to see it.

7. Either create a second button or overwrite the script of the existing button with the following script:

```
on mouseUp
    put "Left edge =" && left of card field 1 ¬
    & return into card field "Where"
    put "Top edge = " & top of card field 1 ¬
    & return after card field "Where"
```

```
        put "Right edge = " & right of card field 1 ¬
        & return after card field "Where"
        put "Bottom edge = " & bottom of card field 1 ¬
        & return after card field "Where"
        put "Top left corner = " & topLeft of card ¬
        field 1 & return after card field "Where"
        put "Bottom right corner = " & botRight of ¬
        card field 1 & return after card field "Where"
        put "Width = " & width of card field 1 & ¬
        return after card field "Where"
        put "Height = " & height of card field 1 & ¬
        return after card field "Where"
    end mouseUp
```

8. Compare the results of these printouts with the **rectangle** of the field as reported in your last run of the previous handler to satisfy yourself that the two handlers essentially produce the same information in different forms.

Notice in the script that we use the **rectangle** function, extract the third and fourth items of it (which point to the lower-right corner), and put them into their own local variable. This makes later command lines more efficient to write than spelling out "item 3 of the rectangle of card field 1." (We subtract 1 from each value to place the drag point inside the rectangle rather than exactly at the corner. This is necessary because of the way coordinates relate to the screen position to which they correspond.) Also notice that we've used the **mouseLoc** function rather than the **clickLoc** function as we advised you to do in Chapter 7. This was done to accommodate an apparent anomaly in HyperTalk: it remembers the mouse click location at the button used to activate the script rather than the one from the new mouse click executed at the script's request while the script is executing. Because there are no instructions between the positioning of the **mouseLoc** and the **drag** command that uses it, this approach works fine and is probably a little quicker than the more usual method of using **clickLoc**.

The *script* property

One of the most powerful features of HyperTalk is the ability to use the **script** property to modify scripts. This self-modification feature is an advanced idea with origins in symbolic processing and AI languages like LISP. Used properly, it can lead to highly personalized HyperCard applications that appear to be quite intelligent about their users.

You can both **get** and **set** the script of any object capable of holding a script. You can access individual elements in the script by placing it into a variable and then treating the script as an ordinary container of text (which it is). The process (which you can experiment with in the next Laboratory exercise) involves a framework like this:

```
put the script of card button 1 into scripter
--use put to modify one or more words or lines
set the script of card button 1 to scripter
```

You may also simply delete the script by using a command like:

```
set the script of this card to empty
```

This might come in handy if you build one or more temporary scripts during execution of an application and you don't want them hanging around the next time the application runs.

By the way, the object whose script is being modified can easily be the object currently being accessed (e.g., a button script can modify itself).

A self-modifying *script*

All you really need for this experiment is a card with a single button. The experiment is more rewarding and easier to follow, however, if you use one of our now-famous one-button, one-field card designs in the Laboratory stack. Again, you can use an existing card or create a new one. After you have such a card, follow these instructions:

1. Open the script editing window of a button in one of the usual ways.

2. Type the following handler into the script editing window. Click OK when you have proofread the script.

```
on mouseUp
  beep 2
    put the script of card button 1 into card field 1
    get word 2 of line 2 of card field 1
    -- use a variable name if you don't have a field
    add 1 to it
    put it into word 2 of line 2 of card field 1
    set the script of card button 1 to card field 1
end mouseUp
```

3. Return to browse mode.

4. Click on the button. Notice that the system produces two short beeps in rapid succession. If you have card field 1 showing, you can see the script appear in the field. But the number on line 2 will become 3. Click the mouse on the button again. This time you hear three beeps and the number in the script changes to 4. This will go on almost forever if we let it!

The *visible* property

The **visible** property is the last shared property we will examine. You can both **set** and **get** it. To check whether an object is presently visible, you can use a construct like:

```
get the visible of card field 2
```

Then, if *It* is false, you can make the field visible as follows:

```
set the visible of card field 2 to true
```

There is little or no penalty in HyperCard for making a visible field visible or making an invisible one invisible.

There are other commands for making a field visible or invisible. You can use the **hide** command to the same effect as setting an object's **visible** property to false. Similarly, you can use the **show** command rather than setting the **visible** property to true.

The *cantDelete* property

Beginning with Version 1.2, HyperCard enables you to protect stacks, backgrounds, and cards from deletion "on the fly." You can set the **cantDelete** property of any object of these types to *true* to prohibit deletion and to *false* to permit it.

   Changing the value of this property changes the setting of the check box in the Info dialog for that property. Therefore, if a card's "Can't Delete Card" box is checked and you set the **cant-Delete** property to *false,* you can delete the card. If you forget to change back the value of this property before closing the stack, the user always is able to delete the card.

Unique Stack Properties

Four HyperCard properties pertain to stacks alone: **size, freeSize, cantModify** and **version**.

The *size* property

You can determine the size in bytes of a stack by using the **get** command with the **size** property. It cannot be **set**. You must tell HyperCard the name of the stack you want to check. If you want the size of the current stack, you must use the key word **this**, as in:

```
get the size of this stack
```

The *freeSize* property

When cards are deleted from a stack, the space they vacate is left open rather than "collapsed" so that all cards are stored contiguously in the file. During stack construction, many events can also cause holes to appear in the stack. If you have ever opened a Stack Info... dialog (see Figure 17-5), you have probably noticed the Free in Stack indicator. This number tells you how many bytes of space are vacant in the script and thus occupying unnecessary disk space.

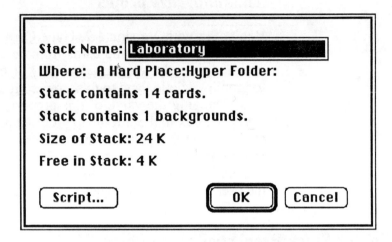

Figure 17-5. Stack Info... dialog box showing free space

You can find the value of the free space in a stack with the **freeSize** property. You cannot **set** its value, however. The only way to modify it is to compact the stack using the Compact Stack option in the File menu. When compaction is complete, the stack's **freeSize** is 0.

Experience shows that when the **freeSize** of a stack exceeds about 15% of the stack's total size as given by the **size** property, compaction results in more efficient stack usage as well as free-ing disk space. In your stacks, you might want to check for this condition in a handler as follows:

```
on closeStack
  if the freeSize of this stack > 0.15 * ¬
  the size of this stack then answer ¬
  "You should compact this stack!"
end closeStack
```

You may, of course, choose to put up the watch cursor and perform the compaction yourself with this command:

```
doMenu "Compact Stack"
```

The *cantModify* property

This property was added with the release of HyperCard Version 1.2. It can be set to *true* or *false*. It has no effect on a locked stack. But if it is set to *true,* the user is prohibited from making any modifications to the stack, including deleting or compacting it.

When the property is true, a padlock symbol appears at the end of the menu bar and the menu options for compacting and deleting the stack are dimmed in the File Menu.

The property remains in the state to which it is set when the stack is closed, so if you intend a change to be temporary in the value of this property, be sure to reset its value on leaving the stack.

The *version* property

You can use the **version** property to obtain useful information about the versions associated with a stack's creation and modification history. The property is read-only and returns five eight-character numbers separated by commas. They are, in order of appearance in a **put** statement:

- the version of HyperCard used to create the stack;

- the version of HyperCard last used to compact the stack;

- the oldest version of HyperCard used to modify the stack since its last compaction;

- the version of HyperCard that last changed the stack;

- the most recent modification date and time, in seconds, of the stack.

If any of the stack values -- i.e., items 1-4 of the list returned by the **version** property -- is less than 1.2, its value in this list will be "00000000."

The fifth value is only updated when the stack is closed, not each time a change is made.

Unique Field Properties

HyperTalk includes five properties that apply exclusively or uniquely to fields. Four — **scroll, wideMargins, lockText,** and **autoTab** — apply only to fields. The fifth, **style,** is common to both fields and buttons but has markedly different values for each.

We should point out, too, that fields have five text properties associated with them: **textAlign, textFont, textSize, textStyle,** and **textHeight**. But these are identical in operation to the same properties as they relate to HyperCard's painting environment, which is discussed in detail in Chapter 13. We will not repeat the discussion of those five properties here.

The *autoTab* property

Beginning with HyperCard Version 1.2, a field may be defined as having an Auto Tab characteristic (see Chapter 4). This property can also be set in a script to be either true or false. If it is true, the Return key acts exactly like the Tab key under some circumstances. If it is false, the Return key always inserts a carriage return in the field.

The **autoTab** property only works with non-scrolling fields. If this property is true for a particular field and the user presses the Return key when he is on the last line of this field, Hyper-Card treats this Return as if it were a Tab. It moves him to the next field on the card (if there is one) and sends the **closeField** message if text has been changed (see Chapter 6).

The *lockText* property

Two types of text can be displayed in a field: editable text and locked text. Generally, when you want to make the text in a field non-editable, you check the Lock Text check box in the Field Info... dialog (see Figure 17-6). But this property can also be changed from within your scripts by modifying the **lockText** property.

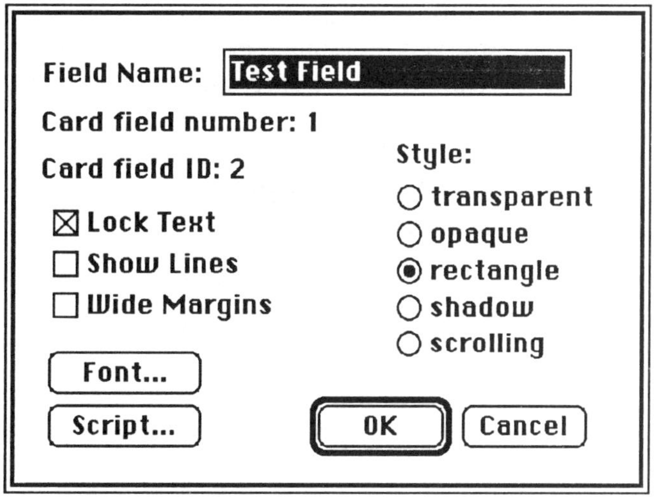

```
┌────────────────────────────────────────────────┐
│  ┌──────────────────────────────────────────┐  │
│  │                                          │  │
│  │  Field Name: ▐Test Field▌                │  │
│  │  Card field number: 1                    │  │
│  │  Card field ID: 2          Style:        │  │
│  │                            ○ transparent │  │
│  │  ☒ Lock Text               ○ opaque      │  │
│  │  ☐ Show Lines              ◉ rectangle   │  │
│  │  ☐ Wide Margins            ○ shadow      │  │
│  │                            ○ scrolling   │  │
│  │  ( Font... )                             │  │
│  │  ( Script... )     (  OK  ) ( Cancel )   │  │
│  │                                          │  │
│  └──────────────────────────────────────────┘  │
└────────────────────────────────────────────────┘
```

Figure 17-6. Field Info... dialog showing Lock Text

The **lockText** property can be true or false. When it is true, it is the same as checking the Lock Text check box in the dialog. This makes the text in the field uneditable. When the pointer moves into a field with locked text, it does not change to the text editing I-beam cursor but remains the browsing pointer. When the **lockText** property is false, the cursor changes to the I-beam when the pointer enters the field, and clicking anywhere in the field makes the text available for editing.

Locked text is used much like painted text, which also cannot be changed by simple editing. But locked text also cannot be changed with paint tools. Standard headings can be placed into locked-text fields. This is particularly useful if part of these headings' contents changes from card to card but you don't want the user to be able to edit them.

One of the best uses of locked text we've seen is in a stack called Xref-Text by Frank Patrick. This shareware stack permits you to create "sticky buttons" in any field of text, so you can create hypertext documents dynamically. The text in a field is locked until the user clicks on a word that he or she wants to use as a hypertext linking word. Then Patrick's script unlocks the field, modifies the word to add an asterisk after it (flagging it as a linked word), re-locks the field, and then continues its processing. (We've made extensive use of Xref-Text and highly recommend it for the creation of first-rate hypertext documents.)

The *scroll* property

The **scroll** property is one of the most interesting properties in HyperCard. Using it in calculations, you can determine how many lines of text have scrolled off the top of a scrolling text field and change the number (and thus the visible contents of the field) in a script. The **scroll** property's value is the number of pixels that have scrolled off the top of the field to which it is attached.

By dividing the value obtained from **get**ting the **scroll** property for a field by the **textHeight** value for that field, you can find out how many lines are in the scrolling field but no longer visible:

```
put the scroll of field 1 / the textHeight of field 1 into invis
```

You can then use **set** to change the number of invisible lines to any value you want by a reverse process:

```
set the scroll of field 1 to 3 / the textHeight of field 1
```

This command scrolls the text in the field so that the first three lines are invisible to the browser. The user can still scroll to see those lines using the arrows and other scroll controls. They are not gone, just temporarily invisible.

Manipulating the *scroll*

This two-phase experiment requires that you create a new Laboratory stack card with a single scrolling text field and a single button. Make the text field relatively small, though large enough to permit two or three lines of text to be visible. When you have things set up, follow these instructions:

1. Open the script editing window of the button in one of the usual ways.

2. Type the following handler into the script editing window. Click OK when you have proofread the script.

```
on mouseUp
  put the scroll of card field 1 / the  ¬
  textHeight of card field 1 into invis
  put invis
end mouseUp
```

3. Return to browse mode.

4. Type a few lines of text into the scrolling field. Make sure that at least five or six lines of text are in the field. Then use the scrolling arrows to position the first three lines of text so they are hidden at the top of the field.

5. Now click the button. The result should resemble Figure 17-7. The Message box contains a 3 because there are three invisible lines above the top of the scrolling field.

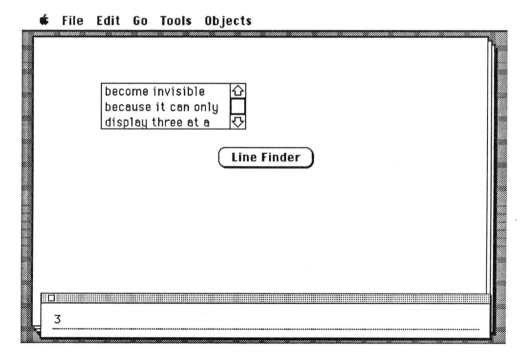

Figure 17-7. Scrolling field test, phase one

6. Scroll a few more lines off the top of the field with the scrolling arrow. Now press the button again and notice that the value in the Message box changes. Experiment with different field depths and perhaps even different fonts and sizes to see how the calculation is affected.

7. Now for the second phase of our experiment. Add a second button. (We labeled the first one Line Finder and the second one Line Reset so we could tell them apart. Choose your own names or use ours, but label them.)

8. Open the script editing window of this button in one of the usual ways.

9. Type the following handler into the script editing window. Click OK when you have proofread the script.

```
on mouseUp
  set the scroll of card field 1 to 0
end mouseUp
```

10. Return to browse mode.

11. Make sure at least one line has scrolled off the top of the scrolling field and then click this new button. The result should resemble Figure 17-8. The top line of text is again visible in the field.

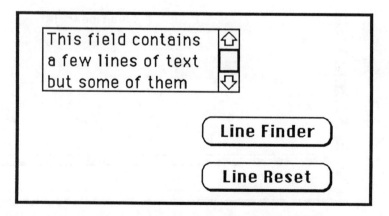

Figure 17-8. Scrolling field test, phase two

The *showLines* property

Like the **lockText** property, the **showLines** property is normally set from the Field Info... dialog. The **showLines** property can be either true or false. If it is true, the lines under each line of text in the window are displayed. If the **showLines** property is false, which is its default condition, the lines are not shown.

The distance between the lines in the text field when **show-Lines** is true is the value of **textHeight**.

This property has no effect on scrolling fields.

The *style* property

Buttons and fields share the **style** property, but the values the property can have associated with it are different between the two types of objects. A field's style, like most other property features we've been discussing, is generally selected from the Field Info... dialog, using the set of radio buttons on the right side of the window. Notice that only one **style** attribute can be set at a time.

The choices for the **style** property in a field are: *transparent*, *opaque*, *rectangle*, *shadow,* and *scrolling*. The first two **style** values produce fields with no visible borders. The difference is whether underlying paint objects can be seen (*transparent*) or not (*opaque).* The next two values, *rectangle* and *shadow*, determine the appearance of a border around the field. The last, *scrolling,* defines a field with a border and scroll bars capable of displaying as much as 32K bytes of information. (Although all HyperCard fields can hold 32K bytes of data, all but scrolling fields are limited to displaying as much as will fit into their physical configuration on the card.)

The *wideMargins* property

The **wideMargins** property is yet another property that is normally set with the Field Info... dialog. It can have a value of true, in which case HyperCard adds some extra space at the left and right margin of each line of text to improve its readability, or false, in which event the full width of the line is used. Figure 17-9 shows you the same field (from our previous Laboratory exercise) with **wideMargins** set to true (on the left side of Figure 17-9) and in its default state of false (on the right).

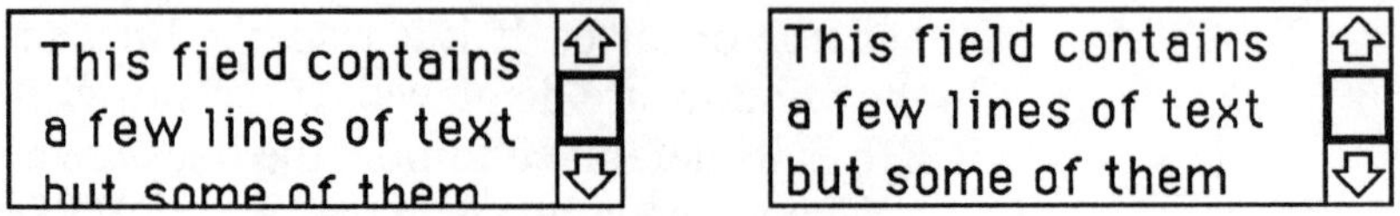

```
┌─────────────────────┬──┐   ┌─────────────────────┬──┐
│ This field contains │⇧ │   │This field contains  │⇧ │
│ a few lines of text │  │   │a few lines of text  │  │
│ but some of them    │⇩ │   │but some of them     │⇩ │
└─────────────────────┴──┘   └─────────────────────┴──┘
```

Figure 17-9. Effect of wideMargins settings

Unique Button Properties

Five HyperCard properties pertain only to buttons: **autoHilite**, **hilite**, **icon**, **showName,** and **style**. In addition, text properties that apply to painting and fields are also pertinent to the text inside buttons.

The *autoHilite* property

The **autoHilite** property, which can be either true or false, is normally set through the Button Info... dialog (see Figure 17-10) using the Auto hilite check box. It determines whether the button will become momentarily highlighted, or inverted, when it is pressed. The default for the **autoHilite** property is false.

Most experienced HyperTalk programmers we know generally change the **autoHilite** property to true because it is more Mac-like to have the button highlighted when it is activated.

The *hilite* property

The **hilite** property is true if the button is presently highlighted and false if it is not. You can use both **get** and **set** with this property, and it can be used from a script or from the Message box. Figure 17-11 shows what a button looks like when its **hilite** property is set to true from the Message box.

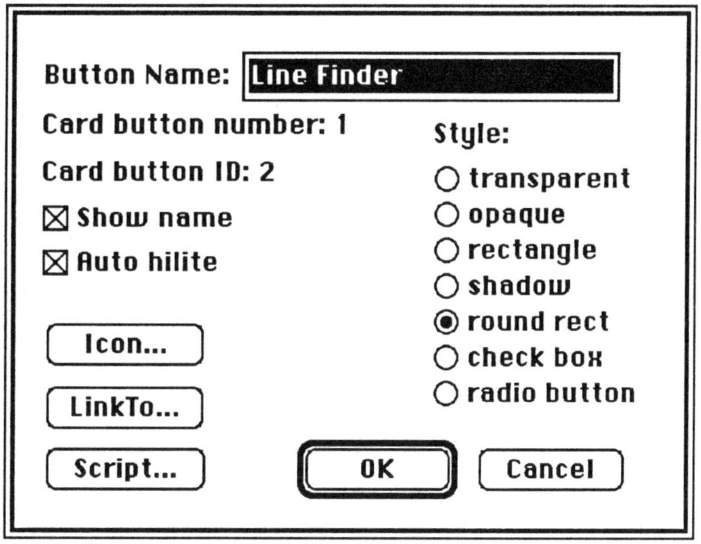

Figure 17-10. Button Info... dialog

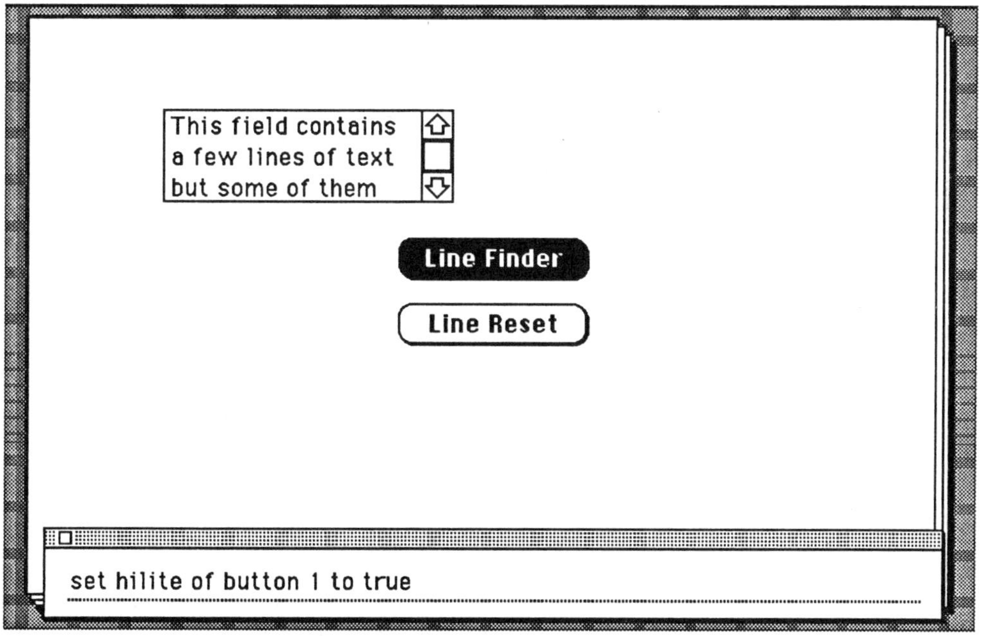

Figure 17-11. Button with *hilite* set to true

The *icon* property

Many buttons in HyperCard stacks have an icon associated with them, though they are not required to do so. Each icon is a resource (see Chapter 21) with an associated name and number. HyperCard uses only the number to identify icons in scripts. The **icon** property contains the number of the icon assigned to a button.

Most of the time, you won't use the **icon** property. But there is at least one occasion you might want to use **set** with the **icon** property to change an icon associated with a button.

Many Macintosh applications, as you know, have icons that invert when they are selected. Others change the icon completely when it is selected. You can achieve these same effects in Hyper-Card applications by including in an **on mouseUp** handler a command to change the icon of the button to indicate activation. There is no point in using this approach only to cause HyperCard to invert the icon because HyperCard can do that as a matter of design. But when you want to achieve a dramatic effect by changing the icon to indicate it is selected, you can do so with a command like:

```
set the icon of button 3 to 1048
```

In the last Laboratory exercise, we created a button called Line Reset. It had a simple one-line script. If you modify that script and enlarge the button, it looks like Figure 17-12 when it is selected. Here is the new script:

```
on mouseUp
    set the icon of card button 2 to 27056
    set the hilite of card button 2 to true
    set the scroll of card field 1 to 0
    wait 10 seconds
    set the icon of card button 2 to 0
    set the hilite of card button 2 to false
end mouseUp
```

Icon 27056 is supplied with HyperCard as one of the icons you can select when you click the Icon button in the Button Info... dialog.

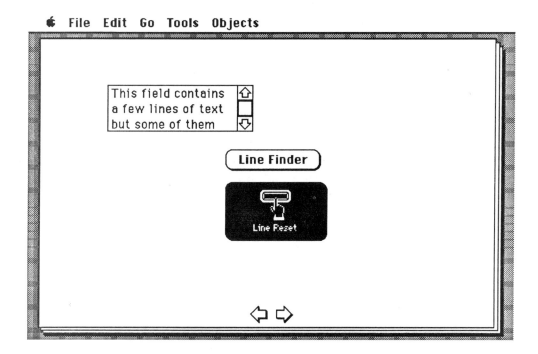

Figure 17-12. Substituting icon when button selected

The *showName* property

The **showName** property is another property that is generally turned on and off through the Button Info... dialog. When it is true, the name chosen for the button in the text edit rectangle at the top of the dialog is displayed inside the button. If the button also includes an icon, the name is displayed under the icon in small type. Otherwise, it is displayed in the text pattern set by a script, or the system default (12-point Chicago centered).

With **showName** set to false, only the icon or underlying painted material shows through the button. The icon is always visible, but paint on the card or background is visible only through a button whose style is *transparent*. Button **style** is discussed in the next section.

The *style* property

Like its field-related counterpart, a button's **style** property is normally set from the Button Info... dialog, using the set of radio buttons on the right side of the window. This property has seven possible values: *transparent, opaque, rectangle, shadow, round rect, check box,* and *radio button.* The first four are identical in effect to their duplicates in a field's **style** property.

The *round rect* style of button is the one that HyperCard uses if you don't tell it to do something else. Like *rectangle* and *shadow*, it affects only the border around the button.

The check box and radio button style buttons are well known to anyone who has used a Macintosh even casually. But if you've programmed the Macintosh in other languages, you should be aware that HyperTalk does *not* handle the management of these button types for you simply because you declare them to be one of these types. If you define a set of radio buttons, your script must manage turning one and only one on at a time. If you use check boxes, you can have more than one in a set selected at one time. That is the fundamental difference, besides shape, in the two types of buttons. We have more to say about handling banks of radio buttons in Chapter 20.

Unique Picture Property

Beginning with Version 1.2 of HyperCard, Apple defined a new quasi-object called a **picture.** (See Chapter 13 for a discussion of pictures and their manipulation.) A single property associated with these new types of objects is provided so that you can determine in your script if a particular card or background picture is visible. This property is the **showPict** property.

In effect, this property is a card or background property, because each card and background can have only one piece of art, which is treated as a single picture.

As you would expect, the value of the **showPict** property is *true* if the picture in question is visible, *false* if it is not.

Your script may **get, put,** or **set** this property. For example, to find out whether the picture on the current card is visible, you can use a command like this:

```
if the showPict of this card is true then…
```

The important thing to note is that even though the property applies to a picture, it is addressed as if it were a card or background property.

Summary

In this chapter, you learned about HyperCard properties and how to manage them. You examined every property that wasn't covered when we discussed painting in HyperTalk scripts in Chapter 13. You saw how to use **get** to find out the current value of a property and how to use **set** to change the values of those properties subject to modification.

Chapter 18 examines the connection between HyperCard and the outside world through telecommunications and telephone links.

CHAPTER

18

HyperTalk Dialing and Communications

In this brief chapter, you will learn about

- HyperTalk's built-in **dial** command and how it can be used in scripts to enable communications with the world outside HyperCard

- the problems in attempting to program stacks to access the Macintosh's serial ports directly for external communications

Of HyperCard, Phones, and Modems

When HyperCard first arrived on the Macintosh scene, one of the first things people noticed about its usefulness was that it included the ability to dial telephone numbers from address stacks and other places in its environment. Visions of easy-to-build and easy-to-use telecommunications and electronic bulletin board systems (BBSes) swarmed around Macintosh user groups.

After some investigation, though, it became clear that HyperCard, in keeping with its role as an information management tool and scaled-down development environment, did not include enough power to access the serial ports of the Mac directly. In short, you could dial the phone — and do so quite adequately — but you were not likely to use unadorned HyperCard for sophisticated telecommunications applications.

Still, a programming language that contains the built-in ability to "reach out and touch" another Mac user is more than a little intriguing. Many HyperTalk programmers have tackled the task of finding new and creative ways of using this power. Maybe you'll be the one who finds the indispensable way of using it and makes a pile...er, stack...of money in the process.

The *dial* Command

There are two ways to dial a telephone with HyperCard: through a special device connected to the Macintosh that uses speaker tones to dial an ordinary telephone or through a modem connected to the modem port on the Mac.

Using *dial* without a modem

Several devices on the market connect to the Macintosh's speaker jack on one end and a telephone line on the other. They use internally generated dialing tones to place calls. HyperCard can activate these devices with the **dial** command in its simplest form:

```
dial "<phone number>"
```

Although you can supply a telephone number explicitly with the **dial** command, you will probably use the standard containers *It* or *selection*, a variable, field name, or a component containing the telephone number. If you do supply a telephone number rather than the place the number can be found, be sure HyperCard doesn't think 555-4232 means subtract 4,232 from 555. You can do this one of two ways. First, you can format the number in the usual way with the separating hyphen and enclose the entire phone number in quotation marks. Second, you can supply the phone number with no internal punctuation, such as 5554232.

Using *dial* with a modem

If you use the **dial** command on a telephone line connected to the Mac serial port through a modem, you must tell HyperCard you are using a modem for the call. You may also want to send some parameters to the modem as part of the dialing process. The syntax for the **dial** command using a modem is as follows:

```
dial "<phone number>" with [modem] ["<modem parameters>"]
```

The presence of the key word **with** tips off HyperCard that you're using a modem. The word **modem** is optional, though if you opt for the usual HyperTalk readability, you will include it. The modem parameters, also optional, consist of a string enclosed in quotation marks. HyperCard sends anything contained in this string to the modem before any attempt is made to dial the phone.

Unless you know what kind of modem the user of your script has, including explicit modem parameters can be a little tricky. Sending the wrong parameters to the modem can result in no connection and can cause the user's blood pressure to rise. If including parameters is important to your script you can use at least two strategies. First, you can require a modem compatible with standards established in the industry by Hayes Microcomputer Products Co. and tell your users they can only use your script without modification if they are using a Hayes-compatible modem. This includes, by the way, both the Apple Modem 300/ 1200 and the Apple Personal Modem. Second, you can supply a setup card with a script that obtains parameters from the user and builds the parameter string as a result.

Modem parameters

Although there is some variation among modems as to the kinds of parameters that can be set with commands, a reasonable amount of standardization has developed around the Hayes command set. Even though some modems may use different commands to effect changes, almost all modems permit the user to set with commands such parameters as type of dialing (pulse or tone), baud rate, mode (answer or call), how long to wait for a carrier after dialing (used only in computer-to-computer communications), and loudness of the modem's built-in speaker.

Because HyperTalk's **dial** command is intended for use only with voice calls, most of these parameters do not have much value in scripts. But you will probably want to set at least three as part of the modem dialing process.

First, you will want to be sure the modem is set for tone dialing, not pulse dialing. In a Hayes-compatible modem, this is accomplished with the *DT* (for dial tones) parameter.

Second, you will probably want to reduce the amount of time the modem stays connected to the line after dialing. Normally, the modem stays connected for about 30 seconds after the dialing process is complete. During this time, it degrades the quality of the phone connection and sometimes sends an annoying, ear-splitting signal as it looks for a computer connection on the other end. The command *S7=1* gives the user one second after dialing to pick up the phone before the modem disconnects the line. You can set this to any value; typical values are between 1 and 30.

Finally, you may want to reduce the volume of the modem's built-in speaker, if it has one, by the command *L0* (that's a zero, not the letter *O*). Some modems are quite loud while dialing, and the noise can be aggravating to others (particularly in a work environment) besides jarring the user who is next to the modem.

With a Hayes-compatible modem, all these commands are set with a single set of parameters enclosed in quotation marks. They start with the letters *AT*, which is the way the Mac gets the modem's attention and informs it that what follows is intended for use by the modem directly and not by the software running in the Mac. To dial a number such as 555-1234 with a modem and the previous settings, place the following **dial** command in your script:

```
dial "555-1234" with modem "ATDTS7=1L0"
```

For the most part, modems are forgiving about spaces and the order in which commands are given.

HyperCard's Smart Dialing Helps

Two facilities in HyperCard assist you in carrying out **dial** commands more easily in your scripts. First, several built-in buttons in the Button Ideas stack are shaped like telephones and have dialing instructions built into them. You can cut and paste these buttons into your stacks and get instant, programming-free access to the program's telephone dialing capability. Second, every copy of HyperCard comes with a Phone stack to select the proper dialing method and other aids to make dialing the phone easy.

Built-in buttons

From the standard Home card, click on the Button Ideas icon. The screen displays an index card containing, among other things, an entry for home and business buttons that looks like Figure 18-1.

 Home, Business

Figure 18-1. Button Ideas stack index entry for phone buttons

When you click on this button, you are taken to a card of buttons that looks like Figure 18-2. Any telephone-shaped button on this card can be cut using the **button** tool and then pasted into your stack. Each of these buttons contains a script like this:

```
on mouseUp
   get the selection
   if it is empty then ask "Dial what number?"
   if it is not empty then
      push this card
      visual effect zoom open
      go to stack "Phone"
      dial it
      pop card
   end if
end mouseUp
```

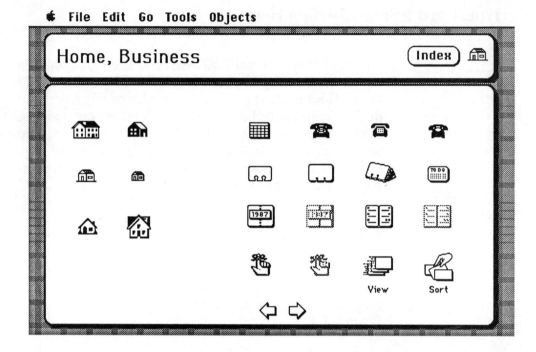

Figure 18-2. Phone buttons in Button Ideas stack

With the exception of the purpose of the Phone stack, which we discuss in the next section, this script is self-explanatory. It looks in the *selection* for a phone number to dial. If the *selection* contains nothing, it then asks the user for the number to dial. You can substitute any other container name for the *selection* or add others to search through before asking the user for the number to dial.

The Phone stack

HyperCard has obligingly built in a stack called Phone, which can take care of some housekeeping chores related to telephone dialing that your scripts can use to great benefit. In a sense, this stack adds some "intelligence" to a phone dialing script's capabilities. You can examine the Phone stack without dialing a number by going to the stack directly with a **go** command or a menu choice. When you open this one-card stack, you see a display similar to that shown in Figure 18-3.

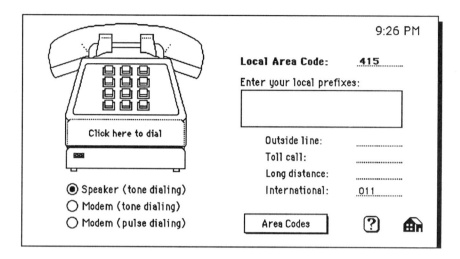

Figure 18-3. One-Card Phone stack

As you can see, this card provides several types of assistance in the dialing process. These include

- selection of type of dialing

- filter for local area code and prefix

- prefix for obtaining access to an outside line

- prefixes for long-distance and international dialing

- a link button to the Area Codes stack

By clicking one of the radio buttons in the lower-left corner of the card, the user can change the type of dialing. The default is tone dialing through a modem.

The local area code filter is quite handy. If your user's Address stack has phone numbers stored so that all of them have area codes, even local calls, the Phone stack will bypass dialing the local area code if it encounters it as the first three digits in a number. This is important because in many parts of the country dialing the local area code results in the call being intercepted by phone company equipment with a recording.

If users of your script are dialing through a central dialing system like a PBX or switchboard, they might be required to dial a 9 to access a public line outside the company's internal lines. HyperCard pre-sets this field to a 9, but you can change it or remove it entirely (as we've done) if you aren't using such a phone system. Similarly, some phone systems require users to dial a 1 for a long-distance call, and others do not. The long-distance prefix field can be used for this 1 or for an access code for a long-distance service supplier. International calls usually require an 011 prefix.

Finally, a button on this card lets the user link to the stack where the area codes for hundreds of American cities are stored. This is not in itself intelligence that is accessible to your script, though you could obviously add a link if you want.

Using HyperCard for Telecommunications

Clearly, HyperCard was not intended to be used to design and build scripts for computer-to-computer telecommunications. Its dialing capability does not include many features needed for such dialing and communication links.

Nonetheless, many early HyperTalk programmers began to work on the idea of developing full-scale telecommunications stacks. To do this, however, you have to design and include external commands and functions (discussed in detail in Chapter 23) to handle many of the tasks for which HyperTalk has no built-in facilities.

Summary

In this chapter, you became acquainted with the HyperTalk **dial** command and how it works for direct phone dialing and modem dialing. You also learned about HyperCard's built-in buttons and Phone stack capabilities, which your scripts can use to make it easy to include useful dialing routines in your stacks.

Chapter 19 is the last chapter that discusses HyperTalk commands and functions. It focuses on language features involved with scripts themselves and with the passing of information in HyperTalk.

CHAPTER

19

Script-Related Commands and User-Defined Functions

In this chapter, you will learn about

- the **edit script** command and its uses

- the **wait** command

- using and manipulating parameters in HyperTalk scripts

- defining your own functions and using them in scripts

Using the *edit script* Command

If you are designing stacks to be used by technical people, particularly utilities for other stack developers to use such as those discussed in Chapter 24, you may find it useful to know how to use the **edit script** command. When HyperTalk encounters this command, it opens the script editing window for the object whose identification is supplied as an argument. Here is the command's syntax:

```
edit script of <object>
```

You should be judicious in your use of this command because it gives the user complete access to the script. If you design a stack for a non-technical user but the script occasionally requires modification or customization, consider using the less intimidating method of **put**ting the script into a variable, modifying the variable, and then **set**ting the script to the contents of the modified variable. This technique is discussed in detail in Chapter 17 where scripts are treated as properties of their associated HyperCard objects.

Although you can enter this command from the Message box, you will probably never do so because it is easier to hold down the Shift key and double-click on a field or button to get at its script. You can use the **edit script** command to edit the script of the present script, card, or background, or some other script, card, or background. If you want to edit a script for an object that is not on the screen, this command can be a good shortcut.

The *wait* Command

We have used the **wait** command quite a few times in the book without explaining it. Its action is quite apparent, but it does have some nuances worth noting.

The command has three forms of syntax:

```
wait [for] <number> [ticks]|seconds
wait until <true/false>
wait while <true/false>
```

Using the first form, the minimal command you can issue looks like this:

```
wait 20
```

This results in the script pausing for 20 ticks, where one tick is 1/60 second. So the pause here would be about 1/3 second.

HyperTalk assumes you want to use ticks unless you supply the word **seconds**, as in:

```
wait 3 seconds
```

If you want to use ticks, you need not supply the label, though you may want to do so for readability. You can also put the word **for** after the **wait** command for readability; it is a throw-away word that HyperTalk ignores.

NOTE

Beginning with Version 1.2, HyperCard recognizes the singular word **second.** This makes the use of one-second delays read more naturally. Seconds may also be abbreviated **secs,** or singularly as **sec.**

The second and third forms of the syntax for the **wait** command use Boolean expressions to determine how long to wait or, more accurately, when to stop waiting. The **wait until** command continues to hold in a waiting state until the expression in the Boolean true/false argument becomes true, then the script continues processing. Conversely, **wait while** continues to wait only as long as the Boolean argument is true, resuming script operation as soon as it becomes false.

An obvious use of the **wait until** command, and one we've used a few times in this book, is to give the user control over when to proceed to the next step in processing. Generally, use the **mouseClick** function to determine when to continue, and let the user know that clicking the mouse ends the pause:

```
wait until the mouseClick
```

Parameters in HyperTalk

Virtually every system message in HyperCard and most messages you design in your scripts include one or more parameters.

When you use a **go** command, for example, you supply one or more parameters naming the destination card, background, or stack:

```
go card "Testing"
go stack "My Contacts"
go first card of stack "My Contacts"
```

When commands and messages involve parameters, you can use built-in HyperTalk functions to find out how many parameters are being sent with the message, place the entire parameter list into a variable or container, or extract and use a specific parameter by its position in the parameter string.

How many parameters?

To determine how many parameters are sent with a message, use **the paramCount.** Because there is only one actively processing message or command at any moment, this function ironically requires no parameters. It simply returns an integer indicating how many parameters were passed with the last message.

You might use this construct, for example, where it is important to your handler that a certain number of parameters be passed before it can carry out its task:

```
on openHandler
  if the paramCount <3 then ask "I need three arguments."
end openHandler
```

Extracting individual parameters

Quite often when a message or command with parameters is sent to a handler you've designed (as opposed to a system message handler), you will need to pull the parameters apart and use them in different ways throughout the script. You can extract any parameter from a string with **the param.** Its syntax looks like this:

```
the param of <integer>
```

To extract the first parameter, you simply code:

```
the param of 1
```

Using this method, you can extract any individual parameter or combination of parameters for later manipulation and analysis in the handler. For example, if you've defined a handler called *grabWords* that receives two parameters, one of which is the number of the first word to be extracted from line 1 of a field and the other of which is the number of the last word to be extracted, you might write something like this (in part):

```
on grabWords
  put the param of 1 into startWord
  put the param of 2 into endWord
  repeat with counter = startWord to endWord
    put word counter of line 1 of field 1 after holder
  end repeat
  --put holder somewhere
end grabWords
```

You can use **the param** to identify the message being sent as well. The message name, which is always one word, is numbered 0 so that extracting it requires a construct like this:

```
put the param of 0 into lastMessageName
```

Storing the parameter string

The third parameter handling function in HyperTalk lets you manage the entire string of parameters as one entity, typically storing it for later use. The function called **the params** returns a string containing the entire message, including the message name. You can then use the usual chunking methods to extract whatever portions of the string you need. This function does not require any parameters.

Normally, you will probably use **the params** function to store the parameter string for later use in a handler that may be sending or dealing with other messages as it executes.

Remember that all three of these parameter-related functions only deal with the most recent message sent (i.e., the one that is being executed or processed at the time).

Defining and Using Your Own Functions

As we have mentioned, you are not restricted to the use of HyperCard's built-in functions and commands. You can define your own messages and handlers, simply by typing the name of the message as the parameter to an **on** construct. (See the discussion of this issue in Chapter 5.)

Similarly, you can define your own functions in HyperCard. After these functions are defined, they can be used similarly to (though not identically with) built-in HyperCard functions. The framework for defining a function of your own looks like this:

```
function <functionName> [parameter[,parameter]]
  -- list of commands that make up the function
  return <result>
end <functionName>
```

The key words **function**, **return,** and **end** are required in any function handler you define. The value following the **return** key word is the value returned by the function when it is called.

After you've defined a new function, it is treated identically with built-in HyperCard system functions. Among other things, this means if you define a function that can be used in many stacks, consider placing its definition in your Home stack. HyperCard searches through the hierarchy for functions exactly the same way as it does for commands. Another implication of this treatment of user-defined functions as being identical to system-defined functions is that if you write a new function with the same name as a system-defined function, the new function supersedes the one supplied by HyperCard. This requires some careful planning and thought, but you can supply customized versions of built-in HyperCard functions this way.

It is also worth noting that we need not use the same parameter names in the function handler itself and in the script line that calls the handler. In our example below, you will see that we name the parameter *theString* in the handler but when we call the function, we supply the parameter's name as *userEntry*. It is the parameter's relative position in the command and not its name that determines how it will be treated.

Here's an example of a user-defined function that takes a string as an argument, closes up any spaces in it, and capitalizes the first letter of each word if they are not already capitalized. We use this function for creating neatly formatted names for objects from user-entered strings that don't always follow our rules for neatness.

```
function makeNeat theString
    put the length of theString into len
    put "False" into newWord
    repeat with counter = 1 to len
        put char counter of theString into currChar
        if newWord is "true" then
          put upperCase(currChar) after outString
          put "False" into newWord
          next repeat
        end if
        if currChar is not space then
          put currChar after outString
        else
          put "true" into newWord
        end if
    end repeat
    return outString
end makeNeat
```

To use this function, treat it like any other HyperCard function. Here is a handler that simply tests the function:

```
on mouseUp
    ask "Enter a string to convert"
    put it into userEntry
    put makeNeat(userEntry)
end mouseUp
```

Just to be complete, here is the other function used by **makeNeat**, called **upperCase**. It looks at a character passed to it as a parameter. If that character is not already uppercase, it converts it to uppercase. Otherwise, it leaves it unchanged.

```
function upperCase letter
    get the charToNum of letter
    if it >= 97 and it <= 122 then
        subtract 32 from it
        return the numToChar of it
    else
        return letter
    end if
end upperCase
```

As we said at the beginning of this discussion of user-defined functions, there is a slight difference between the way your functions and HyperCard's built-in functions are called. When you call a HyperCard function, you usually must precede it with the word **the,** then you simply supply the name of the function and its parameters as a string. For example:

```
return the numToChar of it
```

But when you call a user-defined function, you must supply the parameters in parentheses. Furthermore, you must supply the parentheses even if the function requires no parameters. The parentheses are HyperTalk's indicator that you are invoking a user-defined function. (You can also use the parenthesized approach to call HyperCard functions in certain cases, but we discourage the practice so that user defined functions are more clearly detectable.)

Note, too, that (as with HyperCard's built-in functions) you cannot simply type the name of the function and its parameter(s), as in:

```
makeNeat("This is a test")
```

You must tell HyperCard what to do with the result of the function. Generally, this involves using a **put** command to store or display the result.

Summary

In this chapter, you learned about some useful, though somewhat miscellaneous, commands that deal with script-level issues. You saw how to use the **edit script** command to give technical users easy and immediate access to scripts they want to change in your stack. You learned about the various forms of the **wait** command and its use in scripts.

You also examined the use of parameter passing operations and the built-in HyperCard functions for manipulating parameter lists. Finally, you learned the form for defining your own functions and saw a detailed example of how to do so.

In Chapter 20, you will find a useful potpourri of Hyper-Talk tips, hints, traps, and techniques assembled from a variety of sources.

HyperTalk Tips, Traps, and Techniques

This chapter includes some suggestions and techniques to improve your scripts and make you more effective and efficient. It includes:

- tips, which are "insider" hints about things you can do to make your stacks snappier and your programming more efficient

- traps, which are potential bugs and pitfalls in HyperTalk

- techniques, which are several handler ideas for carrying out tasks that you might have occasional or even frequent need to do but which may not be entirely self-evident

Wherever possible, we've given the source of information on these suggestions and ideas. Many of them we created and others were thought of or suggested by several people or are relatively trivial. The absence of credit does not mean we claim the idea as original.

This chapter cannot possibly contain all the tips that an experienced scripter develops over months and years of experience with HyperTalk. Consider joining a user group, signing up for an electronic bulletin board system, or contacting Apple Computer about becoming a Certified Developer so that you can keep abreast of new hints, techniques, and developments in Hyper-Card.

Power Tips

Let us begin with some tips about using and scripting in Hyper-Talk.

Pop-up fields

Although HyperCard is a highly graphic and visual environment, it is often used to present information in text or hypertext form. With scrolling fields capable of storing 32,000-plus characters of information, the amount of text content in a card or stack can become overwhelming. The careful HyperCard stack designer looks for ways to minimize the impact of large amounts of text. One excellent way is to use *pop-up fields* on cards.

A pop-up field is one that stays hidden until summoned to the forefront, generally by some action of the user. The advantage of such fields is that they stay out of the way until needed and retreat politely into the ether when they are no longer required. The disadvantage is that it is all but impossible to guarantee browsers will ever see them unless they want to do so. As a result, you should not use pop-up fields for essential information. Typical uses include help functions and About boxes.

Users generally activate pop-up fields by pressing a button. Often, the button is associated with an icon like one of those shown in Figure 20-1. When users click on one of these buttons, the pop-up field appears. After users have read the field's contents, they generally expect to be able to click on the field to close it, though you may supply a visible button to close the field.

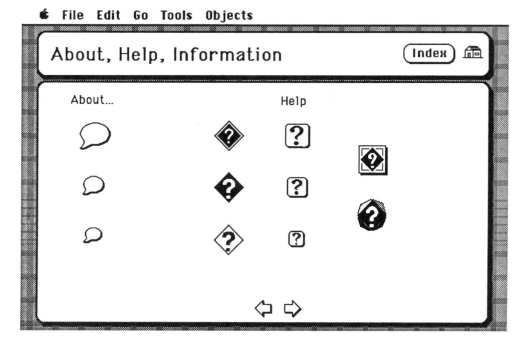

Figure 20-1. Icons for About and Help buttons

To create a pop-up field and the appropriate management buttons on a card, follow these steps.

1. Create a new field.

2. Select the type, size, and position of the field. Your choices depend on how you want the pop-up field to blend or contrast with surrounding objects on the card. Then use the browse tool to enter some text into the field at least for testing.

3. Create two new buttons. Use icons if appropriate.

4. Attach the following script to one of the buttons:

```
on mouseUp
  show card field 1
  show button "Close It"
end mouseUp
```

5. Name the second button Close It and attach this script to it:

```
on mouseUp
  hide button "Close It"
  hide card field 1
end mouseUp
```

6. Put the following script at the card, background, or stack level as appropriate (depending on where this action is most efficiently carried out):

```
on openCard -- or other system message name as appropriate
  hide card field 1
  hide button "Close It"
end openCard
```

7. Open the card so that the field is hidden (see Figure 20-2).

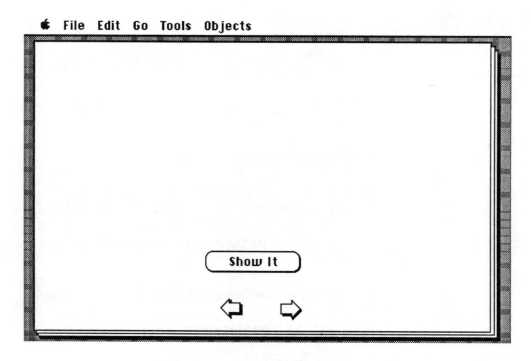

Figure 20-2. Pop-up field hidden on card

8. Press the first button (we've labeled it Show It), and the field and its associated close button appears. See Figure 20-3.

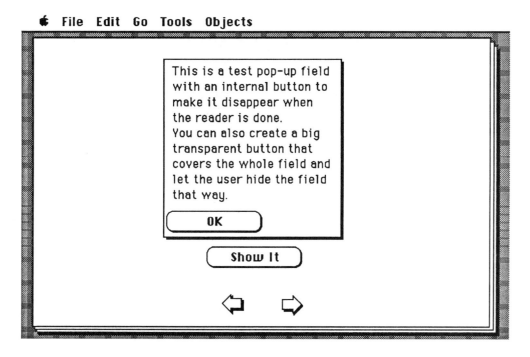

Figure 20-3. Pop-up field and related button displayed

There is no overhead associated with the card-level script at step 6; if the field and the button are already hidden, throughput is slowed negligibly, if at all. Putting it there assures that the user doesn't push the Show It button, read the field, and then move to the next card without closing it. Alternatively, you can put a reverse script to hide the field and button on a **closeCard** condition.

To make the entire field a button on which the user can click to close the field, create a large transparent button to cover the field, but recognize that the user cannot edit the underlying text. You can also use a **wait until the mouseClick** command to enable the user to click anywhere to hide the field.

Saving disk space with pictures

Pictures occupy relatively large amounts of disk space. In the interest of keeping your stacks as small as possible, think carefully about the use of art in your stacks. For example, if you have a picture that appears on many cards with a particular background but not on all of them, it may seem that you should just copy and paste the picture onto each card where it's needed. But it is usually more efficient to store the picture on the background and then simply obscure it on the cards where it is not needed.

To do this, just follow these steps:

1. Get into background editing mode by typing Command-B or choosing Background from the Edit menu.

2. Create the artwork.

3. Return to normal card editing mode by again typing Command-B or choosing Background from the Edit menu.

4. Get to a card on which you do not want the artwork to appear.

5. Use one of the selection tools to select the area to be obscured on this card.

6. Choose Opaque from the Paint menu.

7. Return to browse mode. The area in question is opaque but still exists on all other cards.

Using this opaquing technique is more efficient than using the eraser because the eraser places more graphics on the card, overlaying the background graphic with a region of white.

Speeding up *show card* operations

The following power-user tip comes from *Windoid* Issue #1. (*Windoid* is a newsletter published by the Apple HyperCard User Group, or AHUG. Details for obtaining it are in Appendix C.) If your script calls for the use of the **show card** command or one of its variations, you can greatly accelerate execution of these commands by pre-caching the cards. HyperCard, as you know, keeps track of the last 42 cards seen by the user. It can move quickly to any card on this list because of the way it manages the memory that points to these cards.

Put a script like the following into your stack and compare the results of using **show card** routines before and after:

```
on openStack
  set lockScreen to true
  show all cards
  set lockScreen to false
end openStack
```

The user is aware of only a slight delay here, but later execution increases noticeably and makes up for this momentary pause.

Traps to Avoid

Here are two obscure traps you should know about.

Watch out for user interruptions

One stack designer we know had a problem with a script that included a **print this card** command in the middle of a handler. If the user typed Command-period to stop the printing of the card, HyperTalk stopped executing the script. That's the behavior you'd expect, but it wasn't what was desired!

There is no way for a script to intercept or disable the Command-period typed by the user. To avoid having this cause a problem with printing, make sure any **print** command is the last one in a handler. If users think they are interrupting the print and end up stopping your handler, you will be back where you expected to be in any event. Printing is one of the few actions users might try to stop with Command-period, so this simple precaution can reduce troubles with interrupts.

Handler names and special characters

You cannot use a special character in a handler name. Hyper-Talk stops parsing when it encounters the special character — even if it is not a reserved word — and generally poses an error message like that shown in Figure 20-4.

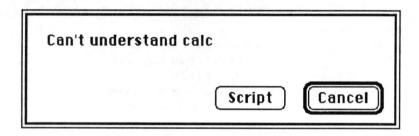

Can't understand calc

Script   Cancel

Figure 20-4. Result of using a special character in a handler name

In the example depicted in Figure 20-4, the handler is called *calc+*, but notice that HyperTalk indicates it is having trouble dealing with *calc*. The plus sign is ignored.

Techniques for Special Needs

The balance of this chapter consists of a dozen useful techniques for doing things in HyperTalk that may not be self-evident.

Double-clicking a button

HyperCard deviates from the previously accepted Apple Human Interface Guidelines in a number of ways. One of the most readily apparent is that it carries out tasks by the single-click of a button rather than requiring the traditional double-click action. The designers of HyperCard found in their studies that some people had trouble double-clicking, so they designed HyperCard to be easier for more people to use.

But what if you *want* the user to double-click on a button to activate something? For example, you might define a transparent button with an icon so that all the user sees is the icon. This stack might be used by someone who is accustomed to double-clicking. (We should note that it is alright for the user to double-click on a button even without special handling because HyperCard simply ignores the second click.)

Here is a script to handle double-clicking on a button. We found this script originally in *Windoid* Issue #1:

```
on mouseUp
 put the ticks into originalTicks
 repeat until the mouseClick
 if the ticks - originalTicks > 30 then exit mouseUp
 end repeat
 -- Put here whatever you want the button to do when
 -- double-clicked
end mouseUp
```

This handler is activated when the user releases the mouse in the object with which the handler is associated. It then stores the value of **ticks** into a local variable and waits for another mouse-button press. If the first and second click occur within 30 ticks (about 1/2 second) of each other, the action called for in the event of a double-click is executed. You can adjust the time delay between clicks by changing the value in the fourth line of the handler.

We modified this handler slightly to allow different actions depending on whether the user single-clicks or double-clicks the icon:

```
on mouseUp
    put the ticks into originalTicks
    wait 30 ticks
    if the mouseClick then
  -- react to a double-click
  else
  -- react to a single-click
  end if
end mouseUp
```

Now you can have one button that works differently depending on whether the user single-clicks or double-clicks on it.

Accumulating card fields into a running total

If your stack involves calculations, you may need to accumulate the values in a field into a special variable or field. The following script accomplishes this task nicely and is flexible and efficient enough for general use. You can use the **put** statement in the last line of the handler to do whatever you want with the accumulated *total*.

```
on mouseUp
  set lockScreen to true
  set lockMessages to true
  put 0 into total
  put the number of cards into loopEnd
  repeat with counter = 1 to loopEnd
    put the number of lines in field 1 into temp
    repeat with newCounter = 1 to temp
      add line newCounter of field 1 to total
    end repeat
    go next
  end repeat
  set lockScreen to false
  set lockMessages to false
  put total
end mouseUp
```

This script works for a stack with any number of cards containing a field with any number of lines as long as each line contains a numeric value. You can also add a check to determine if the line contains a number and branch if it does not.

Tool selection with the keyboard

During the design of a stack, you probably find yourself switching back and forth among the browse, button, and field tools and perhaps among one or more painting tools as well. The tear-off

Tools menu certainly makes this selection easy, but if you don't want that windoid around while you design something or if you prefer not to take your hands off the keyboard, you've probably wished for keyboard equivalents for the tools.

Wish no longer. Here are two techniques for changing the tool currently in use to the one you want without using the mouse.

The first uses a keystroke followed by a carriage return to select a specific tool in any order. Because Command-Tab always picks the browse tool, we don't include a handler to choose it. Put these scripts in the Home stack if you want them always available. Then, any time you want to use the button tool, just press *b* and Return. (Case, as usual, is insignificant.)

NOTE

It is not possible without extending HyperTalk with an XFCN or XCMD (see Chapter 22) to trap for a single keypress event. So you'll have to be content with the two-key sequence described here unless you're adventuresome enough to generate an external routine to handle the one-key approach. Frankly, we haven't felt the savings would be worth the effort.

The pattern for the handlers is the same in all cases:

```
on letter
  choose toolName
end letter
```

What letters you assign to the tools is up to you. We use mnemonics, but you may want to use, for example, the numbers on the numeric keypad in some configuration that's easy to remember.

```
on b
  choose button tool
end b
on f
  choose field tool
end f
on l
  choose lasso tool
end l
on e
  choose eraser tool
end e
on h
  choose brush tool
end h
on t
  choose text tool
end t
on s
  choose spray can tool
end s
on m
  choose select tool -- "m" for "marquee"
end m
on d
  choose line tool -- "d" for "drawing"
end d
on x
  choose rectangle tool - "x" for "boX"
end x
on o
  choose oval tool
end o
on p
  choose bucket tool -- "p" for "paint bucket"
end p
```

With these handlers in place on your Home stack, you can press *t* and the Return key any time you wish and immediately be using the text tool. This can be pretty handy.

```
┌─────────────────────────────────────────────────┐
│                      NOTE                         │
│                                                   │
│  For this approach to be useful, you must turn on│
│  the **blind typing** property on your Preferences│
│  card in the Home stack. Otherwise, the Message  │
│  box will have to be visible anytime you want to │
│  use this technique. If it's not, you'll simply  │
│  be greeted by one of the Mac's beep sounds (or  │
│  some other sound if you have a Mac II). Also,   │
│  you cannot activate any tool once you are using │
│  one of the paint tools. HyperCard effectively   │
│  disables blind typing when a paint tool is in   │
│  effect to enable you to use power keys, even if │
│  you have not turned the power keys feature on in│
│  the Preferences card of the Home stack.         │
└─────────────────────────────────────────────────┘
```

To facilitate selection of a smaller number of tools in a fixed rotation, you can use the Enter key to move from tool to tool. The following script allows you to rotate among the browse, button, field, and text tools. It comes in two handlers. The first sets up the list of tools and initializes the counter to use the browse tool. The second increments a counter each time the Enter key is pressed, resets it to 1 if it goes past 4, and chooses the tool next in the rotation. Put these handlers at the Home card level and you can use the Enter key technique anywhere during stack design.

```
on openCard
  global toolList, enterCount
  put "browse" && "button" && "field" && "text" into toolList
  put 1 into enterCount
end openCard

on enterKey
  global toolList, enterCount
  add 1 to enterCount
  if enterCount=5 then put 1 into enterCount
  put word enterCount of toolList into toolChoice
  do "choose" && toolChoice && "tool"
end enterKey
```

You can customize these handlers. You can add or change the tools that are selectable and the order in which they are selected. If you make the list longer than four tools, change the line in the **on enterKey** handler that resets the *enterCount* variable to 1 so that the variable is reset when the value is one higher than the number of tools you are including. If you want to be flexible, you can use **put** to find out how many tools are currently in the *toolList* and then use that variable for the test. In that event, the **on enterKey** handler would look similar to this:

```
on enterKey
  global toolList, enterCount
  put number of words in toolList into maxTool
  add 1 to enterCount
  if enterCount=maxTool + 1 then put 1 into enterCount
  put word enterCount of toolList into toolChoice
  do "choose" && toolChoice && "tool"
end enterKey
```

Incidentally, we could carry out this processing without defining a global variable by testing for the value of the current tool and changing to the next one in the cycle:

```
on enterKey
  if the tool is "browse tool" then choose button tool
  -- and so on for the other tool combinations
end enterKey
```

Script-modifying scripts

In an advanced stack design — one, for example, that implements an expert system — it may be necessary for a script to modify another script before it is executed.

> ### WARNING
>
> It is considered bad programming style to write programs that modify themselves or other programs. This is no less true of HyperTalk than it is of, for example, LISP or Pascal. You should generally try to find a way other than dynamic script modification to accomplish your task. The text contains a brief discussion of such alternatives.

When you have a script that modifies itself, be aware that the modified script does not execute until the next time its message is received. Let's take a simple example:

```
on enterKey
  put script of me into tempScript
  put "beep 5" into line 5 of tempScript
  set script of me to tempScript
  beep 1
end enterKey
```

It would *seem* from an examination of this script that the third line modifies the number of beeps to be sounded before the **beep 1** line is encountered. You might therefore expect to hear five beeps the first time you execute this handler. But that is not the case. While HyperCard is executing a script, it puts the script into a special buffer. When you modify the script, you are modifying the stored copy but the original continues to execute. However, after you carry out the previous script, you can open the script and find that line 5 has indeed been changed to **beep 5**. The next time you press the Enter key, you'll hear five beeps.

Using **put** commands, you can carry out major surgery on a script as a consequence of executing it or another script. You can add new commands with **put before** and **put after** or, as we have seen in our small example, modify existing lines by replacing them with **put into** commands.

Most of the time when script modification seems like the best or only way to accomplish something, you can find a better, safer way. Programs and scripts that modify themselves or are modified by other scripts "on the fly" can pose maintenance nightmares. In this example, you might think you need to change the script under some circumstances so that it beeps more than once. But by defining a global variable, you can accomplish the same thing without script modification. For example, if you want to modify the number of beeps only if today is Thursday, you might modify the previous script example as follows:

```
on enterKey
  put the date into today
  convert today to dateItems
  if item 7 of today=5 then -- 0=Sunday; 5=Thursday
    put script of me into tempScript
    put "beep 5" into line 13 of tempScript
    beep 5
  end if
  beep 1
end enterKey
```

But it is more straightforward and safer to set up the handler like this:

```
on enterKey
 put the date into today
 convert today to dateItems
 if item 7 of today=5 then beep 5 else beep 1
end enterKey
```

Clearly, you would never modify a script dynamically for something this trivial. But if you examine situations where you believe you need to carry out such modifications, you will usually find that you can avoid the seeming necessity by changing a variable or installing some new logic.

One place script modification is probably defensible is in set-up routines. Suppose you have a handler that executes only the first time a user opens your stack, and you don't want it to execute later. You can simply delete it from the script so that it won't appear on all subsequent uses of the stack. This can be a good way to post a notice about piracy, for example.

Making words in fields active

There are many occasions when we want to let the user click on a word in a field and then do something depending on which word is clicked. But there's an apparent dilemma here. The mouse messages — **mouseDown**, **mouseStillDown**, and **mouse-Up** — are only sent to a field if its **lockText** property is set to true. But when the field's text is locked, the user can't click on anything in the field because the cursor never becomes the I-beam, which lets the user edit the text.

The solution is to fool HyperTalk into thinking that the word has been double-clicked after the text has been unlocked, then resetting the lock on the text. Here's a skeleton of such a handler:

```
on mouseDown -- note:  not a mouseUp handler!
  set lockText of me to false -- must start out locked
  click at the clickLoc
  click at the clickLoc
  -- process the selection (see text discussion)
  set lockText of me to true
end mouseDown
```

After the two **click** lines execute, the word that is at the **clickLoc** is highlighted. In HyperCard terms, that means it is now identified by the special variable the *selection*. So you can now do whatever you need to do based on the content of the *selection*. In the following example, we've used this technique to create what amounts to a field used as a menu from which the user chooses an action. Figure 20-5 shows what the rudimentary card looks like. The field is used as a list of choices from which the user makes a selection by clicking once.

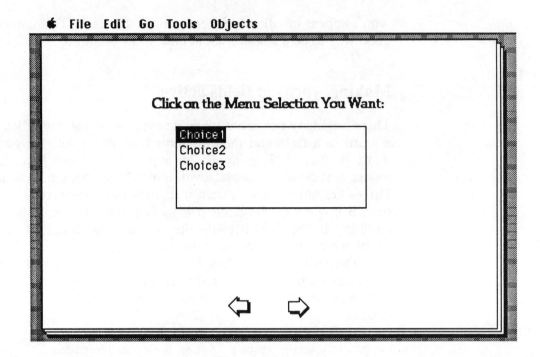

Figure 20-5.   Using a field as a menu

First, the field script:

```
on mouseDown
    set lockText of me to false
    click at the clickLoc
    click at the clickLoc
    if the selection is empty then
        set lockText of me to true
        exit mouseDown
    end if
    send the selection
    set lockText of me to true
end mouseDown
```

Note that the framework of this script is identical to the handler outlined earlier. Unless the *selection* is empty (as would happen if the user clicks on a blank line in the field), the handler simply **send**s the message so that an appropriate handler can deal with it. Here's the simplified but instructive card script that accompanies the field script:

```
on Choice1
   play "boing"
end Choice1
on Choice2
   play "harpsichord"
end Choice2
on Choice3
   beep 3
end Choice3
```

Obviously, your script will do something more exciting or useful than play sounds, but the pattern will be the same. It is also not necessary that any or all of the handlers for the menu selections be on the same card or background as the field — as long as they are higher up the HyperTalk hierarchy or you use an explicit **send** command to get the message to the right handler.

Making navigation buttons zoom

Here's a quick technique we've found useful. You can make any navigation button double as a zoom button by adding a handler similar to the following to its existing script:

```
on mouseStillDown
  wait 30
  go next
end mouseStillDown
```

Now if users click on a button to move forward through your stack (a right arrow), they move one card. But if they hold down the button, they move swiftly through the stack a card at a time. You can use a **go previous** in place of line 3 of this sample script on a left-pointing arrow and get the same effect. By experimenting with the delay in line 2, you can make the movement very fast or quite slow.

Note that this script works only if the navigation button is a background button, but such buttons are usually on the background.

Highlighting text when selected

One problem with having the user select text in a field is there is
no feedback to indicate that text has been selected. If you are using the *selection* to indicate the word the user has clicked on, the
highlighting of the selected text gives that feedback. But you are
limited to actions in fields with locked text, and then only one
word at a time.

Another problem is that inverting text — i.e., making text
white on a black background — is sometimes distracting and not
aesthetic. When you want to provide visual feedback on text
being selected, you can use the technique described in this
section. It highlights the text with a rectangle when the mouse
button is pressed on top of the text and removes it when the
button is released. This unobtrusive form of highlighting works
well for fields where the text is locked.

The key to this technique is changing the **style** property of
the field surrounding the text by means of a button script like
this:

```
on mouseUp
    set style of card field 1 to transparent
end mouseUp
on mouseDown
    set style of card field 1 to rectangle
end mouseDown
```

This button overlays the text to be highlighted, and the text in
turn is all contained in one field. You can use adjacent fields to
permit the user to select any of several words or phrases. Each
field then has its own button.

Finding text by first letter of field

If you have a stack sorted alphabetically on the contents of a
field, you may want to be able to move directly to the cards
whose sorted field starts with a specific letter. But using Hyper-
Card's **find** feature won't do the trick because it stops on every
card that has the designated character anywhere in the field.

This script stops only on cards that have the desired letter in the first position of background field 1:

```
on locate letter
  set lockScreen to true
  repeat with counter = 1 to number of cards
    find letter in field 1
      if first character of field 1 is letter
        then
        -- process accordingly
      end if
    go next
  end repeat
  set lockScreen to false
end locate
```

Send the message **locate "h"** to this handler and it locates each card in which *h* or *H* is the first letter of background field 1.

Check box selection

Macintosh users are accustomed to seeing check boxes on lots of screens. Unlike radio buttons (discussed next), check boxes are not mutually exclusive. Of any given set of such button shapes, any number from zero to all of them can be selected. Also unlike radio buttons, a check box should de-select itself if it is selected when the user presses on it and select itself if it isn't already selected. There is a very efficient way of dealing with this requirement:

```
on mouseUp
  set the hilite of me to not the hilite of me
end mouseUp
```

The **not** turns the **hilite** property of the button into the opposite of what it was before the button was pressed.

Radio button management

Radio buttons are very much a part of the Macintosh interface. Many dialog boxes include one or more sets of these buttons, and users have become accustomed to using them to select an

option. Radio buttons are generally grouped into sets of two or
more mutually exclusive alternatives in such a way that selecting
one and "turning it on" results in all the others in the same group
being de-selected, or turned off. They get their name from the resemblance between them and car-radio station-selection buttons,
where pushing any one of them selects a specific station and de-
selects the previously selected station.

The management of radio buttons is one aspect of Mac programming that HyperTalk does not automate. You have to
handle it yourself. You define a set of buttons as a group simply
by the way you treat the user's interaction with them. Your script
has to turn off a selected button when another, incompatible one
is selected by the user.

In HyperTalk, there is one additional issue. If you put radio
buttons in the background of a stack but you want those buttons
to have card-specific values, you need to override HyperTalk's
normal processing, which is to have a background button appear
the same on all cards.

Grouping and selecting radio buttons. Let's look at a small
example of a card containing two sets of radio buttons, each set
having two buttons. This is small enough to be manageable, and it
demonstrates all the principles and techniques in dealing with
radio buttons in HyperTalk. The card we will work with is shown
in Figure 20-6. The two-button set on the left controls sound
effects. (This could be done with one button, with on meaning
sound effects are on and off meaning sound effects are off, but this
configuration serves our learning purposes better.) The right
group lets the browser decide to send information to a disk file or
the printer.

When we click on Sound Effects On, we expect the Sound
Effects Off button to be turned off. The opposite is also true.
Here are the portions of the scripts that handle this processing,
with the Sound Effects On button's script listed first:

```
on mouseUp
  set hilite of me to true
  set hilite of button "Sound Effects Off" to true
end mouseUp
```

```
on mouseUp
  set hilite of me to true
  set hilite of button "Sound Effects On" to false
end mouseUp
```

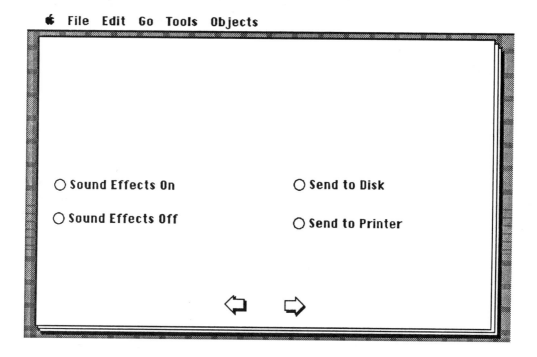

Figure 20-6. Radio button demonstration card

Similar scripts would manage the other group of buttons. Notice that even if the alternate button is already off or the selected one is already on, the handler sends appropriate **hilite** messages. There is little or no overhead to doing so, and this is more efficient than checking the status of a button before deciding whether it needs to have a message sent to it.

Where you have groups of several buttons, you will probably find it more efficient to design a repeat loop to turn off the other buttons. In this case, using the buttons' numbers, rather than their names, is appropriate. For example, suppose you have four buttons numbered 5-8. You want buttons 5, 7, and 8 to turn off when 6 is selected. Button 6's script could look something like this:

```
on mouseUp
 turnOn 6
end mouseUp
```

The handler that deals with the **turnOn** message, then, would be at the card level or higher and could look like this:

```
on turnOn buttonNo
 repeat with counter = 5 to 8
  if buttonNo=counter then set hilite of button counter to true
else set hilite of button counter to false
 end repeat
end turnOn
```

This approach can be generalized to account for any button group as long as the buttons have consecutive layer numbers. You might pass two parameters with the **turnOn** message, the first parameter is the selected button's number and the second identifies its group:

```
on mouseUp
 turnOn 6,radioGroup1
end mouseUp
```

Now the **turnOn** handler needs to set the range of button numbers in each group. Otherwise it is identical to our previous handler:

```
on turnOn buttonNo, groupID
 if groupID = "radioGroup1" then
  put 1 into start
  put 5 into endButton
 else
  put 6 into start
  put 11 into endButton
 end if
 repeat with counter = start to endButton
  if buttonNo=counter then ¬
  set hilite of button counter to true else ¬
  set hilite of button counter to false
 end repeat
end turnOn
```

Setting card-specific values. If you have a series of cards with a common background and the background contains a set of radio buttons, you almost certainly want to be able to vary the contents of those buttons from card to card. But if you simply set up the stack and scripts as described previously, you won't achieve this objective. Each time you change the value of a radio button on one card, it changes on all cards. This is not the way HyperCard handles background buttons, so some scripting is required to get your stack to do what you want.

Basically, the strategy is simple. You store the values of all the buttons on a card in an invisible background field when the card is closed and restore the buttons' values based on those settings when the card is opened. One way to do this that is easy to understand and keep track of requires a hidden field where each line contains the word true or false and corresponds to the button number on that card (i.e., line 1 of the field has the value of button 1, line 2 that of button 2, and so forth).

Here is a sample of the handler that sets up the buttons correctly when the card is opened:

```
on openCard
  repeat with counter = 3 to 5
    set hilite of background button counter to ¬
    Line counter of field "Button Values"
  end repeat
end openCard
```

In this example, the radio button group consists of buttons 3-5 on the background. We leave the first two lines of the field blank (or put false in them because they're used for the two navigation arrows in this case) and then put true or false into the lines. You have to set up each field's initial values when you create the invisible field to contain the button values.

Now here's the handler that stores the buttons' values into the field Button Values when the card is closed:

```
on closeCard
  repeat with counter = 3 to 5
    put hilite of background button counter into ¬
    Line counter of field "Button Values"
  end repeat
end closeCard
```

Make the Button Values field invisible on each card and the user will not be distracted by its appearance and changing values.

Summary

In this chapter, you have picked up a few hints about dealing with scripting problems and their solution. Chapter 21 turns our attention to making HyperCard more powerful by adding to and supplementing the resources associated with it.

Extending HyperTalk with Resources

In this chapter, you will learn

- what resources are and how they figure in stacks

- where to find and how to create resources

- two techniques for moving resources into stacks

- how to use resources after they are in your stack

Resources and HyperTalk

The idea of a *resource* is central to any Macintosh programming. If you were developing applications on the Mac without the benefit of HyperTalk, you'd be spending a good deal of time defining, setting up, and managing resources. As it is, HyperTalk does all required resource management for you. But adding things like special sound effects, icons, and cursors to your stacks can make your stacks more interesting and effective.

What's a resource?

"Everything is a resource." That statement is only a slight simplification of the crucial role played by resources in Macintosh programming. All icons, cursors, windows, dialog boxes, controls, menus, and other visible elements of a Mac program are or can be resources. In addition, program code itself is a resource (we'll have more to say about code resources in Chapter 22).

In some ways, resources resemble HyperCard fields and buttons. They have a type, a name, an ID, and a position relative to their surroundings.

Where are resources stored?

But just saying "everything is a resource" and enumerating things that are resources hardly defines the term in any helpful way. You can think of resources in another way that might help you understand them better. But to understand this discussion, we need a slight diversion into the world of Macintosh files.

Every Macintosh file, without exception, has two *forks*: a data fork and a resource fork (see Figure 21-1). The data fork is managed by the program without any built-in or automatic assistance from Macintosh system software. The resource fork, on the other hand, is managed and accessed by means of the system's Resource Manager, a part of the powerful and extensive User Interface Toolbox that exists primarily in ROM on a Mac.

Quite often, a Macintosh program has an empty data fork. We don't know of any applications that have empty resource forks, though documents often do, particularly if they contain only text.

The non-empty resource fork of any Macintosh file has a structure like that shown in Figure 21-2. Each resource in a fork has two entries: a *resource map* entry that tells the system the type, number, name, and attributes of the resource, along with a pointer to the resource data itself and a *resource data* entry that completely describes the resource. Each type of resource — and there are several dozen identifiable types, some application-defined — has its own resource data format.

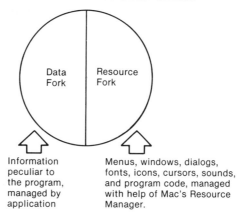

Figure 21-1. Two forks in a Mac file

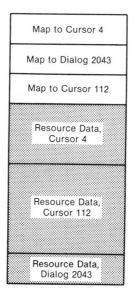

Figure 21-2. Structure of the resource fork

When you add resources to a stack, you are simply bringing in a new resource data entry describing that resource, and the Resource Manager builds an entry in the resource map to access that resource. Then, when you want to use the resource, all you do is tell the Resource Manager, in effect, "Go get me cursor 4," and it knows where to find it and what to do with it.

The role of resources in HyperCard

When you define a new button and click on the Icon button in the Button Definition dialog, you may notice that the buttons to which HyperCard takes you have numbers associated with them (see Figure 21-3). Each number is a resource identifier. In Figure 21-3, the icon has ID number 7012. Cursors and sound effects are also stored as resources in HyperCard.

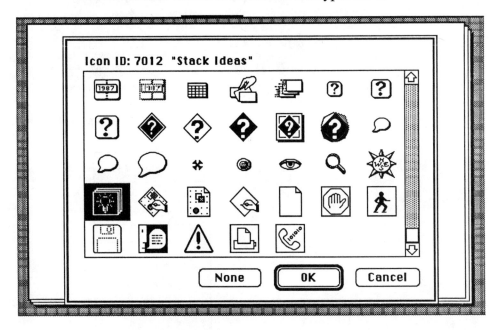

Figure 21-3. An icon has a resource number

Where Do Resources Come From?

Now that you have an idea about what resources are, you might be interested in adding some nifty new resource to the prize-winning stack you're constructing. But where do you find resources? There are at least four sources of resources:

- HyperCard itself includes quite a number of resources.

- Other people's stacks often contain useful resources you can copy using one of the techniques described later in this chapter. Even non-HyperCard applications have usable resources you can obtain. (Remember the caveat we mentioned earlier about copyrighted material; some resources are copyrighted.)

- Some special stacks contain only resources that you can use in your stacks. (Again, be sure about ownership before you use these in a commercial product.)

- You can create your own resources using specialized tools, including some designed specifically for use with HyperCard.

If you use a stack or another Macintosh application that has an icon or a cursor you particularly admire or find suitable for your stack, and assuming the owner of the resource permits its use, you can use one of the techniques defined in the next section to copy that resource directly into your stack.

Special stacks for resource use

From the early days of HyperCard, many people began to build stacks with the express purpose of offering resources you could use in your own stacks as well as some excellent facilities for moving these resources into your stacks. Three that are particularly noteworthy because of their elegance and wide availability help you change the cursor, dabble with sophisticated-sounding music, and add simulated speech to your stacks.

A stack called, directly enough, Cursor Stuff has found its way onto many bulletin boards and into many user group public domain libraries. This nifty little stack contains 63 different cursor shapes (see Figure 21-4). Each cursor's resource ID number is shown in the only card in the stack. Using ResCopier or ResEdit, you can move any or all of these cursor shapes into your own stack and then use them as you wish.

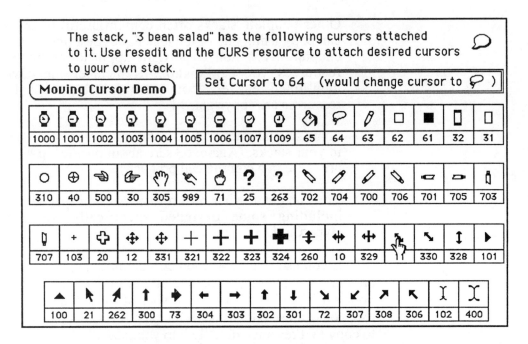

Figure 21-4. Cursor Stuff stack's 63 cursor shapes

Another stack we grew to love early in our HyperTalk scripting days is called Sound Advice and is the product of the fertile mind of Paul T. Pashibin. The stack includes a number of delightful sounds that you can add to your stacks simply by copying the appropriate button (see Figure 21-5). This approach to resource relocation in HyperCard seems to be catching on; look for many more stacks to offer such facility.

Finally, Dennis C. DeMars has created a product called HyperMacintalk that lets you add speech to your stacks. This is a sophisticated, yet easy-to-use stack that translates human-language text into *phonemes* that you can then edit to refine pronunciation. Figure 21-6 shows the main card in this stack, and Figures 21-7 and 21-8 display the vowel and consonant sounds and their phonemes. You can see that it is possible to refine the pronunciation of words quite nicely with this program. The stack consists of a collection of external commands (XCMDs, the primary topic of Chapter 22) that you can add to your stacks so that they, too, can talk.

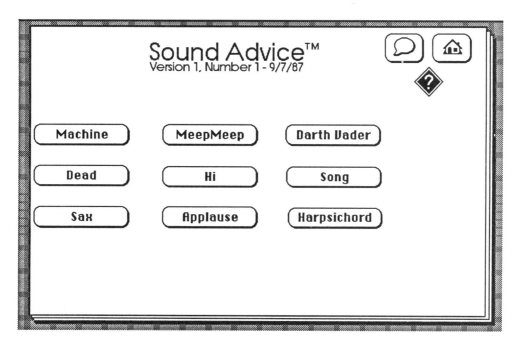

Figure 21-5. Sounds in Sound Advice stack

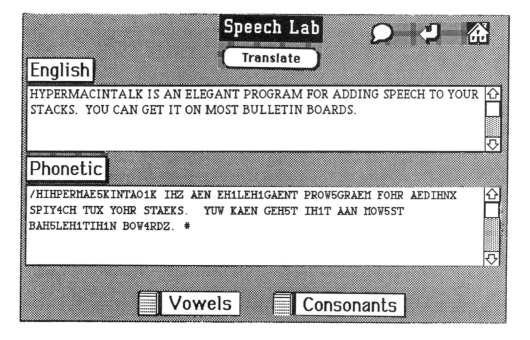

Figure 21-6. HyperMacintalk action card

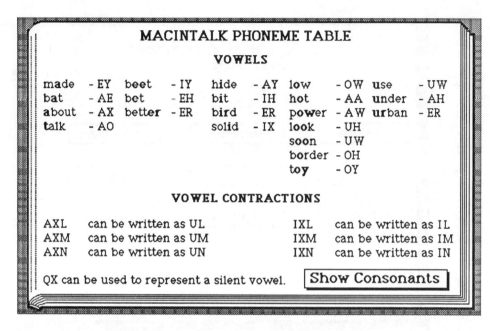

MACINTALK PHONEME TABLE

VOWELS

made	- EY	beet	- IY	hide	- AY	low	- OW	use	- UW
bat	- AE	bet	- EH	bit	- IH	hot	- AA	under	- AH
about	- AX	better	- ER	bird	- ER	power	- AW	urban	- ER
talk	- AO			solid	- IX	look	- UH		
						soon	- UW		
						border	- OH		
						toy	- OY		

VOWEL CONTRACTIONS

AXL	can be written as UL	IXL	can be written as IL
AXM	can be written as UM	IXM	can be written as IM
AXN	can be written as UN	IXN	can be written as IN

QX can be used to represent a silent vowel. | Show Consonants |

Figure 21-7. Vowel phonemes in HyperMacintalk

MACINTALK PHONEME TABLE

CONSONANTS				SPECIAL SYMBOLS	
but	- B	soup	- S	pity (tongue flap)	- DX
dog	- D	table	- T	kitt_en (glottal stop)	- Q
fed	- F	very	- V	call	- LX
guest	- G	wax	- W	car	- RX
hole	- /H	axe	- KS		
judge	- J	yak	- Y	1 - 9	are stress marks
kitchen	- K	zipper	- Z	.	sentence terminator
lot	- L	check	- CH	?	sentence terminator
must	- M	loch	- /C	,	clause delimiter
new	- N	rush	- SH	-	phrase delimiter
push	- P	pleasure	- ZH	()	noun phrase
quit	- KW	thin	- TH		
rat	- R	then	- DH		Show Vowels

Figure 21-8. Consonant phonemes in HyperMacintalk

NOTE

You may be tempted to copy these resources into
your Home stack where they will always be accessible to all your stacks. That is an acceptable strategy
provided you remember that when you sell or copy
the stack to someone else, you move the needed resources out of your Home stack and into the new
stack. Otherwise, the user is going to have trouble
running your stack.

Creating your own resources

Several commercially available and public domain or shareware
programs enable you to create resources. Apple Computer
distributes a program called RMaker through the Apple
Programmers and Developers Association (see Appendix C for
information on how to contact APDA). It is part of the
Apple-developed Macintosh Programmers Workshop (MPW)
product line.

Other programs range from the easy-to-use Icon Maker by
Steve Fine to the powerful and relatively sophisticated Icon
Hacker by Joe Mastroianni. Both of these products are share-
ware and are widely distributed on bulletin board systems.

Creating sound effects is a little more difficult, as you can
imagine, but there are some commercial products to assist you.
One of the most versatile and affordable approaches is Farrallon
Computing's MacRecorder. This product consists of a sound
digitizer with a built-in condenser microphone and a jack for
connecting it to external sound sources such as stereos. It comes
with two major pieces of software to facilitate both the editing
and customizing of recorded sounds and their conversion to appropriate formats for HyperCard use. Many HyperCard designers have adopted MacRecorder as their sound digitizer of choice.

In Chapter 24, we look at a stack called Menus for Hyper-
Card! from Nine to Five Software. It is not, strictly speaking, a
resource creator, but because menus are generally viewed as resources in Mac applications, we felt it deserved a mention here.

Moving Resources

A number of programs on the market enable you to move resources such as icons, sound effects, and cursors between Macintosh files. The most widely used is probably Apple Computer's own ResEdit (for Resource Editor). Figure 21-9 shows a typical ResEdit screen with an icon selected and ready to be copied to another application. ResEdit can be obtained through your Apple dealer or APDA (Apple Programmer's and Developer's Association; see Appendix C). It is relatively easy to use, though you will occasionally need some technical knowledge to understand what is going on.

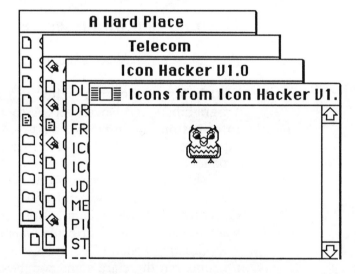

Figure 21-9. Typical ResEdit icon selection session

After you have located the icon or other resource you want to move with ResEdit, simply use the Edit menu commands to Copy it, then open the file in which you want to include it, and Paste it into the right resource type. (This is something of a simplification; you must be concerned about conflicting resource numbers as well, but a complete discussion of the detailed use of ResEdit is not our objective here. If you want to use the program, read the documentation and only work on copies of files that you don't mind damaging if you encounter some difficulty.)

If the resource you want to move is not located in another HyperCard stack, you have to use ResEdit or a program like it. (MiniServant, an application available on the HyperCard Goodies 1 disk through user groups and bulletin boards, has facilities for such tasks as well. And there are dozens of programs to make the relocation of icons, in particular, easier. Check with knowledgeable Mac programmers in your area for advice and assistance.)

But if you want to shift a resource from one HyperCard stack to another, you may prefer a superb stack called ResCopier written by Steve Maller. Maller is a well-known Mac guru, author, and trainer who works for Apple Computer outside the Hyper-Card area. The stacks and products he wrote that we discuss here and elsewhere in this book are not officially supported Apple products, but rather his own work. Like most of the other products we mention in this book, ResCopier can usually be found on your local bulletin board, on one of the national BBSes, or at a user group meeting. This stack operates much like Apple's useful Font/DA Mover and is well-documented on-line. Figure 21-10 shows the process of moving a sound resource from one Hyper-Card stack to another. The process is as simple as clicking the mouse a few times.

This discussion of resource movement in HyperCard has not been exhaustive. Additionally, the world of HyperCard programming tools is increasing quite fast, so by the time you read this there may be a dozen slick new ways of moving resources. With the assistance of tools like those discussed here, you can do a lot to make your stacks more effective and efficient without having to do a great deal of heavy-duty Macintosh programming. Consider this a starting point, not the final word.

Using Resources

After a resource has been added to a stack, you can use it like any other resource that was there when you obtained HyperCard or a specific stack. HyperCard cannot tell the difference between "original equipment" and "added accessories" when it comes to resource files.

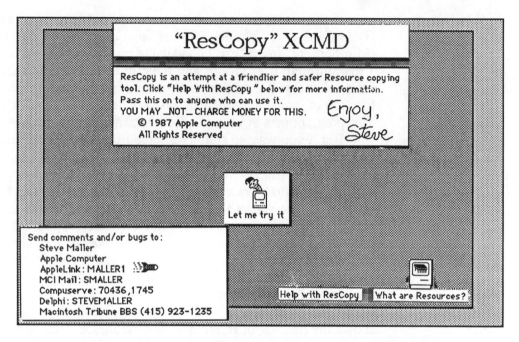

Figure 21.10. Using ResCopier to move resources between stacks

Thus, if you add a new icon to the repertoire of those available in HyperCard, you can use it like any standard icon. For example:

```
set icon of button 4 to "Smiling Face"
```

The same is true of new cursors:

```
set cursor to 603
-- Any valid cursor resource number can be used.
```

Sounds are treated the same way as built-in sounds, called into effect with the **play** command:

```
play "Applause"
```

and can even use the tempo and note-value arguments that are normally associated with "music." Some startlingly good sound effects are available in sources such as those outlined earlier in this chapter.

Summary

Extending the look, feel, sound, and utility of your stacks with resources you create or with resources borrowed from others can be fairly easy and quite effective. In this chapter, you learned what resources are, how they are used in HyperCard, and how to move them from other applications and other stacks into your own stacks. You also saw that, from HyperCard's perspective, there is no difference between these added resources and the ones it originally had, so they are used the same way.

In Chapter 22, we delve into the extension of HyperTalk by the special kind of resource called a *code resource* through the use of mysterious-sounding XCMDs and XFCNs.

Extending HyperCard with XCMDs and XFCNs

HyperTalk is a plainly powerful and obviously elegant programming language. HyperCard is a powerful, and forgiving development environment. So why would you want to extend its capabilities? In this chapter, we will answer that question and address such other issues as

- how XCMDs and XFCNs differ from full-blown Macintosh applications and desk accessories

- the basic principles of design in XCMDs and XFCNs

- the nature of the tools furnished by Apple through APDA for the design and implementation of external routines and their incorporation into HyperTalk

- using the HyperCard Developer's Toolkit from APDA and the Apple-supplied routines it contains to build XCMDs and XFCNs in Pascal and C

- compiling and linking external routines under MPW

403

- traps and pitfalls to avoid in building external routines for inclusion in your stacks and those of others

A caveat before we begin: the material in this chapter involves programming in more conventional programming languages such as C and Pascal. It is more technical than the rest of the book. If you don't understand C or Pascal or if you do not see a need to extend the language capabilities of HyperTalk, you can safely skip this chapter. Nothing that follows this chapter assumes you have read and understood it.

Incidentally, at this writing there are no files available to allow you to create external routines for HyperCard in BASIC, LISP, Prolog, Logo, or other popular languages. But a number of software publishers have discussed with us their plans to create such files. If your favorite language isn't listed here, contact the manufacturer of your software. The chances are good that they will be publishing the necessary routines.

What Are XCMDs and XFCNs?

An XCMD is a command added to HyperTalk's vocabulary by a program written outside HyperCard, typically in C or Pascal but also in assembly language, and incorporated, or "glued," into HyperCard. An XFCN is the same as an XCMD except it is a function that returns a value rather than a command that is not expected to return a result.

These external routines are similar to Macintosh programs in that they are written in traditional high-level languages and perform some function. They differ from applications because they have no header bytes. They differ from desk accessories in much the same way, though they more closely resemble desk accessories than they do full-blown Mac programs. (Actually these external routines can include header bytes as long as the first byte they contain is executable code. The same is true of desk accessories, but in practice this turns out to be a fine point most programmers ignore.)

XCMDs in particular, but also XFCNs, typically rely heavily on HyperCard to furnish a hospitable and manageable environment in which they can reside. Most routines use the user interface built into HyperCard rather than make calls to the Macintosh's ROM Toolbox routines themselves. This means they differ markedly from full-scale applications, which manage the entire user interface. Generally, Mac applications are much larger and more complex than XCMDs and XFCNs.

This is not to say, however, that XCMDs and XFCNs are trivial. On the contrary, we have seen several XCMDs that were more than 1000 lines long. Such XCMDs can carry out sophisticated processing that is beyond the scope of what HyperCard and HyperTalk were designed to do.

Why design external routines?

HyperCard creates a specialized environment for itself. In doing so, it isolates the programmer from the myriad details contained in more than 900 ROM toolbox calls that facilitate and define the Mac's distinctive user interface. On one hand, this isolation is good; it frees the programmer to concentrate more on solving the problem and less on presenting the solution to the user.

On the other hand, if you need to accomplish something in a script that is outside the range of HyperTalk's built-in commands, you could be quite frustrated were it not for the ability to extend the language through XCMDs and XFCNs. For example, there is no way in HyperTalk to find a file outside HyperCard by name with the usual file-opening dialog. As we will see later in this chapter, a perceived need for such a facility led to the development of an XCMD set to handle files in a more comfortable, Mac-like way.

Specialized math routines, management of color and color QuickDraw (on the Macintosh II), and the like are all candidates for XCMDs and XFCNs. If you are scripting along and find a need for a command that isn't built into HyperTalk, you might consider tackling the design and construction of an XCMD or XFCN.

Using external routines

After an external routine — XCMD or XFCN — has been "glued" into a stack, the commands it contains or the functions it defines can be used as if they were HyperTalk built-ins. As we saw in Chapter 19 when we described the process of defining your own functions, these additions become, for most practical purposes, part of the HyperTalk fabric.

Thus, as we will see, if an XCMD called *fileName* has been defined and glued to the stack and requires that the name of a file be supplied as an argument, we can easily code right in Hyper-Talk:

```
fileName(<arguments>)
```

and expect that the XCMD will perform some specified file function. In the case of the example later in the chapter, the *fileName* XCMD is used to gain access to files in a way that is identical to the way you access files outside HyperTalk.

Designing External Routines

The process of designing external routines for HyperTalk is not difficult or obtuse. You simply approach it as you would any other programming problem.

You can write XCMDs and XFCNs without knowing much about programming the Macintosh in detail, particularly if you use sets of libraries of functions that will undoubtedly become available. If, on the other hand, you're writing an XCMD that demands the use of a number of Mac interface routines, you may have to delve deeply into the inner workings of the machine. In that event, you will need more help than this chapter provides. You should pick up copies of Stephen Chernicoff's comprehensive *Macintosh Revealed* and Scott Knaster's highly readable and practical *How to Write Macintosh Software*. Both are available through Howard W. Sams & Co. The ultimate authority on Macintosh programming is Apple's own *Inside Macintosh* library. If you are a Certified Developer (see Appendix C for details), you can also receive frequent Technical Notes from Apple Computer to keep you abreast of changes, bugs, and other important information.

In most ways, designing an external routine for HyperCard's use is not much different from designing any other Macintosh program. The key difference is that an XCMD or XFCN must be a standalone module that can be brought into HyperCard as a *code resource* and has no header bytes. In many ways, XCMDs and XFCNs are similar to the popular Macintosh FKEYs, which began appearing in the past year or so. HyperCard requires that these externally generated commands begin with executable code at the first byte of their location.

Connecting these code resources into HyperCard then requires the use of a resource relocating program such as Apple's ResEdit or Steve Maller's ResCopier. (See Chapter 21 for a brief discussion of resources on the Mac.) You can, of course, supply a button in a stack that automates the movement of resources.

Tools for Adding External Commands

In designing HyperTalk, Dan Winkler created an interface that accommodates interaction between HyperCard and the outside world represented by code resources. The APDA-distributed *HyperCard Technical Reference* has three components, one of which is a disk of examples and some brief documentation on how to design and connect external commands. With interface routines supplied in the APDA package, you can send HyperCard a message, perform other useful conversions, and retrieve or change field values. (As with other product-specific information, this description is of course subject to change as the documentation and toolkit evolve.)

Two key files make up the interface between your external program code and HyperTalk:

- HyperXcmd.p (or HyperXcmd.h for C programmers), which contains the definitions for the interface routines between HyperTalk and Pascal (or C)

- XCmdGlue.inc (in Pascal or C), which defines those interface routines

A total of 29 interface routines are in these files. A discussion of the entire set of interface procedures is beyond the scope of this book; if you are interested in the subject, buy the *HyperCard Technical Reference* from APDA. We will look at four of the most frequently used routines. An examination of how they work can be directly applied to the other XCMD and XFCN interface routines in the APDA manual. The four we will discuss are

- **SendCardMessage**

- **EvalExpr**

- **PasToZero**

- **ZeroToPas**

SendCardMessage

The **SendCardMessage** routine takes a single argument, a zero-terminated C-type string, and sends it to the currently active card in HyperCard. The string can be any valid message, including parameters, that you could send to the card if you were in the HyperCard Message window or running a HyperTalk script. For example, if your XCMD needs to create a new card in Hyper-Card, it can execute an instruction like this one:

```
SendCardMessage('doMenu "New Card"');
```

There is no need for you to define these messages. Because you are effectively *in* HyperCard when the message is sent, HyperTalk handles the message as if it had come from any HyperCard object.

EvalExpr

The **EvalExpr** command is a very powerful interface command. It allows you to evaluate HyperCard functions and expressions within your external routine. A simple example of its use is checking the HyperCard variable **the result** to see if a **find** or **go to** operation has succeeded:

```
thingsOK := EvalExpr('the result');
```

This command causes HyperCard to look at **the result** and put its value into a memory location from which your XCMD can retrieve it. (Because this memory location is established by the interface routines, your program need not be concerned with it.)

PasToZero and *ZeroToPas*

The last two interface routines translate Pascal-type strings to and from C strings. The maximum length of a Pascal string is only 255 characters. Strings in HyperCard, on the other hand, can be arbitrarily long. So the interface routines between Hyper-Card and the outside world require the conversion of strings that do not comply to the standard definition of a C string (i.e., those that are not null-terminated). Similarly, if you are working in Pascal, you need to convert returned strings from HyperCard into strings with which Pascal can work.

If you are sending information to HyperCard, use **PasToZero**. It converts the string supplied as an argument into a null-terminated string and returns a handle to the converted string. If you are dealing with a string returned by HyperCard to your pro-gram, use **ZeroToPas** to convert the null-terminated string into one with which Pascal can deal.

A Template for XCMDs and XFCNs

Here is a blank-form template for the creation of XCMDs and XFCNs, written in Pascal syntax, though adapting it to C would not be difficult. Items of particular interest or items peculiar to the HyperCard interface process are discussed in comments to the code.

```
{$S Segment-Name} (* The segment name must be the name you intend
                    users to use when they call the command. *)

UNIT WhoCaresWhat Name (* Required for form, but name is immaterial *)

PROCEDURE ENTRYPOINT(paramPtr: XCmdPtr);
(* Lets HyperCard know where to call you back. *)
```

```
IMPLEMENTATION

TYPE Str31 = String[31];
(* Required by XCmdGlue.inc - do not  omit!*)
(* other implementation TYPE declarations you need *)


PROCEDURE Segment-Name(paramPtr: XCmdPtr);
FORWARD; (* must declare your procedure as FORWARD; see next
            instruction*)

(* The following code must appear substantially as shown, though you
must substitute the name of your procedure in the Segment-Name
slot.  This makes your XCMD re-entrant as required for interaction
with HyperCard.*)

PROCEDURE ENTRYPOINT(paramPtr: XCmdPtr);
BEGIN
  Segment-Name(paramPtr);
END;


PROCEDURE Segment-Name(paramptr: XCmdPtr);
VAR
  (* declare your local variables *)
  {$I XCmdGlue.inc}   (* must appear after your VAR declarations and
                         must not be omitted *)
BEGIN
  (* your procedure goes here *)
END;

END.
```

Nature of External Commands

XCMDs and XFCNs, because of their unique nature and unique interaction with HyperCard, have some intriguing and important character traits you need to understand if you are planning to write external routines. Steve Maller, author of the sample XCMD we'll discuss later in this chapter and several other programs involving the extensive use of XCMDs, says, "XCMDs and XFCNs are strangers in a strange land. They are only moderately welcome visitors there, and it is essential that they not only abide by the rules but keep in mind their status."

For example, an external routine cannot define new global variables that are recognized by HyperCard. Consequently, your external routines must not assume that they are still known entities after they have executed once and are about to be re-invoked. Unless you have a script with your XCMD — in which case you can do a lot more but are more subject to user modifications — you just cannot be sure what the state of the Mac environment is as your XCMD begins to run. In fact, you can't even be sure where your code was called, especially if your XCMD relocates stacks and cards as part of its processing.

Memory allocation is critical to the proper design and use of external routines in HyperCard as well. You should allocate and deallocate memory as you need it and dispose of any handles your code either directly generates or requests from HyperCard.

Finally, notice that XCMDs are modal. This poses some special problems. For example, if your XCMD doesn't run in a window or dialog, you must be certain that the program is and remains in the front window, especially with the advent of Multi-Finder and the different ways it causes Mac programmers to treat software design.

An Example XCMD

One of the first things requested by early HyperCard users and HyperTalk designers was the ability to open Macintosh files within HyperCard without having to know their names. Steve Maller, among other people, responded to that need. He agreed to permit us to publish the Pascal source code for his XCMD called fileName (with his sometimes-whimsical comments left intact).

```
{$S fileName }

UNIT Snoopy_Vs_TheRedBaron; (*obviously this is irrelevant*)
   INTERFACE

      USES
         {$LOAD HD:Hyper:XCMDs:PasSymDump}
         MemTypes, QuickDraw, OSIntf, ToolIntf, PackIntf,
            HyperXCmd;
```

```
    PROCEDURE EntryPoint(paramPtr: XCmdPtr);

IMPLEMENTATION

    TYPE
        Str31 = String[31];

    PROCEDURE FileName(paramPtr: XCmdPtr);
        FORWARD;

    PROCEDURE EntryPoint(paramPtr: XCmdPtr);

        BEGIN
            FileName(paramPtr);
        END;

    PROCEDURE FileName(paramPtr: XCmdPtr);

        VAR
            myWDPB: WDPBPtr;
            myCPB: CInfoPBPtr;
            myPB: HParmBlkPtr;
            fullPathName: Str255;
            numTypes: Integer;
            reply: SFReply;
            typeList: SFTypeList;

            {$I XCmdGlue.inc }

        FUNCTION TheyChoseAFile: Boolean;

            VAR
                pt: Point;

            BEGIN
                TheyChoseAFile := FALSE;
                pt.v := 60;
                pt.h := 82;
                SFGetFile(pt, '', NIL, numTypes, typeList, NIL, re-
            ply);
(* have 'em pick a file *)
                IF reply.good THEN
(* if they didn't choose Cancel *)
                BEGIN
                    TheyChoseAFile := TRUE;
```

```
                    fullPathName := reply.fName;
(* start the ball rolling *)
            END;
    END;

PROCEDURE BuildThePathName;

    VAR
        name: Str255;
        err: Integer;

    BEGIN
        name := '';
            (* start with an empty name *)
        myPB^.ioNamePtr := @name;
            (* we want the Volume name *)
        myPB^.ioCompletion := pointer(0);
        myPB^.ioVRefNum := reply.vRefNum;
(* returned from SFGetFile *)
        myPB^.ioVolIndex := 0;
(* use the vRefNum and name *)
        err := PBHGetVInfo(myPB, FALSE);
(* fill in the Volume info *)
        IF err <> noErr THEN
            Exit(FileName);
```

(* Now we need the Working Directory (WD) information because we're
going to step backwards from the file through all of the folders
until we reach the root directory *)

```
        myWDPB^.ioVRefNum := reply.vRefNum;
(* this got set to 0 above *)
        myWDPB^.ioWDProcID := 0;
(* use the vRefNum *)
        myWDPB^.ioWDIndex := 0;
(* we want ALL directories *)
        err := PBGetWDInfo(myWDPB, FALSE);
(* do it *)
        IF err <> noErr THEN
            Exit(FileName);

        myCPB^.ioFDirIndex := - 1;
    (* use the ioDirID field only *)
        myCPB^.ioDrDirID := myWDPB^.ioWDDirID;
    (* info returned above *)
```

```
            err := PBGetCatInfo(myCPB, FALSE);
        (* do it *)
            IF err <> noErr THEN
                Exit(FileName);
```

(* Here starts the real work - start to climb the tree by
continually looking in the ioDrParId field for the next directory
above until we fail... *)

```
            myCPB^.ioDrDirID := myCPB^.ioDrParId;
        (* the first folder*)
            fullPathName := Concat(myCPB^.ioNamePtr^, ':',
                reply.fName);
            REPEAT
                myCPB^.ioDrDirID := myCPB^.ioDrParId;
                err := PBGetCatInfo(myCPB, FALSE);
        (* the next level *)
```

(* Be careful of an error returned here - it means the user chose a
file on the desktop level of this volume. If this is the case, just
stop here and return "VolumeName:FileName"; otherwise loop until
failure *)

```
            IF err = noErr THEN
                fullPathName := Concat(myCPB^.ioNamePtr^, ':',
                    fullPathName);

            UNTIL err <> noErr;

        END;   (* PROCEDURE BuildThePathName *)

    BEGIN    (* PROCEDURE FileName *)
```

(* First we allocate some memory in the heap for the parameter
block. This could in theory work on the stack, but in reality it
makes no difference as we're entirely modal (ugh) here... *)

```
        fullPathName := '';

        myCPB := CInfoPBPtr(NewPtr(SizeOf(HParamBlockRec)));
        IF ord4(myCPB) <= 0 THEN
            Exit(FileName);
    (* Rats! Not enough room *)
        myWDPB := WDPBPtr(myCPB);
    (* icky Pascal type coercions follow *)
        myPB := HParmBlkPtr(myCPB);
```

```
numTypes := 1; (* for SFGetFile *)
WITH paramPtr^ DO
   BEGIN
      IF paramCount = 0 THEN
         numTypes := - 1
(* FileName() - get all files *)
      ELSE
         BlockMove(params[1]^, @typeList[0], 4);
(* FileName("TYPE") *)

      IF TheyChoseAFile THEN
         BuildThePathName;
         returnValue := PasToZero(fullPathName);
   END; (* WITH paramPtr^ DO *)

DisposPtr(pointer(myCPB)); (* Clean Up Your Heap! *)

END;     (* PROCEDURE FileName *)

END.
```

This program was written in MPW Pascal. To use it after it's included in a stack, simply type its command name followed by an optional file type:

```
fileName("fileType")
```

For example, if you want to look only at HyperCard stacks, code a command like this:

```
fileName("STAK")
```

To look at all files, regardless of type, use:

```
fileName()
```

Maller provides the following example of the use of this command in a script:

```
on mouseUp
  put fileName("TEXT") into theFile
  if theFile is not empty then
    open file theFile
    read from file theFile for 2000
```

```
      put it into bkgnd field 1
      close file theFile
   end if
end mouseUp
```

When the **mouseUp** script encounters the XCMD fileName, it opens a standard dialog (called, in Mac parlance, an SFOpen box because the Mac uses that command to open a standard file open window and the SF stands for standard file). The user selects a file name and processing continues.

NOTE

The Mac only supports Pascal strings for full path names, so they must be limited to 255 characters.

An Example XFCN

One of our favorite add-on programs for HyperCard is Menus for HyperCard! from Michael Long and Nine to Five Software. The program's operation is described in some detail in Chapter 24, but reproduced here is the Pascal source code for one of the XFCNs it contains. This function implements a **newMenu** command. The comments are sufficiently liberal that you can probably figure out what's going on from reading them.

```
{$R-}

UNIT DummyUnit;

(* This XFCN implements a NewMenu function for HyperCard.  It re-
turns 0 if it was unable to create a menu, or a reference number so
the menu can be accessed again by other menu commands.

Written by:
  Michael Long of Nine To Five Software on September 1, 1987*)
```

```
INTERFACE

USES
        {$LOAD Hyper.LOAD }
            MemTypes, QuickDraw, OSIntf, ToolIntf, PackIntf,
            HyperXCmd;

PROCEDURE ENTRYPOINT(paramPtr: XCmdPtr);

IMPLEMENTATION

    CONST
      MaxMenus          = 16;
      MenuStart         = 7777;

    TYPE
      MDHandle          = ^MDPtr;
      MDPtr             = ^MyDataRecord;
      MyDataRecord      = RECORD
                            kind : OSType; {used to identify our data}
                            next : MDHandle;  {next mdh handle in list}
                            handles : Array[1..MaxMenus] of handle;
                          END;
PROCEDURE AddMenu(paramPtr: XCmdPtr);
FORWARD;

PROCEDURE ENTRYPOINT(paramPtr: XCmdPtr);
  BEGIN
    AddMenu(paramPtr);
  END;

FUNCTION GetDataHandle(which:OSType):MDHandle;
    CONST
        windowList        = $9D6;
        messageWindow     = 5;
    VAR
        wPeekPtr          : ^WindowPeek;
        wPeek             : WindowPeek;
        mdh               : MDHandle;
        i                 : integer;
    BEGIN
        wPeekPtr := pointer( windowList ); {find window of handle}
        wPeek := wPeekPtr^;
        WHILE wPeek^.refcon <> messageWindow DO
            wPeek := wPeek^.nextWindow;
```

```
      mdh := MDHandle( wPeek^.dataHandle ); {get handle to list}
       WHILE (mdh <> NIL) &  {find old data if exists}
          (mdh^^.kind <> which) DO mdh := mdh^^.next;
      IF mdh = NIL THEN BEGIN {if doesn't exist then create it}
          mdh := MDHandle( NewHandle(SizeOf(MyDataRecord)) );
          IF mdh <> NIL THEN WITH mdh^^ DO BEGIN
             kind := which; {save our type and put it into list}
             next := MDHandle( wPeek^.dataHandle );
             wPeek^.dataHandle := handle( mdh );

             FOR i:=1 TO MaxMenus DO {initialize private data}
                 handles[i] := NIL;

          END; {if not nil}
        END; {if nil}
      GetDataHandle := mdh;
   END;

PROCEDURE AddMenu(paramPtr:XCmdPtr);
 VAR
   mdh            : MDHandle;    {our mdh handle}
   menuIndex      : integer;     {index into menu array}
   zsp            : ptr;         {pointer to a zero-delimited string}
   str            : str255;      {pascal string}
   menuID         : integer;     {id of new menu}
   mh             : menuHandle;  {menu handle for new menu}
   i              : integer;     {for loop index}
   count          : integer;     {number of parameters passed}

 PROCEDURE DoJsr(addr: ProcPtr); INLINE $205F,$4E90;

 FUNCTION  PasToZero(str: Str255): Handle;
     BEGIN
        WITH paramPtr^ DO
          BEGIN
            inArgs[1] := ORD(@str);
            request := xreqPasToZero;
            DoJsr(entryPoint);
            PasToZero := Handle(outArgs[1]);
          END;
      END;
   PROCEDURE ZeroToPas(zeroStr: Ptr; VAR pasStr: Str255);
      BEGIN
        WITH paramPtr^ DO
          BEGIN
```

```
              inArgs[1] := ORD(zeroStr);
               inArgs[2] := ORD(@pasStr);
               request := xreqZeroToPas;
               DoJsr(entryPoint);
            END;
       END;


   PROCEDURE Error(err:boolean);
      BEGIN
         IF err THEN BEGIN
            paramPtr^.returnValue := PasToZero('0');
            Exit(AddMenu)
            END;
      END;


 BEGIN
      paramPtr^.passFlag := FALSE;   {we handle this}
      count := paramPtr^.paramCount;   {get count}
      Error(count<1);    {exit if not enough parameters}
      mdh := GetDataHandle('MENU');    {get data handle}
      Error(mdh=NIL);   {exit if GetDataHandle failed}
      menuIndex := 1;   {find first free handle}
      REPEAT
          IF mdh^^.handles[menuIndex]=NIL THEN LEAVE;
          menuIndex:=menuIndex+1;
      UNTIL menuIndex>MaxMenus;
      Error(menuIndex>MaxMenus); {exit if none free}
      menuID := MenuStart;   {get a menu id that isn't being used}
      REPEAT
          menuID := menuID+1;
          mh := GetMHandle(menuID);
      UNTIL mh=NIL;
      zsp := paramPtr^.params[1]^;   {get and convert menu name}
      ZeroToPas(zsp, str);
      mh := NewMenu(menuID, str);   {make a new menu record}
      mdh^^.handles[menuIndex] := handle(mh); {save it for later}
      FOR i := 2 TO count DO BEGIN
        {get, convert, and install menu items}
          zsp := paramPtr^.params[i]^;
          ZeroToPas(zsp, str);
          AppendMenu(mh, str);
          END; {for}
      InsertMenu(mh, 0);   {insert the menu into the list}
      DrawMenuBar;          {draw the new menu bar}
      NumToString(menuIndex, str);   {return reference to this menu}
```

```
        paramPtr^.returnValue := PasToZero(str);
  END; {addmenu}
```

```
END.
```

This routine also illustrates how to reserve permanent memory in HyperCard. An example of the command is:

```
put NewMenu("MyMenuName","MenuItem1","MenuItem2") into myMenu
```

Compiling and Linking XCMDs and XFCNs

The process of compiling and linking external routines for inclusion in HyperCard varies with the compiler. This discussion uses MPW Pascal. We assume you understand how to compile and link Pascal code and provide no explanation of the process or the command set, which is fairly straightforward.

To compile Maller's fileName stack, type these commands:

```
pascal fileName.p
   link -m ENTRYPOINT -rt XFCN=913 -sn MAIN=fileName ∂
     -t STAK -c WILD ∂
     fileName.p.o ∂
     mpw:libraries:Interface.o ∂
     mpw:libraries:Paslib.o ∂
     -o "hd20:hyper:stacks:TestXFCN"
```

NOTE

The special character appearing at the end of all but the last line of the previous command list is created with an Option-D key combination. It tells MPW that the command continues on the next line. It thus facilitates making such command lines more readable.

The number assigned to the XFCN is arbitrary. The last three lines may be associated with fuller directory path names and will vary depending on how you have set up your files.

Insights, Tips, and Techniques

This concluding section discusses insider tips and special techniques, as well as some traps and pitfalls, in designing and writing XCMDs and XFCNs.

Checking the system

The Mac System File, in its most recent incarnations, includes a special Toolbox command called **SysEnvirons** from which you can obtain information about the operating situation in which your XCMDs and HyperCard are running. Such data as the type of CPU, whether there is a math coprocessor, the version of the System File, and whether color QuickDraw is in effect can be gathered by a call to this command.

By using this command, you can easily adapt your stacks to the specific operating environment — Mac Plus, MAC SE, or Macintosh II with color or monochrome display — in which they are implemented. Like all Toolbox commands, **SysEnvirons** can only be called from an XCMD or XFCN, not from HyperCard itself.

Making sure the screen re-draws

All XCMDs and XFCNs operate as modal applications, which means they don't allow the user to leave until he or she *does* something. Most external routines run in a window of their own because they can't run directly in HyperCard cards. When the user quits your external process or it terminates by some other means, HyperCard does not know about the window's disappearance. As a result, it doesn't re-draw the underlying bit image. Users are left with a large white space in the middle of their card.

You can avoid this problem by including three lines in your XCMD, just after its window closes and before it returns control to HyperCard:

```
sendHCMessage('set lockScreen to true');
sendCardMessage('go to this card');
sendHCMessage('set lockScreen to false');
```

The simple act of **go**ing to the card redraws it on the display. With **lockScreen** set to true, the user won't see any of this activity.

Memory checking on a large external routine

If your external routine is particularly large, you may run out of memory, perhaps even before the routine is loaded into RAM. HyperCard is a notorious user of memory resources. To make matters worse, HyperCard makes a copy of external routines before it executes them. If you have a 20K-byte routine, for example, you need 40K bytes just to load and begin to execute it.

A good strategy for large routines is to segment the command or function into two or more code blocks. Make the first one fairly small and design it so that it checks available memory when it is loaded into memory. If there is not enough memory to handle the entire command, display an alert dialog and gracefully exit, leaving the user's original activities intact. If memory is adequate, your first segment can load the second.

Besides checking for enough memory on a large routine, you should also consider being sure you have a minimum of 64K bytes available (for a small external routine) before you try to execute your command or function. HyperCard does some memory management "behind your back," as it were, and it is safe to bet that if you are closer than 64K to the point of being out of allocatable memory, you may want to stop processing and give the user a safe exit.

Allocating and deallocating memory

Your external routines should allocate all the memory they need and deallocate it when they are finished running. Disposing of handles created by your program or in response to a HyperCard command your program invokes is the task of your program. Failure to "clean up" after yourself when your routine ends can be a source of great difficulty in HyperCard's memory-intensive environment.

Accessing *It* from an external routine

Because your external commands and functions cannot use HyperCard's global variable space, they cannot access directly the value of the ubiquitous variable *It*. So you have to do some neat side-stepping. For example, if you want to send an **answer** message and retrieve the response, you have the problem of getting at *It*. Your XCMD would send the message:

```
sendCardMessage("answer 'Are you ready?' with 'Yes' or 'No'");
```

But HyperCard puts the user's reply to the **answer** command into *It*, which is not directly accessible from your XCMD. So you have to send two more commands to HyperCard to retrieve this value:

```
sendCardMessage('put It');
sendCardMessage('get the message');
```

Now *It* is returned as a normal value from HyperCard, and your external routine can use it as needed.

Using quotation marks in messages

Because of the way HyperCard scans strings, you cannot use double quotation marks inside strings. HyperCard stops searching for the end of the string the instant it encounters a second quotation mark. That creates a probable syntax error because HyperCard does not receive part of the command. The problem is that HyperCard just displays a syntax error message and ends execution of your XCMD or XFCN. This makes debugging such errors extremely difficult.

Experienced Pascal programmers use a simple routine that puts a string into a packed array of characters and scans for quotation marks, replacing any it finds with single quotation marks.

Duplicate resource numbers

In a Macintosh resource fork, you can have two resources of the same type with the same name, as long as the two have different identification numbers (or *resource IDs*). Thus it is not uncommon to have two menus with the same name that perform slightly different tasks and are swapped as needed by the program that accesses them.

But because the resource name of an XCMD or XFCN is also that command or function's name as used within HyperCard, duplicate names will pose a problem. HyperCard only executes the first such command it encounters in the resource fork, and there is no direct way to force it to do otherwise. So it is important that you do not allow duplicate resource names with XCMDs and XFCNs.

The best way to avoid such conflicts is to use a resource moving program like ResEdit or ResCopier (see Chapter 21) to move the code resource into the stack. Those routines check for duplicate names and flag them for you as they relocate resources.

Don't hide HyperCard

The entire time your XCMD is executing, HyperCard is still running. Users of your command have a right to know that and in fact may need to know it. To be sure they don't get confused on this point, make sure any dialogs or windows you create don't cover the entire screen area. Leave enough showing under your application so that HyperCard is still visible.

Not all events are for you

In a normal Macintosh application setting, your application traps for events that go on in the system and handles those that pertain to it. If your application is the top window on the stack and a window-related event is detected, you are expecting it to be for your application. In HyperCard, that isn't always the case. You need to be sure the message you are handling is intended for your routine and not for HyperCard.

Summary

No single chapter in a book about HyperTalk could make you an expert in designing and constructing XCMDs and XFCNs, which are really mini-applications on the Macintosh. But in this chapter, you saw the general process involved, were given a Pascal template to follow in creating your own, saw an example of a working XCMD and how it was written, linked, and compiled, and were given some practical advice about designing and implementing external routines.

CHAPTER

Designing Stacks

In this chapter, you will be given a number of tips related to the design of HyperCard stacks. These tips include such topics as

- how the nature of the data your stack will contain relates to its design

- the trade-offs between multiple stacks and multiple-background stacks

- consistency in card and background layout and in stack design

- user-oriented button design

- communicating with the user

Two Caveats

There are two general ideas to keep in mind as you read this chapter. First, suggestions in this chapter are just that — suggestions. They are neither rules nor official guidelines. They are just ideas that grew out of examining hundreds of stacks, creating a dozen or so of our own, and talking to lots of other HyperTalk scripters. They also grow out of our several years' experience using and writing about the Macintosh.

Second, Apple Computer will undoubtedly publish official stack design guidelines. Apple has pioneered the issuance of formal guidelines through its Human Interface Group. When those guidelines are published, you should get them, read them, and take them to heart. If what they say conflicts with what's in this chapter, Apple is probably right.

Before You Begin Stack Construction

Designing a stack is not totally dissimilar from other programming tasks you may have undertaken. At the beginning of any task involving information management, it's a good idea to ask yourself two basic questions:

- Who is the ultimate end user of this program and what does he or she know?

- What approach to the organization and management of this information will best enable the user to find and use it?

In this case, the user's identity is reasonably well known. Your stack's users will almost certainly be people who have used the Macintosh previously. There's also a good chance they will have at least a passing acquaintance with HyperCard. It is possible that your stack will be used by someone to whom both the Mac and HyperCard are new. Helping such users get started in the use of your stack may take a fair amount of effort and perhaps some written documentation or an orientation stack.

Less predictable than the likely end user of your stack is the nature of the data that the stack contains. With HyperCard, you can store data in a single stack or in a group of connected stacks that are closely related, loosely related, or virtually unrelated. If the information is related, you may connect it in any of several ways, including:

- linearly (sequentially)

- hierarchically (tree structured)

- non-linearly (quasi-randomly)

- combination of these

Each type of informational relationship can influence the way you organize your stacks. For example, if the data in your stack is linear — i.e., if the user is likely to want to view it in sequence most or all of the time — you will use straightforward navigation approaches to movement. This means not much exotic linking is involved and probably very little programming is needed to accomplish navigation-related tasks. Figure 23-1 is a schematic of a sequentially organized stack.

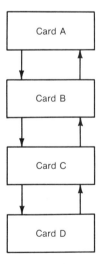

Figure 23-1. Linear stack organization

Hierarchically structured data, on the other hand, implies that the browser has multiple options at many points in the navigation process. Figure 23-2 depicts this type of data organization. Quite often one or more of these multi-path cards calls for a different background to differentiate it and to make it operate as expected. In addition, navigation not only requires forward and backward buttons but also links to other points in the stack or in related stacks.

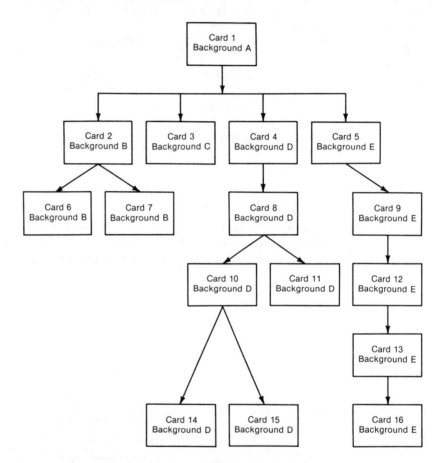

Figure 23-2. Hierarchical stack organization

When data chunks — typically stored as cards in Hyper-Card — have multiple entry and exit connecting points, the data is organized non-linearly, as shown in Figure 23-3. In this kind of stack, navigation is ad hoc, and each card probably has no buttons to move to the next card or a previous card, but may have many linking buttons. This kind of information requires a sophisticated level of thinking and planning.

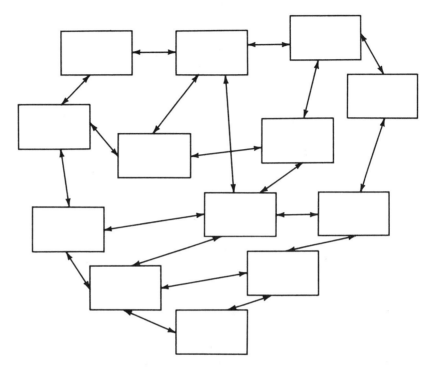

Figure 23-3. Non-linear stack organization

Much of the data we work with in everyday life, whether it is stored in HyperCard or on 3x5 index cards, is organized by a combination of linear and non-linear means. Such a structure can be conceptualized as looking like Figure 23-4. The horizontal portion of the structure has a linear organization in the illustration, and the vertical portion is somewhat tree-structured, though also quite linear. Yet the overall structure is neither tree-structured nor linear.

If the data you are working with requires a mixed organization, navigation controls require both back and previous buttons as well as linking buttons. The impact of the type of data organization is not confined to navigational issues, but these are the ones that are most obviously and directly affected as a rule.

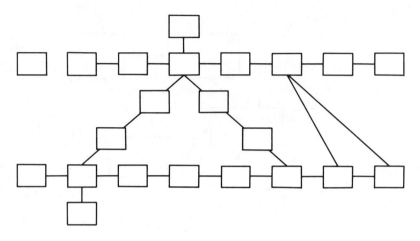

Figure 23-4. Mixed stack organization

Add Stacks or Backgrounds?

When you have data of more than one type in a stack, you typically must decide how to treat the different types of information so that the user understands it and the amount of programming, disk space, and execution time is minimized. There are two approaches:

- create separate stacks and link them at appropriate points in the navigation or execution process

- stay with one stack and create separate backgrounds for different types of data

Neither approach is inherently better than the other, and sometimes you may want to mix the two approaches, using separate stacks with stacks that have cards of two or more backgrounds. How will you make these decisions? There are no hard-and-fast rules, but here are some principles you can use in deciding on the best approach for your stack.

STACK VERSUS BACKGROUND PRINCIPLES

1. A single stack with multiple backgrounds increases retrieval speed, reduces scripting and makes copying and downloading easier than when multiple stacks are used.

2. Multiple stacks make the best sense when data can be subdivided and some or all users might not want or need to access certain parts of the data.

3. The minimum overhead for a stack is about 8K of disk space, so using multiple stacks can become costly in terms of disk storage.

4. The standard HyperCard **find** command will not work across stack boundaries, so if this is the primary or sole means for your user to navigate through your application, a single stack is dictated. (You can write a handler to extend HyperCard's **find** command to cross stack boundaries.)

5. The same is true of the **print** command. If the user needs a report containing information of more than one type, you have to use a single stack with multiple backgrounds, modify the **print** command with your own handler (a difficult task at best), or use one of the reporting routines discussed in Chapter 24.

Consistency in Layout and Design

You should strive for consistency in your stack designs so that users are comfortable with how your stacks work and focus on their content and substance rather than their form. Consider this consistency issue in relation to background layouts, navigation techniques, restoring the system to its original state, and the user interface.

Background layouts

Basic stack design begins with the background. Most stacks have only one background, though easy but clever approaches can make them appear to have more than a single background.

An easy mistake to make in designing stacks, particularly when you first begin to explore the power of HyperCard, is to over-design the backgrounds. If you have too many varieties of backgrounds or backgrounds that are simply too intricately designed and cluttered, you will confuse the user. When you analyze the data the stack will present, you can generally find ways of dividing the information conceptually into a small number of subclasses. Use backgrounding or separate stacks for those divisions and leave the rest of the stack as a unified, consistent-looking whole.

Navigation techniques

As users navigate through the stack, they should be comfortable with each card as new information of the same kind is presented. The only time the stack or card design should cause the user to stop simply flowing along with the presentation of information is when the nature of the information changes. For example, when you move from the annual calendar to the weekly calendar to the daily appointment list or notes, the background should be different. The user needs to be aware that the rules may have changed; navigation is different now and the information is different as well. On the other hand, if you have different backgrounds for June's calendar and December's, you ought to have a very good reason for that and the reason ought to be one your user can understand.

Leaving things as they were

Another aspect of consistency has to do with a fundamental principle of HyperTalk design: leave things as they were. If the Message box was visible when the user started using your stack, make sure it's still there when the user quits your stack. If the user's access level was set to authoring (i.e., 4) before the user opened your stack, be sure to return it to that level at the end of your stack.

If you do anything to alter the environment during your stack's execution, do yourself and your user a favor. Store the original state of things, and return to that original state as part of an **on closeStack** handler. Be sure to include in this original state the tool that was in use. This will almost always be the browse tool, but be certain that users don't find themselves unable to do something just because you've changed the tool and failed to return it to its original state.

Usage management

During usage of your stack, be sure that things the user notices and uses are consistent from card to card and background to background. This usually requires moving handlers higher up the hierarchy than might at first seem necessary.

For example, if a field on a card is always the one users want to enter information into first, make sure the insertion point always appears in that field when users change cards or add a card. This usually means that the handler that puts the insertion point in the right place belongs at the background or stack level and not at the card level where it could be inadvertently modified during development or later maintenance. With the object-like nature of HyperTalk, later modifications are much easier if you keep these handlers high enough in the hierarchy rather than distribute them throughout the cards.

A tip: protect the form

It is important that you design your stack so that the casual browser cannot inadvertently change something that makes the stack work consistently and predictably. Lock elements of the design that you don't want users to modify. If there will be an occasional need for users to modify the design, give them the means — probably with a password check — to do so.

You can lock text fields, cards, or backgrounds using the appropriate Info... option from the Objects menu. Stack protection was discussed in Chapter 9.

User-Oriented Button Design

Virtually all of the user's interaction with your stack — at least in terms of directing its activities and processing — comes through pressing buttons on cards and backgrounds. It is therefore important that the design and use of buttons be well thought-out as part of your script design. Consider the issues of consistent use of standard HyperCard buttons, feedback when the user pushes a button, and standard implementation of familiar Macintosh button types.

Using HyperCard buttons consistently

The HyperCard buttons that most stacks include are

- arrow buttons (forward, backward, beginning of stack, end of stack, and return to where the user came from last)

- the Home button

Many other buttons are arguably HyperCard "standard" buttons, but they are used far less frequently than these.

Good stack design dictates that you use arrow buttons as users expect in each stack. An arrow pointing to the right ought to result in users feeling that they have turned a page or moved one step farther into the stack (see Chapter 13 for a discussion of accompanying visual effects). Similarly, a left arrow should move users toward the top of the stack and give the impression of flipping the pages of the book back toward the front cover.

This is not to say you can't be creative with button design for navigation. But if you decide to do so, be sure your creative choices are intuitive to the user and you don't use a standard but-ton in a way that is non-intuitive.

The Home button is not furnished in all stacks but probably ought to be. Users can always get to the Home stack with a Com-mand-H key sequence, but why not make life easier and more HyperCard-like for them? Don't have a house icon on the stack mean anything other than "go to the Home stack," either. We've seen one stack that uses the Home button to take you back to the beginning of the stack. That approach is bad HyperCard design.

Feedback to the user

All buttons that are not transparent — and some that are — should probably highlight when the user presses them. Unfortunately, HyperTalk is designed in such a way that automatic highlighting is turned off for buttons, so you almost always have to turn it on.

In addition to highlighting buttons when they are pressed, consider whether a sound effect accompanying a button's push might have value. The user of your stack feels more comfortable when, having pushed a button, something happens fairly soon. This is especially important in view of HyperCard's very delib-erate (and good) design decision to have most actions require only a single click when most users are accustomed to double-clicking. If the user doesn't get some feedback on a single click, you may find your stacks not working properly because the user continues to click and ends up activating something accidentally by pushing a button on the next card.

Consistency with Mac interface

Anyone who uses a Macintosh for any length of time becomes closely acquainted with check boxes and radio buttons. It is therefore important that your stack's use of these buttons is con-sistent with the "normal" Macintosh approach users expect.

Don't use radio buttons or check boxes for navigation or to pass commands. These buttons are primarily useful for setting up parameters and properties. The difference between the two types is that only one radio button in a collection of such buttons can be selected, or "on," at one time, but in any group of check boxes, as many as the user wants can be checked at the same time.

Another aspect of consistency with the Macintosh interface involves the use of Cancel in **ask** commands and in other places where the user is providing some information to your script. This is particularly important in HyperCard since the program automatically saves changes while it runs. The user needs a way to say, "I didn't mean that!"

Communicating with the user

It is generally not a good idea to use the Message box to communicate information to the user. Too often the information you want to convey is overtyped the instant the user presses a key. At the very least, it is impossible to prevent the user from typing information into the Message box, so it is bound to happen at inopportune times.

Use **ask** and **answer** dialogs (see Chapter 11) to get information from the user when you really need it. On the whole, however, interrupt the user to obtain information only when there is no smooth way to let the user supply data without interruption.

Other Design Considerations

This chapter has scratched the surface of design issues in building HyperCard stacks. We hope it has supplied some insights that may not have occurred to you before.

Keep an eye on other people's stacks. When you find yourself working with a stack intuitively and smoothly, with the substance dominating the form, analyze the reasons for it and then try to emulate some of those design approaches in your own stacks.

Summary

In this chapter, you learned about the basic ideas in HyperCard stack design. You saw that the design of a stack is quite often related to the nature of the data and how it is best organized. You also looked at some of the trade-offs in deciding whether to add backgrounds or stacks when data becomes complex.

You learned how to make your stacks consistent internally and consistent with the user's expectations. Finally, you learned some principles of good user-oriented button design and how to use dialogs to communicate with the user from your script.

Chapter 24 focuses on some readily available HyperTalk programming tools.

Programming Tools

In the first few months that HyperCard appeared on the market, it attracted an unusually large number of programming tools, many of which were quite useful and nicely designed. In this chapter, we will look at a sampling of those programs, including:

- several that assist you in working with scripts

- three that "spruce up" scripts with added facilities

- one that enables you to import text files and create database-like cards directly from the input

This discussion cannot encompass all programming tools. If it even tried to do that, it would be obsolete as soon as the book was printed. Join APDA and a local user group and sign up for one of the national bulletin board services (see Appendix C) if you are serious about developing stacks.

In addition, Chapter 26 contains a programming tool that we designed for this book and that we trust you will find a useful addition to your scripting arsenal.

Script-Working Programs

We've seen three programs that are particularly useful in developing substantial stacks with more than a handful of scripts. Two are quite similar and are discussed together first. The third is radically different.

Stack listers

If you've done much scripting, you've probably encountered a situation where you wanted a listing of all scripts in your stack so that you could read the scripts like a more traditional program listing. Finding places where messages are sent incorrectly is greatly simplified by such a process. Debugging stacks when scripts are scattered among a few or even a few dozen objects can be a tasking chore.

If you're particularly enterprising, you might have realized that you could simply open each script, select it all, copy it, open a new card or even a text-only document with a desk accessory or as a separate application under MultiFinder, and build your own collection of scripts in one document. If you're *really* into scripting, you may even have found a way to write a script for this purpose.

Both Script Report and scriptView are low-cost shareware products that automatically retrieve, format and display, print, or save all scripts in a stack. They are quite similar and can be obtained from national and local bulletin boards and user groups.

Script Report was written by Eric Alderman and is available for a suggested shareware contribution of $10. Eldon Benz asks for a $5 contribution for his scriptView stack.

Figure 24-1 shows you the opening screen of Script Report. To use it, you just click on the big button in the lower center part of the screen, tell the stack which file you want to examine, and then sit back and wait. After a few minutes and a fair amount of screen activity, a single window with all the scripts in it appears. You can then choose to print this listing or save it on disk.

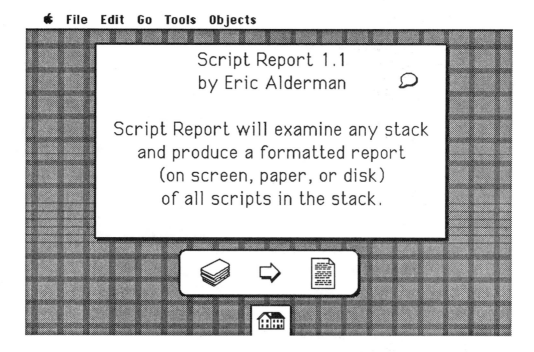

Figure 24-1. Script Report opening screen

Figure 24-2 shows the opening screen of scriptView. It works similarly to Script Report. Press on the Begin button and tell scriptView which stack you want to look at. In a few minutes, your script appears in a window, ready to be printed or saved (see Figure 24-3).

You can't go wrong with either of these programs, and we don't see how you can do successful scripting of any complexity without one of them or something similar. The slight differences between these two stacks are trivial. Neither is faster nor better than the other in any important respect we've been able to detect.

Stack Detective

A different kind of scripting help can be obtained by the use of Stack Detective by Peter Olson. This is not a stack but rather an external program that must be run outside HyperCard (it can be launched from inside HyperCard as well with the **open** command). It can be obtained for a $10 shareware donation through local and national bulletin boards and user groups and from Heizer Software.

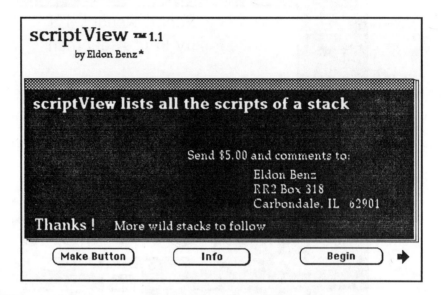

Figure 24-2. scriptView opening screen

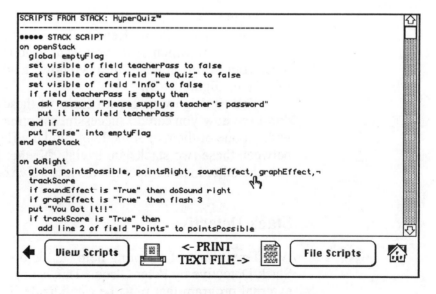

Figure 24-3. Typical scriptView listing

Stack Detective probes every nook and cranny of your stack and its scripts and produces a generally voluminous report that tells you a great deal about how the stack is structured internally. Each time Olson releases a new version of the program, he's found out more about the internal and undocumented structures of HyperCard files.

One of the most convenient aspects of Stack Detective is that it permits you to choose from a range of options to determine what kinds of objects the program will look at and attempt to translate, what kinds of files to open, what to do with the resulting output, and many other powerful choices. Figure 24-4 shows the basic options set-up screen for Stack Detective. Figure 24-5 displays one of several detailed screens for choosing various settings.

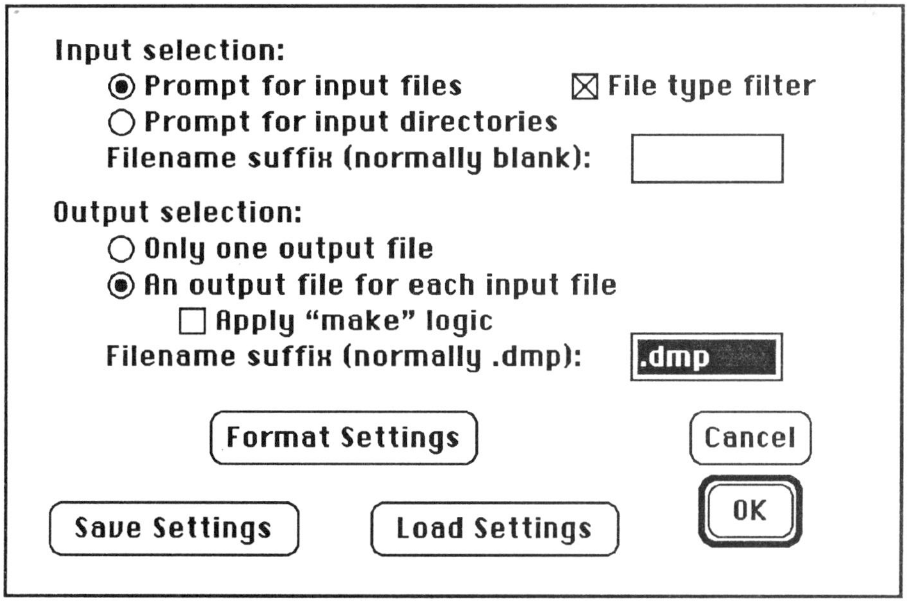

Figure 24-4. Initial options for Stack Detective

When Stack Detective has finished analyzing your stack, it produces an output file that is almost always larger than the stack itself and quite often substantially larger. The beginning of the file looks something like Figure 24-6. A more detailed look at a specific object is provided by such information as shown in Figure 24-7.

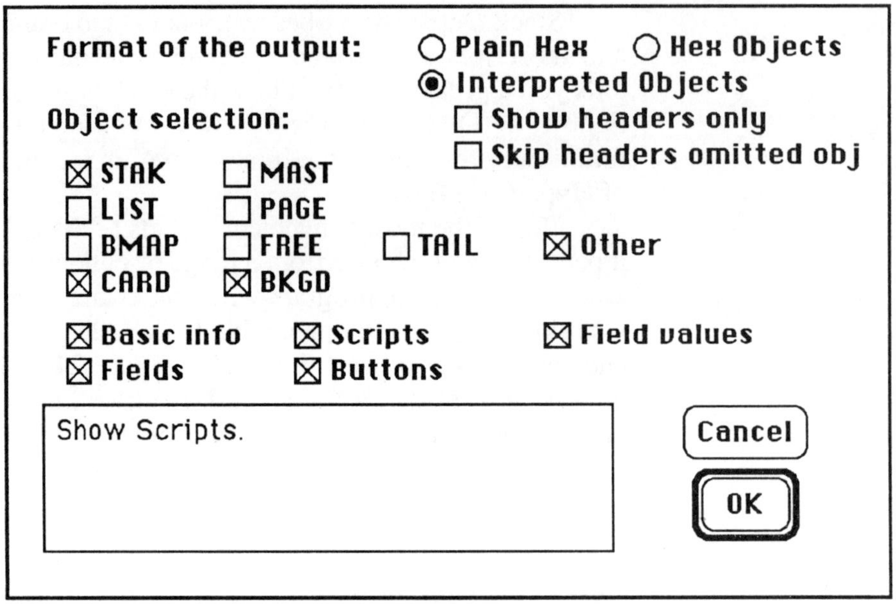

```
┌──────────────────────────────────────────────────────────────┐
│                                                                │
│   Format of the output:    ○ Plain Hex    ○ Hex Objects        │
│                            ⊙ Interpreted Objects               │
│   Object selection:        ☐ Show headers only                 │
│                            ☐ Skip headers omitted obj          │
│      ☒ STAK    ☐ MAST                                          │
│      ☐ LIST    ☐ PAGE                                          │
│      ☐ BMAP    ☐ FREE     ☐ TAIL     ☒ Other                  │
│      ☒ CARD    ☒ BKGD                                          │
│                                                                │
│      ☒ Basic info    ☒ Scripts        ☒ Field values           │
│      ☒ Fields        ☒ Buttons                                 │
│                                                                │
│   ┌────────────────────────────────┐     ┌──────────┐         │
│   │ Show Scripts.                   │     │  Cancel  │         │
│   │                                 │     └──────────┘         │
│   │                                 │     ┌──────────┐         │
│   │                                 │     │    OK    │         │
│   └────────────────────────────────┘     └──────────┘         │
│                                                                │
└──────────────────────────────────────────────────────────────┘
```

Figure 24-5. Settings screen in Stack Detective

Although Stack Detective will let you analyze and read the scripts of protected stacks, it does not affect the protected nature of the stack or the password.

Stack Enhancers

We talked in Chapter 21 about HyperMacintalk, the shareware program that lets you add speech to your stacks. Here, we focus on two other products from a single company that let you enhance your stacks with menus and add value to your stacks with powerful and attractive reports. Both of these products were developed by Nine-to-Five Software of Greenwood, Indiana. The first, Menus for HyperCard!, is freeware and can be obtained from local and national bulletin boards and user groups. The second, called Reports for HyperCard, can be ordered through your Macintosh software dealer.

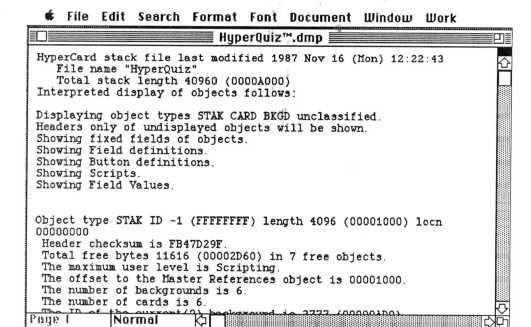

Figure 24-6. Basic stack analysis output

Menus for HyperCard!

The Menus for HyperCard! program (see Figure 24-8) is actually a collection of external commands (XCMDs, as discussed in Chapter 22) that enable you to modify the HyperCard menu bar and menu options in your stacks. The program adds menu options to the menu bar but does not alter or replace any of HyperCard's built-in menus. You can then use these commands in any script exactly as if they were built-in HyperCard commands. This can give your stackware a real Macintosh look and feel.

After this program is installed, you can use any of the following commands:

- **NewMenu**, to add and display menus and menu items to the menu bar

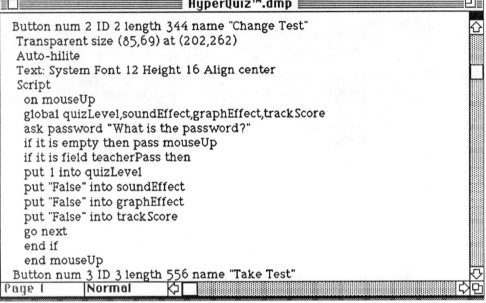

Figure 24-7. Detailed object analysis output

- **ShowMenu,** to display menus and items you add after HyperCard has redrawn its own menu bar (e.g., when the user selects a paint tool)

- **ChangeMenu,** to change the name of an item on a menu you've added

- **DeleteMenu,** to remove a menu you've created

- **EnableMenu,** to turn individual menu items on and off

- **CheckMenu,** to add and remove check marks next to menu items

These XCMDs can be added to any stack you design with the simple click of a button on the Menus for HyperCard! opening screen.

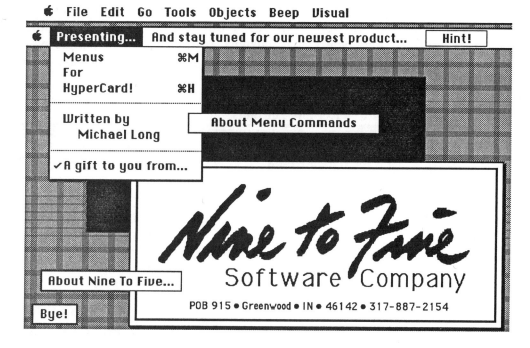

Figure 24-8. Menus for HyperCard! opening screen

Although the HyperCard interface is undoubtedly strong, and in some ways even an improvement over the popular Mac interface standard, there is no doubt that some users will expect to be able to use pull-down menus. This program lets you add such menus to your stacks and give your users that Macintosh"feel."

Reports for HyperCard

HyperCard was not intended to be a database development environment. Apple Computer specifically positioned it as system software and downplayed its data management capabilities. There were a number of good reasons for this. But even the best of reasons didn't prevent a great many people from comparing HyperCard with popular Macintosh database programs and using HyperCard for data management tasks.

When those applications began to appear, one glaring shortcoming in HyperCard became painfully evident. Its reporting capabilities are somewhat primitive. Although the standard

HyperCard report dialog (see Figure 24-9) gives you a great deal of flexibility in producing reports within its parameters, its parameters are somewhat restrictive. For example, you cannot include graphics, change fonts, calculate totals and subtotals, or perform conditional page-breaks.

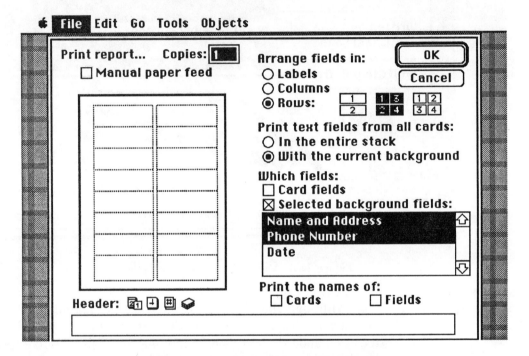

Figure 24-9. Standard HyperCard report dialog

Michael Long saw this "hole" as an opportunity and created Reports for HyperCard. It has quickly become one of the most popular and successful HyperCard add-ons. Reports for Hyper-Card is available at most computer dealers. It is a commercial HyperCard stack from Imaginetics (formerly Activision). Its suggested retail price at this writing is $99.95. Developers can obtain run-time licenses to include Reports functionality in their stacks without requiring their users to buy the program.

With Reports for HyperCard, you can easily build reports from multiple stacks, define subtotals on fields, and lay out the report to print fields anywhere you like on the form. The basic Reports for HyperCard window in which report design takes place is shown in Figure 24-10. You may have seen other

Macintosh programs that work with database design and permit you to develop reports in a similar fashion.

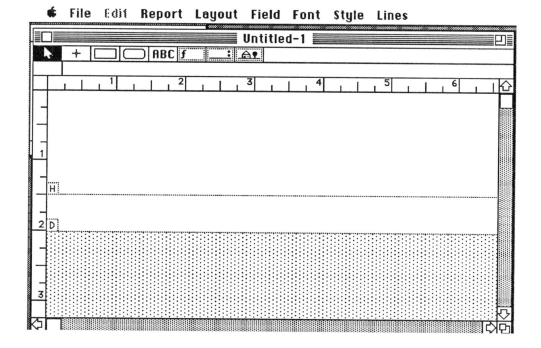

Figure 24-10. Reports for HyperCard design window

There is additional functionality built into Reports for HyperCard. For example, you can build in detailed custom programming via the program's built-in script editor. Before the program prints any section of the report, it calls a handler named after that part of the printout. You can modify this handler, enabling you to customize the report process completely.

Figures 24-11 a and b show portions of several reports produced using the Reports for HyperCard program. As you can see, you can achieve a great deal of flexibility in report design. Look for more programs that add power to HyperCard to become available in coming months.

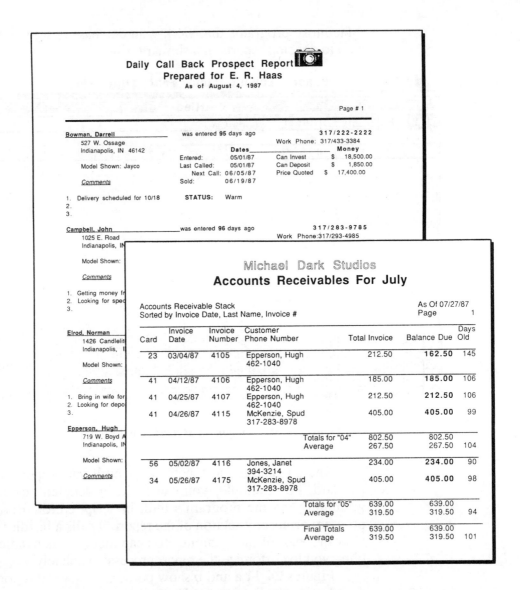

Figure 24-11 a. Sample reports produced with Reports for HyperCard

Michael Dark Studios 📷
Accounts Receivable as of 07/27/87
Prepared by Dana J. Andrews

Second Notices are sent at 30 days.
Third Notices are sent at 60 days.
Final Notices are sent at 90 days.

Accounts Receivable Sorted by Month of Invoice Date, Last Name, and Invoice #   Page # 1

INVOICE DATE	INV #	CUSTOMER'S NAME	PHONE #	TOTAL INVOICE	BALANCE DUE	AGE	COMMENTS
03/04/87	4105	Epperson, Hugh	317-881-1234		$ 212.50	$ 162.50	1 4 5	Will pay Friday
04/12/87	4106	Epperson, Hugh	317-881-1234	$ 185.00	$ 185.00	1 0 6	Will Pay Friday
04/25/87	4107	Epperson, Hugh	317-881-1234	$ 212.50	$ 212.50	9 3	will Pay Friday
04/14/87	4115	McKenzie,Spud	317-283-8978	$ 405.00	$ 405.00	1 0 4	Will Pay Saturday
Total For Month 04				$ 802.50	$ 802.50		Total Open Invoices... 3
Average For Month 04				$ 267.50	$ 267.50	1 0 1	
05/02/87	3223	Brown, David	317-861-7511	$ 157.50	$ 157.50	86	Will Pay Tuesday
05/30/87	4108	Epperson, Hugh	317-881-1234	$ 267.50	$ 267.50	58	Will Pay Friday
05/12/87	3412	Hardy, Florence	317-899-4731	$ 450.00	$ 450.00	76	Will Pay Thursday
05/06/87	3349	Jones, Kim	317-763-6129	$ 185.00	$ 140.00	82	Will Pay Tuesday
05/13/87	3347	Shaw, Cindy	271-5552	$ 640.00	$ 400.00	75	Will Pay Monday
05/27/87	2298	Webb, Jimmie	556-4500	$ 240.00	$ 240.00	61	Will Pay Saturday
05/30/87	2995	White, Beckey	317-462-5599	$ 560.00	$ 560.00	58	Will Pay Monday
05/07/87	3434	Zion, Joannie	317-861-6248	$ 90.00	$ 90.00	81	Will Pay Wednesday
Total For Month 05				$ 2580.00	$ 2305.00		Total Open Invoices... 8
Average For Month 05				$ 322.50	$ 288.13	72	
06/03/87	4098	Bowman, Darrel	317-462-3551	$ 65.00	$ 65.00	54	Will Pay Wednesday
06/27/87	3484	Campbell, John	317-861-6523	$ 612.50	$ 612.50	30	
06/03/87	3348	Dye, Wayne	936-5720	$ 240.00	$ 160.00	54	Will Pay Friday
06/03/87	4104	Elrod, Norman	317-271-0023	$ 267.50	$ 267.50	54	Will Pay Tuesday
06/15/87	4100	Englund, Richa	462-5315	$ 235.00	$ 235.00	42	Will Pay Tuesday
06/01/87	4109	Epperson, Hugh	317-881-1234	$ 212.50	$ 212.50	56	Will Pay Friday
06/02/87	4110	Epperson, Hugh	317-881-1234	$ 212.50	$ 212.50	55	Will Pay Friday
06/01/87	4101	Faut, Ken	317-273-3829	$ 612.50	$ 612.50	56	Will Pay Monday
06/23/87	4103	Fleming, John	244-2348	$ 185.00	$ 185.00	34	Will Pay Thursday

Figure 24-11 b. Sample reports produced with Reports for HyperCard

Importing Text Intelligently

One of the first things many early HyperCard users wanted to do was move information they had stored in another program's data file into this impressive new environment. Many public domain and shareware programs were constructed specifically to assist with this task, and more are being developed all the time.

Although a discussion of text importing programs may seem out of place in a chapter on programming tools, we have found that many stack developers need such a capability early in their experience as scripters. Given HyperTalk's ability to deal with text in many different forms, it is not a difficult task to write your own script to deal with these needs. On the other hand, if someone else has done the work, and done it well and flexibly enough to accommodate your needs, why reinvent the wheel?

We have experimented with several of those programs, and many of them work quite well. As an example of how such programs can work and help you, we've chosen to discuss Importer 1.1, a $10 shareware program written by Stephen Michel of Albany, California. It is one of the easiest to use and most intelligent of the import programs we've seen. Its early version was limited to importing tab-delimited files, but the author is at work on accessing files with other well-documented formats. Check your local or national BBS or user group for information on the latest version and what file types it handles.

Using Importer 1.1 is a real joy. The author automates virtually the entire process. You click on a button and answer two questions – dealing with the names of the output and input files – and then the stack looks at your file and reports back. It tells you how many fields there are and gets ready to import the contents. This is where the program gets smart and helpful.

If the first line of your text-only, tab-delimited file contains the names of the fields you want to use in your stack, Importer 1.1 lets you use those names with a click of the mouse (see Figure 24-12). Or you can change them, as you would want to do, for example, if the first line of the file contains real data rather than column labels or if you just don't like the labels someone has put into the file.

After you've given the field a name or accepted the one suggested by the first line of your file, you are asked to indicate where on the card layout you want to put this field. Simply click at the upper-left corner of where you want the field located. Importer 1.1 then creates the field and positions it where you indicated. You can later re-size the field, make it into a scrolling field, change the border, or make other modifications.

Aside from the inability to import files that are not tab-delimited, the only major design drawback to Importer 1.1 that we've experienced is that you cannot import text to an existing stack. Given the relative difficulty of merging two stacks, this is a potential problem. But if you have a lot of data to move, you are probably creating a new stack with the data. So import the text fields, then build the card around the data.

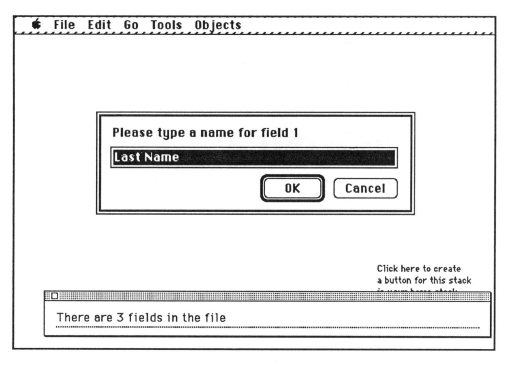

Figure 24-12. Using file's first line as field labels in Importer 1.1

Developer Stack

One of the most innovative and useful programming tools we encountered as we were going to press is "Developer Stack" from ART Incorporated and Steve Drazga. This stack is available via CompuServe and other BBSes. It incorporates many of the external commands and functions described in Chapter 22 into a single, easy-to-use environment. You can link the Developer Stack to the stack on which you are working so that you can move back and forth between them with a single button-click.

In addition to XCMDs and XFCNs, the Developer Stack also includes a number of handy HyperTalk handlers. There is even a single-button method for incorporating Importer 1.1 directly into a stack. All scripts are accessible and therefore modifiable to meet your specific needs. This stack is nearly 150K bytes large so downloading time can be lengthy but it's freeware and well worth the download cost if you're developing serious stacks.

Figure 24-13 shows the opening screen of Developer Stack, with the lower left corner displaying the names of some of the XFCNs, XCMDs and HyperTalk functions available for one-step integration into your stacks.

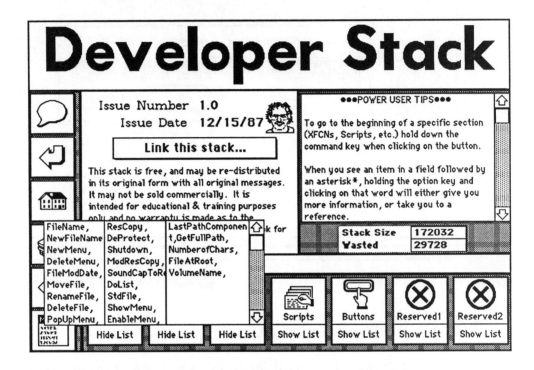

**Figure 24-13. Opening screen from Developer Stack
with XCMD, XFCN, and function lists**

Summary

In this chapter, you looked at some of the most useful programming tools available for HyperTalk. As you can tell, we are great believers in supporting user groups and having access to national bulletin board services. In a field as dynamic as HyperCard, this kind of real-time support is invaluable.

An Educational Script

This chapter contains the cards and scripts for a HyperCard stack we created for this book. It's called *HyperQuiz* and is offered as a free program here and on CompuServe, GEnie, and other bulletin boards around the country.

The script includes numerous comments and the cards are labeled so that you can see what buttons activate what scripts and which fields are involved. Rather than present all the same information again in the text, we will provide an overview of how the script works and then step aside and let you roll up your sleeves and start scripting.

Two Users

There are two potential types of users for HyperQuiz: teachers, who build quizzes, and students, who take them. When teachers use the system they see Cards 1-5 as they set up the parameters for the quiz and enter the questions. When students use it, they see the questions on cards like Cards 3-5 and at the conclusion of the quiz they see Card 6 where their performance is assessed.

Teacher use

The first time a teacher uses the stack, he or she must enter a password to protect against students being able to alter the quiz or to create new ones. Thereafter, any time the Create a New Test button or the Change This Test button is pressed, the user will have to enter a password to match the one entered by the instructor or access will be denied.

Once in the stack, the instructor selects the type of question to be entered from the three buttons in the middle of Card 2: True/False, Multiple Choice and Fill-In. Then HyperQuiz takes the teacher to a blank card of the appropriate background. After entering the question and, in the case of the multiple choice question, 2-4 alternatives for the student to choose from, the teacher presses the Done button. HyperQuiz then goes through some wrap-up questions involving the addition of a note or help to the question (more later), supplying the correct answer and asssigning the point value for the question.

The teacher can also turn sound effects, graphics effects, and scoring on or off for a given quiz. We have supplied rudimentary sound and graphics and indicated where in the script these can be enhanced if you are interested in more elaborate feedback.

Student use

A student can only access the stack via the Take This Test button. The student is then taken to the true-false question if there are any, then to the multiple-choice questions, then to the fill-in questions, and finally to the scoring screen. At each screen, the student either provides an answer or presses the question-mark button. In the latter case, a new field appears containing either a note or hint provided by the teacher or the message "Sorry, but no hints are available for this question!"

The Cards

There are six cards and six backgrounds in the stack. Cards 3-5, which are the question cards, appear differently for the teacher and for the student. The global variable **quizLevel** determines which view the user sees.

Card 1 has one information field, Field 2, which occupies so much of the card that we have shown it as a separate figure. Cards 3-5 have a "Notes" field that you can put wherever you like; it will inevitably cover some of the material on the card so we have omitted it from the figures.

Figures 25-1 through 25-10 reproduce the screens, with all fields and buttons labeled to make reading the script easier. You can, of course, design these cards any way you like as long as you preserve object names.

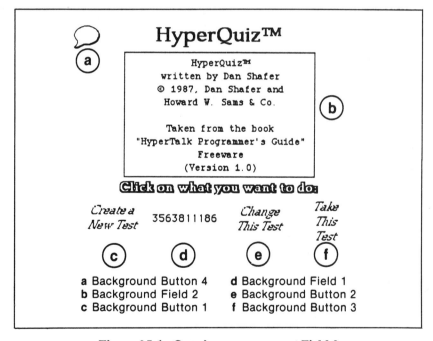

Figure 25-1. Opening screen except Field 2

To create a new test with HyperQuiz™, this script will create a copy of itself and store that copy under whatever name you type when you are asked to do so. Once that is done, you will be returned to this card. At that point, choose " Open Stack... from the File Menu and select the quiz stack you have just created.

Then click on the middle button, "Change This Test" to begin creating the questions for the new test.

Click the mouse anywhere to create the new quiz.

Figure 25-2. Field 2 from opening screen

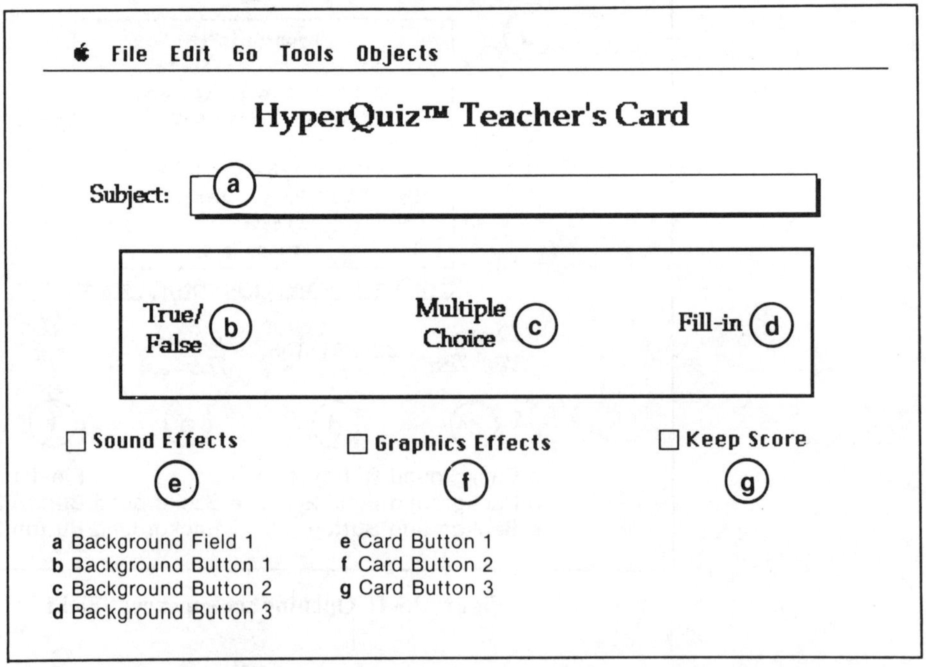

Figure 25-3. Teacher's card

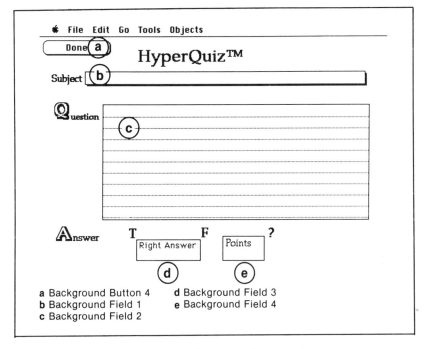

Figure 25-4. True/False card, teacher's view

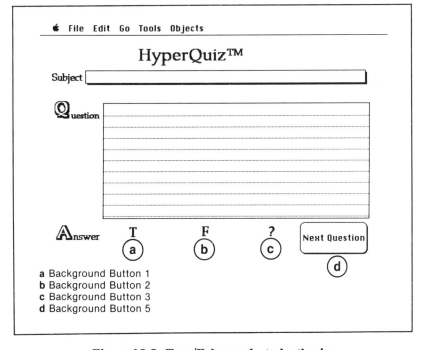

Figure 25-5. True/False card, student's view

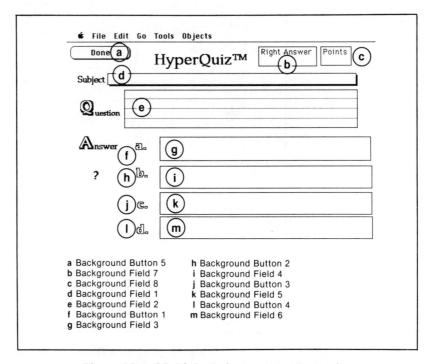

Figure 25-6. Multiple choice card, teacher's view

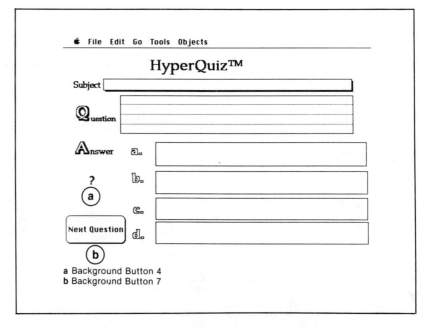

Figure 25-7. Multiple choice card, student's view

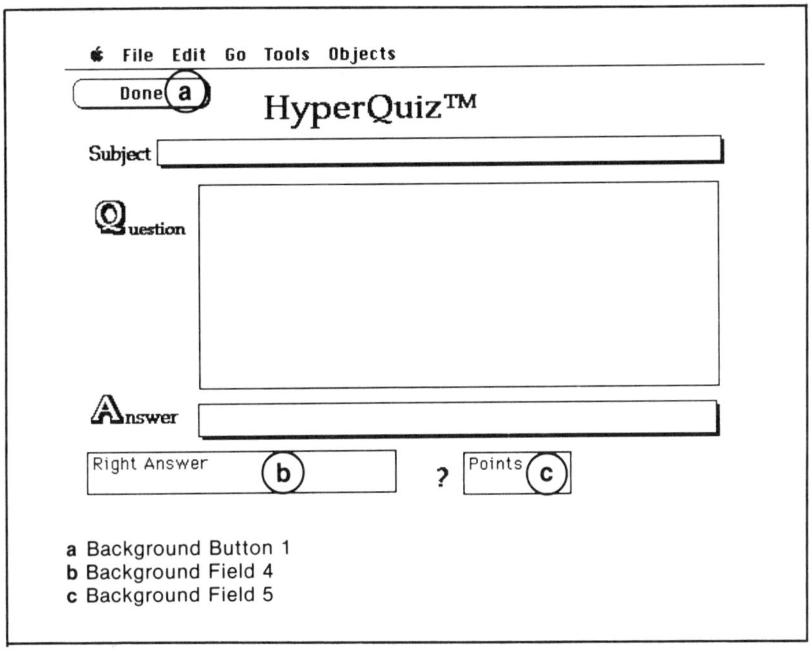

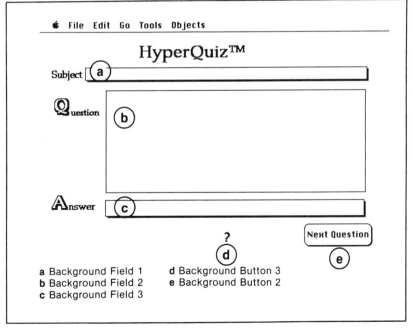

Figure 25-8. Fill-in card, teacher's view

🍎 File Edit Go Tools Objects

HyperQuiz™

Done (a)

Subject

Question

Answer

Right Answer (b)   ?   Points (c)

a Background Button 1
b Background Field 4
c Background Field 5

Figure 25-8. Fill-in card, teacher's view

🍎 File Edit Go Tools Objects

HyperQuiz™

Subject (a)

Question (b)

Answer (c)

?
(d)   Next Question (e)

a Background Field 1   d Background Button 3
b Background Field 2   e Background Button 2
c Background Field 3

Figure 25-9. Fill-in card, student's view

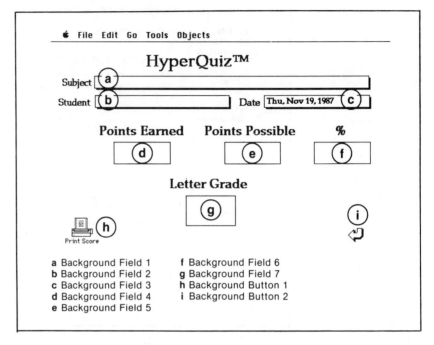

Figure 25-10. Final scoring card

The Scripts

The scripts are reproduced here. Comments are preceded by the double-hyphen (--) marker. (The original listing of these scripts was produced using Eric Alderman's Script Report, discussed in Chapter 24.)

```
SCRIPTS FOR STACK: HyperQuiz
=========================================================


** STACK SCRIPT **********************************
on openStack
  global emptyFlag
  set visible of field teacherPass to false
  set visible of card field "New Quiz" to false
  set visible of  field "Info" to false
  if field teacherPass is empty then
    -- if you get a copy with a non-empty teacherPass field,
    -- try "cj0420," the password we used in the original version!
```

```
      ask Password "Please supply a teacher's password"
        put it into field teacherPass
      end if
      put "False" into emptyFlag
    end openStack

    -- Handler to use when student gets question right
    on doRight
      global pointsPossible, pointsRight, soundEffect, graphEffect,¬
      trackScore
      if soundEffect is "True" then doSound right
      if graphEffect is "True" then flash 3
      -- improve on the above graphic effect with your own design,
      -- either by adding several lines in the if...then construct
      -- or by defining a new handler called, e.g., "doGraphic"
      -- We don't furnish a graphics effect for wrong answers.
      put "You Got It!!" -- can eliminate this and the "wait" below
                         -- for faster student use if you like
      if trackScore is "True" then
        add line 2 of field "Points" to pointsPossible
        add line 2 of field "Points" to pointsRight
      end if
      wait until the mouseClick -- can be eliminated; see above
      hide the message box -- eliminate if you do away with the box
    end doRight

    -- Handler to use if student answer is wrong
    on doWrong
      global pointsPossible, pointsRight, soundEffect, graphEffect,¬
      trackScore
      if soundEffect is "True" then doSound wrong
      put "Sorry, but that's not right."
      if trackScore is "True" then add line 2 of field "Points" ¬
      to pointsPossible
      wait until the mouseClick
      hide the message box
    end doWrong

    -- Very rudimentary sound effects.  Use resources and 'snd' files
    -- as described in Chapter 21 to make this far more interesting.
    on doSound response
      if response is "right" then play harpsichord "c e"
      if response is "wrong" then play boing "e c"
      wait until the sound is "done"
    end doSound
```

```
-- Most of the processing of the student's interaction with the
-- program takes place in this handler.
on nextQuestion
  global emptyFlag
  if emptyFlag is "False" then checkAnswer
  set lockScreen to true
  set lockMessages to true
  put "False" into emptyFlag
  go next
  send openCard to this card
  -- above line is here because of an anomaly in HyperCard that
  -- sometimes prevents the "openCard" message from being sent
  -- when we move from the last card of one background to the
  -- first card of another background.  Subsequent versions may
  -- fix this but it is known to exist in 1.1.
  if the short name of this card is "Final Card" then
    testOver
    exit nextQuestion
  end if
  if  field "Question" is empty then
    put "True" into emptyFlag
    nextQuestion
  else
    put "False" into emptyFlag
    set lockScreen to false
    set lockMessages to false
  end if
end nextQuestion

on testOver
  global pointsPossible,pointsRight
  set numberFormat to "0#"
  put pointsPossible into field "Possible"
  put pointsRight into field "Right"
  put pointsRight/pointsPossible * 100 into field "Pct."
  -- We use the traditional 10-pct. divisions.  It would be trivial
  -- for you to change these if your grading system is different.
  if field "Pct." >= 90 then
    put "A" into field "Grade"
    cleanExit
  end if
  if field "Pct." >= 80 then
    put "B" into field "Grade"
    cleanExit
```

```
  end if
   if field "Pct." >= 70 then
     put "C" into field "Grade"
     cleanExit
   end if
   if field "Pct." >= 60 then
     put "D" into field "Grade"
     cleanExit
   end if
   if field "Pct." <=59 then
     put "F" into field "Grade"
     cleanExit
   end if
end testOver

on checkAnswer
   global answer,emptyFlag
   put "False" into emptyFlag
   if answer is line 2 of field "Right Answer" then doRight ¬
   else doWrong
   wait until the sound is "done"
end checkAnswer

-- Used wherever we are exiting mid-handler
on cleanExit
   set lockScreen to false
   set lockMessages to false
   exit to HyperCard
end cleanExit


** BKGND #1, BUTTON #1: Create Test
**********************************
on mouseUp
   ask password "What is the password?"
   if it is empty then pass mouseUp
   -- May have to enter one yet
   if it is field teacherPass then
     set visible of card field "New Quiz" to true
     -- displays contents of Field 2, which explains that to create
     -- a new quiz, we copy this stack to a stack of the teacher's
     -- named choice.  Then we return to Home and the teacher selects
     -- the newly named stack and selects "Change This Test" from the
     -- first card.  Could use Steve Maller's "fileName" XCMD to
     -- keep track of the file and go there automatically but this
```

```
  -- is easy enough and takes up less space!
    wait until the mouseClick
    set visible of card field "New Quiz" to false
    doMenu "Save a Copy..."
    go "Home"
  else
    answer "Sorry, you're not authorized!" with "Shucks!"
  end if
end mouseUp


** BKGND #1, BUTTON #2: Change Test
*************************************
on mouseUp
  global quizLevel,soundEffect,graphEffect,trackScore
  ask password "What is the password?"
  if it is empty then pass mouseUp
  if it is field teacherPass then -- initialize parameters
    put 1 into quizLevel
    put "False" into soundEffect
    put "False" into graphEffect
    put "False" into trackScore
    go next
  end if
end mouseUp


** BKGND #1, BUTTON #3: Take Test
*************************************
on mouseUp
  global studentName,quizLevel,pointsPossible,pointsRight
  -- Even if this is a teacher, during quiz-taking we want students
  -- to leave it set so that the persons using it can walk through
  -- the questions, and not find themselves in question-entry/edit
  -- mode.
  put 0 into quizLevel
  -- Initialize the scoring variables
  put 0 into pointsPossible
  put 0 into pointsRight
  ask "What's your name?"
  put it into studentName
  set lockScreen to true
  go to second card of background "True/False"
  -- First card of background is blank, so we start questions with
  -- the second one. If result comes up non-empty, it means there is
  -- no true/false question, so we move to the next type of
  -- question. This allows creation of quizzes that don't have all
```

```
   -- three types of questions in them.
   if the result is not empty then go to second card of background¬
   "Multiple Choice"
   if the result is not empty then go to second card of background¬
   "Fill-In"
   if the result is not empty then
     beep
     put "Sorry, but this test seems to be empty!"
   end if
end mouseUp
```

```
** BKGND #1, BUTTON #4: Info Button
*************************************
on mouseUp
  set visible of  field "Info" to true
  wait until the mouseClick
  set visible of  field "Info" to false
end mouseUp
```

```
** BKGND #2, BUTTON #1: TF Select
*************************************
on mouseUp
  global subject
  set lockScreen to true
  put field "Subject" into subject
  go first card of background "True/False"
  doMenu "Copy Card"
  doMenu "Paste Card"
  put subject into field "cardSubject"
  set lockScreen to false
  type tab & tab -- put teacher into the question field and await
input
end mouseUp
```

```
** BKGND #2, BUTTON #2: MC Select
*************************************
on mouseUp
  global subject
  set lockScreen to true
  put field "Subject" into subject
  go first card of background "Multiple Choice"
  doMenu "Copy Card"
  doMenu "Paste Card"
  put subject into field "cardSubject"
  set lockScreen to false
```

```
  type tab & tab
end mouseUp


** BKGND #2, BUTTON #3: Fill-in Select
**************************************
on mouseUp
  global subject
  set lockScreen to true
  put field "Subject" into subject
  go first card of background "Fill-In"
  doMenu "Copy Card"
  doMenu "Paste Card"
  put subject into field "cardSubject"
  set lockScreen to false
  type tab & tab
end mouseUp


** BACKGROUND #3: True/False *************************************
on openCard
  global quizLevel
  -- All of the question-entry backgrounds are nearly the same.
  -- We set up the fields and buttons so the ones the teacher needs
  -- are visible and the ones the student needs are invisible if
  -- quizLevel=1 (i.e., quiz entry is in process) and vice versa if
  -- quizLevel=0 (i.e., student is taking quiz).
  hide the message box
  set visible of field "Notes" to false
  set lockScreen to true
  if quizLevel is 1 then
    set visible of field "Right Answer" to true
    set visible of field "Points" to true
    set lockText of field 1 to false
    set lockText of field "Notes" to false
    set visible of background button "Done" to true
    set visible of background button "Next Question" to false
  else
    set visible of field "Right Answer" to false
    set visible of field "Points" to false
    set lockText of field 1 to true
    set lockText of field "Notes" to true
    set visible of background button "Done" to false
    set visible of background button "Next Question" to true
  end if
  set lockScreen to false
end openCard
```

```
** BKGND #3, FIELD #5: Notes *********************************
on closeField
  set visible of me to false
end closeField

** BKGND #3, BUTTON #1: True *********************************
on mouseUp
  global answer
  put "True" into answer
end mouseUp

** BKGND #3, BUTTON #2: False ********************************
on mouseUp
  global answer
  put "False" into answer
end mouseUp

** BKGND #3, BUTTON #3: ? ************************************
on mouseUp
  global quizLevel
  show field "Notes" -- Displays any hint and waits for a mouseClick
  wait until the mouseClick
  hide field "Notes"
end mouseUp

** BKGND #3, BUTTON #4: Done *********************************
on mouseUp
  if field "Question" is empty then -- Maybe changed mind?
    beep
    answer "Cancel this entry?" with Yes or No
    if it is "Yes" then
      set lockScreen to true
      doMenu "Delete Card"
      go to card "Teacher Card"
      set lockScreen to false
    else
      exit mouseUp
    end if
  else
    if field "Notes" is empty then -- It's OK, but check to be sure.
      answer "Do you want to leave a hint or help?" with "Yes" or "No"
      if it is "Yes" then
        show field "Notes"
        click at the loc of field "Notes"
        exit mouseUp
```

```
      else
        put "Sorry, but no hints are available for this question!"¬
        into field "Notes"
      end if
    end if
    answer "What's the right answer?" with "True" or "False"
    put it into line 2 of field "Right Answer"
    ask "How many points is this question worth?" with "1"
    put it into line 2 of field "Points"
    go to card "Teacher Card"
  end if
end mouseUp


** BKGND #3, BUTTON #5: Next Question
*************************************
on mouseUp
  nextQuestion
end mouseUp


** BACKGROUND #4: Multiple Choice
*************************************
on openCard
  global quizLevel
  -- see comments under "True/False", Background #3
  hide the message box
  set visible of field "Notes" to false
  set lockScreen to true
  if quizLevel is 1 then
    set visible of background button "Done" to true
    set visible of field "Right Answer" to true
    set visible of field "Points" to true
    set lockText of field 1 to false
    set lockText of field "Notes" to false
    set visible of background button "Next Question" to false
  else
    set visible of background button "Done" to false
    set visible of field "Right Answer" to false
    set visible of field "Points" to false
    set lockText of field 1 to true
    set lockText of field "Notes" to true
    set visible of background button "Next Question" to true
  end if
  set lockScreen to false
end openCard
** BKGND #4, FIELD #9: Notes *************************************
```

```
on closeField
  set visible of me to false
end closeField

** BKGND #4, BUTTON #1: Answer a
***********************************
on mouseUp
  global answer
  put "a" into answer
end mouseUp

** BKGND #4, BUTTON #2: Answer b
***********************************
on mouseUp
  global answer
  put "b" into answer
end mouseUp

** BKGND #4, BUTTON #3: Answer c
***********************************
on mouseUp
  global answer
  put "c" into answer
end mouseUp

** BKGND #4, BUTTON #4: ? *************************************
on mouseUp
  global quizLevel
  show field "Notes"
  wait until the mouseClick
  hide field "Notes"
end mouseUp

** BKGND #4, BUTTON #5: Done *************************************
on mouseUp
  -- if there's no question and not at least two answers,
  -- you don't really have a multiple-choice question
  if field "Question" is empty or field "Answer a"¬
  is empty or field "Answer b" is empty
  then
    beep
    answer "Cancel this entry?" with "Yes" or "No"
    if it is "Yes" then
      set lockScreen to true
      doMenu "Delete Card"
```

```
     go to card "Teacher Card"
       set lockScreen to false
     else
       exit mouseUp
     end if
   else
     if field "Notes" is empty then
       answer "Do you want to leave a hint or help?" with "Yes" or "No"
       if it is "Yes" then
         show field "Notes"
         click at the loc of field "Notes"
         exit mouseUp
       else
         put "Sorry, but no hints are available for this question!"¬
         into field "Notes"
       end if
     end if
     ask "What's the right answer?" with "a"
     put it into line 2 of field "Right Answer"
     ask "How many points is this question worth?" with "1"
     put it into line 2 of field "Points"
     go to card "Teacher Card"
   end if
end mouseUp


** BKGND #4, BUTTON #6: Answer d
***********************************
on mouseUp
  global answer
  put "d" into answer
end mouseUp


** BKGND #4, BUTTON #7: Next Question
***********************************
on mouseUp
  nextQuestion
end mouseUp


** BACKGROUND #5: Fill-In ***********************************
on openCard
  global quizLevel
  -- For comments, see "True/False", Background #3
  hide the message box
  set visible of field "Notes" to false
  put empty into field "Answer"
```

```
  set lockScreen to true
   if quizLevel is 1 then
     set visible of field "Right Answer" to true
     set visible of field "Points" to true
     set visible of background button "Done" to true
     set lockText of field 1 to false
     set lockText of field 3 to true
     set lockText of field "Notes" to false
     set visible of background button "Next Question" to false
   else
     set visible of field "Right Answer" to false
     set visible of field "Points" to false
     set visible of background button "Done" to false
     set lockText of field 1 to true
     set lockText of field 3 to false
     set lockText of field "Notes" to true
     set visible of background button "Next Question" to true
   end if
   set lockScreen to false
end openCard
** BKGND #5, FIELD #6: Notes ************************************
on closeField
  set visible of me to false
end closeField


** BKGND #5, BUTTON #1: Done ************************************
on mouseUp
   if field "Question" is empty then
     beep
     answer "Cancel this entry?" with "Yes" or "No"
     if it is "Yes" then
       set lockScreen to true
       doMenu "Delete Card"
       go to card "Teacher Card"
       set lockScreen to false
     else
       exit mouseUp
     end if
   else
     if field "Notes" is empty then
       answer "Do you want to leave a hint or help?" with "Yes" or "No"
       if it is "Yes" then
         show field "Notes"
         click at the loc of field "Notes"
         exit mouseUp
```

```
      else
        put "Sorry, but no hints are available for this question!"¬
        into field "Notes"
      end if
    end if
    ask "What's the right answer?"
    put it into line 2 of field "Right Answer"
    ask "How many points is this question worth?" with "1"
    put it into line 2 of field "Points"
    go to card "Teacher Card"
  end if
end mouseUp


** BKGND #5, BUTTON #2: Next Question
***********************************
on mouseUp
  global answer
  put line 1 of field "Answer" into answer
  nextQuestion
end mouseUp


** BKGND #5, BUTTON #3: ? *************************************
on mouseUp
  global quizLevel
  show field "Notes"
  if quizLevel is 1 then set lockText of field "Notes" to false
  else
    set lockText of field "Notes" to true
  end if
  wait until the mouseClick
  hide field "Notes"
end mouseUp


** BKGND #6, BUTTON #1: Print Score
***********************************
on mouseUp
  print this card
end mouseUp


** BKGND #6, BUTTON #2: Return **************************************
on mouseUp
  go to first card
end mouseUp


** CARD #2: Teacher Card **************************************
```

```
on openCard
  tabKey
end openCard
** CARD #2, BUTTON #1: Sound Effects
**********************************
on mouseUp
  global soundEffect
  set hilite of me to not hilite of me
  -- if the button is on, turn it off; if it's off, turn it on
  put not soundEffect into soundEffect
end mouseUp

** CARD #2, BUTTON #2: Graphics Effects
**********************************
on mouseUp
  global graphEffect
  set hilite of me to not hilite of me
  put not graphEffect into graphEffect
end mouseUp

** CARD #2, BUTTON #3: Keep Score
**********************************
on mouseUp
  global trackScore
  set hilite of me to not hilite of me
  put not trackScore into trackScore
end mouseUp

** CARD #6: Final Card ***********************************
on openCard
  global studentName,subject
  put subject into field "cardSubject"
  put studentName into field "Name"
  put the abbrev date into field "Date"
  set lockScreen to false
end openCard
```

Changes and Additions

As it stands, we hope you'll find HyperQuiz to be a helpful and useful program. It is not, however, a commercially finished product, nor is it intended to be. Its real purpose here is to illustrate scripting techniques involving multi-background stacks. But you could do a number of things to "spruce it up." Here are some ideas. (If you do improve on our program, we'd appreciate you sending us a copy. We are constantly amazed by the quality of feedback we get from readers and users and we enjoy the dialog!)

Time limit

You could add a time limit check box to Card 2 and then keep track of the time it takes the student to answer the questions in the quiz. The teacher would be asked for a time limit in minutes and then just use HyperTalk's powerful time-management commands to deal with tracking the elapsed time.

Teacher help

As it now stands, the student can get hints and help during quiz-taking if the instructor provides it. But the teacher is pretty much on his or her own. Arguably, the process of entering the questions is sufficiently self-evident that help is not needed. But adding a teacher's help button would be a relatively easy task. We omitted it primarily because the fields would have resulted in more script length than we felt you'd want to type into HyperCard.

Better graphics

We point out in the script where you can improve the graphics effect of a right answer. You might also add visual effects as you move from card to card, particularly as you change backgrounds.

Skipping questions

It might be helpful to add a new button to the student versions of the question cards to permit them to skip a question and come back to it later. The logic for handling this would require you to put the card IDs of the skipped questions into an invisible field so you could track through them again when the last question is reached.

Bugs

We don't claim to write bug-free code, even in HyperTalk, which is more forgiving of many kinds of programming errors than other languages. If you find bugs and fix them, please let us know. The Preface tells you how to reach us.

Summary

This chapter has presented a finished, non-commercial educational application including its cards and scripts. We trust you have learned something and enjoyed the process.

26

Semi-Automatic Programming

The script in this chapter enables you to program a substantial portion of your HyperTalk scripts simply by pushing buttons. It takes a lot of the possibility of syntax errors out of the process of scripting while making the generation of scripts much faster by providing you one- or two-click access to major commands and properties.

The idea for this script originated in our experience with Omnis3+, an eminently powerful database management system for the Macintosh from Blyth Software. It incorporates a powerful programming language and the only way to build programs with it is to use push-button methods. As you press one button, a new screen, containing only those commands and parameters that are syntactically compatible with the command you chose, is displayed. You select another level of the command and continue this until you've built a valid command line.

Using the Stack

This stack, which is a kernel of a commercial program we've developed called ScriptExpert consists of one main card and six related cards, all with one background. At the opening card, you must indicate to the system whether you are defining a handler or a function. You must then give it a name. It fills in the **on** and the name of the handler or function in the scrolling field at the top of the card and you can begin programming.

As you press buttons on the various cards you'll answer questions posed in dialog boxes, you will find your script building in the window. Most often, the program fills in a structure and you can then edit in your own parameters, but some functions and commands are self-contained or obtain enough information from you that they are complete as they appear in the editing window.

When you finish your script, press the Done button and tell the program where to store the text file containing your script. From there, you can copy it and paste it into the script-editing window of the object to which you want it attached. Press the tab key and you can see if it's properly formatted and completed.

The Cards

Figures 26-1 through 26-7 show the cards in the stack, with labels to identify which buttons are which. We've only labeled those buttons whose names are different from those shown on the cards. If you see a button with no label, its name is the same as that on the card.

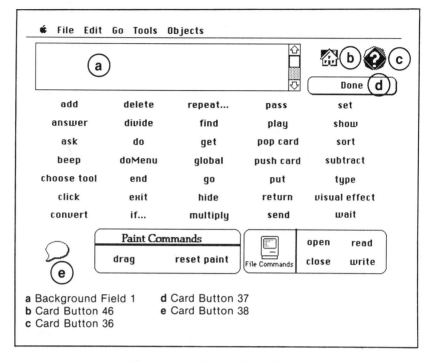

a Background Field 1
b Card Button 46
c Card Button 36
d Card Button 37
e Card Button 38

Figure 26-1. Main Card of stack

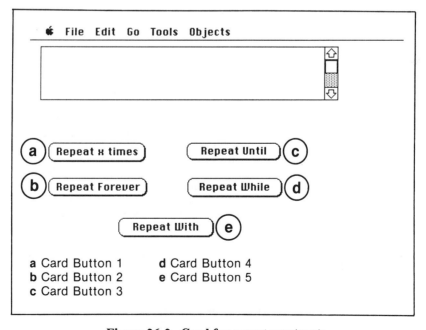

a Card Button 1
b Card Button 2
c Card Button 3
d Card Button 4
e Card Button 5

Figure 26-2. Card for *repeat* constructs

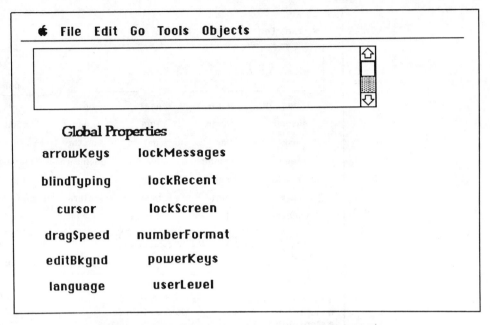

Figure 26-3. Card for *set* command, globals only implemented

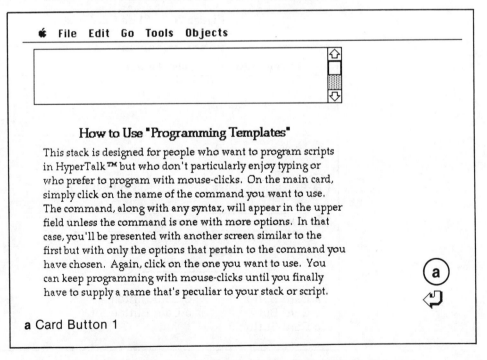

Figure 26-4. Card explaining how to use the stack

File   Edit   Go   Tools   Objects

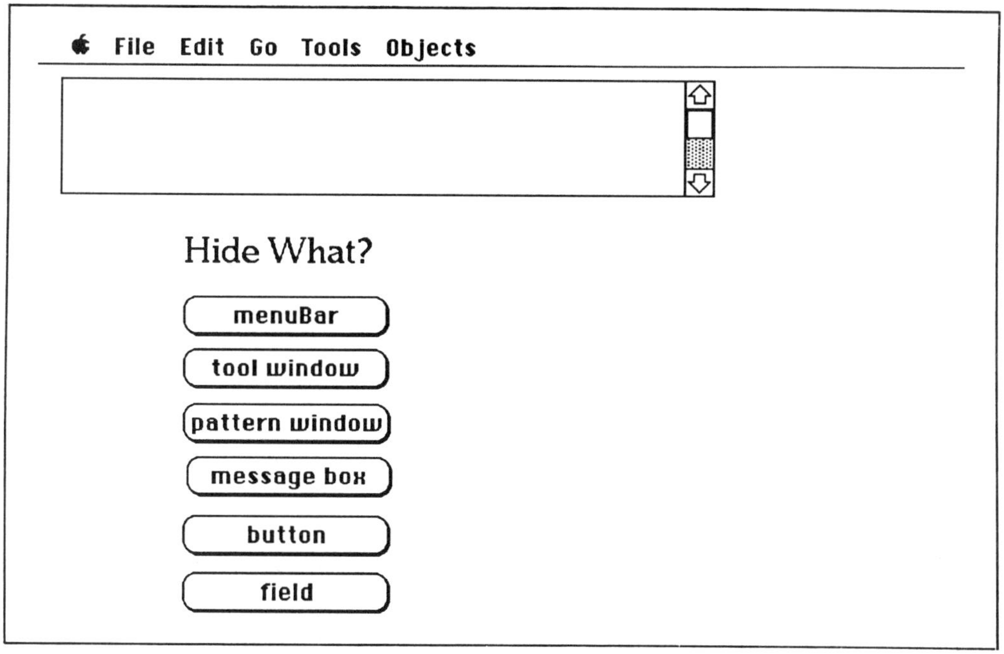

Hide What?

(menuBar)

(tool window)

(pattern window)

(message box)

(button)

(field)

Figure 26-5. Card for *hide* command

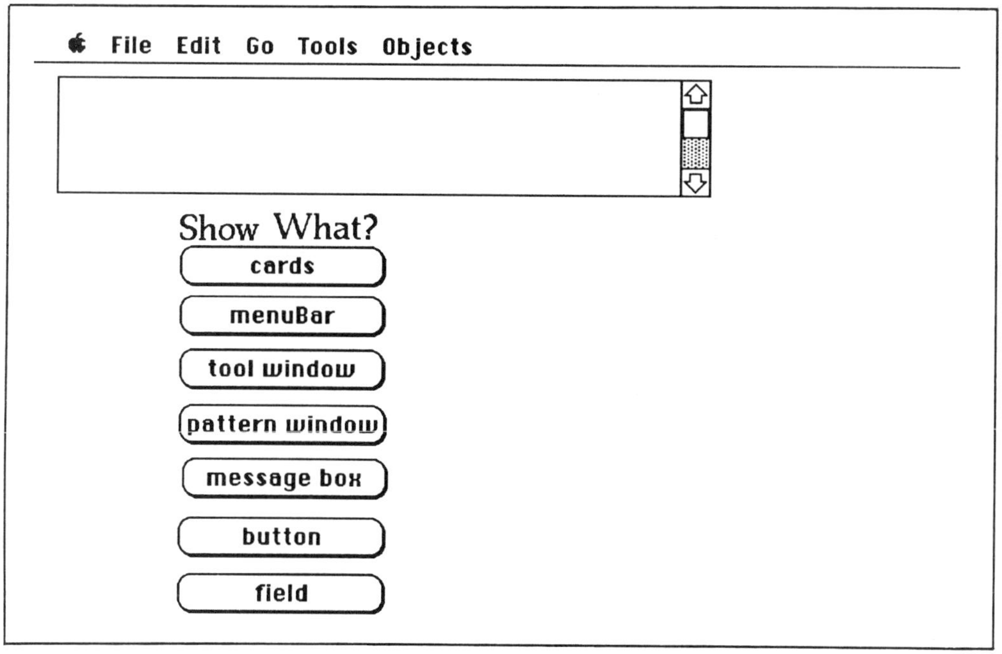

 File   Edit   Go   Tools   Objects

Show What?

(cards)

(menuBar)

(tool window)

(pattern window)

(message box)

(button)

(field)

Figure 26-6. Card for *show* command

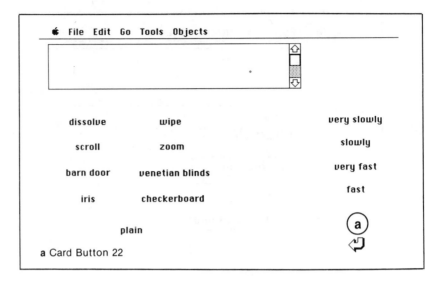

Figure 26-7. Card for *visual effect* command

The Scripts

The scripts for this relatively simple but useful portion of the stack follow. Comments are inserted where necessary, but because the subject of this script is largely explained in the rest of this book, extensive commentary is superfluous.

```
SCRIPTS FOR STACK: Program Templates
==========================================================

** STACK SCRIPT ***********************************
on openStack
  global scriptName,type
  hide the message box
  put empty into field "Script-it" of card "Main Card"
  answer "Build a handler or a function?" with "Function" or "Han-
dler"
  put it into type
  ask "What is the message name?"
  put it into scriptName
  put "on " & scriptName & return into field "Script-it"
end openStack
```

```
** CARD #1, BUTTON #1: add ***********************************
on mouseUp
  put "add  to  " & return after field "Script-it"
end mouseUp

** CARD #1, BUTTON #2: answer *********************************
on mouseUp
  ask "Type your question:"
  put it into query
  put "answer" && quote & query & quote & "with " into holder
  put holder & return after field "Script-it"
end mouseUp

** CARD #1, BUTTON #3: ask ************************************
on mouseUp
  ask "What question do you want to ask?"
  put it into query
  put "ask" && quote & query & quote & return into holder
  put holder after field "Script-It" of card "Main Card"
end mouseUp

** CARD #1, BUTTON #4: beep ***********************************
on mouseUp
  ask "How many times should I beep?" with "1"
  put "beep" && it & return after field "Script-It" of card "Main Card"
end mouseUp

** CARD #1, BUTTON #5: choose tool
*************************************
on mouseUp
  put "choose  tool" & return after field "Script-It" ¬
  of card "Main Card"
end mouseUp

** CARD #1, BUTTON #6: click **********************************
on mouseUp
  put "click at  with  key" & return after ¬
  field "Script-It" of card "Main Card"
end mouseUp

** CARD #1, BUTTON #7: convert ********************************
on mouseUp
  put "convert  to  " & return after ¬
  field "Script-It" of card "Main Card"
end mouseUp
```

```
** CARD #1, BUTTON #8: delete ********************************
on mouseUp
  put "delete " & return after ¬
  field "Script-It" of card "Main Card"
end mouseUp

** CARD #1, BUTTON #9: repeat...
***********************************
on mouseUp
  global holder
  put "repeat" into holder
  push this card
  visual effect wipe right
  go to card "Loops"
end mouseUp

** CARD #1, BUTTON #10: pass **********************************
on mouseUp
  put "pass " & return into holder
  put holder after field "Script-It" of card "Main Card"
end mouseUp

** CARD #1, BUTTON #11: set **********************************
on mouseUp
  global holder
  put "set " into holder
  push this card
  visual effect wipe right
  go to card "Properties"
end mouseUp

** CARD #1, BUTTON #12 **********************************
on mouseUp
  put "divide  by  " & return after ¬
  field "Script-It" of card "Main Card"
end mouseUp

** CARD #1, BUTTON #13: do **********************************
on mouseUp
  put "do " &quote && quote & return after ¬
  field "Script-It" of card "Main Card"
end mouseUp

** CARD #1, BUTTON #14: doMenu **********************************
```

```
on mouseUp
  put "doMenu " & quote && quote & return after ¬
  field "Script-It" of card "Main Card"
end mouseUp


** CARD #1, BUTTON #15: end **********************************
on mouseUp
  put "end " & return after ¬
  field "Script-It" of card "Main Card"
end mouseUp


** CARD #1, BUTTON #16: exit **********************************
on mouseUp
  put "exit " & return after ¬
  field "Script-It" of card "Main Card"
end mouseUp


** CARD #1, BUTTON #17: if... **********************************
on mouseUp
  answer "What kind of 'if' construct?" with "Simple" or "If-Then" or ¬
  "With Else"
  put it into ifKind
  if ifKind is "Simple" then
    put "if " & return after ¬
    field "Script-It" of card "Main Card"
    exit mouseUp
  end if
  if ifKind is "If-Then" then
    put "if " & return & return & "then" & return & return ¬
    & "end if" & return after field "Script-It" of card "Main Card"
    exit mouseUp
  end if
  put "if " & return & return & "then" & return & return ¬
  & "else" & return & return & "end if" & return after ¬
  field "Script-It" of card "Main Card"
end mouseUp


** CARD #1, BUTTON #18: find **********************************
on mouseUp
  put "find " into holder
  answer "Find string,  word or characters?" with ¬
  "word" or "chars" or "String"
  if it is "String" then
    put quote && quote & return after holder
    put holder after field "Script-It" of card "Main Card"
```

```
  else
     put it && quote && quote & return after holder
     put holder after field "Script-It" of card "Main Card"
  end if
end mouseUp


** CARD #1, BUTTON #19: get ************************************
on mouseUp
  put "get " & return into holder
  put holder after field "Script-It" of card "Main Card"
end mouseUp


** CARD #1, BUTTON #20: global *************************************
on mouseUp
  put "global " & return after holder
  put holder after field "Script-It" of card "Main Card"
end mouseUp


** CARD #1, BUTTON #21: go ************************************
on mouseUp
  put "go  card  of " & return into holder
  put holder after field "Script-It" of card "Main Card"
end mouseUp


** CARD #1, BUTTON #22 ************************************
on mouseUp
  global holder
  put "hide " into holder
  visual effect wipe right
  push this card
  go to card "Hide Items"
end mouseUp


** CARD #1, BUTTON #23: multiply
************************************
on mouseUp
  put "multiply  by " & return into holder
  put holder after field "Script-It" of card "Main Card"
end mouseUp


** CARD #1, BUTTON #24: play ************************************
on mouseUp
  put "play " into field "Script-It"
end mouseUp
```

```
** CARD #1, BUTTON #25: show ************************************
on mouseUp
  global holder
  put "show " into holder
  visual effect wipe right
  push this card
  go to card "Show Items"
end mouseUp

** CARD #1, BUTTON #26: pop card
**********************************
on mouseUp
  answer "Pop into container?" with "Yes" or "No"
  if it is "Yes" then put "pop card into " & return into holder ¬
  else put "pop card" & return into holder
  put holder after field "Script-It" of card "Main Card"
end mouseUp

** CARD #1, BUTTON #27: push card
**********************************
on mouseUp
  answer "Which card to push?" with "recent" or "this one"
  if it is "recent" then put "push recent card" & return after ¬
  field "Script-It" else put "push card" & return after ¬
  field "Script-It"
end mouseUp

** CARD #1, BUTTON #28: put ************************************
on mouseUp
  put "put " & return after field "Script-It"
end mouseUp

** CARD #1, BUTTON #29: return ***************************************
on mouseUp
  global type
  if type is not "function" then
    beep
    answer "Sorry, but this can only be used in a function."
  else
    put "return " & return after field "Script-It"
  end if
end mouseUp

** CARD #1, BUTTON #30: send ************************************
on mouseUp
```

```
  put "send  to " & return after field "Script-It"
end mouseUp

** CARD #1, BUTTON #31: sort **************************************
on mouseUp
  answer "Sort in what order?" with "ascending" or "descending"
  put "sort" && it & " " into holder
  answer "Usual text sort?" with "Yes" or "No"
  if it is "Yes" then
    put "by " & return after holder
  else
    answer "What type of sort?" with "numeric" or "dateTime" or ¬
    "international"
    put it && "by" && return after holder
  end if
  put holder after field "Script-It"
end mouseUp

** CARD #1, BUTTON #32: subtract
**********************************
on mouseUp
  put "subtract  from  " & return after field "Script-It"
end mouseUp

** CARD #1, BUTTON #33: type **************************************
on mouseUp
  put "type" && quote && quote after field "Script-It"
end mouseUp

** CARD #1, BUTTON #34: visual effect
**********************************
on mouseUp
  global holder
  put "visual effect " into holder
  visual effect dissolve
  push this card
  go to card "Visuals"
end mouseUp

** CARD #1, BUTTON #35: wait **************************************
on mouseUp
  answer "What kind of wait command?" with "for time" or ¬
  "until" or "while"
  put "wait" && it into holder
  put empty into third word of holder
```

```
  put holder & return after field "Script-It"
end mouseUp


** CARD #1, BUTTON #36: use help
**********************************
on mouseUp
  visual effect iris open
  push this card
  go to card "Use Help"
end mouseUp


** CARD #1, BUTTON #37: Done ***********************************
on mouseUp
  global scriptName
  put "end " & scriptName & return after field "Script-it"
  ask "Name a file to put the script into:"
  put it into fileName
  open file fileName
  write field "Script-It" to file fileName
  close file fileName
  answer "Ready for you to cut and paste"
  visual effect dissolve
  go "Home"
end mouseUp


** CARD #1, BUTTON #38: About ***********************************
on mouseUp
  show card field "Info"
  wait until the mouseClick
  hide card field "Info"
end mouseUp


** CARD #1, BUTTON #39: File Commands
**********************************
on mouseUp
end mouseUp


** CARD #1, BUTTON #40: drag ***********************************
on mouseUp
  put "drag from  to " & return after field "Script-It"
end mouseUp


** CARD #1, BUTTON #41: reset paint
**********************************
on mouseUp
```

```
  put "reset paint" & return after field "Script-It"
end mouseUp

** CARD #1, BUTTON #42: open ************************************
on mouseUp
  put "open file" && quote && quote & return after ¬
  field "Script-It"
end mouseUp

** CARD #1, BUTTON #43: close ************************************
on mouseUp
  put "close file" && quote && quote & return after ¬
  field "Script-It"
end mouseUp

** CARD #1, BUTTON #44: write ************************************
on mouseUp
  answer "What kind of wait command?" with "for time" or ¬
  "until" or "while"
  put "wait" && it into holder
  put empty into third word of holder
  put holder & return after field "Script-It"
end mouseUp

** CARD #1, BUTTON #45: read ************************************
on mouseUp
  put "read from file " && quote && quote into holder
  answer "How should the read end?" with "A Character" or ¬
  "No. Chars"
  if it is "A Character" then put " until " after holder ¬
  else put " for " after holder
  put holder & return after field "Script-It"
end mouseUp

** CARD #1, BUTTON #46: Go Home!
************************************
on mouseUp
  if field "Script-It" is empty then
    go "Home"
    exit mouseUp
  else
    answer "Are you sure you want to abandon the script?" with ¬
    "No" or "Yes"
    if it is "Yes" then
      go "Home"
```

```
      exit mouseUp
    end if
  end if
end mouseUp

** CARD #2, BUTTON #1: Repeat x times
**********************************
on mouseUp
  global holder
  put " times" & return & return & "end repeat" after holder
  put holder & return after field "Script-It" of card "Main Card"
  visual effect wipe left
  pop card
end mouseUp

** CARD #2, BUTTON #2: Repeat Forever
**********************************
on mouseUp
  global holder
  put return & return & "end repeat" & return after holder
  put holder after field "Script-It" of card "Main Card"
  visual effect wipe left
  pop card
end mouseUp

** CARD #2, BUTTON #3: Repeat Until
**********************************
on mouseUp
  global holder
  put " until " & return & return & "end repeat" & return after
holder
  put holder after field "Script-It" of card "Main Card"
  visual effect wipe left
  pop card
end mouseUp

** CARD #2, BUTTON #4: Repeat While
**********************************
on mouseUp
  global holder
  put " while " & return & return & "end repeat" & return after
holder
  put holder after field "Script-It" of card "Main Card"
  visual effect wipe left
  pop card
```

```
end mouseUp

** CARD #2, BUTTON #5: Repeat With
**********************************
on mouseUp
  put "with counter =  to  " & return & return & "end repeat" ¬
  & return after holder
  put holder after field "Script-It" of card "Main Card"
  visual effect wipe left
  pop card
end mouseUp

** CARD #3: Properties *************************************
on TorF
  global holder,propName
  answer "Set " & propName & " to what?" with False or True
  put space & it & return after holder
  put holder after field "Script-it" of card "Main Card"
  visual effect wipe left
  pop card
end TorF

** CARD #3, BUTTON #1: arrowKeys
**********************************
on mouseUp
  global holder, propName
  put "arrowKeys" into propName
  put " arrowKeys to " after holder
  TorF
end mouseUp

** CARD #3, BUTTON #2: lockMessages
**********************************
on mouseUp
  global holder, propName
  put "lockMessages" into propName
  put " lockMessages to " after holder
  TorF
end mouseUp

** CARD #3, BUTTON #3: blindTyping
**********************************
on mouseUp
  global holder, propName
  put "blindTyping" into propName
```

```
  put " blindTyping to " after holder
    TorF
end mouseUp

** CARD #3, BUTTON #4: cursor *************************************
on mouseUp
  global holder
  put " cursor to " after holder
  ask "What cursor number?"
  put it after holder
  put holder & return after field "Script-it" of card "Main Card"
  pop card
end mouseUp

** CARD #3, BUTTON #5: dragSpeed
***********************************
on mouseUp
  global holder
  put " dragSpeed to " after holder
  ask "What speed (pixels per second)"
  put it & return after holder
  put holder after field "Script-it" of card "Main Card"
  pop card
end mouseUp

** CARD #3, BUTTON #6: editBkgnd
***********************************
on mouseUp
  global holder, propName
  put "editBkgnd" into propName
  put " editBkgnd to " after holder
  TorF
end mouseUp

** CARD #3, BUTTON #7: language *************************************
on mouseUp
  global holder
  ask "What language?" with "English"
  put " language to " & it & return after holder
  put holder after field "Script-it" of card "Main Card"
  pop card
end mouseUp

** CARD #3, BUTTON #8: lockRecent
***********************************
```

```
on mouseUp
  global holder, propName
  put "lockRecent" into propName
  put " lockRecent to " after holder
  TorF
end mouseUp


** CARD #3, BUTTON #9: lockScreen
**********************************
on mouseUp
  global holder, propName
  put "lockScreen" into propName
  put " lockScreen to " after holder
  TorF
end mouseUp


** CARD #3, BUTTON #10: numberFormat
**********************************
on mouseUp
  global holder
  put " numberFormat to " after holder
  ask "How many digits of precision?" with "2"
  put it into precision
  answer "Display a zero before the decimal?" with Yes or No
  put it into displayZero
  if displayZero = "Yes" then put "0" into format
  put "." after format
  repeat with counter = 1 to precision
    put "#" after format
  end repeat
  put quote & format & quote & return after holder
  put holder after field "Script-it" of card "Main Card"
  pop card
end mouseUp


** CARD #3, BUTTON #11: powerKeys
**********************************
on mouseUp
  global holder, propName
  put "powerKeys" into propName
  put " powerKeys to " after holder
  TorF
end mouseUp


** CARD #3, BUTTON #12: userLevel
```

```
*************************************
on mouseUp
  global holder
  put "userLevel to " after holder
  ask "What level of use?" with "5"
  put it after holder
  put holder & return after field "Script-It" of card "Main Card"
end mouseUp

** CARD #4, BUTTON #1: Go Back **********************************
on mouseUp
  visual effect iris close
  pop card
end mouseUp

** CARD #5, BUTTON #1: menuBar **********************************
on mouseUp
  global holder
  put "menuBar" & return after holder
  put holder after field "Script-It" of card "Main Card"
  visual effect wipe left
  pop card
end mouseUp

** CARD #5, BUTTON #2: tool window
*************************************
on mouseUp
  global holder
  put "tool window" & return after holder
  put holder after field "Script-It" of card "Main Card"
  visual effect wipe left
  pop card
end mouseUp

** CARD #5, BUTTON #3: pattern window
*************************************
on mouseUp
  global holder
  put "pattern window" & return after holder
  put holder after field "Script-It" of card "Main Card"
  visual effect wipe left
  pop card
end mouseUp

** CARD #5, BUTTON #4: message box
```

```
*********************************
on mouseUp
  global holder
  put "message box" & return after holder
  put holder after field "Script-It" of card "Main Card"
  visual effect wipe left
  pop card
end mouseUp

** CARD #5, BUTTON #5: button *********************************
on mouseUp
  global holder
  answer "What kind of button?" with "background" or "card"
  put it && "button" & return after holder
  put holder after field "Script-It" of card "Main Card"
  visual effect wipe left
  pop card
end mouseUp

** CARD #5, BUTTON #6: field *********************************
on mouseUp
  global holder
  answer "What kind of field?" with "background" or "card"
  put it && "field" & return after holder
  put holder after field "Script-It" of card "Main Card"
  visual effect wipe left
  pop card
end mouseUp

** CARD #6, BUTTON #1: menuBar *********************************
on mouseUp
  global holder
  put "menuBar" & return after holder
  put holder after field "Script-It" of card "Main Card"
  visual effect wipe left
  pop card
end mouseUp

** CARD #6, BUTTON #2: tool window
*********************************
on mouseUp
  global holder
  put "tool window" & return after holder
  put holder after field "Script-It" of card "Main Card"
  visual effect wipe left
```

```
 pop card
end mouseUp

** CARD #6, BUTTON #3: pattern window
***********************************
on mouseUp
  global holder
  put "pattern window" & return after holder
  put holder after field "Script-It" of card "Main Card"
  visual effect wipe left
  pop card
end mouseUp

** CARD #6, BUTTON #4: message box
***********************************
on mouseUp
  global holder
  put "message box" & return after holder
  put holder after field "Script-It" of card "Main Card"
  visual effect wipe left
  pop card
end mouseUp

** CARD #6, BUTTON #5: button ***********************************
on mouseUp
  global holder
  answer "What kind of button?" with "background" or "card"
  put it && "button" & return after holder
  put holder after field "Script-It" of card "Main Card"
  visual effect wipe left
  pop card
end mouseUp

** CARD #6, BUTTON #6: field ***********************************
on mouseUp
  global holder
  answer "What kind of field?" with "background" or "card"
  put it && "field" & return after holder
  put holder after field "Script-It" of card "Main Card"
  visual effect wipe left
  pop card
end mouseUp

** CARD #6, BUTTON #7: cards ***********************************
on mouseUp
```

```
  global holder
    ask "How many cards (or all)?" with "all"
    put it && "cards" & return after holder
    put holder after field "Script-It" of card "Main Card"
    visual effect wipe left
    pop card
end mouseUp
```

```
** CARD #7: Visuals ***********************************
-- This card shows some effective use of hiding and showing buttons,
-- giving the appearance of animation as it unveils new buttons that
-- are appropriate to the first selection.  Thus if the user picks
-- "scroll," the buttons called "up," "down," "left," and "right"
-- appear.  This is a technique you might find quite useful in your
-- stacks.
on openCard
  repeat with counter = 10 to 17
    hide button counter
  end repeat
end openCard
```

```
** CARD #7, BUTTON #1: dissolve *************************************
on mouseUp
  global holder
  put "dissolve " after holder
  repeat with counter = 18 to 21
    show button counter
  end repeat
end mouseUp
```

```
** CARD #7, BUTTON #2: scroll **************************************
on mouseUp
  global holder
  put "scroll " after holder
  repeat with counter = 10 to 13
    show button counter
  end repeat
end mouseUp
```

```
** CARD #7, BUTTON #3: barn door
***********************************
on mouseUp
  global holder
  put "barn door " after holder
  repeat with counter = 14 to 15
```

```
    show button counter
  end repeat
end mouseUp

** CARD #7, BUTTON #4: iris ************************************
on mouseUp
  global holder
  put "iris " after holder
  repeat with counter = 14 to 15
    show button counter
  end repeat
end mouseUp

** CARD #7, BUTTON #5: wipe ************************************
on mouseUp
  global holder
  put "wipe " after holder
  repeat with counter = 10 to 13
    show button counter
  end repeat
end mouseUp

** CARD #7, BUTTON #6: venetian blinds
**********************************
on mouseUp
  global holder
  put "venetian blinds " after holder
end mouseUp

** CARD #7, BUTTON #7: zoom ************************************
on mouseUp
  global holder
  put "zoom " after holder
  repeat with counter = 14 to 17
    show button counter
  end repeat
end mouseUp

** CARD #7, BUTTON #8: checkerboard
**********************************
on mouseUp
  global holder
  put "checkerboard " after holder
end mouseUp
```

```
** CARD #7, BUTTON #9: plain ***********************************
on mouseUp
  global holder
  put "plain " after holder
end mouseUp


** CARD #7, BUTTON #10: up *************************************
on mouseUp
  global holder
  put "up " after holder
end mouseUp


** CARD #7, BUTTON #11: down ***********************************
on mouseUp
  global holder
  put "down " after holder
end mouseUp


** CARD #7, BUTTON #12: left ***********************************
on mouseUp
  global holder
  put "left " after holder
end mouseUp


** CARD #7, BUTTON #13: right **********************************
on mouseUp
  global holder
  put "right " after holder
end mouseUp


** CARD #7, BUTTON #14: open ***********************************
on mouseUp
  global holder
  put "open " after holder
end mouseUp


** CARD #7, BUTTON #15: close **********************************
on mouseUp
  global holder
  put "close " after holder
end mouseUp


** CARD #7, BUTTON #16: in *************************************
on mouseUp
  global holder
```

```
  put "in " after holder
end mouseUp


** CARD #7, BUTTON #17: out *********************************
on mouseUp
  global holder
  put "out " after holder
end mouseUp

** CARD #7, BUTTON #18: very slowly
***********************************
on mouseUp
  global holder
  put "very slowly" after holder
end mouseUp


** CARD #7, BUTTON #19: slowly *********************************
on mouseUp
  global holder
  put "slowly" after holder
end mouseUp


** CARD #7, BUTTON #20: very fast
***********************************
on mouseUp
  global holder
  put "very fast" after holder
end mouseUp


** CARD #7, BUTTON #21: fast ***********************************
on mouseUp
  global holder
  put "fast" after holder
end mouseUp


** CARD #7, BUTTON #22: Go Back *********************************
on mouseUp
  global holder
  put holder & return after field "Script-It" of card "Main Card"
  visual effect dissolve to inverse
  pop card
end mouseUp
```

Changes and Additions

The commercial version of this script contains many enhancements and occupies far more space than would be possible or practical to print here. You can obtain the commercial version through Hyperpress Publishing (see Appendix C) or your Macintosh software dealer. But you might want to consider adding such features as the following to make the script even more usable:

- paint, card, field, and button properties to the Properties card or to their own cards

- built-in HyperTalk functions programmed the same way as the commands that are already included

- more automatic movement of the finished script to the user's object

As with the stack in Chapter 25, if you make changes we'd love to see them. Contact us as explained in the Preface.

Summary

This concludes our study of HyperTalk. You've learned all the major commands, operators, functions, and properties, a considerable number of programming strategies, and some design techniques. You should now be ready to tackle the production of stacks for sale or sharing.

Let us know what you're doing!

APPENDIX

HyperTalk Vocabulary

This appendix lists in alphabetical order all the commands, functions, operators, key words, and identifiers used in HyperTalk. The type of word or phrase, its syntax, and notes about its use and effect are also supplied. For page references, see the index.

Because this appendix is different in nature from the rest of the book, I have introduced some new uses for italics, brackets, braces, and other special typographic techniques. The appendix differs in these respects from the rest of the text in the book.

Italics in this appendix act as cross-references to words and phrases used elsewhere in the appendix. We have italicized only those words that are explained in some depth here and that are particularly relevant to the command or phrase under discussion. Brackets continue to indicate optional material, as in the text. Curly braces, on the other hand, mean that one of the options they contain must be chosen.

Word/Phrase	Type	Syntax	Notes
&	Operator	string-value & string-value	Concatenates the two string-values together with no intervening space added. See &&.
&&	Operator	string-value && string-value	Concatenates a space, then the second string-value onto the end of the first string-value.
*	Operator	number * number	Returns the product of the two numbers.
+	Operator	number + number	Returns the sum of the two numbers.
-	Operator	number - number	Returns the difference between the two numbers.
/	Operator	number / number	Returns the first number divided by the second number.
<	Operator	value < value	Compares two values and returns *true* if the first number is smaller than the second, *false* if the second number is smaller.
<=	Operator	value <= value value ≤ value	Compares two values and returns *true* if the first value is smaller than or equal to the second, *false* otherwise. The second form of the operator is created with Option-comma.
>	Operator	value > value	Compares two values and returns *true* if the first is the larger of the two, *false* if the second is larger.
>=	Operator	value >= value value ≥ value	Compares the two values and returns *true* if the first is larger than or equal to the second, *false* if the second is larger. The second form is created with Option-period.
^	Operator	number ^ number	Returns the first number raised to the power indicated by the second number.
abbreviated	Format	abbr[ev[iated]] date	Used with *convert* to reformat a date field or value. Also used with functions. An abbreviated date formats as Fri, Nov 6, 1987.
abs	Function	the abs of number abs(number)	Returns the absolute value of a number (i.e., its value with a positive sign regardless of its original sign).
add	Command	add number to container	Container must have a number in it or an error occurs. Result of addition replaces former value of container.

Word/Phrase	Type	Syntax	Notes
after	Preposition	None	Used with *put* to insert material behind (following) current contents of destination container or variable.
all	Adjective	all cards	Used with *show* and *print* primarily. Any place a number could be used with *cards*, *all* can appear.
and	Operator	expression and expression	Returns *true* if both expressions are true, *false* if either is false.
annuity	Function	annuity(rate,periods)	Highly accurate way of calculating the annuity function. Arguments must be numeric. Used to calculate present and future value. See *compound*.
answer	Command	answer "prompt-string" [with option [or option [or option]]]	Displays a dialog with a default OK button if all "with" parameters are omitted. Otherwise, fills the dialog box button row from right to left with parameters. User presses button and result of the button press is stored in It. See *ask*.
any	Selector	any chunkExpression	Used in commands to identify, select, or test a random element or chunk.
arrow	Identifier	set cursor to arrow	One of 8 pre-defined cursor shapes in Version 1.2 and later.
arrowKey	System Message	arrowKey left | right | up | down	A system message sent to a card when the indicated arrow key has been pressed.
ask	Command	ask "prompt-string" [with answer] ask password "prompt-string" [with answer]	Displays a dialog displaying the message in "prompt-string" and allows user to enter text in response. Places string into It. If password form is used, password is encrypted before being returned.
atan	Function	the atan of angle atan(angle)	Returns the arc tangent of the *angle*, which must be expressed in radians.
autoHilite	Property	None	Tells whether a button will highlight when pressed. Values are *true* and *false*. Read/write.
autoTab	Property	None	Tells how a Return key will be treated when pressed in the last line of a non-scrolling field. Values are *true* and *false*. If *true*, then HyperCard treats such a return as a Tab. If *false*, it inserts a carriage return. Read/Write. Added in Version 1.2.

Word/Phrase	Type	Syntax	Notes
average	Function	average(number-list)	Returns the average value in the list of numbers supplied as an argument.
back	Identifier	None	Points to card immediately before the current card in the Recent list. Equivalent to *recent card*.
barn door	Visual Effect	barn door {open | close}	No default value.
beep	Command	beep [number]	Causes the system to beep number of times. If number omitted, beeps once.
before	Preposition	None	Used with *put* to insert material ahead of current contents of destination container or variable.
bg[s]	Abbreviation	None	Can be used wherever the term "background[s]" would be allowed.
bkgd	Abbreviation	None	Can be used wherever the term "background" would be allowed.
black	Adjective	visual effect to black	Alters the way *visual effects* work. Creates a black screen as an intermediate point for the visual effect before going to the destination card.
blindTyping	Property	None	Global property that indicates whether blind typing is available to the user. Read/write.
bot[tom]Right	Function	the bot[tom]Right of Object bot[tom]Right(Object)	Returns two integers separated by a comma, indicating the point that defines the lower right corner of the rectangle of the Object. Version 1.2 and later only.
bot[tom]	Function	the bot[tom] of Object bot[tom](Object)	Returns an integer indicating the rightmost point of the rectangle of the Object. Version 1.2 and later only.
browse	Tool Name	None	None
brush	Tool Name	brush tool	None
brush	Painting Property	None	Holds a value of 1-32, defining the shape of the brush to be used in paint operations. Read/write.
btn[s]	Abbreviation	None	Can be used wherever the term "button[s]" would be allowed.
bucket	Tool Name	None	None

Word/Phrase	Type	Syntax	Notes
busy	Identifier	set cursor to busy	One of 8 pre-defined cursor shapes in Version 1.2 and later. (Referred to as the "beach ball".)
button	Tool Name	button tool btn tool	None
cantDelete	Property	None	Stack, card or background property that determines whether a user can delete the object to which it is related. True/false. Read/write.
cantModify	Property	None	Stack property that determines whether a user can compact, delete, or change the contents of the stack. If the stack is not physically locked, this property is read/write. True/false.
card	Multiple	None	Used in chunk expressions, in *go* commands, with *show*. Also used with *visual effect*, where it is default mode.
cd[s]	Abbreviation	None	Can be used wherever the term "card[s]" would be allowed.
centered	Painting Property	None	When true, draws shapes from their centers out rather than from their top-left corners. When false, uses standard top-left corner anchor for shape drawing. Read/write.
char	Identifier	char[acter]	A character or a group of characters can be selected using one of the chunking techniques. See *word*, *line*, and *item*.
charToNum	Function	the charToNum of character charToNum(character)	Returns the ASCII value of the *character*.
checkerboard	Visual Effect	None	None
choose tool	Command	choose tool-name tool	Selects the named tool exactly as if chosen from the Tools menu. The userLevel must be set to appropriate value to allow access to the named tool.
click	Command	click at point [with keyList]	Simulates the user clicking the mouse at the screen address given in *point*. Modifier keys may be added in combination, separated by commas.
clickH	Function	the clickH	Returns the address of the horizontal point on the screen where the mouse was most recently clicked. See *clickLoc* and *clickV*.

Word/Phrase	Type	Syntax	Notes
clickLoc	Function	the clickLoc	Returns the address of the point on the screen where the mouse was most recently clicked. Point is in format (h,v).
clickV	Function	the clickV	Returns the address of the vertical point on the screen where the mouse was most recently clicked. See *clickLoc* and *clickH*.
close printing	Command	close printing	Terminates printing and flushes the print buffer to ensure all cards are printed.
closeBackground	System Message	None	Sent to card when movement causes the background to change. Can occur on any *go* command or on a *Quit*.
closeCard	System Message	None	Sent to a card when it is closed.
closeField	System Message	None	Sent to a field when the user tabs or clicks out of it and its contents have been changed.
closeStack	System Message	None	Sent to a card when the stack is about to be closed by the user opening another stack.
commandKey	Function	cmdKey	Returns status of Command Key as *up* or *down*.
compound	Function	compound(rate,periods)	Returns the compound interest factor at *rate* over the number of *periods* indicated. Used in calculating present and future values of annuities. See *annuity*.
contains	Operator	container contains value	Returns *true* if the text on the left side of the operator is found in the string or container on the right, *false* if it is not. The *contains* operator and the *is in* operator are synonymous except that the order of arguments is reversed.
controlKey	System Message	controlKey key-number	A system message sent to a card, indicating that the Control Key has been pressed. Always accompanied by an argument that indicates which key was held down along with the Control Key. The argument is the ASCII value of the accompanying key.
convert	Command	convert container to format	Changes format of date/time information in container to format specified: seconds, dateItems, long date, short date, abbrev[iated] date, long time, or short time.

Word/Phrase	Type	Syntax	Notes
cos	Function	the cos of angle cos(angle)	Returns the cosine of the angle supplied as an argument and expressed in radians.
cross	Identifier	set cursor to cross	One of 8 pre-defined cursor shapes in Version 1.2 and later.
cursor	Property	None	A string or number identifying a cursor resource in the current environment. Write only.
curve	Tool Name	None	None
date	Function	the [short | long | abbrev[iated]] date	Returns a string representing the current date in your Mac, using one of the formats shown if it is supplied and defaulting to the short format. See *short, long,* and *abbrev[iated]*.
dateItems	Format	None	Used with *convert* to cause HyperCard to put a date/time field into a comma-delimited string for extraction and calculation purposes. Returns year, month, day, hour, minute, second, and day of week (Sunday = 1).
dateTime	Sort Type	None	Used with *sort* to sort stack by treating a chunk expression as a date/time value.
delete	Command	delete chunk [of card]	Deletes text described by *chunk* expression from current card unless *of card* parameter is supplied and identifies a different card.
deleteBackground	System Message	None	Documented but not functional in any version of HyperCard.
deleteButton	System Message	None	Sent to a button indicating it is about to be deleted.
deleteCard	System Message	None	Sent to a card indicating it is about to be deleted.
deleteField	System Message	None	Sent to a field indicating it is about to be deleted.
deleteStack	System Message	None	Sent to a card indicating its stack is about to be deleted.
dial	Command	dial number dial number with modem dial number with modem modem-string	Attempts to dial the telephone using built-in speaker tones if *modem* omitted or with a modem if included in command. Optionally, may supply modem-initialization commands as *modem-string*.

Word/Phrase	Type	Syntax	Notes
diskSpace	Function	the diskSpace	Returns the number of bytes left on the currently logged disk drive.
dissolve	Visual Effect	None	None
div	Operator	number div number	Returns truncated quotient of first number divided by second number.
divide	Command	divide container by number	The *container* must have a number in it or an error occurs. Contents of container replaced by quotient.
do	Command	do "text string"	Gets whatever is in text string or source of text string and interprets it as a HyperTalk command.
doMenu	Command	doMenu "menuItem"	Simulates user selection of indicated menu item. *menuItem* must correspond exactly to the name of a selection of a currently active and available menu. The userLevel must be set to permit access to the menu containing the item.
done	Predefined Value	None	The value returned by the *sound* function if no sound is playing.
down	Constant	None	One of the possible values of the mouse button and many keys whose status can be checked with functions. See *up*.
drag	Command	drag from point to point [with keyList]	Simulates dragging with the tool currently in use. Dragging occurs from first point to second. Optional keyList can contain modifier keys, separated by commas. See *choose tool*.
dragSpeed	Property	None	Global numeric property that determines the rate at which dragging will occur, in pixels per second. Read/write. On *idle*, reset to 0.
edit script	Command	edit script of object	Opens script of *object* for editing by user. The userLevel must be set to 5 (scripting) or nothing happens.
editBkgnd	Property	None	Global property that determines whether operations are currently being performed on the background of the current card. Read/write.
eight	Constant	None	Use in place of number 8.
eighth	Selector	eighth chunkExpression	Used in commands to identify, select or test the eighth element or chunk.

Word/Phrase	Type	Syntax	Notes
empty	Predefined Value	None	Equals the null string, "". Used most often with *put* and with conditional tests on variables, containers, and fields.
end	Identifier	end handler-name	Required at the end of all event and function handlers. See *on, function.*
enterInField	System Message	enterInField	A system message sent to a field whenever the user presses the Enter key with the pointer positioned in that field. (Version 1.2 and later.)
enterKey	System Message	enterKey	A system message sent to a card indicating the Enter key is pressed.
eraser	Tool Name	None	None
exit	Command	exit handler-name	Leaves a handler before the *end* is reached.
exit repeat	Control Structure	exit repeat	Used to exit a repeat loop before the condition arises that would normally terminate it.
exit to HyperCard	Command	exit to HyperCard	Quits all levels of handlers immediately and stops HyperTalk completely.
exp	Function	the exp of number exp(number)	Returns the constant *e* raised to the power represented by number.
exp1	Function	the exp1 of number exp1(number)	Returns the value one less than the *exp* of the number.
exp2	Function	the exp2 of number exp2(number)	Returns the value of 2 raised to the power specified by the number.
false	Constant	None	One of the two Boolean values returned with true/false tests. See *true.*
fast	Adjective	None	Used with *visual* to cause the next visual effect to execute quickly.
field	Tool Name	None	None
fifth	Selector	fifth chunkExpression	Used in commands to identify, select, or test the fifth element or chunk.
filled	Painting Property	None	When true, any shapes drawn are filled with the currently selected pattern as they are drawn.

Word/Phrase	Type	Syntax	Notes
find	Command	find target [in field field-name] find char[acter]s target [in field field-name] find word target [in field field-name] find whole target [in field field-name] find string target [in field field-name]	The target is a text string. Field-name, if present, must be the name, number, or ID of a field. Without qualifiers, *find* locates target at the beginning of words. With *chars*, it finds string anywhere in word. With *word*, it finds only whole words that match the target string. With *whole*, added in Version 1.2, it finds only exact matches, including spaces, with word order significant, and requires that the target be found entirely within one field. With *string* and arguments with spaces, performance improvement is obtained in Version 1.2 and above.
first	Selector	first chunkExpression	Used in commands to identify, select, or test the first element or chunk.
five	Constant	None	Use in place of number 5.
fld[s]	Abbreviation	None	Can be used wherever the term "field[s]" would be allowed.
formFeed	Constant	None	Can be *put* or concatenated into a string with & to cause the printer to eject a page when this command is encountered. See *lineFeed*.
forth	Identifier	None	Points to the next card in the Recent list. If the current card is the last card in the Recent list, returns to Home stack.
foundChunk	Function	the foundChunk	Returns a chunking expression that identifies the location of the last text found with a *find* command. (Version 1.2 and later)
foundField	Function	the foundField	Returns the identification of the field in which the last text was found with a *find* command. (Version 1.2 and later)
foundLine	Function	the foundLine	Returns the field number and line number on which the last text was found with a *find* command. (Version 1.2 and later)
foundText	Function	the foundText	Returns the last text found with a *find* command. (Version 1.2 and later)
four	Constant	None	Use in place of number 4.
fourth	Selector	fourth chunkExpression	Used in commands to identify, select, or test the fourth element or chunk.

Word/Phrase	Type	Syntax	Notes
freeSize	Property	None	Global property indicating how much free space is in the current stack. Read-only.
functionKey	System Message	functionKey number	A system message sent to a card indicating that the function key whose number is indicated has been pressed.
get	Command	get source-expression	Puts the value of any literal, constant, function, or container into *It*. See *put*, which is more useful. *get* is not used often and is left over from earlier versions of HyperTalk for compatibility.
global	Command	global name-list	Identifies one or more variables as global in nature, i.e., known and accessible outside the current handler. Command must appear before variable it names is used.
go	Command	go [to] card-name go [to] stack stack-name go [to] card-name of stack-name go [to] card-name of background-name [of stack-name]	Changes the display to show the designated card in the current or designated stack with the current or designated background.
gray	Adjective	visual effect to gray	Alters the way *visual effects* work. Creates a gray screen as an intermediate point for the visual effect before going to the destination card. (Alternate spelling, grey, is allowed after Version 1.2.)
grid	Painting Property	None	When *true*, constrains some painting operations to a grid with lines at eight-pixel intervals, forcing everything to line up on those grid lines (visible or invisible). Read/write.
hand	Identifier	set cursor to hand	One of 8 pre-defined cursor shapes in Version 1.2 and later.
heapSpace	Function	the heapSpace	Returns the amount of space currently available on the application heap.
height	Function	the height of Object height(Object)	Returns an integer indicating the distance in pixels between the top and bottom of the rectangle of the Object. Version 1.2 and later only.
help	Command	help	Takes user to HyperCard's built-in Help stack.

Word/Phrase	Type	Syntax	Notes
help	System Message	None	Sent to a card to indicate that Help has been selected from the Go menu.
hide	Command	hide menuBar hide window hide object	Removes the designated window or object from view. See *show*. The *window* may be *tool window* or *pattern window* or any valid address for the *Message box*.
hilite	Property	None	Indicates whether a button is highlighted or not. Read/write.
home	Identifier	None	Points to first card in Home stack. (There must be a stack called Home for HyperCard to operate.)
iBeam	Identifier	set cursor to iBeam	One of 8 pre-defined cursor shapes in Version 1.2 and later.
icon	Property	None	Number of icon resource associated with a button. Read/write.
id	Property	None	Numeric ID of a background, card, field, or button. Read-only.
idle	System Message	None	Sent to a card when no other message is being sent and no other action is taking place. Alternates with *mouseWithin* if the mouse is over a button or a field.

if	Control Structure	if true/false then
		  statement-list
		[else
		  statement-list
		end if]
			If only one statement in either or both statement-lists, no need for *end if*. *else* is optional. *then* is required.

international	Sort Type	None	Used with *sort* to sort a stack by treating a chunk expression as text but using international sort-sequence standards rather than ASCII. See *text*, *numeric*, and *dateTime*.
into	Preposition	None	Used with *put* to replace current contents of destination container or variable with value supplied in command.
inverse	Adjective	visual effect to inverse	Alters the way *visual effects* work. Creates a screen that is the inverse of the destination card as an intermediate point for the visual effect before going to the destination card.
iris	Visual Effect	iris {open | close}	No default value.

Word/Phrase	Type	Syntax	Notes
is in	Operator	text is in container	Returns *true* if *text* is found in *container*, *false* if not. The *is in* operator is synonymous with *contains* except the order of arguments is reversed.
is not in	Operator	text is not in container	The logical opposite of *is in*. May also use *not (text is in container)* to accomplish this goal.
it	Identifier	None	Default container used by several retrieval and chunking commands. Can also be used explicitly. See *put* and *get*.
items	Identifier	None	An item is defined as any arbitrary text separated by a comma from other text in a field, line, container, or variable.
language	Property	None	Global property containing the language in which activities take place. Read-write. Must be a language interpreter for the chosen language or an error results. Read/write.
lasso	Tool Name	None	None
last	Selector	last chunkExpression	Used in commands to identify, select, or test the last element or chunk.
left	Function	the left of Object left(Object)	Returns the leftmost position of the object's rectangle as an integer.
length	Function	the length of text length(text)	Returns the number of characters in the string of *text* supplied as an argument.
line	Tool Name	None	None
line	Identifier	None	A line is a block of text in a field that ends with a carriage return.
lineFeed	Constant	None	Can be used with *put* or concatenated with & to cause the printer to skip a line when it is encountered. See *formFeed*.
lineSize	Painting Property	None	Defines thickness in pixels of a line drawn in painting as one of the following values: 1, 2, 3, 4, 6, or 8. Read/write.
ln	Function	the ln of number ln(number)	Returns the natural (base-*e*) logarithm of *number*.
ln1	Function	the ln1 of number ln1(number)	Returns the natural (base-*e*) logarithm of 1 + *number*.

Word/Phrase	Type	Syntax	Notes
location	Property	[the] loc[ation]	A set of two screen coordinates that define the center of a field or window, or the upper center of a button's outline. Read/write.
lock	Command	lock screen	Equivalent to setting the *lockScreen* property to *true*.
lockMessages	Property	None	Indicates whether *open* and *close* messages will be sent to the card. True/false. Read/write. On *idle*, reset to false.
lockRecent	Property	None	Global property that determines whether the Recent stack, which shows the most recent cards navigated up to a depth of 42 cards, will be updated or not. True/false. Read/write. On *idle*, resets to *false*.
lockScreen	Property	None	Global property that determines whether the screen will reflect navigation and other on-screen activities that alter the appearance of the screen. True/false. Read/write. On *idle*, resets to *false* with no levels of lock and unlock pending. (See *lock* command).
lockText	Property	None	Field property that determines whether the user can enter information into the field or not. True/false. Read/write.
log2	Function	the log2 of number log2(number)	Returns the base-2 logarithm of the *number*.
long	Format	long {date | time}	Used with *convert* to reformat a date or time field or value. Also used with functions. Long dates format as Friday, November 6, 1987. Long times format as 9:50:10 PM or 21:50:10.
max	Function	max(number-list)	Returns the highest value in *number-list*, which must be a list of two or more numbers separated by commas.
me	Identifier	None	Points to object to which the script is attached. In Version 1.2 and later, is also a container into which information can be placed and that can be used to access the contents of the object when that object is a field.
Message box	Object	[the] message [box | window] [the] msg [box |window]	A windoid that stays on top of the display at all times.

Word/Phrase	Type	Syntax	Notes
middle	Selector	mid[dle] chunkExpression	Used in commands to identify, select, or test center or middle element or chunk. Always rounds up if chunkExpression has even number of elements.
min	Function	min(number-list)	Returns the smallest value in *number-list*, which must be a list of two or more numbers separated by commas.
mod	Operator	number mod number	Returns only the decimal remainder of the division of the first number by the second.
mouse	Function	the mouse	Returns current status of the mouse button as *up* or *down*. See *mouseUp* and *mouseDown*.
mouseClick	Function	the mouseClick	Returns *true* if the mouse button has been clicked since this handler began executing, *false* otherwise.
mouseDown	System Message	None	Sent to an object indicating mouse button is down and located within its boundaries.
mouseEnter	System Message	None	Sent to a button or field when the mouse enters its boundaries. See *mouseLeave*.
mouseH	Function	the mouseH	Returns current location of the mouse pointer in pixels from the left side of the card window. See *mouseV* and *mouseLoc*.
mouseLeave	System Message	None	Sent to a button or field indicating the mouse has left its boundaries. See *mouseEnter*.
mouseLoc	Function	the mouseLoc	Returns the horizontal and vertical coordinates of the point in the card window where the mouse is currently located. The horizontal position is given first in a two-number list, separated by commas. See *mouseH* and *mouseV*.
mouseStillDown	System Message	None	Sent to an object indicating that the mouse button has remained down and within its boundaries since the last time it was checked.
mouseUp	System Message	None	Sent to an object indicating that the mouse button has been released within its boundaries after having been pressed there. See *mouseDown*.

Word/Phrase	Type	Syntax	Notes
mouseV	Function	the mouseV	Returns the current location of the mouse pointer in pixels from the top of the card window. See *mouseH* and *mouseLoc*.
mouseWithin	System Message	None	Sent to a button or field indicating that the mouse pointer has moved within its boundaries.
multiple	Painting Property	None	When *true*, creates multiple images of a shape as the cursor is dragged after user selects a shape tool. Read/write.
multiply	Command	multiply container by number	The container must hold a number or an error results. Product of multiplication replaces contents of container.
multiSpace	Painting Property	None	Determines the number of pixels (1-9) between multiple images drawn when *multiple* is *true*. Read/write.
name	Property	None	String identifying a stack, background, card, field, or button by the name assigned by the developer or the user, or the default value if none is assigned. Read/write.
newBackground	System Message	None	Sent to a card indicating that a new background is about to be created.
newButton	System Message	None	Sent to a button as soon as it has been created. To be of practical use, must be in a script at card level or higher.
newCard	System Message	None	Sent to a card as soon as it is created. To be of practical value, must be at the background level or higher.
newField	System Message	None	Sent to a field as soon as it is created. To be of practical value, must be at the card level or higher.
newStack	System Message	None	Sent to a card indicating a new stack is being created. To be of practical value, must be at the Home stack level or higher.
next	Identifier	None	Points to next card in current stack.
next repeat	Control Structure	next repeat	Used to cause part of a repeat control structure not to execute and the control value to increment if one is in use. See *repeat*.
nine	Constant	None	Use in place of number 9.

Word/Phrase	Type	Syntax	Notes
ninth	Selector	ninth chunkExpression	Used in commands to identify, select, or test the ninth element or chunk.
none	Identifier	set cursor to none	One of 8 pre-defined cursor shapes in Version 1.2 and later. (Blank cursor.)
not	Operator	not (true/false)	Returns the opposite of the result of the true/false expression.
number	Function	[the] number of objects [the] number of cards of background [the] number of chunks in text-source number(objects)	Returns the number of card or background buttons or fields on the current card, the number of backgrounds or cards in the current stack, or the number of cards sharing a current or specified background. When dealing with chunks, returns number of characters, words, items, or lines in a string, variable, or container.
number	Property	None	Backgrounds, cards, fields, and buttons have a number associated with them that indicates the layer within which they are found on the card. This property holds this number for each object. Read-only.
numberFormat	Property	None	Global property that uses zeros, decimal points, and pound signs to format numbers for output in the stack. Read/write. On *idle*, resets to "0.######".
numeric	Sort Type	None	Used with *sort* to sort a stack by treating a chunk expression as a numeric value. See *text*, *international*, and *dateTime*.
numToChar	Function	the numToChar of number numToChar(number)	Returns character whose ASCII equivalent is *number*. You can only use one argument even with the second form.
offset	Function	offset(text,string-source)	Returns the number of characters from the beginning of *string-source* at which *text* begins. If *text* is not present in *string-source*, function returns 0.
on	Identifier	on handler-name parameter-list statement list end handler-name	See *end*, *function*.
one	Constant	None	Use in place of number 1.
open file	Command	open file file-name	Opens any ASCII file called *file-name*, which can be a string or a container storing a string. See *read from file* and *write to file*.

Word/Phrase	Type	Syntax	Notes
open printing	Command	open printing [with dialog] print card-name close printing	Initiates a print job, prints cards that appear in *print* statements before the *close printing* statement. Optionally opens print dialog for user's input.
openBackground	System Message	None	Sent to a card when it is opened and its background is different from that of the immediately previously shown card. See *closeBackground*.
openCard	System Message	None	Sent to a card when it is opened by going to it.
openField	System Message	None	Sent to an unlocked field when it has been clicked in or tabbed into.
openStack	System Message	None	Sent to a card when its stack is opened. To be of practical value, usually placed at the stack level or higher.
optionKey	Function	the optionKey	Returns status of Option key as *up* or *down*.
or	Operator	expression or expression	Returns *true* if either expression is true, *false* only if both are false.
oval	Tool Name	None	None
param	Function	the param of number param(number)	Returns the parameter in the *number* position of the parameter string passed to the currently executing handler. The message name is numbered 0.
paramCount	Function	the paramCount	Returns the number of parameters passed to the currently executing handler.
params	Function	the params	Returns the entire parameter list, including the name, of the message passed to the currently executing handler.
pass	Command	pass handler-name	Sends the handler-name message or command to the next level up the hierarchy.
pattern	Painting Property	None	Sets the current number to a value from 1-40 corresponding to the palette patterns. Read/write.
pattern window	Identifier	None	Used to *get* and *set* properties of the pattern window used during graphics operations.
pencil	Tool Name	None	None
pi	Constant	None	Value of pi = 3.14159265358979323846

Word/Phrase	Type	Syntax	Notes
pict	Abbreviation	None	Can be used wherever the term "picture" would be allowed.
picture	Identifier	None	One of HyperCard's object types. Can be a *background* picture or a *card* picture.
plain	Visual Effect	None	None
play	Command	play "sound name" [tempo]["note-list"] play stop	Uses voice identified in sound name to play sounds through the Macintosh built-in speaker or external speaker port. Any sound resource can be used as the sound name. Sound plays until done unless *play stop* is encountered and stops the music immediately. If note-list is empty, middle C is played. See *sound* function.
plus	Identifier	set cursor to plus	One of 8 pre-defined cursor shapes in Version 1.2 and later.
polygon	Tool Name	poly[gon] tool	See *regular polygon*.
polySides	Painting Property	None	Determines how many sides the regular polygon tool will draw. Must be between 3 and 50. Read/write.
pop	Command	pop card [{into I before I after} destination]	Retrieves a card previously *pushed*. If a destination is furnished, card's contents are placed there; otherwise a *go* to the *pop*ped card is implied. See *push*.
powerKeys	Property	None	Global property that determines whether a user with painting level or higher access can use one-key power keys during paint operations. True/false. Read/write.
previous	Identifier	prev[ious]	Points to previous card in current stack.
print card	Command	print card print {number I all} cards print card-name	Part of *open printing* construct. Orders HyperCard to print the current card, some number of cards in the stack, all cards in the stack, or a specific card whose name, number, or ID is supplied. See *open printing*, *close printing*.
push card	Command	push card	Saves current card's ID information in memory for later retrieval with *pop card*.

Word/Phrase	Type	Syntax	Notes
put	Command	put [expression] [{into | before | after} destination]	With only an *expression*, replaces contents of Message box with *expression* value. With *destination*, places *expression* contents in place of, preceding, or following contents of *destination*. If *expression* contains an arithmetic expression, it is evaluated first.
quit	System Message	None	Sent to a card when Quit HyperCard is selected from the File menu. To be of practical value, must be at the Home stack level.
quote	Constant	None	Used primarily in concatenation with & and && to place a quotation mark in a string.
random	Function	the random of number random(number)	Returns a random integer value between 1 and *number*.
read from file	Command	read from file file-name {until character | for number}	Reads from a text-only ASCII file previously opened with *open*, placing results into *It*. Reading continues until a specified character is reached or until a specific number of characters have been read, depending on form used.
recent card	Identifier	recent card	Points to the card immediately before the current card in the Recent list. Identical to *back*.
rectangle	Tool Name	rect[angle] tool	None
rectangle	Property	rect[angle]	Holds the upper-left and lower-right corner coordinates for a field, button, or window as four digits separated by commas. Read/write.
regular polygon	Tool Name	reg[ular] poly[gon] tool	See *polygon*.
repeat	Control Structure	repeat [for] [number] [times] repeat with variable = start to end repeat with variable = start downTo end repeat while true/false repeat until true/false	Used alone, means "repeat forever." Minimum form is repeat number. See *end repeat, exit repeat, next repeat* for ways of ending control structure looping.
reset paint	Command	reset paint	Returns painting parameters to their original default conditions.

Word/Phrase	Type	Syntax	Notes
result	Function	the result	Returns a string explaining any error caused by the previous command. If no error occurred, the value of *the result* is *empty*.
resume	System Message	None	Sent to a card to indicate that HyperCard has resumed operations after being *suspend*ed.
return	Command	return result	Used in function handlers (see *function*) to identify the value to be sent to the calling handler routine.
return	Constant	None	Used primarily in concatenation with & and && to place a carriage return in a string.
returnInField	System Message	returnInField	A system message sent to a field whenever the user presses the Return key with the pointer positioned in that field. (Version 1.2 and later.)
returnKey	System Message	returnKey	A system message sent to a card indicating that the Return key has been pressed.
right	Function	the right of Object right(Object)	Returns an integer indicating the rightmost position that defines the rectangle of the Object. Version 1.2 and later only.
round	Function	the round of number round(number)	Returns *number* rounded to the nearest integer.
round rectangle	Tool Name	round rect[angle] tool	None
screenRect	Function	the screenRect	Returns four integers separated by commas indicating the top left and bottom right corners of the screen. Version 1.2 and later only.
script	Property	None	Enables the retrieval and modification of the script of any object: stack, background, card, field, or button. Read/write, but must use a container for modification.
scroll	Visual Effect	scroll {left | right | up | down]	No default value.
scroll	Property	None	Field property that determines the number of pixels of text that have scrolled above the top of the field's visible area. Read/write.
second	Selector	second chunkExpression	Used in commands to identify, select, or test the second element or chunk.

Word/Phrase	Type	Syntax	Notes
seconds	Format	None	Used with *convert* command to cause HyperCard to change a date/time field to total number of elapsed seconds since 12:00:00 a.m. on January 1, 1904. Used for calculations.
second[s]	Function	the second[s] the sec[s]	Returns an integer containing the number of seconds between the Macintosh start date of midnight, January 1, 1904, and the date currently set in your system.
select	Tool Name	None	None
select	Command	select object select [before | after] location of field select [before | after] text of field	First form selects the appropriate tool (field or button), then the designated object. Second form uses location as a chunking expression to position the cursor in a field, selecting the text designated by position if *before* and *after* are omitted or inserting a blinking cursor *before* or *after* the chunking expression. Third form selects all text in a field or positions the cursor at the beginning (*before*) or end (*after*) of the field.
selectedChunk	Function	the selectedChunk	Returns a chunking expression that identifies the location of the currently selected text, if any. Returns *empty* if no text is selected. (Version 1.2 and later)
selectedField	Function	the selectedField	Returns the identifier of the field in which the currently selected text is located. Returns *empty* if no text is selected. (Version 1.2 and later)
selectedLine	Function	the selectedLine	Returns the line and field numbers of the currently selected text, if any. Returns *empty* if no text is selected. (Version 1.2 and later)
selectedText	Function	the selectedText	Returns the currently selected text, if any. Returns *empty* if no text is selected. (Version 1.2 and later)
selection	Container	None	Contains the text currently highlighted (selected) on the card.
send	Command	send message-name [parameters] to object	Directs a message-name at a particular object in the hierarchy, overriding normal passage of control. Message-name must be one word with no spaces. It must not end with a special character.

Word/Phrase	Type	Syntax	Notes
set	Command	set property of object to value	Alters condition of *property* associated with *object* so that it equals *value*. If no change is needed, none is made.
seven	Constant	None	Use in place of number 7.
seventh	Selector	seventh chunkExpression	Used in commands to identify, select, or test the seventh element or chunk.
shiftKey	Function	the shiftKey	Returns status of Shift key as *up* or *down*.
short	Format	short {time | date}	Used with *convert* to reformat a date or time field or value. Also used with functions. Short dates format as mm/dd/yy. Short times format as 9:50 PM or 21:50.
show	Command	show menuBar show window [at point] show object [at point] show card window [at point] show {number | all} cards	Displays a specified object or window at an optionally specified location on the screen. Displays a specified number of cards or all cards in the current stack. If *card window* is shown, point is in global coordinates, with upper-left corner of screen 0,0 and *point* giving offset of upper-left corner of card.
showLines	Property	None	Field property that determines whether the lines within a field will be visible or invisible. Has no effect on a scrolling field. True/false. Read/write.
showName	Property	None	Button property that determines whether the button's name will be shown as part of the button display. True/false. Read/write.
showPict	Property	None	Card or background property that determines whether the corresponding *picture* is visible or invisible. True/false. Read/write.
sin	Function	the sin of angle sin(angle)	Returns the trigonometric sine of the *angle*, which must be expressed in radians.
six	Constant	None	Use in place of number 6.
sixth	Selector	sixth chunkExpression	Used in commands to identify, select, or test the sixth element or chunk.
size	Property	None	Stack variable holding the size of the stack in kilobytes. Read-only.
slowly	Adverb	slow[ly]	Used with *visual* to cause the next visual effect to execute slowly.

Word/Phrase	Type	Syntax	Notes
sort	Command	sort [ascending | descending] [sortType] by sortValue	Sorts all cards in a stack. Assumes ascending order. *sortType* may be *text*, *numeric*, *international*, or *dateTime*, and if omitted defaults to *text*. The *sortValue* can be any field identifier or chunk expression or a source of such an identifier or expression.
sound	Function	the sound	Returns the name of the currently playing sound or *done* if none is playing.
space	Constant	None	Used primarily in concatenation with & and && to place a blank space in a string.
spray	Tool Name	spray [can] tool	None
sqrt	Function	the sqrt of number sqrt(number)	Returns the square root of *number*.
stackSpace	Function	the stackSpace	Returns the amount of memory currently available in your system's stack.
startUp	System Message	None	Sent to the first card shown when HyperCard is started. Normally, this is the top card in the stack called Home, but it will be passed if no handler for it is present in this card.
string	Identifier	find "string"	Used only with the *find* command to gain a performance improvement when searching for combinations of characters including spaces.
style	Property	None	For buttons, determines whether button is transparent, opaque, rectangle, shadow, or scrolling. For fields, determines whether the field is opaque, rectangle, round rect, check box, radio button, or scrolling. Read/write.
subtract	Command	subtract number from container	The *container* must hold a number or an error condition results. The result of the subtraction replaces the contents of *container*.
suspend	System Message	None	Sent to a card when HyperCard is about to be suspended by operation of the *open* command that launches another application.
tab	Constant	None	Used primarily in concatenation with & and && to place a tab in a string.

Word/Phrase	Type	Syntax	Notes
tabKey	System Message	None	A system message sent to a card indicating the Tab key has been pressed.
tan	Function	the tan of angle tan(angle)	Returns the trigonometric tangent of the *angle*, which must be expressed in radians.
target	Function	[the] target	Returns a string identifying the original recipient of the current message. In the case of card, background, field, or button, returns a string like "card field id 2578" but may also return "this stack." If message has been passed up hierarchy, use this function to identify the original recipient. The use of *the* is required in versions earlier than 1.2. After Version 1.2, *target* accesses the contents of *the target*, which continues to refer to the object itself and not its contents.
ten	Constant	None	Use in place of number 10.
tenth	Selector	tenth chunkExpression	Used in commands to identify, select, or test the tenth element or chunk.
text	Sort Type	None	Default type of *sort*. Sorts stack by ASCII sort sequence. See *numeric*, *international*, and *dateTime*.
text	Tool Name	text tool	None
textAlign	Property	textAlign [of object]	Sets alignment of text in an object to left, right, or center. If no object is specified, it is a painting property. Read/write.
textArrows	Property	None	Global property implemented in Version 1.1 that determines if arrow keys will be used as cursor-moving keys in text editing mode or only for navigational purposes. True/false. Read/write.
textFont	Property	textFont [of object]	Sets the font to the resource font name to be used. If no object is specified, this is a painting property. Read/write.
textHeight	Property	textHeight [of object]	Determines the line height (leading) between baselines of text. If no object is supplied, this is a painting property. Read/write.
textSize	Property	textSize [of object]	Determines the font size of text. With no object specified, this is a painting property. Read/write.

Word/Phrase	Type	Syntax	Notes
textStyle	Property	textStyle [of object]	Sets the style of text to any combination of bold, italic, underline, outline, shadow, condense, extended, or plain. If the object is omitted, this is a painting property. Read/write.
then	Control Structure	None — part of structure	See *if*.
third	Selector	third chunkExpression	Used in commands to identify, select, or test the third element or chunk.
this	Identifier	None	Points to current card.
three	Constant	None	Use in place of number 3.
tick[s]	Function, Identifier	the tick[s]	With *the*, returns number of ticks (1 tick = 1/60 second) since the Macintosh was turned on or re-booted. Without *the*, designates the number of 60ths of a second to perform some action. Second variation often used with *repeat*.
time	Function	the [short	long] time	Returns the current time as a text string. See *short* and *long* for those formats.
tool	Function	the tool	Returns the name of the currently selected tool. See *choose*.
tool window	Operator	None	Used to *get* and *set* properties of the Tool Window used during graphics operations.
top	Function	the top of Object top(Object)	Returns an integer indicating the topmost location that defines the rectangle of the Object. Version 1.2 and later only.
topLeft	Function	the topLeft of Object topLeft(Object)	Returns two integers separated by a comma indicating the point that defines the upper left corner of the rectangle of the Object. Version 1.2 and later only.
true	Constant	None	One of the two Boolean values returned with true/false tests. See *false*.
trunc	Function	the trunc of number trunc(number)	Returns integer portion of *number* without rounding. See *round*.
two	Constant	None	Use in place of number 2.
type	Command	type text [with key-list]	Simulates character-by-character typing of *text* as if from the keyboard, using one or more optional modifier keys in a comma-separated list.

Word/Phrase	Type	Syntax	Notes
unlock	Command	unlock screen [with [visual effect] *visual effect*]	Unlocks the screen after a *lock screen* or *set lockScreen to true* command has been issued. Alternatively, may include a *visual effect* to be displayed as the screen is unlocked. In latter case, the key words *visual effect* are optional.
up	Constant	None	One of the possible values of the mouse button and many keys whose status can be checked with functions. See *down*.
userLevel	Property	None	Global property containing a number between 1 and 5 and determining the user's level of access to HyperCard. Read/write.
userModify	Property	None	Global property that can be set to *true* to allow the user to make temporary changes to a locked stack. Changes made by the user will not be retained. Ignored in an unlocked stack. Reset to *false* when user leaves a stack. True/false. Read/write.
value	Function	the value of string value(string)	Evaluates *string* as a numerical expression and returns the result.
venetian blinds	Visual Effect	None	None
version	Function	the version the version of (stack) the long Version the long Version [of HyperCard]	Returns the version number of HyperCard or the current stack in use. When used with a stack name or identifier, returns five numbers separated by commas indicating the HyperCard version that created the stack, the version last used to compact the stack, the oldest version of HyperCard; used to change the stack since its last compaction, the version that last changed the stack, and the date of the most recent modification in seconds.
very fast	Adverb	None	Used with *visual* to cause the next visual effect to execute more quickly than when the adjective *fast* is used. Difference probably only noticeable on a Macintosh II.
very slowly	Adverb	very slow[ly]	Used with *visual* to cause the next visual effect to execute more slowly than when *slowly* is used.
visible	Property	None	Determines whether a field, button, or window is visible or invisible to the user. Read/write.

Word/Phrase	Type	Syntax	Notes
visual	Command	visual [effect] effect-name [speed] [to image]	Defines visual effect to take place on next card switch. The *effect-name* must be a valid effect. The *speed* parameter can be *very slow[ly]*, *slow[ly]*, *fast*, or *very fast*. The *image* parameter can be *white*, *gray*, *black*, *card*, or *inverse*. Effects can be accumulated and stay in effect until replaced in another handler.
wait	Command	wait [for] number [seconds] wait until trueFalse wait while trueFalse	Pauses script execution either for a specific amount of time or based on Boolean expression value. If *seconds* is not added, ticks (1 tick = 1/60 second) are assumed. With *until*, waits for *trueFalse* to become true; with *while*, waits for *trueFalse* to become false.
watch	Identifier	set cursor to watch	One of 8 pre-defined cursor shapes in Version 1.2 and later.
white	Adjective	visual effect to white	Alters the way *visual effect*s work. Creates a white screen as an intermediate point for the visual effect before going to the destination card.
whole	Identifier	find whole	Used only with *find* to force HyperCard to locate target string only where it appears exactly as provided in argument, in same word order, in same field.
wideMargins	Property	None	Field property that determines whether text abuts both the left and right margin or is indented slightly. True/false. Read/write.
width	Function	the width of Object width(Object)	Returns an integer indicating the distance in pixels between the left and right of the rectangle of the Object. Version 1.2 and later only.
wipe	Visual Effect	wipe {left | right | up | down}	None
word	Identifier	None	A word is defined as any string beginning and ending with a space.
write to file	Command	write text to file file-name	Writes *text* on a previously opened file. See *open file*, *read from file*, and *close file*.
zero	Constant	None	Use in place of number 0.
zoom	Visual Effect	zoom {open | out | close | in}	No default value.

Macintosh ASCII Chart

Decimal	Character	Decimal	Character
0	None	13	None (Return)
1	None	14	None
2	None	15	None
3	None (ETX)	16	None
4	None	17	None
5	None	18	None
6	None	19	None
7	None	20	None
8	None (Backspace)	21	None
9	None (Tab)	22	None
10	None (Line Feed)	23	None
11	None	24	None
12	None (Form Feed)	25	None

Decimal	Character	Decimal	Character
26	None	54	6
27	None (Escape)	55	7
28	None	56	8
29	None	57	9
30	None	58	:
31	None	59	;
32	Space	60	<
33	!	61	=
34	"	62	>
35	#	63	?
36	$	64	@
37	%	65	A
38	&	66	B
39	'	67	C
40	(	68	D
41	)	69	E
42	*	70	F
43	+	71	G
44	,	72	H
45	- (Hyphen)	73	I
46	.	74	J
47	/	75	K
48	0 (Zero)	76	L
49	1	77	M
50	2	78	N
51	3	79	O
52	4	80	P
53	5	81	Q

Decimal	Character	Decimal	Character
82	R	110	n
83	S	111	o
84	T	112	p
85	U	113	q
86	V	114	r
87	W	115	s
88	X	116	t
89	Y	117	u
90	Z	118	v
91	[	119	w
92	\	120	x
93	]	121	y
94	^	122	z
95	_ (Underscore)	123	{
96	`	124		(Vertical bar)
97	a	125	}
98	b	126	~
99	c	127	None
100	d	128	Å
101	e	129	Å
102	f	130	Ç
103	g	131	É
104	h	132	Ñ
105	i	133	Ö
106	j	134	Ü
107	k	135	á
108	l	136	à
109	m	137	â

Decimal	Character	Decimal	Character
138	ä	166	¶
139	ã	167	ß
140	å	168	®
141	ç	169	©
142	é	170	™
143	è	171	´
144	ê	172	¨
145	ë	173	≠
146	í	174	Æ
147	ì	175	Ø
148	î	176	∞
149	ï	177	±
150	ñ	178	≤
151	ó	179	≥
152	ò	180	¥
153	ô	181	µ
154	ö	182	∂
155	õ	183	Σ
156	ú	184	Π
157	ù	185	π
158	û	186	∫
159	ü	187	ª
160	†	188	º
161	°	189	Ω
162	¢	190	æ
163	£	191	ø
164	§	192	¿
165	•	193	¡

Decimal	Character	Decimal	Character
194	¬	206	Œ
195	√	207	œ
196	f	208	-
197	≈	209	—
198	Δ	210	"
199	«	211	"
200	»	212	'
201	…	213	'
202	(Non-break space)	214	÷
203	À	215	◊
204	Ã	216	ÿ
205	Õ		

APPENDIX

C

Other Sources of HyperCard Information

This appendix contains listings for several organizations where you can obtain additional information about HyperCard. Also listed are the national electronic bulletin board systems (BBSes) where software mentioned in the book can be downloaded. The list of sources of HyperCard information is growing all the time; use the BBSes as a way of staying informed of new companies and organizations entering the market.

Apple Computer

If you are serious about developing stacks and scripts, you'll want to join the Apple Programmers and Developers Association (APDA). It's the only sure way to get "plugged into" the latest news and software you'll need to stay successful. Membership is just $25 in the U.S., $35 elsewhere, and includes a whole list of benefits. Contact APDA at:

541

APDA
290 SW 43rd Street
Renton, WA 98055
(206) 251-6548

You might also want to become an Apple certified developer. For more information about this program, write to:

Apple Developer Services
Apple Computer
20525 Mariani Avenue
Mail Stop 27/W
Cupertino, CA 95014
(408) 973-4897.

Magazines

At the time this book was published, two full-color, nationally distributed magazines devoted to HyperCard and related hypertext and hypermedia topics had already appeared. By the time you read this, there may be several more.

The first magazine we became aware of was *HyperLink*. It is published six times a year by Publishers Guild Inc. For subscription information:

HyperLink Magazine
PO Box 7723
Eugene, OR 97401
(800) 544-0339 (credit card orders)

Dave Brader is the editor of this magazine and I am its regular HyperTalk columnist.

The other magazine is *HyperAge*, a monthly publication that made its debut about the same time as *HyperLink*. For subscription information:

HyperAge
5793 Tyndall Ave.
Riverdale, NY 10471
(212) 601-2832

Electronic Bulletin Board Systems

CompuServe has a special HyperCard Forum called APPHYPER where stacks and discussions are provided. Most of the stacks and programming tools described in this book can be obtained from CompuServe. Many knowledgeable stack designers are frequent contributors.

> CompuServe
> 5000 Arlington Centre Blvd.
> PO Box 20212
> Columbus, OH 43220

Like CompuServe, GEnie has a special area of interest to Macintosh owners and users. On GEnie, this area is reached by menu choices. A special area for HyperCard files, discussions, and question-and-answer sessions has been set up on this service as well. Sponsored by General Electric USA, Inc.

> GEnie
> Voice contact: (800) 638-9636
> Call (800) 638-8369 for sign-on or on-line information
>   At prompt, type HHH
>   At next prompt (U#), type GENIE and press Return
> *Note: Use half-duplex for GEnie connection*

You may then sign up for service or request information.

The BIX (Byte Information Exchange) bulletin board, sponsored by *Byte* Magazine, is one of the more technical BBSes in the country. Frequent discussions are held on programming aspects of HyperCard and the HyperTalk language.

> Customer service for information (voice): (800) 227-2983

Newsletters and User Groups

Many local, regional, and national Macintosh User Groups have special interest groups (SIGs) concerning HyperCard and HyperTalk. Contact Apple Computer's User Group office for information about groups in your area. Following are some specific activities.

The Apple HyperCard User's Group is not officially sponsored by Apple Computer, but it involves a fair number of Apple HyperCard and HyperTalk support and engineering people in its ranks. You can get more information about this group from:

AHUG
c/o Dave Leffler
Apple Computer, Inc.
Mail Stop 27AQ
10500 N. DeAnza Blvd.
Cupertino, CA 95014

If you are an Apple developer and have an AppleLink account, you can reach the AHUG folks at address HYPERBUG$.

This group also publishes a monthly newsletter called *Windoid* that is free to anyone who requests a copy at the previous address and sends along a self-addressed, stamped envelope with 25 cents postage.

The Walking Shadow Press publishes a newsletter called *The Open Stack* and also publishes both stacks and documentation about HyperCard and HyperTalk. The newsletter, as well as a special developer's program that offers solutions to HyperTalk questions and problems, is free. They can be reached at:

Walking Shadow Press
PO Box 2092
Saratoga, CA 95071

Hyperpress Publishing publishes stacks and a helpful Pocket Reference Card. They are also interested in publishing stacks, particularly programming tools and artificial intelligence products. Write to the company at:

Hyperpress Publishing
P. O. Box 8243
Foster City, CA 94404
(415) 345-4620

HyperNews is a stackware newsletter published electronically and distributed on CompuServe and elsewhere by Harry Jones and Beccy Callaghan. It is free and includes a catalog of stacks and utilities marketed by the company. Each monthly issue also has interviews, product reviews, editorials, stacks, and a number of other features.

Books

The original source of information about HyperCard is *The Complete HyperCard Handbook* by Danny Goodman, published simultaneously with the release of the product and available at most computer and book stores.

The Walking Shadow Press, mentioned earlier, publishes a book called *HyperCard Scripting* by Jeff Stoddard, which is available directly from the publisher for $16.95 at the previously listed address.

At the time this is being written, several other books are in preparation.

Index

How to Write Macintosh® Software, Second Edition
Scott Knaster

Written for professional developers and serious hobbyists, this is the best source of information on the intricacies of the Macintosh operating system, and in particular the Memory Manager.

This new edition explains how applications programs on the Macintosh work, how to create and debug professional-quality programs, and how to use C to program the Macintosh. Many new topics, including Macintosh II, Macintosh SE, MultiFinder, Macintosh Programmer's Workshop, and the 68020 and 68030 microprocessors, are included as well as revised and updated information on all its previous topics. Its in-depth discussion of high-quality debugging makes it the preferred reference for programmers and software applications developers.

Topics covered include:

- Getting Started
- Adding Features
- Writing a Program
- Using C
- Loops
- Functions, Subroutines, and Subprograms
- Using Macintosh Features

600 Pages, 7¾ x 9¼, Softbound
ISBN: 0-672-48429-3
No. 48429, $27.95

MacAccess: Information in Motion
Dean Gengle and Steven Smith

This book examines the software and hardware required for successful data transfer and offers a step-by-step discussion of a sample telecommunications session, clearly explaining how to send and receive text files. During detailed presentation of the telecommunications session, the focus is set on solutions to common communications problems.

It includes in-depth discussions on connecting the Macintosh® to other computers, sharing and transferring data between machines, protocols, cabling, and conversion procedures.

With this book, you can easily and efficiently share data between your Macintosh and other computers and keep your vital information flowing to where it will do you the most good.

Topics covered include:

- Information in Motion
- Executives Backgrounder
- Telecommunications
- A SofTour of MicroPhone
- Communication Command Languages
- Links and Hints
- Telephone Management
- Advanced Topics by Section
- Appendices: Mac ASCII Chart, File to File Import/Export Charts, Sources Directory, Families, Bibliography for Further Reference, and Feedback and CTG Newsletter Sheet

304 Pages, 7¾ x 9¼, Softbound
ISBN: 0-672-46567-1
No. 46567, $21.95

MPW and Assembly Language Programming for the Macintosh®
Scott Kronick

This introduction to MPW for programmers is the first to teach Macintosh assembly language! Macintosh Programmer's Workshop (MPW) is the new programming development system for the Macintosh and one of the most sophisticated microcomputer programming development systems in existence.

Topics covered include:

The Macintosh Programmer's Workshop
- A Sample Program in Assembly Language
- Fundamental File Commands
- StartUp and Files
- Command Language
- Make and Structured Commands

The Assembly Tutorial
- Slots
- First Lines of Assembly Code
- The ABC's of Blocks of Code
- QuickDraw Inside the Window
- Structured Programming with Blocks
- The Keyboard
- Menus

The MPW and Assembly Dictionaries
- The MPW Shell Command Language
- The 68000 Instruction Set with Directives and Toolbox Traps

352 Pages, 7¾ x 9¼, Softbound
ISBN: 0-672-48409-0
No. 48409, $24.95

The Macintosh® Advisor
Cynthia Harriman and Bencion Calica

Newly updated to include MultiFinder™, this book provides advice on shortcutting some of the Macintosh's elementary procedures to use it more productively.

MultiFinder is the first multitasking operating system for the Mac which allows users to work with multiple applications at the same time. Learn how to increase the performance and speed of computing tasks by gaining a better understanding of the Finder, RAM disks, memory management, and other features. The book also examines powerful hardware options such as hard disks, RAM upgrades, and the LaserWriter™ and includes troubleshooting procedures for quickly isolating and solving computer problems.

Topics covered include:

- The Finder: Macintosh's Operating System
- Speeding Applications
- Desk Accessories and FKeys
- Customizing Applications
- Disk Management Utilities
- RAM Upgrades and Hard Disk Drives
- Options for Better Input and Output
- IBM to Mac: Transferring Data
- Troubleshooting
- Appendices: Shopping Lists, Sources, Technical References

320 Pages, 7¾ x 9¼, Softbound
ISBN: 0-8104-6569-8
No. 46569, $19.95

Visit your local book retailer, use the order form provided, or call 800-428-SAMS.

Object-Oriented Programming for the Macintosh®
Kurt J. Schmucker

With this book, gain insight into the fundamental object-oriented concepts of objects, classes, instances, message passing and method calls, and into advanced topics like metaclasses and multiple inheritance.

Learn to customize MacApp and avoid programming resizable windows, dialog boxes, and scroll bars from scratch. Investigate QuadWorld and the major Macintosh object-oriented languages.

Topics covered include:

■ Why Object-Oriented Programming?
■ The Basics of Object-Oriented Programming
■ Object Pascal
■ Introduction to MacApp
■ Mini-QuadWorld—A Small MacApp Application
■ The Most Frequently Asked Questions about MacApp
■ The Flow of Events in MacApp
■ QuadWorld—A Full MacApp Application
■ Advanced MacApp Features
■ Advanced Concepts in Object-Oriented Programming
■ Smalltalk
■ Lisa Clascal and the Lisa Toolkit
■ An Overview of Other Object-Oriented Languages on Macintosh

624 Pages, 7¾ x 9¼, Softbound
ISBN: 0-8104-6565-5
No. 46565, $34.95

Programming the 68000
Rosenzweig and Harrison

This prime resource for programmers fully examines the power of the Motorola 68000 microprocessor. It details the assembly language processes of coding, editing, compiling, linking, and resource compiling, with thorough explanations of the 68000 instruction set and addressing modes.

Topics covered include:

■ Introduction to Assembly Language
■ The Addressing Modes of the 68000
■ The 68000 Instruction Set
■ Sample Programs
■ A Programmer's Overview of the 68000 Hardware
■ Macintosh Tools
■ The Macintosh ROM Calls
■ SimpleCalc—A Sample Application
■ Some Advanced Subroutines Not in SimpleCalc
■ Appendices: The Binary and Hexadecimal Numbering Systems, Instruction Format & Cycle Timing, Condition Codes, Error Messages, Using the Lisa Workshop, Samples of Trap Calls into the ROM, SimpleCalc Program Code

416 Pages, 7¾ x 9¼, Softbound
ISBN: 0-8104-6310-5
No. 46310, $24.95

Artificial Intelligence Programming on the Macintosh®
Dan Shafer, The Waite Group

This author presents the fundamentals of artificial intelligence (AI) programming theory and techniques through a step-by-step introduction to the next frontier in computer usage. The programming student and hobbyist will be fascinated by the possibilities of music generation, robotics, and problem solving. . .all available through AI on today's microcomputers.

Containing ten exciting programs, the book is written in easy-to-learn Logo for use on the Macintosh, but is also generalized for use on other computers. The book describes the basics of AI programming techniques and concepts.

Topics covered include:

■ Artificial Intelligence Programming Techniques
■ Micro Logician
■ The Digital Poet
■ Artificial Intelligence Data Bases
■ A Prolog Interpreter
■ Artificial Intelligence Languages
■ Logo and LISP
■ Prolog Tutorial
■ Appendices: LISP Listings of Selected Programs, Converting Between Mac Logos, and Suggestions for Further Reading

304 Pages, 7½ x 9¾, Softbound
ISBN: 0-672-22447-X
No. 22447, $24.95

Understanding HyperTalk™
Dan Shafer

Understanding HyperTalk brings the power and fascination of programming in HyperTalk to those Macintosh® owners who want to customize their environment with Apple® 's HyperCard™.

Written by the author of the best-selling *HyperTalk Programming*, this book will be most useful to people who are deciding whether to buy HyperCard and to people who want to teach themselves or others HyperCard programming and stacks.

Topics covered include:

■ Programming Basics
■ Object-Oriented Programming Ideas
■ HyperCard Refresher
■ HyperTalk Building Blocks
■ System Messages
■ Input/Output
■ Loops and Conditional Processing
■ Navigational Commands
■ Data Management Commands
■ User Interface Commands
■ Graphics and Visual Effects
■ Sound and Music
■ Math Functions and Operators
■ Action-Taking Commands
■ Property
■ Interface to the Outside World
■ Stack Design Considerations

300 Pages, 7 x 9, Softbound
ISBN: 0-672-27283-0
No. 27283, $17.95

Visit your local book retailer, use the order form provided, or call 800-428-SAMS.

IBM® PC and Macintosh® Networking Featuring: TOPS™ and AppleShare™
Stephen L. Michel

IBM PC and Macintosh owners and users who want to combine the power of their machines will welcome this complete resource for networking the IBM PC and the Macintosh using TOPS and AppleShare.

This book details the specifics of using the Macintosh and the IBM PC on the same network, including transferring files, sharing printers, transporting data from IBM software to Mac and vice versa, and mixing word processing and spreadsheet programs.

Full of networking details, this thorough coverage of TOPS software (one of *PC Magazine's* "The Best of 1986" products) details how to create useful files and share printers and external disk drives.

Topics covered include:

- How the Macintosh and PC Really Differ
- TOPS
- AppleShare
- Coexistence
- Managing the Network
- Appendices: Glossary, ASCII Character Sets, Using PostScript Printers

328 Pages, 7¾ x 9¼, Softbound
ISBN: 0-672-48405-6
No. 48405, $21.95

Macintosh® Hard Disk Management
Charles A. Rubin and Bencion J. Calica

This is the ideal companion book for all Macintosh owners who have a hard disk or are considering the purchase of one.

Readers will discover how the disk works, as well as pick up important information on how to recover files, rebuild the desktop, replace files, and install fonts and desk accessories.

Topics covered include:

- Hardware
- The System Folder Files
- The Finder
- Fonts, DAs, and the Font/DA Mover
- Organizing Hard Disk Files
- Sharing Files with a Hard Disk
- Using File or Disk Copying Programs
- Printing from a Hard Disk
- Backing Up a Hard Disk
- Disk Optimizing Utilities
- Font and Disk Accessory Extenders
- Fkeys, Inits, and Chooser Resources
- Finder Alternatives
- Preventive Measures
- Troubleshooting and Repairs
- Appendices: Glossary of Terms, List of Products

300 Pages, 7¾ x 9¼, Softbound
ISBN: 0-672-48403-X
No. 48403, $19.95

HyperTalk™ Tips and Techniques
Dan Shafer

Written for programmers and developers, this book is a collection of more than 100 helpful pieces of information about HyperTalk, the programming language built into Apple® 's HyperCard™. It offers readers with some experience in HyperTalk programming a chance to learn the ins and outs of programming from one of the best-known and widely recognized HyperTalk scripting experts.

Solutions to dozens of bugs, deficiencies, and pitfalls lying in wait for the unsuspecting HyperTalk programmer are documented as are suggestions for handling some of the most often needed HyperTalk tasks. The book provides special shortcuts, speed-ups, and enhancements and a wealth of additional information that isn't available from any other source.

Topics covered include:

- Creating an Invisible Cursor
- Building an Index of Stack Contents Automatically
- Checking a Field's Content for Data Type
- Multiword and Multifield Signs
- Protecting a Stack and Script from Misuse
- How to Construct HyperText Applications in HyperCard
- Dealing with HyperCard's Limits and Performance Issues

300 Pages, 7¾ x 9¼, Softbound
ISBN: 0-672-48427-7
No. 48427, $21.95

The Waite Group's HyperTalk™ 2.0 Bible
Mitchell Waite, Stephen Prata, Ted Jones

An entry-level tutorial for people wanting to learn scripting, this book explains Apple's new programming language in an easy-to-read style that includes end-of-chapter quizzes and exercises.

The reference section includes an alphabetical listing of all HyperTalk commands, functions, operators, properties, messages, and reserved names. Each command is explained in terms of its syntax, shown in several typical usages, and followed by a set of graduated examples that show various ways to use the command.

Topics covered include:

- HyperCard Refresher
- Card Navigation
- Objects and Simple Properties
- Handlers and Messages
- Simple Visual and Audio
- Values, Simple Math, Messages
- Mouse, Keyboard and User Interface
- Decisions and Logic, Loops, Strings
- Advanced Math, Date and Time
- User and Advanced Functions
- Sound
- Global and Window Properties
- Simulation and Object Properties
- Graphics and Paint Properties
- File Input and Output, Printing
- X Commands and X Functions
- Advanced HyperTalk

600 Pages, 7½ x 9¾, Softbound
ISBN: 0-672-48430-7
No. 48430, $24.95

Visit your local book retailer, use the order form provided, or call 800-428-SAMS.

Media Genics

415 329 0800
tech assistance #3

If You Use HyperCard, You Need *Reports*

Reports for HyperCard

THE COMPLETE REPORT
GENERATOR FOR HYPERCARD

HYPERWARE™ FROM
MEDIAGENIC

Reports for HyperCard, the complete report generator for HyperCard, turns your HyperCard data into useful information. Use it to organize, analyze, and print what you want, where you want.

You select the information from any card or stack, and design the report with an easy-to-use layout editor. *Reports for HyperCard* does the rest.

Once created, your reports can be printed at any time from any HyperCard application. *Reports for HyperCard* will create calculated fields, totals and subtotals, averages, and counts – even update your stacks – while printing.

Reports for HyperCard features include—

Graphics-oriented layout editor for easy custom report design – you can even design reports for pre-printed forms like invoices and checks. ·

Up to 5 levels of sorts and breaks in any report for precise grouping of information.

Unlimited card selection criteria, including =, ≠, >, >=, <, <=, **Contains, Excludes, Is in,** and **Is not in.**

Flexible print formatting for complete control of every report's appearance.

Plus graphics in your reports. Paste in graphics from HyperCard stacks or other applications. Use the built-in drawing tools to create lines and boxes.

HyperTalk "shorthand" lets you simply pull down menus and select commands – *Reports* automatically writes the corresponding script segments for you.

Put the power of HyperCard in print. With *Reports for HyperCard,* the complete report designer and generator for HyperCard. $99.95 suggested retail price. ₹119.95

To order direct, call 800-345-2888, Operator 300, or return the coupon below with your check or money order.

Reports for HyperCard requires an Apple® Macintosh™ Plus, SE, or II with minimum 1 Mb RAM, two disk drives, and HyperCard™ software. Hard drive recommended.

HyperWare™ From
M E D I A G E N I C

800 227 6900

To order by phone, Call 800-345-2888, Operator 300.

Name _____

Address _____

City _____ State _____ Zip _____

MAIL TO: MEDIAGENIC, Inc.
P.O. Box T, Gilroy, CA 95021-2249

Canadian orders, add $4.00
No COD orders.
Allow 4-6 weeks for delivery.

METHOD OF PAYMENT

QTY.	TITLE	PRICE EACH		TOTAL	
	Reports for HyperCard	$99	95		
	SUBTOTAL				
	For orders shipped to CA add 6.5% sales tax.				
	SHIPPING CHARGES			$3	50
	TOTAL				

☐ Check or Money Order enclosed (payable to MEDIAGENIC, Inc.)
☐ MASTERCARD   ☐ VISA   ☐ AMERICAN EXPRESS

Credit Card Number

Expiration Date: ☐☐☐☐
Month   Year

PHONE ( ) _____

Signature (required for all credit card orders)

DISK OF PROGRAMS AVAILABLE

If you prefer to have the scripts in Chapters 25 and 26 on a Macintosh diskette rather than typing them into your Mac, you can order a disk from Apricot Press. The disk will, as a free bonus, include all of the freeware and shareware programs mentioned elsewhere in the book, which will save you the cost of downloading these programs from a BBS. There is no charge for these programs but **please honor the shareware fee** requests made by the authors of the programs if you use them.

If you wish to order the disk, send a check or money order for $20 to:

Apricot Press
277 Hillview Avenue
Redwood City, CA 94062

For orders outside the continental United States we require $26.00 in U. S. Funds, drawn on a U. S. Bank, or $24.00 U. S. Currency. For orders shipped to CA, add 6.5% sales tax. Please allow two to four weeks for delivery.

- .

Please send me the disk to accompany *HyperTalk Programming Revised Edition,* by Dan Shafer. I am enclosing a check or money order in the amount of _____ to cover costs, postage, tax, if applicable and handling.

NAME: _____

COMPANY: _____

ADDRESS: _____

CITY: _____ STATE: _____ ZIP: _____

TELEPHONE: (___) _____

set userLevel to 5

X comel called mergestack